Ruth Hanna McCormick

Ruth Hanna McCormick

A LIFE IN POLITICS 1880–1944

Kristie Miller

University of New Mexico Press
Albuquerque

Library of Congress Cataloging-in-Publication Data

Miller, Kristie, 1944–
    Ruth Hanna McCormick : a life in politics, 1880–1944 /
Kristie Miller.—1st ed.
        p.   cm.
    Includes bibliographical references and index.
    ISBN 0–8263–1333–7
    1. Simms, Ruth Hanna McCormick, 1880–1944.
2. Politicians—United States—Biography.
3. Women political activists—United States—Biography.
4. Presidents—United States—Election—1940.
I. Title.
E748.M452M55   1992
973.91'092—dc20
[B]   91–28230
                                                            CIP

McCutcheon cartoon "Bound to Come Sooner or Later"
© Chicago Tribune company. Reprinted with permission.

Designed by Cynthia Welch

For Sander and Ellen

Contents

Foreword   ix

Acknowledgments   xiii

Introduction   1

1. Her Father's Daughter: 1880–1903
   An Upbringing in the Political Seraglio   9

2. Chicago: 1903–1912
   Municipal Housekeeping: "Back of the Yards"   33
   Carl Jung: "The Work Is in Good Hands"   44
   The Bull Moose Campaign: "My Money's on the Mare"   48

3. Woman Suffrage: 1913–1914
   Illinois: The Big Four   73
   The Congressional Committee:
   "Lincoln Used to Be My Patron Saint, But Now It's Job"   82

4. The Irreconcilables: 1915–1919
   "Tantrums on the Hill"   101

5. Women Voters: 1920–1924
   Apprenticeship in the Republican Party:
   "Politics Never Is a Game of Solitaire"   123

Republican National Committeewoman:
"We've Carried Water for the Elephants Long Enough" 135

6. On Her Own: 1925–1927
      "You Are the Man for the Job" 149

7. Congresswoman-at-Large: 1928–1929
      "Nobody Asked Me to Run" 185
      "No Favors and No Bunk" 196

8. The Senate Campaign: 1930
      "Bound to Come Sooner or Later" 207

9. New Mexico: 1931–1939
      "The Duchess of Albuquerque" 235

10. A Master of Politics: 1940–1944
      The Dewey Campaign:
      "Politics Is a Capacity for Infinite Detail" 257
      The War Years:
      Politics—"My Right and My Pleasure" 279

      Epilogue 289
      Notes 291
      Bibliography 329
      Index 335

Foreword

NANCY LANDON KASSEBAUM

In any age, in any circumstance, Ruth Hanna McCormick would be recognized as an extraordinary woman. The possessor of boundless energy and enthusiasm, she grew up in a political world with an apprenticeship from a master, her father, Mark Hanna. However, Ruth's success came from her ability to use with great skill her own political instincts. If some people are born with perfect pitch and others are called natural athletes, then Ruth Hanna was a natural politician who seldom hit a wrong note or made a wrong move. Given her family and upbringing, she could have chosen a life of ease. Instead Ruth was drawn to the give and take, the maneuvering and compromise of the political fray. If no female role models were around, no matter—she didn't need them. She would learn what she could from her father and his associates and then set her own standards and goals.

Understanding the importance of contacts and organization long before networking had been defined, she recognized the limitations of single-issue organizations and candidates. She was comfortable with people at all levels of the political spectrum and not in the least awed by the notables of the day. Even now, how many young women would have the presence of mind to deny a request by the president of the United States to change the date of her wedding to accommodate his schedule!

Ruth's political acumen was backed by intelligence, curiosity, dedication, and supreme self-confidence. An effective participant in the Suffrage Movement, she made the transition to mainstream politics while others in the movement remained behind with limited goals and perspectives. Ruth was ready for a larger stage and in a few short years she accumulated a lot of firsts. One of her firsts was the cover of *Time* in 1928. It was not until 1959 that another woman in politics, Margaret Chase Smith, made the cover. Ahead of her time, Ruth was leading the charge of an army of one—herself—and the rest of us had to catch up.

A man of considerable accomplishment in diverse fields is called a Renaissance Man. Well, there have always been Renaissance Women: we just did not have to wait until there had been an age to define a person of many talents. In earlier times, women's achievements were, for the most part, within the family circle. Technology has made the world a smaller, more complex place. Women today direct their talents and energy into the community and beyond. Society has been the beneficiary of their efforts and now more and more women are seeking and performing with distinction in elected and appointed office at all levels of government.

The question has long been asked why it has taken so long for women to provide leadership. Frankly, countless theories abound and books have been written exploring this question. Lack of funds or time or opportunity . . . the list goes on with a lot of truth in all these conjectures. Virginia Woolf wrote of the "liberty of experience," something that women in earlier eras seldom had, something that is not all that abundant today. Regrettably, women all too often don't learn of their own inner resources and strengths until an outside circumstance requires it—the death of the breadwinner, a family illness, for example. In times of war or famine or upheaval, it has repeatedly been the woman who kept the family together and found the wherewithal for survival. American women were spared many of the immediate horrors of World War II, yet they kept the home fires going and took over jobs essential to the war effort. Once newfound strengths and abilities had been tapped and women had tasted the "liberty of experience," they were not willing to accept major retreats to prewar roles and expectations.

Without that liberty of experience, women did not have the luxury to try and fail and try again and, in the process, develop the self-confidence and courage for the leap of faith to pursue personal goals. If Ruth Hanna McCormick had any reservations about her chances for success, she kept them to herself. Like the song in *Chorus Line*, "I can do that . . . ," Ruth could and did. Indeed, in explaining her decision to seek office she said, "No one asked me to run. I choose to run." And win she did. The depression may have later brought an end to her quest for elective office, but it never dampened her ardor for the political process. If one avenue was closed off, she opened another.

"What goes around, comes around," is a popular contemporary observation. It may be that history is like the old Slinky toy, with almost concentric circles inching forward, retreating briefly, only to advance again. The circle of Ruth Hanna McCormick, grandmother of author Kristie Miller, intersected her life by a brief three weeks. In Kristie's youth, her grandmother was but a shadow. With time came the realization that she had been an individual of note. Where once it was not important to know that one's traits, talents, and interests could be the legacy from a family member of another era, these discoveries would now be endearing and enduring. Wisely, Bazy, Ruth's daughter and Kristie's mother, ignored pleas to tell her about her grandmother. Kristie later was given the rare opportunity to make her own discoveries and draw her own conclusions. It is not surprising, therefore, that the person she discovered was not the mother Bazy remembered or that Bazy's memories differed greatly from her sister's. Each had known a different individual.

Kristie found a grandmother who had been a consummate politician, community leader, publisher, rancher, and supporter of the arts. In reading this fascinating account, I was struck by some similarities in Ruth Hanna McCormick's life in the political arena and my own. For example, when she was seeking office, she received a letter that stated, "I would not think of voting for a woman for Congressman-at-Large any more than to vote for one of my cows for such a responsible office." The *London Times* reported my election to the Senate as happening "in Kansas where a man's a man and a woman's his cook." This is, of course, merely a superficial observation, an anecdote, but other similarities run much deeper. We both had fathers involved in politics. At an early age, we both enjoyed listening in on their conversations and in working for local candidates. Neither one of us wanted to be considered "a woman's candidate." Going back to the idea of the Slinky, I was pleased to learn that one of Ruth's circles had crossed my family's. One of four speakers, she seconded Dad's nomination for the presidency in 1936 and went on to campaign for him in the Midwest.

Now, years later, her granddaughter's circle has intersected mine, introducing me to a woman of achievement. Who knows where the future circles will connect? We may at times come full circle, but each one advances in ways we could never predict—and therein lies the adventure.

Acknowledgments

When I was about twelve years old, it began to dawn on me that my mother's mother, whom I had never known because she died when I was less than one month old, was a Personage.

"Who was she?" I asked my mother. "Tell me about her."

This she steadfastly refused to do.

"One of two things may happen," she explained. "You might think you could coast on her achievements. Or you might be intimidated by her accomplishments. When you are older, you will find out about her, if you want to." I think my mother was wise.

I forgot about my grandmother, except as the principal agent of some wonderful practical jokes my mother would occasionally recall. I lived overseas off and on for fifteen years, working as an English teacher. Finally, when my own children were of school age, and I couldn't face schoolchildren morning, noon, and night, I began to think of another occupation.

My mother suggested I write her mother's biography.

"People were always telling Mother to write her memoirs, and she'd say airily, 'Oh, my daughter Bazy will do it.' I'm sixty-five and I'm a rancher. I'm not going to do it. Why don't you do it?"

So I did.

I am grateful to my mother, Bazy Tankersley, for giving me the idea and telling me all she could remember. I am especially grateful that, in 1950, she asked Elizabeth Manchester to interview a number of her mother's friends and relations, all long dead by the time I started the project thirty-five years later.

I also wish to thank friends of Ruth Hanna McCormick Simms who gave me personal interviews and shared many wonderful stories about her:

Fern Atencio, George Baldwin, the Honorable Herbert Brownell, Edward Burling, George Byrnes, Ann Simms Clark, Robert Dietz, Paul Horgan, Henriette Wyeth Hurd, Edwin Jaeckle, Janet White Barnes Lawrence, Florence Mahoney, Robert Mann, Olive Moses, Lillian Rosse, Elizabeth Wood Seymour, Albert Simms II, and Harry Thomas.

Very special thanks are due to my father, Peter Miller, Jr., my aunt and uncle, Katrina and Courtlandt Barnes, and to Irene Corbally Kuhn, for many interviews and much valuable advice.

I also want to thank for their valuable criticism: Tom Allen, Jim Dickson, Terry Fife, John A. Gable, Karen Goldbaum, Sally Graham, Louise Hutchinson, and Helen J. Twaddell. I owe an enormous debt of gratitude to Dr. Robert J. Hellman and Dr. Lewis L. Gould for a crash course in writing history.

Thanks to Susan Mary Alsop, for being my best role model, and for lending me her house while I worked at the Library of Congress; Ardene Blakeslee, for arranging all the travel this book required; Barbara Guth and David Holtby, my editors at UNM Press; Tom Hill at the Thomasville Historical Society; James Hillman, editor of *Spring*; Melanie Jackson, literary agent; Millicent Joseph, who chased children so I could work; Karl Kabelac of the University of Rochester Rare Book Collection; Charles J. Kelly of the Library of Congress Manuscript Reading Room; John McCutcheon, of the *Chicago Tribune* archives; Mary Ellen McElligott, editor of the *Illinois Historical Society*; and to Edmund Morris, Sylvia Jukes Morris, Lola Romanucci-Ross, Anna Curtenius Roosevelt, Burton R. Rubin, Joanna Sturm, Sheridan Sweet, Laurence R. Tancredi, Peter C. White, III, and the Biography Group of Washington D.C., for all manner of help and encouragement.

Affectionate thanks to my husband, T. L. Hawkins, without whose distracting attention this book would have been finished in half the time.

Introduction

"She learned the law of the jungle," read the caption on the cover of *Time* magazine. The red-bordered picture above it, a woman in a cloche hat with a wide grin and flashing brown eyes, was of Ruth Hanna McCormick, the most successful woman politician in the decade after women won the vote. It was April 1928, and Ruth McCormick had just defeated seven men in the Republican primary for Congressman-at-Large from Illinois. When she carried the entire state in November, ahead of the runner-up by ninety thousand votes, McCormick bid fair to become the first woman senator in 1930.

Ten years later, Ruth Hanna McCormick Simms again broke new ground when Thomas E. Dewey appointed her to manage his campaign for the Republican presidential nomination. This was an accomplishment that would not be equalled for almost fifty years. Raymond Moley, a *Newsweek* political analyst of the time, called her "the only woman in North America with a political technique."

In her half-century in politics, Ruth McCormick had the widest-ranging political career of any woman of that era. She had started out in the same manner as dozens of other civic-minded women of her generation, founding reform groups during the Progressive period, then moving on to fight for suffrage when it became clear that women would never get the reform legislation they wanted without the vote. Even after they won the vote, however, women found it hard to win political office. Male incumbents were hard to displace, and many women avoided party politics altogether, fearing that they would be co-opted by the men. Women often found themselves in a double bind: openly criticized if they tried to form a bloc of women voters, and ignored if they did not form one. Women struggled, too, against the social convention that a woman's personal commitments should always come before her career. Small wonder that volunteer politics continued to be women's principal political activity.

Most politically active women in the teens and twenties believed, along with Eleanor Roosevelt, that women succeeded best in politics if they followed a "service ideal." Eleanor Roosevelt, as well as other highly influential women like Molly Dewson, Belle Moscowitz, and Frances Perkins, enjoyed political power but thought that women should enter politics on the strength of issues, not personalities. The late Joseph Alsop, recalling Ruth's career, said, "It was uncommon then, as now, to meet a woman who talked politics, not morals."

Ruth Hanna McCormick had learned from intimate contact with powerful men how to cultivate a political personality, the sine qua non for elective politics in America. Her father, Marcus Alonzo Hanna, William McKinley's campaign manager and one of the most powerful men in the Senate, had trained Ruth as his personal assistant. Ruth had married Medill McCormick, who left his family-owned *Chicago Tribune* to become a Progressive legislator and, eventually, an influential senator himself. Ruth McCormick was her husband's valued political ally from the time he entered politics during the Bull Moose campaign of 1912 until his death in 1925. Theodore Roosevelt, whose legendary daughter Alice was her close friend, recognized Ruth McCormick's political instincts and corresponded with her minutely on Progressive party matters. Lacking female role models, Ruth, like the scant score of women in state and national politics in the twenties, had learned political techniques from male mentors.

Ruth McCormick always believed that women could and should participate equally with men, once the vote was won. "I am a suffragist, not a feminist," she liked to say. Many of the women who had worked for suffrage chose to continue in separate groups like the League of Women Voters and the Woman's Party. The term "feminist" in the 1920s and 1930s applied to those women who supported such separatist groups and worked for the Equal Rights Amendment. Women who successfully worked with men in the realm of elective politics, women like Ruth McCormick, Eleanor Roosevelt, Frances Perkins, and Molly Dewson, did not consider themselves "feminists." Ruth McCormick saw her primary mission as bringing women into the partisan political process.

Although Ruth McCormick was accepted by men as a working politician, she was still a woman, and the women of Illinois were her power base. To help her husband's Senate race in 1924, she had organized a network of Republican women's clubs across Illinois, and after his death the following year she made this considerable machine her own. Such grass-roots support enabled her to go to Congress, and later, to wrest the Senate nomination from a popular incumbent. A conventional and feminine woman who dressed beautifully and was the mother of three, Ruth McCormick made politics respectable for the many women who still considered the political process a rough, masculine affair. She was never in the vanguard of the women's movement of her day, but she filled an important role as a leader of the mainstream.

Her predilection for the middle ground became apparent in 1913 and 1914 when she began to campaign for suffrage. Her controversial activities in this movement have been examined here in depth, partly to dispel the popular myth that women in the suffrage campaign were united to achieve a common goal. Also, it was in the suffrage campaign that Ruth McCormick's techniques, first in Illinois and then as the head of the Congressional Committee of the National American Woman Suffrage Association, foreshadowed her life-long commitment to working within existing political structures. Her attempt to balance the separatist and integrationist tendencies in the women's movement continued throughout her career.

Ruth McCormick charged into party politics as soon as the Nineteenth Amendment was passed. She became the first woman on the Executive Committee of the Republican National Committee, and the first National Committeewoman from Illinois, as well as the first woman to win a national state-wide election, the first woman to run for the Senate on a major party ticket, and the first woman named as a presidential campaign manager.

Much of her success at politics came, not from a sense of moral uplift, but from the competitive zest that made her an expert poker player. Few women in the twenties had the personal ambition necessary to seek elective office, but after she was widowed, Ruth McCormick aspired to public office herself. "Nobody asked me to run," she said during her first campaign. "I choose to run." She plunged into the maelstrom of Illinois politics despite her background of wealth and influence. In fact, most women who entered public life in the teens and twenties were well-to-do. But the presence of even such unusual women in an arena traditionally reserved to men was one of the greatest accomplishments of the women's movement of her generation.

Ruth McCormick was a fortunate woman, but she always worked extremely hard, as if to justify her fortune. Nor did she work exclusively at politics. She had boundless enthusiasm for any new undertaking: in addition to her political work, she was a successful dairy and cattle rancher for thirty years, a newspaper publisher for more than fifteen years, and during the depression, she discovered and promoted many young artists, writers, and musicians who were struggling during the hard times. Often she ignited projects, turned them over to someone else, and then went on to a new venture. "How can you organize this woman's life?" her son-in-law wondered. "She was like a pea on a griddle." She might have accomplished more had she dedicated herself to a single goal. But then, as Yeats wrote, "The intellect of man is forced to choose/ Perfection of the life, or of the work."

Ruth McCormick's life was far from perfect. She faced many misfortunes. Her husband and soul-mate Medill McCormick was a manic-depressive who turned to alcohol to alleviate his mood swings, and at the age of forty-seven, killed himself. Their only son died mountain climbing when he was twenty-one. Her second marriage to Albert Simms grew loveless and lonely. And, of course, like any politician, she suffered her share of bitter defeats. But she prided herself always on her ability to cope with any crisis. Mark Hanna had been reared by a strong and capable woman, whom he loved and admired; he trained his own daughter to be strong and capable, too. He was stingy with praise, and from her early adolescence Ruth learned to be stoic and resourceful, for these were qualities that her father admired.

Although the success of Ruth McCormick's campaigns was essentially dependent on her ability to project her appealing personality, there were two key issues for which she worked all her life: women's rights and keeping America out of foreign wars. It would be wrong, however, to judge these ideas by the standards of our own time. Ruth McCormick thought that women should be equal to men, but not the same as men; along with many women of her generation, she believed that women had special abilities and special duties. But although she did relatively little work on specific legislation for women, she strove for over three decades to bring women into the world of partisan politics, believing that it was the only practical way for women to achieve their political goals. And it is clear that she believed her own electoral victories would pave the way for the success of future women politicians.

It is also possible to oversimplify Ruth McCormick's view of America's military obligations by labelling it positively as "pacifism" or negatively as "isolationism." Neither description would be entirely fair. Her father's Quaker background may have influenced her to some degree, but so did

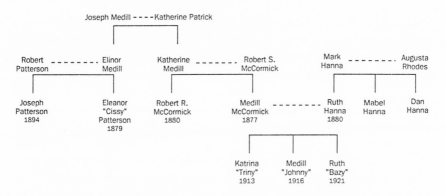

Theodore Roosevelt's call for "preparedness" during World War One. After that war, however, Ruth McCormick became disillusioned with the European situation. She was convinced that there would be constant warfare in Europe and that America had nothing to gain and a great deal to lose by interfering. She was a visible part of a strong anti-war movement that disappeared like smoke after Pearl Harbor, but which deserves to be better understood, especially at a time when ethnic antagonisms in Europe threaten to reappear in our own post–Cold War era.

When women first appeared on the political scene, Ruth McCormick was uniquely qualified to take advantage of the new opportunities, and her career illustrates the possibilities and limitations defining women's expanding role in politics before the Depression and the Second World War. For nearly fifty years, she was involved in most of the significant and colorful political events in this country: the settlement house movement, the Bull Moose party, the struggle for suffrage, the League of Nations fight, women's entrance into party politics, the depression, and the Republican Party's resurgence at the end of the depression. However, the depression, World War II, and the cult of home making in the fifties eclipsed the achievements of Ruth's generation. By the seventies and eighties, when the newest women's movement was looking for role models in politics, Ruth Hanna McCormick had been forgotten.

Too little is known today about women's political activities in the years after they won the vote. Too many women today seem to think that ours is the only pioneer generation. They forget that we owe a great deal of credit to those who came before us. It is, perhaps, unsettling to realize that progress is not constant and that advances may be partially reversed, as many of these women's were. Nevertheless, people like Ruth McCormick are the spiritual ancestors of the women of the modern period, working to bring women into existing political structures, learning the techniques of real politics, and how they can work for us. Ruth McCormick's values and strategies still have importance today.

Raymond Moley, asked in the late forties why there were so few successful women politicians a quarter of a century after women had won the vote, responded, "Success comes only to those who spend long years in the novitiate." In the twenties it was hoped that individual successes among exceptional women would lead to permanent changes in the power structure. That did not happen for many years, partly because lives like Ruth McCormick's were still so unusual.

Until you've been in politics, you've never really been alive. It's rough, and sometimes it's dirty, and it's always hard work and tedious detail. But it's the only sport for grown ups. All other games are for kids.

—Robert Heinlein

1
Her Father's Daughter: 1880–1903

AN UPBRINGING IN THE POLITICAL SERAGLIO

An upbringing in the political seraglio is like any other; one's father's business is an awful bother.

Thomas Beer, *Hanna*

Ruth Hanna was growing indignant. She had not minded when President Theodore Roosevelt had asked her father for an invitation to her upcoming wedding to Medill McCormick. After all, Ohio's Senator Mark Hanna had worked closely with the president for two years, and Roosevelt was a frequent visitor to their house, just across Lafayette Square from the White House. And she had not minded very much that the newspaper copy about her nuptials dwelt less on her trousseau than on Roosevelt's probable desire to secure Hanna's support for the presidential nomination, a difficult mission given that Hanna was Roosevelt's only serious rival. But now the president was planning a speaking tour through the West and had suggested Ruth postpone her wedding.

"The wedding has been set for the tenth of June," she coolly reminded the press. "It cannot be postponed. I am sure, if Mr. Roosevelt understands this, he will arrange to reach Cleveland by that time." The president meekly changed his itinerary. At twenty-three, Ruth Hanna already felt herself on equal terms with men, even with the most august political figures of her day. It was a day in which women were not often at ease with politicians. But Mark Hanna's daughter was different.[1]

Ruth Hanna was born in 1880, the year her father entered politics. Mark Hanna was already a settled and successful businessman of forty-two, beginning to feel there was more excitement to be got out of life than just making money. Her mother, Gussie, was a dignified matron of thirty-eight, with prematurely grey hair. Ruth was an afterthought baby, whose brother Dan was already thirteen, her sister Mabel just a bit younger. But in her father's old age, Ruth became his darling and his protégé, at a time when Mark Hanna dominated the politics of the Gilded Age. In time she became his political heir.

Perhaps this was only appropriate, for in many ways, Ruth resembled her father. She had the same piercing brown eyes and small, restless hands. They were both impulsive, generous, enthusiastic. Like her father, Ruth was impatient with mere books and learned directly from talking to people, all sorts of people. By the time she was sixteen, she had begun to take part in Hanna's political life, when he successfully managed William McKinley's presidential race against William Jennings Bryan. For the next seven years, she lived across from the White House, and considered the president a close friend. When Mark Hanna died, in Ruth's twenty-fourth year, she inherited his political allies, many of his political concerns, and his extraordinary political technique. For a woman in the early twentieth century, it was a unique legacy. It would be impossible to understand Ruth Hanna McCormick's career without a look at her famous father.

When Ruth was born, there was no hint in her parents' comfortable married life of their turbulent courtship. Young Mark Hanna had started out in his family's modest grocery and shipping business in Cleveland, Ohio. He was not, however, a single-minded businessman like his class-mate, John D. Rockefeller, but preferred to spend his leisure time at card parties, dinners, dances, or the boat club, of which he was the captain. At his father's insistence, Mark had enrolled in Western Reserve University but was suspended in the middle of his first year for a satire of the solemn Junior Exhibition. He was far happier working on the docks in his overalls, where he learned a great deal from talking to all sorts of people.

Mark's father was disappointed. Leonard Hanna, one of six strapping boys known collectively as "42 Feet of Hanna," was the only one who had gone to college, having trained as a physician at Rush Medical College in Philadelphia. But a fall from a horse in early manhood had injured his spine, and instead of practicing medicine he went into business with his brothers.

Leonard, a Quaker, had married Samantha Converse, a Presbyterian schoolteacher from Vermont, well-educated herself, with considerable executive ability. Her husband was often away on business trips or speaking tours (he took a prominent part in the temperance movement, mostly

on medical grounds.) In his absence Samantha exerted a powerful influence on her children. She was a sociable woman who loved having
important visitors to dinner. Their children were raised with more tol-
erance and less discipline than was usual in American homes of that
period.

When Leonard died at fifty-six, his widow capably reared and educated
the six children who were still at home. Mark was fond of his mother
and usually did what she wanted him to do. But in 1861 Mark and his
mother clashed over his wish to join the Union army. Mark had cast his
first vote for Abraham Lincoln and wanted to fight for his president. But
Samantha knew her husband was dying, and only Mark, the eldest boy,
understood the family's business affairs. After two months of tedious
wrangling, his younger brother went to war and Mark stayed home. He
tried to compensate by entertaining his friends on leave at dinners or at
the theater. If a soldier's son applied to him for a job, he would try to
find him one or send him to another firm with a note of recommendation
and a couple of dollars.[2] From his mother's example, young Mark learned
to respect the capabilities of women. Perhaps he was also influenced by
the Quaker tradition that stressed the equality of all human beings before
God. Quaker women preachers were not uncommon in the nineteenth
century, and this tradition produced a number of active feminists, such
as the Grimké sisters, Lucy Stone, Lucretia Mott, and Florence Kelley.

In the spring of 1862, Mark, a jolly, auburn-haired, freckled-faced
young man of twenty-six, met Charlotte Augusta Rhodes at a bazaar.
Gussie was the only daughter of Daniel Rhodes of Cleveland, who had
made a small fortune in coal and iron. She was nineteen years old, just
returned from three years at a finishing school in New York, tall, dignified,
and lovely; much too good, thought her father, for the likes of Mark
Hanna. Possibly Daniel Rhodes objected to the fact that the Hannas
were not as rich as he. But what was worse, they were Republicans.
Rhodes was half-cousin to Stephen Douglas, arch-enemy of the Hanna
hero, Abraham Lincoln. At that time, a man's party profoundly influenced his view of men and events, and Rhodes turned young Hanna out
before he even had time to plead his case. The two lovers persevered,
with Mark dispatching secret notes to Gussie at a dollar apiece via the
gardener's son. Finally, after two years, Rhodes relented. By then, Mark
had been conscripted, and he went off, an engaged man, to a hundred
days of service at the end of the Civil War.[3]

Mark Hanna, at the height of his political career some thirty years
later, was often portrayed by the opposition press as a callous brute. In
fact, the record shows he could be quite tender-hearted, even sentimen-

tal. At night, bivouacked near the Potomac, the young Union soldier fantasized about his wedding day. "How will you feel," he wrote Gussie, "when for the first time I take you in my arms and whisper in your ear 'my own darling wife' . . . when I can love and caress you to your heart's content . . ." He insisted on "an arrangement whereby you shall agree to do your share of that kind of business—for I am just as fond of it as you can possibly be."[4]

They were married soon after Hanna was mustered out, in September 1865. Immediately after the ceremony, Dan Rhodes turned to his son-in-law. "It's all over now, Mark," he said, "but a month ago I would like to have seen you at the bottom of Lake Erie." Hanna eventually went into business with his father-in-law, however, and prospered; until 1880 he devoted practically all his time to the coal and iron trade. Perhaps it is a measure of his way with people that although he had six thousand employees, there was little serious labor trouble. Typically, he made a point of going out among his men, and whenever one of them came to Hanna's office, he was shown in ahead of everyone else in the waiting room. When the business suffered its one bad strike in 1876, the governor called out the militia to put it down, and a striker was shot. Hanna was horrified and resolved to find a better method to solve differences. He became the first operator in the bituminous coal industry to recognize arbitration and also paid half-salary to men who were sick or injured, an uncommon practice at the time.[5]

After a period of depression, business picked up at the end of the 1870s, and Hanna expanded his activities. He bought a newspaper, organized a bank, and took over the little street railway company that served his neighborhood. On a whim, he even acquired a theater. Hanna was fond of plays and fascinated by players. He liked their gaiety and good fellowship. Edwin Booth, Henry Irving, Ellen Terry, Ethel Barrymore, and many other notable actors of the day were his good friends.[6]

Thus it was into ever-widening family horizons that the new baby girl was born in the early morning hours of March 27, 1880. Her parents had planned to call her Samantha Sophia after her grandmothers, but the visiting actor Lawrence Barrett protested, and they finally called her Ruth. Growing up, Ruth Hanna never went to sleep in a silent house. There was always jovial conversation and waves of laughter from below. Mark Hanna's favorite recreation was companionship, and he entertained not only his friends and business associates, but any prominent or interesting people who came to Cleveland. From an early age, Ruth would be stationed at the nursery window before dinner to count the carriages coming in, so that her mother would have some notion of how many to feed. Gussie had reluctantly learned to cope with the demands of so much entertainment. She had persuaded her parents' talented cook, Maggie Maloney, to accompany her when she left to be married, but there were times when Mrs. Hanna confessed to being "a weary house-keeper, tired of the momentous question, 'What shall we have to eat?'"[7]

Hanna relished company not just for the pleasure it gave him, but for what he could extract from his guests. He told Ruth, "If you surround yourself with your cronies, you may not learn anything from them." Ruth quickly showed herself as gregarious as her father. She was nothing at all like her mother, who was gentle and retiring. But since Mark had little time for the children, it was Gussie who supervised their upbringing; she was a permissive soul, and whenever Mark tried to impose discipline the children could always coax her to intercede. Ruth adored her father, but she was always considerably in awe of him.[8]

Sometimes Mark could show his concern for his little daughter, as when she became seriously ill on a family trip to Atlantic City the year she was eight. Hanna put off all business for six weeks to be with her until she was well enough to travel. But this indulgence was unusual. More typical was the time when Ruth was thrown from a horse and broke her arm. She consoled herself with the thought that her father would feel sorry for her, but when Hanna came home that night he took one look at her and barked, "What happened to you?"

"Oh Father," she wailed, "I fell off my horse and broke my arm." Ruth always remembered that he gave her a cold look and merely said, "I'll get you a riding master who will teach you how to fall off without breaking your arm." And then he walked out. It was hard to gain her father's attention, but she was determined to do it.[9]

Ruth was a high spirited and energetic child. The Hannas lived outside of town beside a lake, in a rambling three-story Victorian house with a round tower and many gables. Ruth and the other girls in the neigh-borhood loved to play Indians on horseback or ride the roller coaster at the end of the street-car line. Ruth was the boldest. She and her cousin Lucia often smoked cigarettes in back of the barn. One night when her parents were out, Ruth even persuaded Lucia to try one of the cigars her father always kept in a big container on the hall table. But when the girls lit up and propped their feet on the front porch, they were caught red-handed by a neighbor. However, he never told and they were not sick. Ruth continued to run a bit wild, feign illness, and skip school. In the summers she enjoyed the freedom of her grandparents' farm in Rav-enna, Ohio, where she romped with her brother Dan's three boys. She loved to ride and was particularly proud of her ability to manage a "four in hand," four horses drawing a coach.[10]

Though she was wild, Ruth was the only child who would not prove a disappointment to their father. The eldest, Dan, had become an attractive man with drive and ability, successful in business, but he drank heavily and was divorced by three wives in scandalous circumstances. The second child, Mabel, was euphemistically said to be "not quite right"; she spent hours sitting in a swing, rolling her eyes and simpering when spoken to. Though Gussie was very protective of her, there was considerable prejudice in that era against "feeblemindedness." Ruth may have tried to ignore her elder sister, and Mabel, for her part, understandably disliked Ruth for being the favorite in the family.[11]

As Ruth grew older, her father took a more active role in her upbringing. In later years, when she had become a politician herself, she liked to recollect a political meeting where she was "put to bed on a pile of overcoats on a desk in an anteroom when she could stay awake no longer." Hanna, absorbed in the issues he had just been discussing, supposedly did not remember his daughter until he was half-way home. Ruth loved a good story, and some of her recollections were highly colored, but it was true was that she soon began to share her father's interest in public affairs. Since Hanna conducted a great deal of business by entertaining at home, Ruth was schooled in political talk from an early age; as she grew older, she joined in the conversations.[12]

In what normally passes for schooling, Ruth was far less advanced. When she was sent off to boarding school in Dobbs Ferry, New York, at fourteen, it was a disaster. Because she had attended elementary school inconsistently, she was poorly prepared and failed nearly everything. Self-conscious over her backwardness, she did not make friends. To console herself, she kept a rabbit in her slop jar, but it was discovered and there was a row. Worst of all, she came down with whooping cough. Finally, she fled to Thomasville, Georgia, where her father was spending the winter, to recover. That visit changed her life.[13]

Thomasville was the premier Southern resort of its day, and for several years Mark Hanna had taken his family there on short winter vacations. That year, they were staying at a small hotel, where Ruth was installed in a bedroom to be nursed by her mother and aunt. Soon the Hannas were coming up after meals with stories of the family at the table next to theirs in the dining room. It seemed there was a slim boy of seventeen who was also convalescing, together with his parents and a deaf grandfather with a huge ear trumpet. The grandfather was Joseph Medill, publisher of the *Chicago Tribune*, With him were his daughter, the beautiful, imperious, red-headed Kate, and her diplomat husband, Robert McCormick. The boy was his grandfather's namesake, Joseph Medill McCormick, heir apparent to the *Tribune*.[14]

Young Medill,* as he was called, and Ruth were sent riding on trails through the pine woods to recover their health with fresh air and exercise. Medill immediately admired her fine horsemanship and the great long braid of hair that flapped between her shoulders when she galloped. Ruth did not ride side-saddle as a Southern lady would; she rode astride, wearing wide divided bloomers. Their companionship was enlivened by the picnics and dances, races and musical entertainments of the popular resort town. By the time the two had recovered their health, and separation loomed, they had fallen in love. They engaged themselves to marry, but were too young to dare tell their parents. Medill went back to Groton, and Ruth returned to her grandparents' farm in Ravenna, Ohio, with a tutor.[15]

Once Ruth had recovered, Hanna expressed his annoyance with her poor performance at Dobbs Ferry and, as punishment, set her to memorize the tributaries of the tributaries of the Mississippi River. After months of intensive study at home, Ruth enrolled in Miss Porter's School in Farmington, Connecticut. She now passed her courses, although she never became much of a student. She soon became popular there, however. "She would have been very handsome," one classmate remembered, "if it had not been for the puffy black shadows under her eyes." They loved her because she was athletic, high-spirited, and full of mischief.[16]

Ruth craved her father's admiration, but she was not going to win it through her studies. She was much more interested in her father's activities. At the end of 1894 Mark Hanna had turned his business interests over to his brother Leonard so he could devote more time to politics. He believed that retired businessmen made more disinterested politicians than men who went into it "for the trade, for what there is in it," and his attitude inspired Ruth with the idea that politics was a worth-while endeavor. Beginning in 1880, the year Ruth was born, Hanna had worked for James A. Garfield, not only because Garfield was Republican, but because he came from the vicinity of Cleveland. Later Hanna backed Ohio Senator John Sherman in two attempts for the presidential nom-

---

*Pronounced med-DILL.

ination. He could not support anyone with whom he was not personally intimate; his success in business was largely due to his network of personal contacts, and his subsequent success in politics was based on similar ties. Ruth's highly personal political style would be patterned after her father's.[17]

By 1891 Hanna had begun to raise money for another Ohio neighbor, William McKinley, a seven-term congressman running for governor of Ohio. In a year of general Republican defeat, McKinley was elected by a huge majority. Even the caustic former Speaker of the House, Thomas B. Reed, was impressed with Hanna's efforts on behalf of his candidate. "If you ever want to coax me to do anything," he wrote McKinley, "you had better send Hanna."[18]

The Democrats became vulnerable when the country was hit by a depression in 1893. Banks and railroads failed, and farmers, who had already suffered several years of drought, lost their farms. Twenty percent of the labor force was out of work, and Coxey's Army of the Unemployed marched on Washington. Those who still had jobs were striking against drastic wage cuts. In 1894 the Republicans, who had been in decline during the second Cleveland administration, took advantage of the situation to win back many seats in Congress. At that point, Hanna withdrew from business and prepared to make his friend Governor William McKinley president of the United States.[19]

McKinley had been very popular at the 1892 Convention and had been reelected governor of Ohio. By 1895 he had strength throughout the country. But as John Hay observed that summer, "A year is a good while in American politics." McKinley was a strong candidate but hardly the inevitable one. Hanna spent over a year of hard work and careful planning to make the nomination certain. His first step was to lease a house back in Thomasville, where Ruth had met Medill. The McKinleys came to visit, claiming the trip was only "a little rest and outing." But everyone knew that nearly half of the votes needed for nomination came from the South, and that he was there "to discuss Little Miss Boomlet."[20]

Every day the two friends sat in the sun parlor receiving visitors. As good Republicans, they drew no color line. Hanna, although politically conservative, believed, along with most Quakers, in equal opportunities, civil and political rights. Back in Cleveland he had put together a network of African-American political leaders with the help of George A. Myers, a black whom Hanna had helped to establish in a barbershop in Cleveland's leading hotel. Later on, as an influential senator living across from the White House, Hanna made the front page of the New York Times when he invited Judson W. Lyons, the black national chairman from

Georgia, with other Republican chairmen to dinner. Ruth grew up with⎫
his attitudes, and some of her strongest supporters would be her African- ⎬
American constituents.[21]

In the summer Governor McKinley and his wife visited the Hannas
in Cleveland, and on the porch overlooking the lake they discussed the
issues of the upcoming campaign with party leaders. Ruth later claimed
to have sat on McKinley's lap as a child and to have taken the place in
his heart of the little daughters who had died. She was surely exagger-
ating, but McKinley was indeed a household familiar. He and his wife
were extremely fond of youngsters, and she probably did talk freely to
McKinley and the other politicians.[22]

Ruth was now sixteen, and was being indoctrinated into old-fashioned
partisan campaigning. She loved the drama of nineteenth-century popular politics. "It was the ambition of my life," she later recalled,

> to walk in a torchlight parade. When I was finally permitted to, I walked
> until my legs nearly fell off. I screamed and yelled until my throat was
> sore. I waved the torch until it dripped on me and my face was black
> and burned.

At this point it is well to remember that most women of her time were
never initiated into the prevailing political culture; twenty-five years
later it would be hard for them to participate in party politics as men of
their age would easily do. Even the suffrage women were never completely
comfortable with partisan politics, and after they won the vote many
joined the Woman's Party or the League of Women Voters. But Ruth
Hanna, no doubt because of these early experiences, was one of the very
few Suffrage leaders who later went into elective politics at the national
level.[23]

McKinley was easily nominated at St. Louis in mid-June, but Hanna,
at fifty-nine, was feeling the strain of the campaign, and looking forward
to a rest. On July 7, however, the Democrats impulsively nominated
William Jennings Bryan in Chicago after his stirring "Cross of Gold"
speech, and, to Hanna's dismay, the whole situation changed overnight.
Bryan's nomination would mean "work and hard work from the start."
The Republicans had no fixed campaign headquarters. Hanna shuttled
between offices in Chicago and New York in his private railroad car;
wherever he happened to be was the party's headquarters. And Ruth
watched him, as he sat with his cane across his knees and a bottle of
mineral water at his elbow, talking to visitors about speakers and brass
bands and educational pamphlets on sound money.[24]

The campaign that Mark Hanna waged for William McKinley in 1896 was a new kind of campaign. Political campaigns after the Civil War had been rallies featuring torchlight parades, campaign clubs, and marching companies. People were influenced by their war memories and were simply urged to "vote as you shot." But liberal reformers in the 1870s wanted to improve government by educating the voters and trying to overcome the ignorance of recent immigrants and the corrupt influence of the party bosses.

While Mark Hanna did not invent the new "educational" or propaganda technique, the scale of his campaign was unprecedented. He sent out a blizzard of campaign literature to point out the cost of inflation to those with pensions, insurance policies, or savings bank deposits. During the entire campaign at least 200 million pamphlets and leaflets were printed, amounting to 14 pieces for each voter, including 275 different items in eleven foreign languages. He organized bureaus for Civil War veterans, first-time voters, and women's departments in the suffrage states. His thorough methods became a model for his daughter's later campaigns.[25]

Large-scale campaigning required large-scale fund raising. Hanna himself had paid most of the preconvention expenses. For the national campaign, however, outside money had to be raised. Easterners were nervous about Bryan, and Hanna coolly assessed each corporation according to what he thought their financial interest in the election should be. Hanna's basic campaigning technique, essentially still used today, featured a central organization, complete media coverage, and controlled exposure of the candidate. McKinley stayed at home, conducting a "front porch" campaign. He would not give up the old-fashioned notion that "the office sought the man," and refused to tour the country making speeches as Bryan was doing. "I might just as well put up a trapeze on my front lawn and compete with some professional athlete as go out speaking against Bryan," he said, adding slyly, "I have to *think* when I speak."[26]

Delegations streamed into McKinley's hometown of Canton, Ohio all summer. The visitors, wearing campaign badges, caps, and neckties, descended from trains and were escorted down Market Street by the smartly uniformed Canton horse troops, to the trampled McKinley lawn where they waited awkwardly for their hero to appear. Presently he would step out onto the famous porch and wave to the cheering throng, then listen raptly to the spokesman whose remarks he had actually edited some time before. Visitors filed up to the porch, shook his hand, and proceeded out the back door, to where the restaurants and souvenir stands of Canton were doing a brisk business. Groups of Ohio girls, including Ruth Hanna, served sandwiches and beer, coffee, and lemonade from the porch to the waiting delegations.[27]

For the first time in recent history, the Midwest, the Far West, and the Pacific Coast all were in doubt, and the Republican National Committee became more important than ever before. Traveling back and forth between New York and Chicago, Hanna, the national campaign manager, began to receive almost as much attention as McKinley. Part of Hanna's success came from the strength of his personality. He entered into projects whole-heartedly, and his success in politics, like his success in business, was based on his ability to communicate his personal energy to others. While he could dominate an encounter, he was also a good listener. The *New York Tribune* commented that he "never displayed nor dissembled his power, but seemed to carry it as naturally as he carried his rolled-up daily paper." Mark Hanna passed these traits on to his daughter, who became the same sort of campaigner her father had been.[28]

The new prominence of the national campaign manager was not without its disadvantages. Hanna's activity attracted attention, and abuse. The Democrats were hesitant to attack the popular McKinley, so they attacked his manager instead. Especially rough was William Randolph Hearst's *New York Journal,* which published the Homer Davenport cartoons depicting Hanna as an obese drunkard in a check suit covered with dollar signs. Many of Davenport's cartoons suggested that Hanna manipulated McKinley, portraying him as a puppet-master or a ventriloquist. But in fact, it can be argued that it was McKinley who had always used Hanna, as he used many of his other associates. Hanna was "just a shade obsequious" around McKinley, according to one mutual friend. Another saw Hanna's attitude toward the nominee "like that of a big, bashful boy toward the girl he loves."[29]

Yet in all the conjecture about him, what really bothered Hanna most was Hearst's portrayal of him as an enemy of the working class, claiming that for thirty years Hanna had "torn at the flanks of labor like a wolf." Hanna was very proud of his good relations with the unions. A friend reported seeing Hanna wince when he read the newspapers. "That hurts," Hanna said.

> When I have tried all my life to put myself in the other fellow's place, when I have tried to help those in need and to lighten the burdens of the less fortunate than myself, to be pictured as I am here, to be held up to the gaze of the world as a murderer of women and children, I tell you it hurts.

He warned Ruth: "To succeed in politics you must have the hide of a rhinoceros. And a sense of the ridiculous."[30]

By November Bryan's populist appeal was more than offset by Hanna's well-organized campaign of education. Still, Election Day was intensely exciting. Turnout exceeded 80 percent of eligible voters in the North. Ruth begged to be allowed to join the family in New York, and an aunt was dispatched from Cleveland to take her to Madison Square Garden.[31]

"Thousands and thousands of people jammed the plaza and whooped and yelled every time a lead of seven or eight was thrown on a wobbly screen that hung suspended against a building," Ruth remembered. At midnight it was announced that McKinley had been elected by the largest popular vote in twenty-four years, and Ruth, already infected by the intense excitement of a political campaign, learned at firsthand the thrill of a decisive victory at the polls.

She went back to school with the memory of her father besieged at the Waldorf Hotel by hordes of Republicans who thought an endorsement from Hanna was the next best thing to an appointment. Many expected Hanna to take the Treasury post, but he scoffed at the idea: "Me in the Cabinet? All the newspapers would have cartoons of me selling the White House kitchen stove!" His brother-in-law, the historian James Ford Rhodes, suspected that Hanna would have disliked the routine and confinement of the office. Hanna preferred something that would give him influence yet preserve his independence. He had always dreamed of becoming a senator, yet had always felt it was beyond his grasp. But when McKinley decided to honor Ohio's aging Senator John Sherman by appointing him Secretary of State, Hanna was nominated to fill the vacancy in the Senate.[32]

The Hannas went to Washington in March for the Inauguration. Ruth, almost seventeen, was there with her cousin Lucia, in a high state of exhilaration. It was a clear, windy day; flags were snapping and bands were blaring. Crowds surged on all sides. The acrid, burning smell of photograph taking hung on the air. On a stand to one side of the Capitol were operators testing Edison's kinetoscope, trying to obtain a motion picture of the event. And right there on the large decorated platform, with the McKinleys and the massive Grover Cleveland, was Ruth's father. Nearly as exciting, for the two girls, was the parade that followed. With the Republicans back in office, the army and navy were glorified as in days of yore. Ruth and Lucia had beaux in the Ohio horse troops, which enjoyed special prestige that year.[33]

The next day Hanna was sworn into the Senate. He became a picturesque and powerful leader in the course of his seven-year tenure, but he took time to establish himself. Most senators at that time were lawyers, and they were deeply suspicious of businessmen. The *New York Times* sniffed, "Mr. Hanna is too deep in business to be broadminded and impartial." Hanna never spoke from the Senate floor the first two sessions he attended.[34]

Ruth had graduated from Miss Porter's School, but she had no interest in going on to college. Her father did not approve of idleness, so he made Ruth his confidential secretary, where, she said, "my education began in earnest." Every day she set off for his Senate office, hat secured with long pins atop her pompadour, and business-like shirtwaist blouse drawn tightly from a stiff white linen collar, to disappear beneath a snug belt. Above her high-topped shoes Ruth affected a "short" skirt for office wear, which daringly cleared the ground.[35]

Hanna had a male secretary, Elmer Dover, to do the clerical work. Ruth was assigned to read and make digests of the bills up for legislation. When Hanna was in committee, he delegated Ruth to sit in the Senate gallery and report to him what happened in debate, as well as the attitude of certain senators to questions under discussion. She learned legislative procedure, as well as the political technique of the Capitol, for example, how a bill gets on and off the calendar. And she learned to love the drama of debate.[36]

Hanna's office was a busy one. He had more callers than any other senator of the time—politicians from all over the country, businessmen, labor leaders, governors, congressmen, fellow senators, even cabinet officers. Vice-President Garrett Hobart lent Hanna his office to receive them all. The one man on whom Hanna called himself was President McKinley. Sometimes Ruth felt "horribly abused" because she couldn't lie abed mornings but had to be up by eight. If she went to a dance, she would feel so sleepy the next day that the work was "more drudgery than ever." Mark Hanna was not an easy man to work for. Hanna's secretary, Dover, reported that "He never found fault; he never praised anybody; he showed his confidence in men by increasing their responsibility." Another campaign worker agreed. "You could go to the office at the end of a hard campaign and he would never say we had done well . . . If you won, you won; if you lost, you lost and that was all." Ruth was treated in the same way. "In all my life I never had one word of praise from my father," she said. "If he accepted the work, it was satisfactory. Otherwise, it came back to me to do over again." Ruth had always wanted very badly to get her father's attention. She tried to do so by imitating him in every way she could.[37]

Ruth's responsibilities continued at home. During their first two years in Washington, the Hannas lived at the Arlington Hotel, across Lafayette Square from the White House, where they had a large suite. Hanna still entertained as much as ever. The suite at the Arlington was fitted with a special kitchen, converted from a bathroom, where their cook Maggie Maloney prepared the small informal dinners Hanna liked to give to men like Elihu Root, William Howard Taft, Vice-President Garrett Hobart, and occasionally John Hay or Henry Cabot Lodge. The best meal of the week, however, was Sunday morning breakfast, with Maggie's famous corned beef hash topped by poached eggs, surrounded by watercress, and accompanied by fragrant coffee and crisp toast. Though Ruth's part was to sit at the end of the table and pour the coffee, the political breakfasts at which her father entertained did much to enhance her understanding of men and affairs. She later protested that her "participation in them has been charmingly and flatteringly exaggerated by the press. They were not part of a deep-laid plan of my father's to make me into a statesman." Still, that was the result.[38]

In addition Ruth became an eyewitness to the history of her times. Her first year in Washington, she experienced the crisis of the Spanish-American War, which Hanna strongly opposed. War went against his Quaker upbringing; furthermore, it threatened the economic improvement he was working for. This adventurous war was championed by Theodore Roosevelt, then Assistant Secretary of the Navy, who flatly told him, "We will have this war for the freedom of Cuba, Senator Hanna, in spite of the timidity of commercial interests." Hanna struggled to keep McKinley neutral. Ruth recalled spending one long night "crumpled up in a big armchair" in the White House, while her father argued with the president. McKinley could not resist the pressure from his party and from the country as a whole, and Roosevelt went off to war with his Rough Riders. Ruth had been deeply influenced by her father's arguments, however, and she would later campaign passionately to keep America out of entangling foreign alliances and out of further wars.[39]

Ruth's life was not exactly one of drudgery, no matter how ill-used she may have felt at times. During the summers, she had ample opportunity to indulge her craving for activities out of doors. One year the family went on a lake cruise and another year to Yellowstone Park. There were pack trips in the Cascades, Wyoming, or Idaho where she could fish and hunt. The most memorable was a visit to the Ojai Valley in California with her mother. They traveled by coach up the narrow valley, flanked by towering, barren mountains. At the top of the pass they stopped to eat and change horses at a small inn, and the passengers strolled around admiring the panoramic view of pine forests and winding streams. At the end of the rest stop, as the coachman was hitching up fresh horses, he was kicked and his arm was broken. The passengers faced spending the night in the desolate spot. Ruth, still just a teenager, offered to drive the horses down, since the coachman still had one good arm to apply the brake. Less than half the passengers were willing to risk it; comments were made about her small hands and how inadequate they seemed to the task. But the coachman saw it as his best chance to get medical help and allowed her to drive the team down the mountain, which she safely did. It was characteristic of Ruth's confidence in herself and her risk-taking ability. Few of her later accomplishments in life gave her so much pride.[40]

Despite Hanna's doubts about the economic effect of the war, by the turn of the century Americans were at last enjoying good times again, and the Republicans planned to take full credit for this happy state of affairs. There was no suspense over the presidential nomination at the 1900 Convention in mid-June, where McKinley was promptly selected for a second term. The real interest centered on his running mate, since Garrett Hobart had died in office, and a new vice-president had to be selected. The New York machine, under "Boss" Thomas C. Platt, wanted to be rid of their troublesome reform governor, Theodore Roosevelt, and were paradoxically promoting him for the job. The delegates, especially the western delegates, inspired by "Teddy's" exploits as a Rough Rider in the recent war, were eager to have him, too. Hanna, who thought Roosevelt too impulsive, fought in vain to control the convention, exclaiming at one point to a Washington correspondent, "Don't any of you realize there's only one life between this madman and the Presidency?"[41]

Hanna was a loyal Republican, though, and after Roosevelt's nomination he planned a vigorous campaign. The senator liked to "make a sure thing doubly sure," and he canvassed the country thoroughly. Most Republicans were taking victory for granted, and Hanna complained that not he, but General Apathy, was in charge. He campaigned personally in the West, responding to occasional hecklers with "a smile that could grease a wagon." Ruth, when she began to campaign herself, liked to encourage stories that she had stumped with her father. Most probably she had not; nowhere in the many detailed accounts of Hanna's activities was she mentioned. But the truth at the kernel of her stories was that she learned his techniques. She became an extremely thorough campaigner, an engaging speaker, and one who could always parry a taunt with a smile.[42]

Hanna's most effective contribution to the election outcome, however, was his mediation of a threatened strike among the anthracite coal workers. It was feared that a strike would swing votes to Bryan, once again the Democratic nominee. Hanna had unique influence with the mine operators, having been one himself, yet he enjoyed good relations with the workers in his own businesses. Indeed, the men on his street railways had refused to join a general strike the year before, in spite of great pressure to do so, so that Hanna could take a much needed rest cure in Europe. Through Hanna's mediation with both parties, a settlement with the mine workers was reached in mid-October 1900. It was the start of a new career for Hanna, and it was one that influenced his daughter as much as his political campaign tactics had done.[43]

The following year, 1901, Hanna associated himself with the National Civic Federation. He had long felt the need for improved communications between employer and employee. Workers, especially new immigrants with a tradition of more hostile labor movements, needed to be educated. He also was convinced that capitalists had to overcome their belief that they had the right to dictate conditions. The National Civic Federation had grown out of the Chicago Civic Federation, started in 1893 by Ralph M. Easley, a reporter for the *Chicago Inter Ocean*, Easley was impressed by Hanna's reputation for fairness as a major employer and his unusual sympathy for labor unions.

The agreement with the coal operators that Hanna helped negotiate in the fall of 1900 lasted only a few months, however. The miners were threatening another strike unless the union was organized and grievance-settlement procedures adopted. Easley and John Mitchell, the president of the United Mine Workers, turned to Hanna. This came at a time when the railroads were also having disputes, and a steel strike was threatened, too. The National Civic Federation worked to clarify the aims of both owners and workers in each industry. This was a novel, almost revolutionary, idea, but entirely suited to the hands-on talents of Mark Hanna.[44]

Although strikes were not always averted, the four main mediators—Easley, Mitchell, Hanna, and Samuel P. Gompers—were able to prevent crippling sympathy strikes. At first Easley had regarded Hanna as "the greatest buccaneer in the country," but he soon discovered that Hanna was a "whole team and willing to work." The mine owners, on the other hand, accused Hanna of acting only to further his political aims. He replied, "Tell them that if they will arbitrate their differences with the miners, I will make an affidavit that I will not only refuse to accept the nomination for president if tendered to me, but, if elected, I will refuse to qualify." Finally, in Theodore Roosevelt's administration, a coal arbitration commission was established.

Though it came late in life, Mark Hanna had become a real reformer, and he believed the work he was doing was more important than any political work, more important than his work in the Senate. Ruth was twenty-one, and could not have failed to be impressed by his passion and his zeal. Hanna became president of the National Civic Federation, and it is no coincidence that after his death, Ruth helped found a women's division of the organization. It was the beginning of her interest in the reform movements that were gathering momentum at the turn of the century and the beginning of her own political career.[45]

Even though he believed his reform work more important, Hanna could not escape politics altogether. By late spring 1901 the Republican nomination for 1904 was already being discussed; both Hanna and Vice-President Roosevelt were mentioned. When, in June, McKinley stopped rumors of a third term by announcing he would not accept another nomination, Roosevelt increased his efforts to find supporters.[46]

Hanna had worried about McKinley's safety during the election. Anarchists were becoming bold; three European heads of state had been assassinated in recent years. His reservations at the convention about the vice-presidential nominee stemmed in part from his very real fears for McKinley's life. Nonetheless, after the election, security precautions had been relaxed. On September 6 McKinley was shaking hands with the crowd at a Pan American Exposition in Buffalo, New York, when a man stepped forward and shot the president with a gun concealed in a bandage over his hand. McKinley died a week later. Roosevelt rushed to Buffalo from a camping trip, to be inaugurated in a nearby house. Hanna visited him immediately afterwards, and Roosevelt recalled their conversation: "As soon as he called on me, without any beating around the bush, he told me he had come to say that he would do all in his power to make the administration a success." However, "there was not in his speech a particle of subserviency, no worship of the rising sun." Hanna was making it clear that his promise of support did not extend to securing Roosevelt the nomination in 1904.[47]

Yet in spite of their rivalry, Roosevelt and Hanna came to work closely together. The senator lobbied for many of the president's programs in the Senate, most notably the Panama Canal Treaty. "There was no important feature of any of my policies which I did not carefully discuss with him," Roosevelt said. "Throughout my term as President . . . I was in very close relations with him. He was continually at the White House, and I frequently went over to breakfast and dinner at his house . . ."[48]

When President Roosevelt visited, he usually sat beside Ruth at table. "He puffed me up terribly with his compliments about my understanding of politics. He would even turn to me for information sometimes concerning some measure in Congress that I had been studying for Father," she said. Roosevelt must have wished that his own pleasure-loving daughter Alice were as politically minded as Ruth, and he almost never went away without telling her that he wanted Alice and her to be chums. They finally did become friends after Alice attended Ruth's wedding.[49]

Ruth Hanna had never wavered from her plan to marry Medill McCormick, and they had corresponded with each other from their boarding schools. After Ruth's society debut in 1901 they met socially in Washington where Medill was beginning his apprenticeship as a reporter for the *Chicago Tribune*. As the eldest grandson, he was expected eventually to run it.*[50]

First, though, Medill had to prove himself a newspaperman, and he had gone to Washington as a correspondent directly following his graduation from Yale in 1900. But after only three months he left to join an old family friend, General Henry Clark Corbin, who was making a study tour of the recently acquired Philippines. During the long days there on horseback and the still longer ones on shipboard, Medill assessed alternatives to the career into which he had fallen at birth. He did not want to be a diplomat like his father, at least not during his youth. He was interested in politics, but thought a political career could wait until after he had "become a person of influence and experience."[51]

When he returned to Chicago, he settled into newspaper work more seriously than before. In a theme that would recur again and again, he begged his father to keep his domineering mother away for "ten or twelve unbroken weeks," complaining that he and his mother were both "nervous persons" and she continually interfered. He was lonely but denied to his father any thought of marriage. He was sure it would be "charming to

---

*Old Joseph Medill had died in 1899, and the paper was being managed by a son-in-law, Robert Patterson. Robert and Elinor Patterson had a son and a daughter. Elinor, fiercely competitive with her sister Kate McCormick, had also named her first-born after their father, Joseph Medill (Joe) Patterson; their daughter Eleanor was known as "Cissy." The four cousins all made a mark in the world; Medill as a politician; Bert as the publisher of the *Tribune*; Joe as the founder of the *New York Daily News*; and Cissy as the editor of the *Washington Herald* and glamorous enfant terrible.

be married," but he did not propose to jeopardize his career "for the sake of being charmed." Medill was writing to his father, though he meant the reassurance for his mother. The spoiled heiress had no notion of sharing her favorite son with anyone, as Medill doubtless realized.[52]

In June 1902 Ruth's sister Mabel was quietly married off to Harry Parsons, an older man who enjoyed designing boats. Mark Hanna made a settlement on Parsons with the understanding that he act as Mabel's guardian and that there be no children—a type of arrangement that was not unknown in those days. A small ceremony at the Hanna home was attended only by their closest friends, but it inspired Ruth and Medill who decided that, after seven years of waiting, their time had finally come.

While visiting Ruth in Cleveland that summer, Medill carefully chose the moment to approach Mr. Hanna, when he was playing solitaire, but it was no use. Hanna ridiculed the idea: any man Ruth wanted at twenty-two, she would not want at twenty-seven, and he refused to discuss the matter further. A battle of wills ensued between father and daughter. Finally, one day in late August Ruth drove her horse down to meet Hanna at the station. He could not walk or drive away because of his rheumatism; he had to hear her out. She asked him to give her one good reason why she couldn't marry Medill McCormick; if not, she declared, she would announce her engagement within two weeks.[53]

Her father said nothing for two weeks. Ruth boldly called the society pages of the paper and told them to print an announcement. She didn't sleep all night and the next morning went down to breakfast feeling sick with anxiety. Her father was reading the paper. "Well, I see you got your ad in," was his only remark. A reporter called Gussie, who confirmed the announcement.

Meanwhile, Medill's father, Robert Sanderson McCormick, by then Minister of the American Legation in Vienna, had just been named Ambassador to Russia. His wife, the new Ambassadress, was even less pleased than the Hannas. Medill had to appeal once again to his father to control Kate, defending his choice:

> Ruth, I think, is able. I know she is only too willing to do her part. Mother must not only be civil to her—she is that—but she must bridle her tongue when she discusses Ruth in the family or out of it.

Medill pointed out that he had forgiven his mother's "bitterness" up until then, but would do so "no more." When Kate tried to have the wedding postponed for six months, even Mark Hanna took the side of the young couple. "I had an experience of a postponed wedding from May to September and know how it is myself," he wrote the senior McCormicks. "So my sympathy is with my children." The wedding was set for June 10.[54]

Even Ruth Hanna's wedding was a political event. At first Mark Hanna had hesitated to invite the president to the ceremony; he did not want him to feel obliged to attend. But Roosevelt had solved the problem by asking to come. Then, before the wedding took place, the two rivals nearly had a falling out. Hanna's political enemies in Ohio had contrived an awkward situation for him at the state convention in late May 1903. During what should have been a routine meeting, these men proposed that the convention endorse Theodore Roosevelt as a presidential candidate for 1904. But the election was more than a year away, and Hanna wanted to keep his options open.

Roosevelt, who was anxious to be elected in his own right, did his best to put Hanna on the spot. He sent Hanna a curt telegram, which he then made public, saying "Those who favor my administration and my nomination will favor indorsing both, and those who do not will oppose." Hanna reluctantly agreed not to oppose the endorsement. Roosevelt was relieved and grateful: "No one but a really big man—a man above all petty considerations—could have treated me as you have done," he wrote Hanna. Although they appeared to be reconciled, Hanna was smarting from the strong-arm tactics, and Roosevelt was still privately uncertain of Hanna's support. Pundits were eager to see what would happen when the two leaders met at the wedding. The *Buffalo News*, marveling at Ruth Hanna's refusal to change her wedding plans to accommodate the president, wondered, "What might have been the result if the subject of the indorsement of the president had been a matter of difference between the Chief Magistrate and Miss Ruth Hanna, instead of her famous father?"[55]

Medill pretended to be put out by the fuss surrounding Roosevelt's attendance at his nuptials. "Everyone tells me that between you and Roosevelt I will pass unnoticed," he wrote Ruth, adding wistfully, "I hope not by you or the parson." But despite such remarks and his repeated assurances to his parents that he intended to work at the *Tribune*, Medill had already become fascinated by politics during two months that he spent in Washington in spring 1903. He was especially intrigued by the Senate. The government of the United States, he concluded, was "an oligarchy tempered by the veto." Power lay not with the president but with the half dozen "oligarchs" who controlled the Senate. He confessed to admiring them: "If I were not going to be a newspaper person, earning a living for myself and my employers, I should like to be an oligarch. It is an easy life and a proud one." He was about to marry into the family that wrote the book on getting oligarchs elected.

His first political step had been to accept the presidency of the Roosevelt Club in Chicago. Before leaving Washington he had called on the president, and he wrote Ruth of waiting in the ante-chamber, listening to Roosevelt make "staccato noises" in the next room. This meeting began a long relationship that would advance the political careers of both Medill and Ruth Hanna McCormick.[56]

Although Medill had enjoyed his exposure to Washington, he felt there was little real work for him there and eagerly returned to Chicago where he had more than enough to do. He was trying hard to get the *Tribune*'s business affairs running smoothly before his wedding, and complained to Ruth that he couldn't find out how many from Chicago were planning to attend the wedding because if he did, he would have to "throw up his job" to do it. He was always contrite after complaining, signing his letters "your 'worthless' old M." He also worried about his difficult family, warning his bride-to-be to say nothing to his cousin Cissy Patterson that she would not want repeated to his mother, and nothing at all about the *Tribune,* which he was not supposed to have discussed with her. Ruth, in the meantime, sensibly avoided undue strain on herself, having suffered from a mild case of typhoid fever in the spring. She declined any bridal showers, saying they left brides-elect too weary to endure the fatigue of a wedding journey. "I propose to enjoy my trip," she declared.[57]

But Ruth Hanna could not hope to restrain her father upon such an occasion. He enjoyed nothing so much as having a crowd of friends and relatives in his house to celebrate a happy event. He did turn away reporters, protecting the privacy of his illustrious guests and refusing to give out a list of presents: "That is none of the public's business, and I have had enough publicity of late." The president, however, was known to have given a gold after-dinner coffee set, and one reporter sourly observed that if Ruth didn't know how to make good coffee, gold cups wouldn't make it taste any better.[58]

The morning of June 10 dawned cool and sunny. President Roosevelt raced through the night on a special train. Mrs. Roosevelt was indisposed, and Roosevelt had drafted his daughter Alice, four years Ruth's junior, to accompany him. The two girls still barely knew one another. Roosevelt had wanted them to become friends, but in Washington they had moved in completely different circles. Ruth thought Alice was "harum-scarum." She had burst upon the world as "Princess Alice," and led a gay, carefree life. Ruth was afraid Alice thought she was a prig, but if Ruth wanted to dance until four in the morning, she was still expected to be in her father's office at nine and be good-natured about it, ready to work all day. Alice was well aware that Ruth was more serious-minded than she and probably that her father preferred Ruth's behavior to her own. Alice thus felt shy about going to the wedding and said so. But her father insisted.[59]

By nine o'clock crowds had begun to gather outside the church. Admission was by ticket only, yet 5000 invitations had been issued and the church sat 1200. The crowd was largely female; many carried umbrellas to protect their complexions. Men and boys climbed trees for a better view. At eleven the bridal party entered their carriages for the five-mile drive at a slow trot. All along the way the president was cheered by the crowds.[60]

The church had been transformed into a grove, with palms, ferns, and vines, columns shrouded in bittersweet, and over ten thousand peonies, suggestive of the magnolia forests in Thomasville where Medill and Ruth had met. Mr. Roosevelt escorted the mother of the bride to her seat. Ominously, the mother of the groom was not present; she claimed to be ill on the eve of departure and remained in Chicago. In any case she would not have enjoyed relinquishing her best-beloved son to another woman. Ruth's matron-of-honor was her sister Mabel Parsons, who, contrasting their weddings, may have felt like the unfortunate Mrs. Rochester when Jane Eyre was a bride.[61]

After the wedding, in tents back at the Hanna estate, guests sat down to a late lunch. At Ruth's table was Alice Roosevelt, who had begun to enjoy herself flirting with Medill's younger brother Bert, and consequently planned "if possible to be engaged to John Ireland before the end of next year . . . Not, however, permanently." Cissy Patterson, who had always been sweet on her handsome first cousin Medill, and who remained jealous of Ruth for many years, was also one of the party. Everyone ate the famous corned beef hash as champagne was served in large crystal pitchers. Hanna toasted Roosevelt, Roosevelt toasted Ruth, while Hanna, his voice unsteady, blessed the newlyweds. Someone toasted Maggie Maloney, the cook, as "the real mistress of the occasion," and when the president rose with the rest of the company, Miss Maloney cried into her apron. Old Charles Foster lifted a glass and whispered, "To the next president—whichever one it is."[62]

By five o'clock, Ruth had changed into a black and white traveling outfit, and Medill had elaborate plans to give his Yale classmates the slip. The pair drove off in a carriage under a rain of shoes, four white slippers resting on the roof. But to the dismay of reporters and Yalies alike, the couple transferred on Viking Street to a big red automobile that "gave a few snorts and glided away at record-breaking speed." Ten miles away a private railroad car awaited them, to be attached to the eight o'clock train to Chicago.[63]

And so Ruth went from her father's house to her husband's, and at the same time, from one political mentor to another. Hanna had given her an appetite for partisan politics and a feel for his personal and thorough style of campaigning. But he was not an idealist and stoutly maintained that you had to take human nature as it came. McCormick, on the other hand, was a sensitive, intellectual, religious man, who inspired his wife with the belief that politics should serve a high ideal. Ruth later said, "I owe all my development to Medill. Except for him, I wouldn't have had the interest or purpose to go on in my profession."[64]

2
Chicago:
1903–1912

MUNICIPAL HOUSEKEEPING

"Back of the Yards"

As he was boarding the train in Washington to go to Ruth's wedding, President Roosevelt had told reporters he was going to "smoke the old man out," to discover Hanna's intentions regarding the 1904 election. But he had not succeeded. No one knew what Hanna intended to do, except Ruth.[1]

Roosevelt had good reason to be concerned. Many of McKinley's supporters considered Mark Hanna, not Theodore Roosevelt, to be the spiritual heir of the "martyred President"; Hanna had strong support from businessmen, many labor unions, and voters throughout the South. Hanna denied on several occasions that he was a candidate, but Roosevelt, who had yet to be elected in his own right, felt uneasy, and kept pressuring the senator for an unconditional endorsement until Hanna complained: "I am tired of putting my hand on my heart and being sworn in. It is not a dignified thing to do. I have played fair with the President, and I think he should accept my word at face value." Privately he told friends who were urging him to run, "Do you want to put me in my grave?" adding, "the office has no charms for me. I have been too close to it to want it."[2] Hanna's hard work on the Panama Canal Treaty the year before had taken its toll on his health, and Mrs. Hanna, weeping, complained that "nobody could make him behave, not even Ruth."[3]

Hanna fell ill of typhoid in late December, and when Ruth arrived in Washington from Chicago to nurse him, he admitted to her why he had seemed cool toward Roosevelt's nomination. She was reading him the newspapers one day, and came across speculation in the editorials as to whether Hanna would seek the nomination. She asked her father point blank if that was what he intended to do. "No," he replied, "I am not working for the nomination, but it is just as well to let them think I am. I am not going to be smoked out. If I say I am not looking for delegates for myself, somebody else will start out to get them. I am holding them for Roosevelt."[4]

Ruth had resented Theodore Roosevelt's behavior toward her father up until that point. But now the president showed his concern over Hanna's health by calling in person at the Arlington Hotel for the latest word on the invalid. Hanna scrawled a note, addressed to "My dear Mr. President";

> You touched a tender spot, old man, when you called personally to inquire after [me] this a.m. I may be worse, before I can be better, but all the same such "drops of kindness" are good for a fellow.[5]

Ruth carried the message across Lafayette Park to the White House herself. The President replied the next day:

> Dear Senator;
> Indeed it is your letter from your sickbed which is touching . . . May you soon be with us again, old fellow, as strong in body and as vigorous in leadership as ever. Faithfully yours, TR[6]

Hanna never saw this reply, but Ruth did. The president's attentions to her father made her love him. She began to see "his marvelous personality and to appreciate his wonderful character."[7]

On the evening of February 15, 1904, Mark Hanna died quietly in his sleep, with Ruth and her sister beside him. Elmer Dover, Hanna's secretary, went down to the crowded hotel lobby to make the announcement. A number of senators and other friends who had been at the hotel all day broke down and wept for their old friend. Throughout the evening there was a steady stream of callers. President Roosevelt came again, walking to the hotel unattended. The next day, he insisted that Alice go to call on Ruth. "I did not want to," Alice remembered. "I did not think I knew her well enough, and was embarrassed to think of going. But I went—and it was not embarrassing." As famous daughters of famous fathers, the two were often compared. They shared an intense love of politics. Ruth was politically more active, but she always trusted her friend's superb political judgment. "I am a politician, but Alice is a statesman," she used to say. They kindled each other's sense of fun and turned to each other in times of trouble. The meeting was the beginning of a life-long friendship, one each came to depend on because their relationships to their husbands would be difficult, and because they would play unusual roles in the political drama of their times. Ruth was the stabilizing influence Alice needed; she referred to her older friend as "Benevolent Despot," or "B.D." Alice, in turn, could always make her more serious friend relax and laugh.[8]

Hanna's death just seven months after Ruth's marriage underscored the importance of her relationship to her husband. Fortunately, Medill's influence complemented Hanna's. Hanna, like Ruth, was practical, resourceful, and energetic, but Medill was more intellectual and provided many of the ideas that inspired Ruth's career. On the other hand, she supplied the vigor and discipline he lacked; sometimes she called him "Muddle."

"He never knew what time it was or what day it was or where he was going," she later observed. "He hated to pack a bag and he loathed money matters. I attended to the practical details of our life, even finances." (Ruth had inherited $100,000 from her father's estate, an amount worth around $1.3 million in 1990. Medill's income was substantially less than his wife's.)[9]

But there was no one Ruth liked to talk to as much as Medill, and they often sat up discussing issues late into the night. They could be very playful together and lived a companionable life, walking to their offices together every morning and back again at night.[10]

Quickly, however, Ruth came to realize that Medill's problems were deeper than mere eccentricities. He was moody and subject to depression, with alternate periods of energy and euphoria. Medill drank heavily to alleviate his symptoms. Indeed, there was a family history of depression: his paternal grandfather, William Sanderson McCormick, had died in a mental institution in Jacksonville, Illinois, where he was being treated for melancholy and "softening of the brain." Compounding Medill's organic problems, his mother continued to make extraordinary demands on him even after his marriage, feigning illness time after time and summoning him to her side. Ruth later said that very soon after their marriage "my relationship . . . became a relationship of protection and mother to him." It was hard for her:

> I was not intended to be that sort of woman. I loved him in the relationship of a mistress rather than a mother of his children but I was given no choice . . . One can't become the mistress of a man who depends upon one for protection.[11]

Still, there was much to interest and amuse them in the early days. It was a great time and place to be young. Chicago was a lively watering hole for writers, artists, architects, journalists, and actors. Theodore Dreiser, Sherwood Anderson, Edna Ferber, Vachel Lindsay, Ring Lardner, Carl Sandburg, and Richard Wright dominated the literary scene. Popular plays included *Peter Pan* with Maude Adams, Sarah Bernhardt in *Camille*, *Hedda Gabler*, and anything by George Bernard Shaw. The young couple had an apartment, with a Chinese man to cook and clean, and hosted modest avant-garde Sunday night suppers. Medill's mother was horrified by their Bohemian life style: such unseemly socializing might undermine her son's health, particularly his mental health.

> Don't forget the horrid possibility which unfortunately all the McCormicks have to face. Hereditary tendencies are *hereditary tendencies* . . . For God's sake stop going to the theatre and giving these late supper parties! . . . It seems to me perfectly disproper, triviale and undignified for you to be asking to your house these painted strumpets and barnstormers . . . paugh! It makes me sick to think of them in my children's house![12]

But their life was not all amusement. Medill had to work very hard in the early days. After a three-year apprenticeship, which he thought "seemed to be spinning out too long," he judged the time had come for him to prove himself. It was proverbial in the family that he was a poor businessman, and he wanted to show them wrong. At first, he was overwhelmed by the job, "the quick decisions, the big lumps of money involved." He told Ruth "I need you terribly to unbosom myself at 6:30 when I leave the shop, and to have you adjust my point of view." He did not want to become "venal" in "the service of Mammon." She, however, must make no demands upon him; he admitted that her part, supporting him undemandingly, was "quite as great and very likely harder" than his. But he feared that

> the man who questions my industry, sees in you the clinching reason for his opinion. He believes that a girl, bred like you, and living the life you have led, will absorb the time and consume the energy of the stoutest.[13]

When Medill was at work, Ruth's days were apt to be dull. So she began to interest herself in the *Tribune*. At first, when Medill turned to her for advice, she felt at a loss.

> I had lived in a world of men and had few ideas about the so-called women's viewpoint . . . imagine my perplexity when Medill sought my assistance in developing women's interest among readers . . . Other pages were of more interest to me.

Although Ruth believed herself "a poor assistant," she dutifully studied the circulation figures and the Sunday magazine. Mary King, who had a long and distinguished career in journalism, became conscious of her interest in work for women:

> I was not especially ambitious when I started to work on the *Tribune* . . . I was working until I got married. When I was transferred from [Medill]'s office to the Sunday department, [Ruth] wrote a letter to me which indicated that she thought it was an important change for me and she made some general observations about the importance and attractiveness of newspaper work for women which . . . gave me a new attitude toward my work.

Many women reporters were inspired by her intelligent interest.[14]

Ruth's growing interest in women's work soon attracted her to the women's club movement that was sweeping the country. These clubs had started in the late nineteenth century, often as literary clubs that provided, in many cases, the higher education women were otherwise denied. They offered women a meeting place where they were able to learn speaking and organizational skills. These clubs also fostered pride in women's new accomplishments and a growing awareness of the sex discrimination that hampered them. By the turn of the century, women in these clubs were beginning to concern themselves with civic reform issues: child labor and juvenile courts, conservation and sewage, minimum wage and factory abuses, and even women's rights.[15]

The women's club movement coincided with, and fueled, the progressive reform movement. With the return of the country to prosperity in the early 1890s, increased production had outpaced improvements for workers. Progressive activists tried to meet the needs of the workers who were being exploited in the rush to industrialization. Progressive leaders were young men—Theodore Roosevelt, Robert La Follett, William Jennings Bryan, Hiram Johnson—but increasingly women were taking part as well. Indeed, it was said that women were naturally predisposed to introduce morality and human concern into politics, a view that would be regarded as sexist today, but which was meant and taken as a compliment then.

Many progressive women leaders in Chicago had started in settlement houses. The first and most famous had been Jane Addams's Hull House in Chicago, established to help the laboring immigrants. At the turn of the century, one-third to one-half of the population of most major cities was made up of poor immigrant families. Jane Addams, like Ruth McCormick, was the daughter of a politician, and, like Ruth, she believed that a purposeless life was an empty one. Because of their backgrounds both women were comfortable in the public arena.[16]

Settlement houses were centers of recreation and education at first but gradually became the focus for reform movements. Most residents at settlement houses were not professional social workers, but students, teachers, and writers who had not yet settled on a career, and who stayed only a year or two. Many joined the movement because the settlements could be intellectually stimulating places to live, where lively debates continued long into the night. Residents often went on to lobby for progressive legislation after observing the squalid conditions of the working-class at first hand. Among them were Florence Kelley, Julia and Edith Lathrop, Sophinisba Breckenridge, and Dr. Alice Hamilton.[17]

Mary McDowell was another active reformer. An energetic Scotch-Irish woman with a delicious sense of humor and a warm, friendly manner, she had founded a settlement house under the sponsorship of the University of Chicago to serve the needs of the meat packers. The University of Chicago's pioneer sociology department wanted a window on the community, and they selected the district just behind the Union stockyards, known as "Packingtown." Mary McDowell became head resident in 1894, and was soon known as the "Angel of the Yards." Immigrant families there lived in overcrowded, unsanitary housing, and competed for jobs by accepting starvation wages and unhealthy working conditions that bred tuberculosis and rheumatism. Children started work at age ten; before that, they played in garbage dumps or on the railroad tracks and often turned to delinquency and thieving. The only recreation for adults was the saloon. McDowell started a day nursery for working mothers, organized clubs and parties for adults and game rooms for children, and sponsored concerts and classes. She encouraged ethnic groups to practice the crafts and music that were part of their cultural heritage. There was a great deal to do.[18]

The McCormicks' close friends Anne and Bill Hard were journalists with connections to these movements. Bill Hard had worked at the *Tribune* as a reporter and editorial writer and later became a successful free-lancer. He had grown up in India; he had yellowish skin and was very short but distinguished-looking, brilliant, and witty. Anne Hard, homely and difficult, but with a vivid personality, wrote under the name Hyde Clements. Bill Hard had spent time at Hull House and the Northwestern Settlement and was one of the early residents of Packingtown. He often returned to the University of Chicago Settlement House for dinner and informal discussions while researching an article for *Outlook* magazine during a stockyards strike in 1904.[19]

In the summer of 1907 Hard talked to Ruth and Medill about the work being done there. The two young idealists decided to try living as residents "back of the yards" under assumed names, to make a survey of conditions. Just the year before Upton Sinclair had exposed Packingtown conditions in his muckraking novel, *The Jungle,* hoping it would be "the *Uncle Tom's Cabin* of the socialist movement." But instead of inspiring reform of the packers' working conditions, it appalled the public about the unsanitary circumstances under which their food was produced, and the Federal Pure Food and Drug Act was speedily passed. Sinclair observed ruefully, "I aimed at the public's heart, and by accident hit it in the stomach." Workers' conditions were still deplorable the following year, 1907, when the McCormicks took up their clandestine residence.[20]

Packingtown was separated from the rest of Chicago by the packing plants and stockyards that dominated its life. After leaving the lake shore district one bumped along on a horse-drawn street car across some forty railroad tracks, through miles of drab prairie covered with squat factories and grimy smokestacks, until the conductor shouted "End of the line!" at the corner of Ashland Avenue and Forty-seventh Street, the heart of the squalid neighborhood. There were only two paved streets in the district, one of them lined with saloons. A monotonous row of two-story houses crowded against plank sidewalks. Everything was grey with smoke and dirt, unrelieved by any trees, grass, or shrubbery. An overpowering stench of rotting hair, scrapings from hides, refuse from the slaughter houses, "Bubbly Creek," and garbage assaulted the newcomers. Even Mary McDowell herself never got used to the odors, claiming that "we must train ourselves not to ignore them," so as to fight harder to get rid of them.[21]

The McCormicks soon learned that working conditions were just as bad as living conditions. Wages were low and work irregular. When work could be found, it was often for twelve or fourteen hours a day. The plants were badly lit and poorly ventilated, there was inadequate drainage, refrigerator units overhead dripped on the workers underneath, and the workrooms were kept just above freezing to prevent spoilage of the meat. Girls would stand in boxes of sawdust to protect their feet from the cold, damp ground. By 1907 the Germans, Irish, English, and Czechs had been able to move on and were being replaced by Poles, Russians, Lithuanians, and Slovaks. McDowell started a school of citizenship, to teach English and civics, as well as vocational and summer school programs. It was obvious, though, that there was little her programs could accomplish without actual reforms of the system. Although she had worked to organize the women's unions, and supported the strike of 1904, reforms were pitifully slow in coming.[22]

The McCormicks came to understand that they could do little in such an atmosphere. ("Plutocrat socialists" one sarcastic senator called them.) Ruth had taken a short-lived job in the stockyards, pushing meat toward a chopper with no guard for protection, but the employment manager, suspicious of her motives, let her go. There were limits to what she could do as a reformer. This realization was brought home one day when she was making a speech to forty or fifty young women workers. Interpreting their silence as "attention and interest," she grew more eloquent and confident. At the end of forty minutes she concluded and awaited applause with the expectant smile of one who had earned it. When none came, she begged the audience to ask questions if they had not understood. Only one young woman brightened enough to stand up, and her question startled Ruth.

> Mrs. McCormick, I have listened to 'most everything you have said, and it is all right, but what practical good do you think you can do us by coming down here and talking? . . . I can see that some of the things you say may be true, but you don't own any interest in the yards, so that your coming down here ain't going to do us any good. Now, if you can interest Mrs. Armour, Mrs. Swift or Mrs. Libby, you can help us, but until then, you cannot do any good.

It seemed to Ruth "that the girl had struck the nail squarely on the head," and she concluded that she needed to approach the task from another angle. Ruth had always favored practical politics and achievable goals, and the time for pretty speeches was over. The expanding club movement was taking an active part in pressing for improved conditions for working women, and Ruth now began to join a number of these clubs.[23] The Women's Trade Union League helped to organize women factory workers, but the women were hard to organize due to high turnover as women left to marry or have children. Then, too, labor unions were widely considered "anarchistic" by nonunion people, and the unionized women were often opposed by male union members, who dreaded competition and feared that unionized women would neglect their duties at home. Only about 3 percent of women in industrial organizations were organized in 1900, and that number actually declined by 1910 to $1\frac{1}{2}$ percent.[24]

Another approach was through public pressure on employers. The Consumers' League was founded to appeal to the conscience of the buying public, protesting wages of two dollars per week, a work day from 7:45

A.M. until midnight six days out of seven, no seats behind the sales counters, no place for lunch except the toilets and the stockrooms. The league asked customers to shop only in "standard" stores where women were paid a minimum of six dollars per week, overtime after 6 P.M. and were provided with seats and lunch rooms. When boycotts proved ineffectual, the league published a devastating report on their investigation of big State Street stores in the pre-Christmas rush. This report led to the famous Louis D. Brandeis brief of 1908, on which the Supreme Court set aside the principle that protective legislation violated liberty of contract.[25]

Such reform-minded women began to realize that they needed the vote to make any significant progress, and Ruth was one of the founders of the Women's City Club of Chicago, a prosuffrage group that worked to show women how government affected daily life. After an effort organized by Mary McDowell to petition the City Council on the subject of Bubbly Creek failed to bring reform, she turned to her fellow members of the Women's City Club, which launched a major campaign on a citywide level. As is often the case, a small group of women in Chicago was active in many different organizations, and Ruth would have met several of the leading women of the Chicago reform group at that time, in several places. Jane Addams and Florence Kelley, head of the National Consumers' League, were, like Ruth, daughters of politicians, who honed their inherited political skills in these women's groups.[26]

Ruth grew especially interested in involving the National Civic Federation, of which her father had been a founder, in women's welfare work. All her life, she liked to tell of how her father had sent her to live with the family of the foreman of one of his coal mines the summer she was sixteen, allegedly to report to him on conditions there. Much later, her cousin Lucia dismissed these stories, with a loud snort, as pure fabrication. But the fact remains that Ruth, like Mark Hanna, felt at ease with people of all classes and made them feel at ease with her.

In spring 1908 Ruth attended a meeting of like-minded women in New York City including Anne Morgan, the daughter of J. Pierpont Morgan, and Daisy Harriman. They wanted to participate in the Welfare Department of the National Civic Federation and approached Ralph Easley, chairman of the NCF Executive council. They organized the Women's Committee to cooperate with the NCF Welfare Department, because, as Harriman said in her opening address,

> We feel this organization comes nearer to our ideal than any other operation along these lines. All of us have an influence. Some are wives

or sisters of employers of large numbers of factory operators. Or perhaps are owners and stockholders in companies. Should not the woman who spends the money which employees help to provide take a special interest in their welfare, especially that of women earners? Should we not frankly recognize our own ignorance of the conditions under which they live and work?" They would not, she insisted, "use coercive methods . . . to secure improvement, but will try to find opportunities to offer friendly suggestions to those in power.[27]

This was not a women's suffrage organization, one of the leaders made plain. "The advanced woman has had her turn for twenty-five years," declared Mrs. Cyrus Pittman Orr. "Now it's the conservative woman who is coming forward, the woman whose chief interest is the welfare of her home. She is better fitted to judge the needs of other women than the professional female reformer."[28] The old radical feminist arguments that challenged the typical roles of women and men were offset by the "municipal housekeeping" philosophy, which argued for the vote on the basis that women's special talents were needed for civic improvements. This difference between the two groups grew into a real division as the suffrage fight gained momentum.[29]

Some of the women in the NCF tried to think of a plan to include laboring women, but Samuel Gompers and other labor leaders believed that wives of union men were unlikely to go into such an organization, whereas members of women's unions would "probably all be socialists." It was decided that members of the NCF Women's Committee should be stockholders or have interests through family members. Ruth was named director of the new organization and was extremely pleased to be allowed to carry on her father's work. Easley was glad to have "the Hanna people" involved in the NCF again and told United Mine Workers chief Mitchell: "Mrs. McCormick represents much of the tact and political instinct of her father." The first meeting of the Women's Committee was held in Washington, D.C., in May. After the meeting, President Roosevelt received them at the White House and appealed to the women to help him get legislation for government workers. He also cautioned them: "If you approach them in a patronizing spirit, they will refuse to be benefitted," suggesting they approach the problem "in the frankest possible fashion from the standpoint of the common interest that they and you and all of us have in the welfare of the country."[30]

The men in the NCF were glad to have the women join them, subscribing to the prevailing belief that women could see more clearly than men what was needed to make a welfare arrangement helpful and acceptable. They anticipated that the new department would stimulate a healthy rivalry. Mitchell pointed out that women could gain access to factories where he or Gompers would be forbidden. Members of the committee were instructed never to go directly to the employer to ask for reforms, but to enlist a wife, daughter, mother, or sister.[31]

Unfortunately, Ruth soon realized that the federation was handicapped by trying to represent too many diverse interest groups. The women's branch was even weaker, as they were cut off from collaborating with their intended beneficiaries, and they were instructed to work, not with the employers directly, but only through influential family members. Little legislation resulted from their careful studies.[32]

In spite of her growing involvement in nonaligned reform groups, Ruth McCormick still had a taste for partisan politics. 1908 was an election year, and the Republicans were meeting in Chicago on June 16, in sweltering heat. Alice Roosevelt Longworth and her new husband, Nick, a congressman from Ohio and speaker of the House of Representatives, Alice's uncle and aunt Robinson, and their daughter Corinne all descended on the McCormicks. Alice Longworth observed,

> The routine business, the keynotes, the nominating speeches are only fun . . . in small doses. The real fun is outside the convention hall, at the Headquarters of the national committee and of candidates, in the conferences that are peppered through the various hotels and are going on day and night.

The two women made fun of the all-night sessions of the committee on resolutions, and Alice noted:

> The members of the Committee seem to take a weary pride in their state of haggard, frowsy fatigue. They never seem to realize that . . . their portentous self-importance . . . presents a comic and accustomed sight to the convention "fan."

Ruth and Alice both relished the sporting aspect of politics. They were delighted that although Will Taft was the expected nominee, any mention of Theodore Roosevelt still brought the loudest and longest applause.[33]

The four even went on to Denver for the Democrats' Convention, joined by *Chicago Tribune* editor Tiffany Blake, whose wife, Margaret, was a close friend of Ruth's, and several others, all "crowded" into a private railroad car. They lived in the car at the railroad yards in Denver. A baggage car containing their trunks was attached, and their maids tried to keep the ladies' clothes as presentable as they could. Ruth had brought her butler, too, whose main job was to hose the roof of the car in an endeavor to give some relief from the heat of Colorado in July. "It was," decided Alice, "a good deal like living in a sweat box." They finally booked a room at a hotel where they could take turns having a bath. The convention was much livelier than the one in Chicago, though, as Alice said, "There was nothing to it but Bryan."[34]

CARL JUNG

"The Work Is in Good Hands"

Ruth McCormick was finding interesting, congenial work, and she could have fun with her friends. But all was not well at home. Medill had obtained an interest in the *Cleveland Leader*, of which he was co-publisher. Although he was just thirty he was already chafing under the leadership of his uncle Robert Patterson, publisher of the *Tribune*, and he may have threatened to leave the *Tribune* altogether, like his cousin Joe Patterson, who had renounced his capitalist connections, espoused socialism, and written a play entitled *A Little Brother of the Rich*. Finally Medill decided to give up the Cleveland interests to devote himself full-time to Chicago. In 1907 Medill reorganized the business and advertising departments and was made vice president, secretary, and treasurer. His uncle was often away for health reasons, leaving Medill in charge. In 1908 Medill was also named auditor and assistant editor-in-chief and was elected vice president of the American Newspaper Publishers Association. But Patterson did not retire, and Medill's mother became increasingly bitter about her sister's husband, who was, she thought, thwarting her son's advance. Medill, under pressure at work and from his mother, began to drink heavily, and finally suffered a nervous collapse. On November 18, 1908, the *Tribune* directors were called to a special meeting to receive Medill's request for a two-month leave of absence, and he and Ruth left almost at once for Europe.[35]

Medill was probably a victim of bipolar mood disorder. Even today, when "manic-depressive" swings can be treated medically, there is a tendency for victims to use alcohol to alleviate the symptoms. At the turn of the century drink was virtually the only palliative. Medill's mother, who drank a fair amount herself, begged him to leave and seek help. "[G]o before [Patterson] returns as we don't want him to see you as you are now," she advised, adding, "It breaks my heart that my brilliant boy should be so smashed down." She enlisted Ruth's help with even more unvarnished language:

It is astonishing to me that you seem so unaware of Medill's physical condition. I was horribly distressed when I saw him last week. You assure and re-assure me that "Medill doesn't drink." Why my dear child he drinks all the time! He drinks at nine at ten at eleven at twelve. He drinks again at two at three at four at five & six. He never stops the whole day! His nervous system is completely degenerated by alcoholic poison. You my dear are face to face with one of two certainties: Either a crazy husband or a dead husband.

She laced her appeal with a threat:

Unless you and Medill (or Medill alone with me) are off for Europe within the next 10 days . . . I shall go to Mr. Beale and ask him to have Medill removed as he is not now competent to do any work of any kind. [36]

Ruth and Medill spent some time in Europe, probably to consult the noted psychiatrist Carl Jung in Zurich. When they returned, Medill, who appeared to be in good health, resumed his duties at the *Tribune*. [37] Ruth took herself off to her brother's farm outside of Cleveland, on a retreat no doubt suggested by Dr. Jung. Unfortunately, Ruth's personality was extraordinarily ill-suited to a retreat; she was an unusually energetic and active woman, and the eleven-day sojourn was a painful exile. She was doing it to help Medill, and when she felt he didn't appreciate her sacrifice, she exploded in anger. The eleven days' rest produced a tempestuous one-sided correspondence.

At first, she was determinedly cheerful. "There is no life in the world like this!" she exulted on Sunday. "My nerves are so quiet and peaceful as if they had never known what life in Chicago meant." Trying to be helpful, she begged Medill to be honest about difficulties with her: "I want you to think quite carefully what it is that I do that gets on your nerves. There is something and either you know it and don't tell me for fear of hurting my feelings or you do not really know just what it is . . ."

By the second day, she was growing anxious at not having heard from him. "The mails seem slow down here as I haven't heard from you at all . . ." She reminded him that her effort was on his behalf: "When you come down if you are not satisfied with me I will remain still an additional week because I am most anxious to be entirely well in your eyes," but asked him to "Please remember the days are long without any word at all." The night she had left Chicago, Medill gave a party, and the following day he left for Washington with his brother Bert.

During the week she became increasingly lonely in her effort. In one letter she begged:

If you could take the time to tell me in detail what your feelings and

emotions are without me at this time it would be of enormous help to me
. . . My entire being is crying out for kindness, sympathy, and understanding . . ."

She wanted him to come down at the end of the week to give her a
break; after a little "human interest" she thought she could endure another
week. "Oh lamb," she wrote, "what Hell we have been through! But if
it only brings us closer together that is my prayer now . . ." But Medill
never came, and he wrote only twice in eleven days. By the eleventh
day, Ruth had reached her limit and lashed out at her unresponsive
husband. "Now I am mad," the letter began, without any greeting:

> Damn it all you might take five minutes out of your valuable day to give
> a little news. You were going to write every morning before you left the
> house . . . You forgot my *Tribune* so that I was without any paper until
> I wired . . . You didn't even wire that you were or were not coming on
> Sunday and when I telephoned complained because I kept you five min-
> utes! If I had treated you like this when you were going through self-
> investigation what would have happened. You are a rotten nasty PIG so
> there and so help me I will not peep or go home until you treat me like
> a human being. No excuse goes because there is none.
>
> Your mad
>
> wife
>
> PS: If you don't wish to take a brace and realize I am among the living
> (and darned healthy at present thank you) I'll find a feller who will. Put
> that in your pipe and smoke it but blow the smoke the other way![38]

How Medill responded is not known, but it was clear that Ruth, although
eager to help Medill, was not going to sacrifice her life to his.

Soon afterwards, Medill suffered another breakdown, and left the *Tribune* for good. At first, Kate McCormick apparently hoped that Ruth,
and not her younger son Bert, would represent her interests at the *Tribune*;
Bert was embarked on a political career and feared the *Tribune* connections would hinder him.

Ruth saw it differently. "Bert's nominal connection with the paper all
ready conflicts with his political friends," she told her mother-in-law,
and although "you told me that you had told him that I should represent
you in the *Tribune* and he in all else," nevertheless, Ruth and Bert had
"had a nice brotherly talk and we agreed that it was better for me not
to serve on the board."[39]

Ruth and Medill returned to Europe and Carl Jung. But perhaps because of her unhappy experiment in "self-investigation," Ruth was now

reluctant to get involved in Medill's treatment. Medill tried to encourage her,

> Be of good cheer, your little nut is perfectly capable of reading and learning a whole lot if you will try. The doctor already suspected resistance of that sort. He had the same experience with his wife, who thought she could not understand his science and paid no attention to it. Now she is his partner in his work.[40]

Since Medill was not interested in a long analysis, Jung took the unorthodox step of discussing his treatment with Ruth, so that she might help her husband herself. Even while they were in Europe, Medill was not inclined to stay quietly in Zurich, but frequently indulged his passion for adventuring, to the distress of both his analyst and his wife. First he went to Petersburg with his flamboyant cousin Cissy Patterson, who had run away from her abusive husband, the Polish Count Josef Gizycki. The count had retaliated by kidnapping their young daughter. Eventually pressure was brought on the count to return the child, and Medill next accompanied Cissy to Vienna to reclaim her.

Jung was very dubious about all this turmoil, and especially about Cissy, who had paid him a surprise visit. "I do not trust Mme. la Comtesse," he confided to Ruth.

> Her influence upon Mr. McCormick and myself seems to be bad . . . Madame has an enormous secret influence upon men and a remarkable lack of moral consciousness.

He thought that Medill did "not entirely examine his feelings about Madame." Jung went so far as to assure Ruth that it was alright to feel jealous, but urged her, too, when talking about the matter to Medill, to "avoid all signs of irritation."[41]

Next Medill proposed a trip to Albania, "childishly pleased that the Albanians are misbehaving." He planned to push on to Budapest, Belgrade, Constantinople, and Salonika. Jung explained to Ruth that Medill's "apparently dangerous desir [sic] to kill a man, to fight or to have any adventures is purely academical and phantastical." The thirst for such adventures was "quite childish" for a man of Medill's poor health.

Medill's "demon," according to Jung, was caused by his "infantile relations with the mother"; it inspired him "to a wild and immoral life." In marriage, "love could suppress the former immoral tendencies," so he "tried to fight against the approaching danger by an unreasonable way of working . . . Mr. McCormick did his mother's work . . . in place of his former immoral life," and so his business life was nearly as dangerous for him as a life of dissipation. Then "the devil became more decent and tried to destroy Mr. McCormick by alkohol [sic] . . ." These, along with the adventures, were all tendencies to self-destruction.[42]

Because of the magnitude of the problem she was coping with, Jung advised Ruth to rest twice a day: "I know how exhausting such an education is." At least Medill was able to stop drinking for some time, and Jung hoped to "disappear in the background," to be "successfully replaced by Mme McCormick, who accomplishes the important work I began . . . That is the natural and necessary end of psychoanalysis. I believe that the work is in good hands."[43]

Medill, however, relapsed after a few weeks, and Jung gave Ruth advice on dealing with future lapses. "The struggle will last for a long time," he predicted.[44]

Throughout his consultations with Jung, Medill was very affectionate in his letters to Ruth. "My wife complex very active," he wrote at one point. By the end of their time in Europe, he begged Ruth "to try another flight in that ill balanced aeroplane of happiness which we navigated."[45]

She came to accept the fact of his alcoholism. "I was faced with the decision of leaving him or living with him," she later told her elder daughter. "I loved him passionately and devotedly . . ."[46] But it had become obvious that Medill could not hope to recover while still at the *Tribune*, in his mother's sphere of influence. Politics offered a clearer field.

THE BULL MOOSE CAMPAIGN

"My Money's on the Mare"

The McCormicks returned from Europe in the spring of 1910, on the same ship that was bringing Theodore Roosevelt back from a fourteen-month African safari. Talks with Roosevelt on shipboard encouraged Medill to think again about the career in politics that had long been tempting him. Ruth also wanted him to take up a life that she knew and loved.[47]

Medill's mother did not accept this decision easily. Medill and Ruth had gone to Washington, to investigate the fledgling Progressive Party under Wisconsin Senator Robert La Follette. Kate was alarmed. Addressing Medill as "Dearest Flirter," she begged: "Don't chase the Roosevelt phantasmagora. You won't be in it!! Even if it materializes!" While she agreed it was not the "psychological moment" for him to return to the *Tribune*, she urged him to

> come to Chicago and show yourself . . . Take off that horrible beard which gives you such a wild look and re-appear the calm, sweet, handsome un-excentric [sic] old Medill of former days. To return to the *Tribune* you can't miss the smallest two spot in playing your game . . .[48]

She was desperate for influence at the paper in a critical time, when there were offers to buy the paper or merge it with the *Herald*.[49] But Medill refused to go along with his mother. Eventually Medill's brother Bert and his cousin Joe Patterson returned to take charge of the paper, and Medill could pursue his interest in politics.

Medill's relationship with Theodore Roosevelt had progressed a long way from the time when he had met the president as head of the newly emerging Roosevelt Club of Chicago. As close friends of his daughter Alice, he and Ruth saw him often. By 1908 they were on a footing that allowed Roosevelt to write to Medill in a bantering tone, and at the end of his presidential term he was urging Medill, "Do come to Washington this winter. I should like to have you go over all my work with me, not by talking about it with me for an hour, but by seeing it at close hand from day to day."[50]

In the fall of 1910 the Republicans lost control of the House of Representatives for the first time since 1894. Many Republicans were disillusioned with Taft, styling themselves Progressives. They wanted direct primaries, campaign reform, and a general reduction in formal party machinery. They were disturbed at the extent of business involvement in dubious political practices, and they also supported woman suffrage. But they differed from Democrats on issues like child labor and pure food and drug bills. Roosevelt went on a three-week speaking tour of the West in the late summer, to "announce" himself "on the vital questions of the day" and to assess possible support. Roosevelt's activity unsettled President Taft. Although the presidential secretary told newsmen, "We don't know what Oyster Bay is going to do, and we don't give a damn," Taft was disconcerted by what one cabinet officer called "the pilgrimage of insurgents to the shrine on Sagamore Hill."[51]

Ruth and Medill McCormick had gone to Washington to work for the insurgents, or Progressives, in the election. For nearly a year the formation of a national league to promote progressive legislation had been under discussion. At the end of 1910 Senator Robert La Follette of Wisconsin drafted a Declaration of Principles, and on January 21, 1911, a Progressive Party was organized at his house in Washington, with Ruth and Medill present. Although there were Progressive movements in many states, they now looked to the Washington group to take the initiative.[52]

Medill had called on La Follette in the fall, to offer his services, especially his knowledge of publishers all over the country, knowledge that would enable him to promote the campaign. He was now given an office at the Washington headquarters, where he was in charge of printing and publicity. At times Ruth worked in the office while Medill went into the field. The New York Times described Medill as "at the head of Progressive headquarters" in Washington.[53]

Medill wrote an article for North American Review in May 1911, listing the "irreconcilable differences" between the Progressive branch and the administration. It was a rallying cry for the insurgents to organize. "Not a fifth of Republicans in Congress look forward to anything but defeat in 1912," he wrote.

> And yet, in the face of the effective organizing of their opponents, they sit inert, making no plans to compose their own differences or to choose a really popular and positive leader for the next campaign.[54]

At that point, Medill was supporting La Follette, but he remained on good terms with Roosevelt, who sent him glowing letters of introduction to influential friends. "This is to introduce one of the best fellows I know," he wrote. "McCormick is for La Follette, and I have told him you disagree with him on that point. But he is a trump and a square man . . . He is our kind of man." The McCormicks did not stay with La Follette long, however. The Wisconsin senator was proving a poor candidate. His congressional duties kept him in Washington until August, and he had to write an autobiography just to earn needed money. He was, in effect, out of circulation until late in the year. He lacked the opportunity or the means to attract those outside of the Midwest who considered him a dangerous radical. At the end of the year Medill took the important step of trying to bring the Progressives around to support Roosevelt and to persuade La Follette's supporters to force a withdrawal in favor of the former president. La Follette flatly refused and was outraged that Medill had abandoned him. But a fair number of other early La Follette supporters, including William Allen White and Gifford Pinchot, also began to work for Roosevelt by the end of 1911.[55]

While Ruth McCormick participated in Medill's work for the Progressives, she also continued to do the kind of work she had done in Chicago before their European sojourn. In Paris she had taken time to study slum work and the economical management of food. She returned to the National Civic Federation in 1909 as the second vice chairman, and worked there on and off for three years.

Shortly after moving to Washington, she and some of her associates opened a lodging house at 2506–8 K Street for working women. Ruth had financed the project, intended as an object lesson for employers. It was cheap, attractively furnished, and presided over by a matron-house-keeper, but was free from "semi-benevolent rules or restrictions." By 1914 she had opened a second one and reported that the two establishments had become self-supporting.[56] Even though Ruth was the mainstay of Medill's emotional life and supported his political ambitions, she always pursued her own agenda and cultivated her own political base.

In late January several Progressives who had been supporting La Follette, Medill among them, met at the McCormicks' apartment in Washington. Walter L. Houser, the manager of the La Follette campaign, believed that the only way to keep the Progressives together and prevent Taft's nomination was for La Follette to abandon his own candidacy and throw his influence and organization to Roosevelt. On the night of February 2 La Follette collapsed while giving a speech, an event that put an end to his candidacy. "There is a scattering of the rats from the sinking ship," reported the *New York Times* four days later. ". . . along with the statement from La Follette headquarters tonight [announcing La Follette's withdrawal] comes a message from Medill McCormick, who has been one of the chief La Follette boomers, urging the Illinois progressives to get aboard the Roosevelt band wagon with all speed and agility."[57]

Roosevelt hesitated, however, to accept the draft. During much of 1911 he had stayed out of sight, believing that La Follette would lose the nomination and Taft would lose the election. Then the election of 1916 would be wide open. But by early 1912 he could hold back no longer. On February 13 the McCormicks went to Alice Longworth's for tea, and Medill told her that he expected her father would be coming out with a statement within a week. "I don't much like it," Alice confessed to her diary. She did not want him to run to satisfy those "to whom he makes a picturesque appeal," nor to support those dissatisfied with the Taft administration, nor to help others running for office on his coattails. "He must make it clear that he is a candidate because he considers his policies the right policies," she insisted.

Alice never hesitated to tell her father what she thought of his positions. In a speech in Columbus, Ohio, he advocated setting aside court decisions by popular vote. "Father, you are all wrong on that," she told him. Ruth was amazed. "I never dared speak to my father like that," she said. Her deference to her father may account for the fact that she often took conciliatory positions, especially in the early years of her political career. Finally, on February 21 Roosevelt declared, "My hat is in the ring, the fight is on, and I am stripped to the buff!"[58] The die was cast and not just for Roosevelt.

During the spring, Roosevelt campaigned for delegates to the convention. In the states that had adopted the new primary laws, he won. In states without them, delegates were usually pledged to the incumbent, Taft. Both Ruth and Medill became active participants in the Roosevelt campaign. They toured the West in the late Spring, carrying Taft's home state, California, for Roosevelt and going up to Puget Sound where Ruth would campaign almost thirty years later.[59] Roosevelt conducted what one partisan called "a free-for-all, slap-bang, kick-him-in-the-belly" campaign. Ruth, whose father had conducted a very different sort of campaign, observed Roosevelt's activities with wonder. A contemporary described "the agreeable excitement" that Roosevelt generated:

> the din, the alarums, the thunderclaps of his denunciations, the lightning strokes of his epithets, his occasional ruthlessness of attack, the quickness of his rally, the adroitness of his parry . . ."[60]

Ruth's later campaigns, unlike her father's, were not heavily issue-oriented; it was her personality that would carry votes for her. Hanna had taught her organization, but Roosevelt doubtless taught her how to project a personality.

The Republican Convention met in Chicago in mid-June. Daisy Harriman, Ruth's colleague in the National Civic Federation, described:

> a flat, flat lake, sizzling asphalt pavements, bands circling and zigzagging along Michigan Avenue, tooting and booming, "Everybody's saying it, Roosevelt, Roosevelt . . ."

Ruth and Alice Longworth were enjoying the political drama. The National Committee met in advance of the convention to seat the delegates. While a large number of the Roosevelt delegates were being contested, Roosevelt rallied his supporters in the Chicago Auditorium. Medill had distributed one hundred thousand admission tickets to ensure a big turnout. The result was not just a crowd, but a crush, packed to suffocation. "We intend to carry our fight to the end," Roosevelt declared. "You are not merely facing a crisis in the history of a party, you are facing a crisis in the history of a nation." He concluded with a stirring plea:

> We fight in honorable fashion for the good of mankind; fearless of the

future; unheeding of our individual fates; with unflinching hearts and undimmed eyes. We stand at Armageddon and we battle for the Lord![61]

Delegates clashed at the Coliseum. Daisy Harriman, her "frock sticking to the back of the chair," wrote of

red-faced, perspiring men . . . coats off and flashing fists—delegates pummeling each other. The sultry air was charged with dynamite. Rumors flashed like lightning. Delegates talked of drawing pistols and knives over the disputed seats. Everybody jostled, pushed, whispered. Day and night the excitement grew, monotonous, continuous . . . The manager of Roosevelt's Indiana contest came out saying the Convention would last a month. We groaned and believed him.[62]

Thursday, June 20, was a hot, humid, grey day, and a discouraging day for the Progressives. An overwhelming majority of Taft delegates were seated at the expense of Roosevelt delegates; from 254 contested delegates, 235 of the Taft men were seated. The *Chicago Tribune* ran a banner headline: "Thou Shalt Not Steal." Frustrated Roosevelt supporters cried, "Steam roller tactics!" Every time a Taft man made a motion, they rubbed sandpaper together and called out "Toot! Toot!" to keep the image vivid.[63]

But the Progressives knew it was over. Friends who had been in the primary fights came by, miserable, to say they could not leave the party. Roosevelt tried to be philosophical. A conference was held in Roosevelt's room that lasted until dawn. Some of the older men, with careers to lose, were opposed to bolting. Younger men like McCormick wanted to split. Ruth joined Alice in trying to persuade her husband Nick, a Republican congressman from Ohio, to join the Progressives, but he was adamant. The next day Roosevelt announced his willingness to accept the nomination of Progressives forming a new party. His supporters withdrew from the GOP convention and held a "rump" convention in Orchestra Hall. Alice found that the "spirit and buoyancy" of this crowd was a marked contrast to the "sullen, shame-faced" regulars being jeered by the galleries in the Coliseum. The Progressives in Orchestra Hall applauded the arrival of leaders and delegates from the Roosevelt camp, chanting, "We want Teddy!" (Privately, Roosevelt disliked the nickname "Teddy." "Even my wife calls me 'Theodore,'" he complained.) The crowd roared, hats flew into the air as Roosevelt appeared.[64]

A committee was organized, and a formal convention was scheduled for August 5. The McCormicks' loyalty and Progressive work was recognized when Medill was put in charge of the western campaign and Ruth was made chairman of a Chicago Committee of 100. Joining the

Progressives was, for Ruth, a serious departure from her father's training. Hanna was a firm believer in party loyalty, especially Republican Party loyalty. But Ruth was able to use what she had learned from her father, and build on it, as her experiences with her husband, among women's reform groups, and with Roosevelt shaped her philosophy.[65]

The McCormicks went to Oyster Bay for strategy sessions. The Roosevelt household could be daunting to the uninitiated. The Roosevelts' new daughter-in-law described her first visit with horror: The house was always full of people. Conferences went on all day. The telephone never stopped ringing. Something was going on every minute:

> The Roosevelt family enjoyed life too much to waste time sleeping. Every night they stayed downstairs until nearly midnight; then, talking at the top of their voices, they trooped up the wide uncarpeted stairs and went to their rooms. For a brief moment all was still, but just as I was going off to sleep a second time, they remembered things they had forgotten to tell one another and ran shouting through the halls . . . The first night I said to myself, "Here it is nearly one o'clock. No one is likely to wake up before eight at the earliest." Eight? By six the younger ones were up, and by seven I was the only one who was not joyously beginning the day . . .[66]

Ruth, who liked plenty of sleep, may have felt equally dismayed.

Conventions were called in forty-seven states to choose delegates and establish a new party. By August 5 they began to assemble in Chicago, again at the Coliseum, where the Republican Convention had met two months before. There was a spiritual quality to the proceedings. Delegates sang "Onward Christian Soldiers" and "The Battle Hymn of the Republic," speakers made frequent Biblical references, Roosevelt's speech was called a "Confession of Faith." Delegates were different from the establishment types who had attended the Republican Convention in June; they included social workers, professors, school teachers, and liberal clergy. And women were everywhere; the Progressives, unlike the major political parties, supported woman suffrage, and one correspondent reported "plenty of women delegates . . . doctors, lawyers, teachers, professors, middle-aged leaders of civic movements or rich young girls who had gone in for settlement work." During his presidency Roosevelt had been uninterested in the women's plight, writing, "I am not an enthusiastic advocate of it because I do not recognize it as a very important matter." When he endorsed suffrage in the Bull Moose campaign, he was challenged by a man who said, "You didn't think that way five years ago,

Colonel," to which Roosevelt replied, "No, I did not know enough then. I was wrong. I know better now."[67]

The *New York Times* ridiculed the delegates:

> Tomorrow at noon there will open in the Coliseum a convention managed by women and has-beens. About everybody here who wears trousers is an ex. There are ex-Senators, ex-Secretaries, and ex-Commissioners galore. Everybody who is not an ex is a woman.

The women's concerns influenced the structure of the convention. Medill presented the report of the Committee on Rules on August 7. It called for four women members-at-large to every state convention, to ensure female representation. Jane Addams, dressed simply in white, rose to second Roosevelt's nomination and drew nearly as many cheers as the Colonel. She had helped draft the Progressive platform. The next day, when Roosevelt accepted the nomination, the hall was packed beyond its 12,500-seat capacity. Albert J. Beveridge of Indiana, slim, well-dressed, and handsome, announced simply: ". . . The hour, the man, Theodore Roosevelt." Roosevelt appeared on the platform and took his place before a giant sounding board under portraits of Washington, Jefferson, and Lincoln. The crowd roared. A sea of waving red bandannas, the Progressive emblem, covered the floor and galleries. Delegates threw their hats into imaginary rings. Some sang. Most yelled. The demonstration lasted nearly an hour. Ruth must have felt she was at last taking part as she was meant to.[68]

Roosevelt, though, felt himself a prisoner of his own momentum. He wrote a friend in London, "Of course while this must not be said publicly, I am leading rather a forlorn hope this year." On another occasion he wrote, "As we grow older we naturally lose the natural feeling of young men to take an interest in politics just for the sake of strife, the same kind of interest one takes in big game hunting or football . . ."

On the other hand, Ruth and Medill, still in their early thirties, were thoroughly enjoying the fray.[69]

All through the fall the McCormicks worked out of a suite of well-appointed offices in the Congress Hotel, confident that Taft would not get enough votes in Illinois "to wad a gun." The *New York Times* reported that Medill was "finding himself" in his new role. Ruth reinforced her ties to Progressive women in Illinois. Jane Addams, Mary McDowell and Margaret Dreier Robins were all active members of the State Progressive Party. Ruth observed that being a Progressive in Illinois was "respectable, but not fashionable." In many other states it was not even respectable.

Nevertheless, she and her husband believed that the Progressive Party would become a permanent, powerful party. [70]

Some feared that because the incomparable Teddy Roosevelt was at the head of the party it was a one-man show. An anxious correspondent queried the *Chicago Record-American* as to whether the plural for Bull Moose was "Bull Mooses" or "Bull Meese," and was assured, "There is no plural for Bull Moose. There is but one Bull Moose." Still, the Progressive Party in Illinois looked very promising. Both of the old parties were widely and publicly discredited as corrupt machines. Some regular Republicans were supporting Roosevelt, even though they themselves did not want to join the new party. Among them was Charles Deneen, who was running for governor. The McCormicks, however, supported Frank H. Funk, calling Deneen "a reluctant reformer." Deneen would run against both the McCormicks in the twenties. He would beat Medill, but he would not beat Ruth. [71]

Although Ruth was an ardent Progressive, she also had a strong sense of female solidarity. Daisy Harriman, who had been appointed Chairman of the Women's Division of the Woodrow Wilson campaign, later wrote,

> One of the first things I pitched off to do was to go west to form branch committees there. It was a tribute . . . to Ruth Hanna McCormick's broadness, bigness, generosity, and ability that without hesitation I went to her at once when I arrived in Chicago and said, "Tell me what Democratic women I ought to see." Engrossed as she was in the Progressive party campaign, she sat down then and there, and gave me hours of advice and furnished me with lists. Every woman she mentioned turned out afterwards to have just the talents and capabilities she commended them for.

The women were almost too successful in this campaign, for in 1916 Harriman would write,

> . . . the very men who used to come into my office four years before to thank me and my reluctant aides for our noble advance on the front page, turned up with ". . . We don't want a woman's department like that any more. They got more advertising in 1912 than did the candidates." [72]

Women like Daisy Harriman, as well as women in the civic reform groups, provided Ruth with models of a new kind of woman, unlike the Victorian stay-at-home her mother had been.

Medill was less happy in his role as a general campaign manager. After the election he wanted to concentrate on what Progressives could do in state politics, and he had run as a Progressive for the Illinois State

Legislature. Although both the Progressives and the Republicans lost to Wilson in the presidential election, Medill was one of twenty-eight Progressives elected to Springfield, giving them the balance of power in the state legislature. Charles S. Deneen had been elected governor. Ironically, the certificate with the big gold seal that certified Medill's election to the State House of Representatives of the Forty-eighth General Assembly was signed by Deneen, the man who later became his opponent and Ruth's.[73]

Roosevelt recognized that Ruth as well as Medill had played a part in the campaign. "My dear Ruth," he wrote her, "I wish I could see you in person to tell you how deeply I appreciate everything you have done, and how very fond I have grown of you." Ruth, for her part, truly admired Roosevelt, and at the end of her life, when she had worked for every other Republican nominee for almost half a century, still considered Roosevelt "the ablest, the most understanding, the one possessed of the widest knowledge." Unlike most of the other suffragists, Ruth willingly took male models for her political style and philosophy. Roosevelt wrote Ruth with advice on Medill's future career. "I can't help wishing that you and Medill would go to Washington as a result of the Senatorial contest." (A vacant seat was being filled by the legislature, this being before direct election of senators.) Ruth disagreed with him on the timing, and said that Medill could "make a record in the legislature for the future." She realized he could not move too quickly: "To live down being a McCormick is a dreadful job." Roosevelt came around to her thinking.

> [I]t would not be a good thing for us to begin making dickers with either of the old parties . . . I am afraid it would be hard to get a Progressive senator from Illinois without making some deal that would lay us open to attack. Medill can do wonderful work in the [state legislature].[74]

As it turned out, both the McCormicks would do good work in the legislature. It is interesting that Roosevelt was writing all this to Ruth. The colonel valued Medill's political vision, but he believed that Ruth, being her father's daughter, had better judgment. At Sagamore Hill one day, he was standing on the piazza with another mid-western leader, Raymond Robins, and they watched the McCormicks walk across a field toward the woods. Roosevelt clicked his teeth, meditatively.

"Raymond," he remarked—click, click, click—"my money's on the ma-r-re."[75]

Marcus Alonzo Hanna.

Augusta Rhodes
Hanna.

Ruth Hanna, c. 1884.

McKinleys and Hannas at Thomasville, c. 1900.

President Roosevelt to Attend Miss Hanna's Wedding

MISS RUTH HANNA

GLENMERE, SENATOR HANNA'S HOME IN LAKE AVENUE · CLEVELAND· WHERE THE WEDDING CEREMONY WILL TAKE PLACE·

MR JOSEPH MEDILL McCORMICK·

Wedding of Ruth Hanna and Medill McCormick, 1903.

Katherine Medill McCormick.

Alice Roosevelt Longworth. Inscribed "To her B. d. from Alice."

Ruth McCormick
(center), Alice
Longworth (far
right), Nick
Longworth (second
from left), 1908.

Medill McCormick,
c. 1909.

Theodore Roosevelt and running-mate Hiram Johnson, 1912.

Ruth McCormick, 1914. Courtesy of the Library of Congress.

Ruth McCormick,
1916.

Medill McCormick,
1916.

Ruth with Triny and Johnny, c. 1918.

Ruth and Medill, Triny, Johnny, Cissy Patterson, c. 1918.

Medill McCormick, 1924.

Ruth McCormick
in widow's "weeds," 1925.

Woman's World Fair. (l. to r.) Edith Rockefeller McCormick, Helen Bennett, Louise Bowen. Courtesy of the Chicago Historical Society.

Woman's World Fair. Estelline Bennett and Emily Dean. Courtesy of the Chicago Historical Society.

3
Woman Suffrage:
1913–1914

ILLINOIS

The Big Four

Ruth Hanna McCormick had her political baptism in the Progressive campaign of 1912, along with many of the reform-minded women of Chicago. They were beginning to realize, however, that the reforms they wanted—improved education, guaranteed pure food and milk, labor legislation to protect women and children, the reform of the criminal justice system—could only be won if women had the vote.[1] After a long period of inactivity, the suffrage movement was reviving, and Ruth McCormick, with her developing skills as a charismatic political leader, was in the forefront of the fight for the ballot, both in Illinois and on Capitol Hill.

Progressive women like Ruth McCormick, Jane Addams, Mary McDowell, Margaret Dreier Robins, Harriet Vittum, and Louise de Koven Bowen had found ample opportunity to speak during the campaign, sometimes three times a day, and to learn party organization. The Progressive Party was supportive of women's political activities. There had been women delegates to the convention, and the Progressive Party platform had included a plank on suffrage. In the nineteenth century the vote had been seen as a threat to women's special status, but by 1912 many women recognized that they needed it to improve the well-being of mothers.[2]

The suffrage movement was changing. It no longer represented a fringe group with a feminist agenda; it was more conservative and had begun to appeal to working-class women and upper-class women who had not been involved before. More women were working but often for poor wages and under appalling conditions. It became obvious that they needed the vote to legislate change. Conservative and upper-class women began to support suffrage for a variety of reforms. By 1910 obtaining the ballot no longer seemed radical in the context of progress by women in many other areas—education, employment, legal rights, and personal behavior. Ruth, who had begun by considering it "a scorned cause and occasional impotent uproar," was now ready to work for the franchise herself.[3] She found that support for suffrage was by no means universal or even extensive.

Although the Progressives supported suffrage, the major political parties did not. In 1910 President William Howard Taft had stunned the Washington suffrage convention by blurting out his true sentiments: "I am opposed to the extension of suffrage to women not fitted to vote. You would hardly expect to put the ballot into the hands of barbarians or savages in the jungle." He lamely concluded that the best women would not vote while the worst would, but his remarks were, not surprisingly, greeted with stony silence. President Woodrow Wilson, in turn, who had confided to journalist David Lawrence that he thought women "too logical" and too unwilling to compromise to be allowed to participate in politics, announced to suffragists soon after his inauguration that he was too busy to be concerned with the matter.[4]

Presidents and presidential candidates could still hold to such views because woman suffrage had not really been a national issue in 1912. Close to one million women were eligible to vote in six states,* but it is doubtful whether Theodore Roosevelt's support of woman suffrage won him many votes or the failure of the major parties to do so cost them any. Nevertheless, by the end of 1912 three more suffrage states had been added: Oregon, Kansas, and Arizona. Suffrage states now represented one-fifth of the Senate, one-seventh of the House, and one-sixth of the electoral votes for president. Up until 1913 the suffrage states were all in the West. Less bound by tradition, more dependent upon competent women, western men were much more amenable to the idea that women should participate in government.[5]

The keynote of the reawakened suffrage movement was a massive suffrage rally held the second week of March 1913 in Washington, D.C. The National American Woman Suffrage Association had appointed a new congressional lobbyist, Alice Paul, a woman with a remarkable news sense. Paul had organized the parade for the day before Woodrow Wilson's inauguration, when the streets of Washington would be full of curious

---

*Wyoming, Colorado, Utah, Idaho, Washington and California

visitors. The *Baltimore American* reported that when Woodrow Wilson reached Washington and found no crowds to welcome him, he asked where the people were and was told they were on Pennsylvania Avenue, watching the suffrage parade.[6]

An estimated eight thousand women marched from the Capitol up Pennsylvania Avenue, past the White House. They had a permit to march, but spectators became unruly, broke through the police cordon, and mauled and insulted the marchers. Women were pulled off floats, tripped up, knocked down, slapped, and spat upon. Troops of cavalry from Fort Meyer had to be rushed in to restore order. The incident showed the strength of the sentiment against suffrage, but it also brought the movement favorable publicity. Some American men had claimed that women didn't need the vote because their men would protect them. The assault showed the weakness of their argument.[7]

Ruth McCormick, however, had not been able to participate in the march. Childless after nearly ten years of marriage, Ruth had conceived in the summer of 1912, after an operation by a woman gynecologist. The very day after the suffrage parade, Katherine Augusta McCormick was born, named, as was customary, after both grandmothers. She was always called "Triny" and legally adopted the name Katrina as an adult. Among the many telegrams her proud parents received were several predicting the baby would be a suffragist when she grew up. Since she had been working for the ten years following her marriage, Ruth wanted to fit the new baby into her working schedule. The following month she attempted to make a speech at Musician's Hall on Washington Street to a mass meeting of female department store clerks seeking a decent wage and improved working conditions. Newspapers had not publicized their demands for fear of losing advertising, and Ruth rose to denounce the papers and to urge the young women to organize.

> The greatest argument of men against women has been that all women are individualists. We've had to be individualists a long time, by nature of our occupations in the home. The only way in which working women, and all other women, can help ourselves is by organizing.

Before she could finish her speech, however, she began to faint, and Mary McDowell rushed to catch her. But nothing kept her down for long. Six months later Ruth joined another strike, supporting restaurant waitresses seeking an eight-hour day. She and other prominent settlement-house women were useful in curbing police brutality, a major feature of both strikes. Finally, the owner capitulated: "There was no use in fighting women," he said.[8]

Ruth also continued to work from her office, writing Theodore Roosevelt,

> The Tax Federation seems to think that if I enclose their request, that it will have great influence in getting you out here. As I do not wish to disabuse their minds of this impression, for future Progressive benefits, I am complying with their request.[9]

Writer Hamlin Garland reported to Roosevelt that he was discussing the Progressive political organization with Ruth, among others.

Having a baby had not diminished her effectiveness in Progressive politics. In fact, Ruth was more involved than ever, since Medill was one of twenty-seven Progressives elected to the State Legislature in Springfield. Progressives held the balance of power, as neither Democrats nor Republicans had a majority. Medill became the leader through the Forty-eighth General Assembly, and Ruth moved down to Springfield with the baby. According to fellow Progressive Harold Ickes, who later became disenchanted with the McCormicks, "Medill proceeded to run things with a high hand . . . He had called a meeting of the state central committee there, planning to control it." Ickes reported that he and others had "operated on Medill and Mrs. Medill, too, be it said." Ickes came to dislike Ruth, but he never underestimated her.[10] He makes it clear that both McCormicks were involved in Illinois politics.

The first order of business was to elect two U.S. senators. (At that time senators were elected by the state legislatures.) A "short term" vacancy had been created by the impeachment of Republican Senator William Lorimer for bribery in his election. Medill considered the seat for himself but Roosevelt warned the Progressives to stay clear of any alliance "containing the least taint of discredit." In the end the Republicans and Democrats made a deal without the Progressives, electing the obstinate Republican Lawrence Y. Sherman to the short term, and a Democrat, James Hamilton Lewis, for the long term. Lewis would face both McCormicks in future campaigns.[11]

Apart from electing senators, Progressive legislators had an ambitious program of social reform, and high on the list was woman suffrage. Back in 1893 the Illinois Equal Suffrage Association had prepared a bill with the advice of attorney Catharine Waugh McCulloch, their legislative chairman, listing all the offices for which the state legislature could grant suffrage. This bill had been introduced in every session of the Legislature for twenty years without success. In 1912 the Illinois suffrage movement changed direction when Grace Wilbur Trout was elected president of the Illinois Equal Suffrage Association (IESA). Trout had become president of the Chicago Political Equality League in 1910; within two years membership had risen from 143 to over a thousand. There were differences of personality between her and McCulloch, and McCulloch resigned as legislative chairman, pleading family duties. Trout then named Elizabeth K. Booth of Glencoe. Later in the spring she added Antoinette Funk, a Chicago lawyer, and Ruth McCormick to her legislative team. The "Big Four," as they were known, devised a completely new strategy.[12]

Governor Edward F. Dunne agreed to support a Presidential and Municipal Suffrage Bill (all that the legislature could grant) if the suffragists promised not to introduce a measure requiring a constitutional amendment; Illinois was limited to one amendment per year, and he wanted an initiative and referendum amendment. In any case, amending the state constitution was a difficult process, so the suffragists decided the compromise was the only plausible strategy at the time. In addition to such tactical concessions, the Big Four also planned a campaign to avoid antagonizing their targets. In the legislature there were many strong opponents of suffrage, a few supporters, and a number of legislators who treated it as a joke. But nearly all disliked the trainloads of women who had descended every year on their proceedings.[13] A more scientific, less strident approach was planned.

After the November elections Elizabeth Booth got the "Illinois Blue Book" and began a study of the men elected. She organized a card catalogue with the man's picture and vital statistics, including his political "boss," his and his wife's suffrage stands, suffragists in his district, and his record on questions like Prohibition. At the time the Illinois Senate was choosing a U.S. Senator, the House was deadlocked for four weeks over choosing a speaker. Booth sat patiently in the gallery, studying the men and revising her catalogue. Illinois legislators usually went home for the weekends, returning to Springfield on a particular train on Sunday night. Every week, Booth rode the train. She was quiet, sympathetic, and friendly, and she sat with them and let them talk about their hobbies. A data file was in the making.

Meanwhile Grace Trout was traveling over the state, rousing the women. Whereas Booth was always ready with the quiet, logical argument, Trout was eloquent, persuasive, and full of touching stories. She won over many whom Booth had not convinced. From the outset, they determined to ignore the die-hards who were against suffrage and concentrate on those who seemed undecided. It was a very modern targeted campaign.

Still, the women faced an uphill fight. Progressive legislator George Fitch described the situation: "The first Democratic governor in twenty years faced a Democratic delegation split into two wildly hostile halves.

The Progressives and the Republicans were irreconcilable." The legislators had an immense work load: to pass the initiative/referendum
amendment; repair the primary and workman's compensation laws; pass
a public utility law; reform the tax law; and consider other important
bills. Back of each bill was a powerful lobby. The women had to "tear
the House away from these distractions and convince it of the necessity
of carrying woman suffrage across the Mississippi."[14] It was a very tall
order.

Matters were not helped when Catharine Waugh McCulloch descended on Springfield on April 2 to introduce a resolution providing
for the very constitutional amendment that Trout had promised the
women would forego. It was killed in committee; Medill McCormick,
according to Trout, "helped greatly in straightening out this tangle." The
presidential suffrage bill passed through the Senate easily on May 7,
1913. But the Senate had passed suffrage bills several times before only
to have them defeated in the House. They would die in the wrong
committee, be amended to death on the second reading, or get to the
third reading just as the session closed.[15] Illinois suffragists had to avoid
all these pitfalls.

Booth and Trout, though politically untried, were experienced "people
movers," and appealed to the men's sense of justice to at least let the
bill come to a vote. Trout then summoned Antoinette Funk, variously
described as "abrasive" or "persuasive," for the next and more difficult
part of the fight. Ruth McCormick, as soon as she had recovered from
childbirth, was named chairman of publicity.[16] It was time to intensify
the pressure.

It was a stiflingly hot summer. In the Leland Hotel, where Antoinette
Funk and Ruth McCormick lobbied the members who had resisted Grace
Trout and Elizabeth Booth, there was a charged atmosphere:

> Natives strode lazily about under their wide slouch hats with waistcoats
> open and cravats loosened. The smoke of cigars hung in the air. The
> sound of many voices, the ring of heavy laughter, the shuffle of feet over
> the tiles, the clang of the clerk's gong, the incessant chitter of the telegraph
> instrument that sped news to Chicago—all these influences surcharged
> the heavy air with a nervous excitement that made men speak quickly
> and their eyes glitter under the brilliant lights of countless electric bulbs.[17]

In this steamy environment, Ruth was cooly effective with the press.
Her studies at the *Tribune* were now paying off. She took the regular
Springfield correspondents into her confidence and made them valuable
allies. Often they withheld or sent out suffrage news as it would best

help the campaign. *Chicago Tribune* executives James Keeley and Teddy Beck gave extensive coverage to woman suffrage, and the editorial writer as well as the political cartoonist John McCutcheon were enthusiastically in favor.[18] In addition to her press work, Ruth frequently lobbied down at the Capitol. One day an anti-suffrage legislator confronted her by saying, "This is no place for a woman, and no work for a woman. You ought to be at home looking after your husband and child." She turned his argument back on him. "I came down to Springfield and took a house during the session so I could be with my husband and make him comfortable. Now," she said, glancing at her watch,

> I am watching the time because I have to go home and nurse my baby. I am fortunately situated so that I can look after my husband and child and still have time to spare. When I come up here to the Capitol and ask you to vote for woman suffrage, I am thinking of women whose husbands and babies are neglected because they have to get out and work for wages that no one would dare offer a voter.

In order to win majority support, women like Ruth were learning to use the argument that the ballot would complement their feminine charter, not undermine it.[19]

The presidential suffrage bill was voted out of committee and passed the first reading without attracting much attention. By the second reading on June 3, the opposition, according to Trout, made a "most desperate attempt to amend and if possible kill the measure." To the surprise of many, there was an impressive majority against every attacking amendment. Few realized how well the Big Four had done their homework; it seems that man after man, in promising his support, had been told to tell no one. An overmatched Anton Cermak, the head of the United Liquor Dealers Association, rushed down to Springfield to direct the fight against the bill, fearing that woman suffrage would bring prohibition.[20] During this period, the women discovered they were being followed by detectives. "We were on guard," wrote Trout, "and never talked about our plans in public places."

Medill McCormick managed to pass a special resolution that changed the order of consideration for the suffrage bill, which otherwise would not have been introduced during the time that remained. Trout recalled the opposition asking Speaker William McKinley to keep the bill from coming to a vote:

> The young speaker . . . looked worn and haggard during these trying days. He told me he had not been allowed to sleep for many nights.

Hundreds of men . . . begged him to never let the suffrage bill come up
for a vote, and threatened him with political oblivion.

He asked Trout to let him know if there were strong suffrage sentiment
in Illinois. Over the weekend, a "telephone brigade" organized by Harriett
Taylor Treadwell, who had taken over as president of the Chicago Political Equality League, called McKinley every fifteen minutes from early
Saturday until Monday afternoon. When he returned to Springfield Tuesday morning, thousands of letters and telegrams awaited him. He announced the suffrage bill would come to a vote June 11, 1913.[21] Other
wavering members had been similarly bombarded by telegrams from constituents. Messages had been sent to every man who had promised to
vote for the bill to be present by Tuesday morning for a Wednesday vote.
There were sixteen suffrage "captains" to see that the men were in their
seats. A cab was reserved so that the women could bring in missing
members. Once again, the Big Four had done meticulous work.

On the day of the vote Elizabeth Booth and Ruth were in the gallery
with a list of representatives; Trout, knowing the doorman was unsym-
pathetic, stood guard at the entrance to the floor of the House to see
that no friendly members left their seats and no unfriendly lobbyists
unlawfully entered. The "Wets" were nervous, delayed the vote, brought
up points, and demanded roll calls on them, hoping the House would
adjourn. Finally after 3 P.M., the voting began. By then, reported Fitch,
the members were "famished and overwrought."[22]

Voting began in the midst of tense silence and proceeded through two
roll calls. Booth dropped a paper to an ally on the floor. It listed seven
men whose votes had not been recorded. "Please see that these men
vote," she ordered. At this point Representative Edward D. Shurtleff,
who had been opposed to woman suffrage, changed his position. Dis-
gusted by a Vice Commission hearing earlier in the session, he decided
that "if that is the best man can do in the legislative halls, it is high
time we took women into our councils." His reversal changed several
Republican minds.[23] Luck as well as good organization was playing a part.

Speaker McKinley was also called on to vote. It was rumored that his
fiancée, Katherine Riley, refused to set the date for their wedding until
woman suffrage passed. When McKinley's "aye" was added, six others
who had refrained from voting added theirs, and the measure passed
eighty-three to fifty-eight. The Capitol rocked with cheers. Men and
women wept.[24] It was a great victory for the Big Four of Illinois.

Two days later the Illinois Equal Suffrage Association gave a banquet at the Leland Hotel for all the legislators and their wives. Some suffragists questioned whether they should invite their enemies. "We have no enemies," said Mrs. Trout diplomatically. Ruth organized the party in that spirit but provided a roll of honor that all those who had voted for the bill were asked to sign. As the guests departed, they took their leave of The Big Four in the lobby. Fitch claimed to be in awe of "the representatives of 1,300,000 votes," but he wryly observed that "with reprehensible frivolity they were eating chocolates from a large box . . . and they declined to be austere."[25]

The landmark suffrage bill was a product of its time. By 1912, according to Inez Haynes Irwin, chronicler of the suffrage period, the suffrage movement was "virile and vital." A popular vote for woman suffrage in Chicago in 1912, though it failed, had taught the women that they could organize a cohesive cross-class alliance. Working-class and upper-class women had joined the final phase. Working women provided the most compelling arguments for the need for the vote, and upper-class women used their social influence to good effect. Their chances in 1913 were improved by having a goodly number of Progressives in the legislature and probably by the fact that two-thirds of the members were freshmen. Also, The Big Four were willing to compromise on a limited suffrage bill, which previous lobbyists had not been. One cynical analyst believed that some legislators thought a limited suffrage bill too trivial to oppose, and that if the bill's importance had been fully grasped, it would have been defeated.[26]

Compromises aside, the first suffrage bill passed east of the Mississippi was considered something of a political miracle, albeit "a miracle made possible by six months of unceasing toil," as one of Ruth's colleagues, Helen Bennett, observed. But it was not mere work that had carried the day. After all, Catharine Waugh McCulloch had been working for twenty years. In part, it was how the women worked. Believing that "there was no class of people for whom politicians had so tender and respectful a regard as . . . constituents," they had organized pressure groups within each man's district. Perhaps most important was the low-key campaign of "education" and the conciliatory manner of the four lobbyists. (McCulloch had outraged all the lawyers in the Illinois legislature, of which there were many, by her public statement that lawyers were unreliable allies because "the lawyer in the legislature is a failure as an attorney." Trout diplomatically characterized McCulloch's outburst as "unfortunate.") Many men professed to fear that political activities would make women "large-handed, big-footed, flat-chested, and thin-lipped." In order to achieve their goals, leaders of the suffrage movement had to win support among the mainstream and even conservative segments of society. During an earlier campaign to secure the municipal franchise for women in Chicago, Jane Addams lauded the "complete absence of the traditional women's rights clamor . . ." Said Booth, "We answered the claim that politics makes women unwomanly by making a quiet pleasant campaign."[27]

Unlike many of the nineteenth-century suffragists who were reacting against male dominance, Ruth McCormick and her colleagues wished to emulate men and be accepted by them on an equal footing. Some were women who, like Ruth, had been reared by men active in politics: Jane Addams' father had been a state senator, and Julia Lathrop's father had drafted a bill enabling Illinois women to be admitted to the bar. A number of the other women leaders had dual careers with their husbands: Mary Ware Dennett, Harriet Laidlaw, and Margaret Dreier Robins. Ruth wrote, "In the Mississippi Valley the suffrage movement encountered a Chinese wall of opposition until, with the help of men, the adoption of men's political methods opened the little gates and broken places in the wall."[28] The hallmark of her political technique from then on was to secure male allies and use men's political techniques.

Their new tactics had helped secure a victory that would contribute to the momentum of the national campaign. Ruth felt the bill had an important effect in Illinois as well. She reported that the effect was nearly immediate:

> the Women's City Club of 17,000 organized women, representing every precinct in the city, for twelve years had asked the city hall to pass fourteen ordinances, affecting the health of children and adults . . . without a single ordinance being passed, . . . [But] the fourteen ordinances were on the statute books within eleven months from the date of the Governor's signature on the Suffrage bill.[29]

The governor, before signing, had wished to have an opinion on the constitutionality of the law. So immediately after the banquet Ruth had hurried to Chicago to consult lawyers. Reassured, the governor promptly signed the bill. Flags were raised throughout the state. Reporters entertained the victorious foursome with cold drinks at the Leland Hotel, and an automobile parade, still something of a novelty, was held afterwards to celebrate. Jane Addams sent Ruth a delegate pin from the International Suffrage meeting at "Budapesth" as a "slight token" of her admiration for Ruth's work at Springfield.[30]

THE CONGRESSIONAL COMMITTEE

"Lincoln Used to Be My Patron Saint But Now It's Job."

Harriet Taylor Upton

But there was no time for Ruth to rest on her Springfield laurels. 1913 had been a watershed year elsewhere on the suffrage front. In Washington the old Congressional Committee of the National American Woman's Suffrage Association was being completely revitalized under the direction of Alice Paul, whose first move had been to organize the 1913 pre-Inauguration march. Since Ruth was drafted to replace Paul on the Congressional Committee at the end of 1913, a closer look at the national movement is required.

Alice Paul was a young Quaker woman, twenty-seven in 1913, with a Ph.D. on the legal status of women. She had lived in England where she met the British suffragists Emmaline Pankhurst and her daughter Christabel and was impressed by their militant tactics. Paul was an ethereal creature with clear white skin and masses of heavy dark hair, but she was charismatic and indefatigable where woman suffrage was concerned. It was said that she had vowed not to think or read about anything that was not related to suffrage until a federal amendment was passed.[31]

A single-minded and energetic woman was badly needed to bring the suffrage lobby back to life. In the nineteenth century Susan B. Anthony had lobbied in Washington, D.C., for a federal amendment granting all women the vote, but gradually women had turned their attention to passing suffrage laws in the individual states. NAWSA had maintained a Congressional Committee in Washington to arrange for hearings before committees in Congress, but only once, in 1887, had the measure been voted on by the Senate and never by the House. For sixteen years there had been virtually no federal activity. In 1912 Alice Paul persuaded the NAWSA Convention at Philadelphia to allow her to go to Washington at her own expense to lobby Congress for a federal amendment. Paul and her friend Lucy Burns went to Washington in January 1913 and gathered several more women including lawyer Crystal Eastman and historian Mary Beard. Within two short months they had organized the 1913 parade that made such a dramatic impression on the national consciousness. A few months later, Paul galvanized Congress into action on the long-dead amendment by canvassing congressional members and holding more large demonstrations. Her work was so effective that woman suffrage was debated in Congress that year for the first time since 1887.[32]

Alice Paul and Lucy Burns wanted a new national organization dedicated to the sole purpose of working for a federal suffrage amendment,
as NAWSA was still working largely with individual states.[33] With the
consent of NAWSA's president, Dr. Anna Howard Shaw, Paul and Burns
founded the Congressional Union.

Paul now proposed a new and highly controversial strategy, threatening
the Democratic Party, which controlled the Congress, that women in
suffrage states would vote against their candidates there unless the Democrats endorsed the federal amendment. Her case was strengthened by
the success of Ruth McCormick and her friends in Illinois; in 1916 Illinois
women would vote for presidential electors, and increased pressure could
be brought on the president. Paul was criticized for this tactic on two
counts. Many thought her strategy unworkable. In England the party in
power could be held responsible for the success or failure of a policy. In
the United States politicians are very loosely connected with their party
and vote individually. In the one-party South such a policy might alienate
the voters completely, and it was generally assumed that at least two or
three Southern states (then solidly Democratic) would be needed to pass
the Amendment.[34] Furthermore, many pro-suffrage politicians were Democrats and would be penalized unfairly. In addition, the whole idea of
coercion and partisanship was repugnant to the mainstream women in
NAWSA.

Matters came to a head about the time Ruth McCormick arrived at
the NAWSA convention in Washington in early December 1913. Paul's
colleague Lucy Burns wanted NAWSA to join the Congressional Union
in pressuring the Democratic party and to support an all-out campaign
for the immediate passage of a suffrage amendment. This conflicted with
NAWSA's continuing support for the policy of state campaigns. NAWSA
officials were also dismayed that Paul had combined the activities and
finances of the Congressional Committee and the Congressional Union.
As more than twenty-five thousand dollars had been raised and spent
that year, it was not an insignificant issue. Not only were the finances
a mess, but people confused the Congressional Committee with the
Congressional Union, an organization over which NAWSA had no control.[35] The first order of business at the convention was getting control
of the Congressional Committee.

A second issue discussed by the convention delegates was President
Wilson's reluctance to endorse woman suffrage. Wilson, in a message to
Congress two days before, had urged extension of the ballot to the
Filipinos and territorial rights for Alaska, but had not mentioned women.
Few of the NAWSA delegates had wanted to comment publicly on

Wilson's message, but Ruth McCormick, the leader of the Illinois delegation, had no such hesitation and moved that the convention wait upon the president to pressure him to make suffrage an administration measure. For a woman who had been an intimate friend of two of the last three presidents, this was a logical step. After a moment's hesitation there was loud applause and many cries of "Second the motion!" It carried with almost no debate, though there were a few suggestions to amend with a view to "putting it stronger." Ruth Hanna McCormick was delegated to arrange a meeting with the president.[36]

There was less agreement on the problem of the intertwined Congressional Committee and Congressional Union. The NAWSA officers wanted to keep the energetic Alice Paul, but they wanted to prevent her overturning their established priorities. Finally Paul was removed, and Lucy Burns and other Congressional Union members resigned. The NAWSA Board wanted to prove that the Congressional Committee could carry on without Alice Paul.[37] They turned to Ruth Hanna McCormick, who had kept a high profile throughout the meetings and was well-known for her work in the Progressive Party and on the Illinois suffrage bill. Her two Illinois colleagues, Antoinette Funk and Elizabeth Booth, were named her assistants.

This appointment was Ruth's first real political work on her own. She had been working for ten years in the settlement and social reform circles as well as in the Progressive Party, where she had earned the respect of Pinchot, Garland, Ickes, and Roosevelt. Perhaps the fact that her children arrived late had given her the chance to develop contacts and work habits so that she could easily continue working after their arrival. She had other advantages, too, that made it easy for her to enter politics. Her money gave her the leisure to work where she wanted and to underwrite causes she supported. And the training she had received as her father's daughter made her comfortable on Capitol Hill. Not everyone was pleased at Ruth's appointment. Mary Ware Dennett, corresponding secretary of the NAWSA, felt there were liabilities in making Ruth chairman of the Congressional Committee: one, she was closely identified with the Progressive Party; and two, she could not be in Washington all the time during the congressional session. Some thought Ruth was simply a society woman, although others were delighted that she could afford to finance organizers and pay headquarter's expenses. The *Boston Transcript* observed that "she has not yet proved what she can do, whereas Alice Paul . . . has to a marked degree demonstrated her ability."[38] Ruth McCormick was facing the first real test of her ability.

The main difference between Alice Paul and Ruth McCormick reflected a split between radical activists and mainstream pragmatists. This went back to the early days of women's activism and the division between the Elizabeth Cady Stanton/Susan B. Anthony suffragists who became disillusioned with the Republican Party in 1869 for not working harder for suffrage, and the Lucy Stone/Henry Blackwell group who felt the Republicans were right in saying woman suffrage could not have been won at that time.[39] It was the age-old battle of ideologue purists and pragmatic realists.

Paul defended her strategy by pointing out that four million women would vote for ninety-one presidential electors in 1916, and that Wilson had been elected by a majority numerically smaller than the strength of the suffrage states. But NAWSA had a long-time commitment to non-partisanship; they did not believe that women could be made to vote as a bloc, and they thought that Paul's tactics would alienate sympathizers. They favored the continuation of activities that had worked in the past, made more effective by organization. They believed the Congressional Union would weaken the suffrage position by making empty threats.[40]

Ruth outlined her tactics in an early memo. The Congressional Committee intended to work in congressional districts through the state organizations, which, according to Dr. Shaw, the Congressional Union was unwilling to do.[41] Ruth made clear her plan to be pragmatic but tough:

> to oppose those men who by their vote clearly disregard the wishes of constituents in opposing suffrage. This makes their defeat a practical possibility and does not make the National amusing, by making empty threats. It is . . . absurd to attempt to defeat men because they belong to the majority party . . . the most difficult party to defeat. It makes suffragists ridiculous to attempt to defeat the best friends they have in the Senate.[42]

Ruth's suggestions, however, were somewhat against NAWSA policy, too, and created a stir when they appeared in print.[43] Ruth transferred the Congressional Committee headquarters to Chicago, rationalizing the move as due to the growth of the movement, the enlargement of the Committee, and the need for closer communication with the various state committees. She wanted the state chairmen to appoint committees in each congressional district to advise their congressmen on the suffrage question. She and Elizabeth Booth proposed to alternate in directing the work of the national lobby in Washington. While it was personally convenient for Ruth to be in Chicago while Medill was a legislator in

Illinois, it cannot have been the most efficient way to lobby Congress, which was her first mandate.[44]

Ruth acknowledged that getting a federal amendment might seem a nearly hopeless task, but for her committee, she said, it was "simply a work of detail." They planned to study the laws in each state as they pertained to women, and "Where women are dealt with unjustly," she said, "we shall arouse their energies to help us fight." The Committee planned to catalog accounts of congressmen's positions, gather information about local issues, provide a speaker exchange, and establish a finance board.[45]

Rumors of a schism between the Congressional Committee and the Congressional Union soon began to appear in the press. At first, both sides tried to minimize their differences. Alice Paul and Lucy Burns extended a cordial greeting to the new Congressional Committee. Ruth denied any rivalry, stating that the two groups "intend to work along entirely different lines." She suggested the rumors had been started by the "antis," who "would be only too happy to have a factional feeling spring up between the Congressional Committee and the Congressional Union."[46]

Ruth arrived in Washington to begin work on January 23, 1914, the very day Alice Paul "declared war on the Democratic Party," threatening in the 1914 election to "try to deprive the Democrats of control" in the Senate, where they had a slim majority of only four seats. Ruth accused Alice Paul of failing to understand American political traditions and harshly denounced the "unscrupulous methods of a most un-American band of women." Finally she exclaimed, "Are we going to allow two girls to run away with the American suffrage movement?" (Alice Paul was twenty-seven, Ruth thirty-three.)[47]

At first, Ruth had been sorry that the Congressional Union had split from the NAWSA Committee, feeling that its members had done good work. But when the Congressional Union petitioned to become an auxiliary member of the NAWSA a month later, Ruth objected.

> When I accepted the chairmanship of this Committee, I did so innocently confident that I should be able . . . to work out if not a completely satisfactory plan, certainly a compromise plan with the Congressional Union . . . If I had not felt this confidence in the future of the work, I certainly should not have accepted the position as Chairman as it has been one of the most disagreeable tasks ever performed.

She even threatened to resign if the Congressional Union were allowed to join the NAWSA. It was not allowed to join, but Ruth was still reluctant even to attend a board meeting with the Union representatives. When she did, however, she was happy to report, "we threshed out all differences," and praised Alice Paul's idea to have simultaneous demonstrations all over the country in May.[48]

Although Ruth had been working in the national arena, she was still active in Illinois suffrage politics and now traveled back to Chicago to help register the new women voters. Arriving at Union Station, she was met by her husband, who proudly told the press, "She's a regular politician now." They proceeded to the City Hall Square Building where they still had adjoining offices. Women had been given the municipal ballot and wanted to focus their attention on parks, state hospitals for the cure of inebriates, and similar issues. Teachers were asked to tell children to have their mothers vote; pastors, priests, and rabbis were asked to tell parishioners to register and use their vote for the public welfare. Ethnic groups were mobilized: the Bohemian women were proud of "the extraordinary parliamentary training" of their lodges, and forty-five "colored" women's clubs, with memberships of between twenty-five and two hundred, had organized into a federation under Ida Wells-Barnett. Suffrage leaders attempted to remove a disqualification from prostitutes (euphemistically known as "resort inmates"), arguing that they were no more to be disfranchised than their male clients. A large number of similar—and now curiously dated—matters had to be worked out. A Handbook for the Women Voters of Illinois, written by a female member of the Chicago bar, pointed out that women could be even better-informed than "the other voters." The author wrote, "the male voter inherits his politics, or he gets it by a sudden conversion as thoro-going [sic] as those Jonathan Edwards used to describe." Women, she said, could be more rational. They were to register in the same manner as male voters but were to use a special "feminized" ballot. A judge even called a conference in his chambers a few days prior to the registration to decide whether or not women had to give their age on registration day. This was not a frivolous point: Grace Wilbur Trout pointed out that prejudice against age might hurt certain businesswomen, but she still urged that no exception be made in favor of women. "We want to be equal and no more," she insisted. On February 3 over 150,000 women registered. Men bestirred themselves to establish a record, too, of 85,161 new and relocated voters.[49] Although there was a great deal happening in Illinois, Ruth McCormick had work to do in Washington.

Ruth's Congressional Committee now decided to lobby for an alternate amendment to the Constitution that would provide the vote for women.

Amendment "Number One," referred to as the "Susan B. Anthony" Amendment by Paul's Congressional Union, simply stated that "The right of citizens of the United States to vote shall not be denied or abridged by the United States or by any State on account of sex." But on February 3 the Democratic Caucus had refused to recommend a House Woman Suffrage Committee, using the excuse that suffrage was a state, not a federal, issue. Amendment "Number Two," which Ruth Mc-Cormick's committee wanted to substitute if the original bill was voted down, would be a compromise with the states' rights advocates. As it was very hard to get state legislatures to adopt suffrage—two-thirds or three-fourths of each legislature was needed to bring an issue to a vote—Ruth's Congressional Committee proposed an amendment (very much in the Progressive mood) whereby a state suffrage measure would have to be submitted to a vote whenever 8 percent of the voting population had signed a petition. In this way, they expected that there would eventually be a majority of members in Congress from suffrage states who would then pass the Federal amendment.[50]

Although the proposed procedure was awkward, Ruth argued that the amendment would quickly pass because it was the logical outcome of the Democratic Party's states' rights policy, especially since both major parties wanted to be rid of the "suffrage albatross." Ruth had worked with a number of senators to devise the plan, again trying for a practical, workable solution. At first the NAWSA board was unhappy with her new approach; she had not checked with them before announcing the new "policy." This independence from the central authority was just what they had deplored in Alice Paul, but finally they grudgingly agreed to support her.[51]

The woman suffrage question was presented to the House Judiciary Committee on March 3. Ruth McCormick, Antoinette Funk, and Mrs. William Kent, representing the NAWSA, proposed the new amendment if the Anthony amendment should fail. This suggestion produced "great consternation among the Union people," according to Antoinette Funk, and Ruth observed that the House committee "pelted questions at [Funk] for some time, showing that they had grasped the meaning of it, and were interested."[52]

Ruth's committee again had to vie with the Congressional Union for the legislators' attention. When Crystal Eastman Benedict, representing the Congressional Union, was introduced to the House Judiciary Committee, Ruth reported that the men

began to straighten their neck-ties, leaning forward in anticipation of

what this beautiful woman was about to say, and were all smirking
attention. This continued for some time until she announced the Union
policy clearly and definitely as going out to defeat the Democrats if they
failed to pass legislation by this session of Congress," then "they grouched
into their chairs and cast surly looks first at the speaker and then at each
other, and bit their lips with impatience.[53]

When Ruth spoke she emphasized that the NAWSA, with its great
membership, was non-partisan. (The Congressional Union never claimed
to have more than 2.5 percent of the NAWSA membership, even at the
height of the suffrage battle.)[54] Her approach won a friendlier reception.

The scene next shifted to the Senate. Ruth was eager for a vote on
the Anthony amendment as soon as possible because, anticipating a
defeat, she wanted time to present the alternate amendment. She also
believed that even if the measure failed to pass, any increase over the
sixteen who had supported the measure in 1887 would help the cause.
And she realized that the vote would help them target individuals against
whom they could campaign in the fall election. "We have been fighting
in the dark," she said. "The Senators have been very polite, but we have
not felt sure of their support."[55]

Ruth McCormick was always publicly optimistic. On March 7 she was
quoted as saying, "Our fight is practically won. After a week of debate
in the Senate, we see victory in the U.S. as plain as day." On the
seventeenth she claimed "a tremendous victory in having so long a
discussion on the floor of the Senate." As she watched the Senate proceedings from the gallery, she observed that "human nature is pretty
much the same everywhere, and that a man who wants to vote in any
particular way can generally find excuses for so voting." Unfortunately,
she did not apply the same conclusion where her compromise plan was
concerned.[56]

When the Anthony Amendment finally came to a vote in the Senate,
nearly one-third of the senators, twenty-six, were absent. Of the sixty-
nine who voted, there were thirty-five yeas and thirty-four nays. Ruth
was pleased that a majority, if not the two-thirds required for passage,
had voted for the bill. Funk observed that eleven more votes were needed
to win and said of their alternate amendment: "We are assured that it
will receive 10 votes from among the 34 who voted against . . . men
who are unalterably opposed to Amendment Number One on account
of states' rights."[57] It may have been naive of the NAWSA committee
to believe that the opponents of the bill really were opposed on the basis
of states' rights. Many of those men proved all too willing to ignore states'

rights when Prohibition came under consideration.[58] But at the time there was widespread optimism about the second bill.

Senator John F. Shafroth of Colorado, a large, loose-jointed man with sandy hair and moustache and a kindly weather-beaten face, characterized himself as an "old timer" on the suffrage issue; he had introduced a resolution for a constitutional amendment eighteen years earlier, in 1896, when he first met Susan B. Anthony. The day after the defeat of the "Anthony" Amendment, he introduced what was at first called the "Shafroth-McCormick" amendment. There was an instant outcry. Senator Joseph L. Bristow of Kansas, sponsor of the "Anthony" Amendment, said the Shafroth Amendment was more a national initiative and referendum than a woman suffrage amendment. Harriot Blatch, Elizabeth Cady Stanton's outspoken daughter, protested that the Shafroth-Palmer Amendment "smacked strongly of having been suggested by Congressmen who wished to give women some political crocheting to occupy their hands and relieve Congress of their disconcerting attentions." The amendment had its critics and reopened many old wounds. The split between the NAWSA and the Congressional Union over the suffrage amendment paralleled the old differences between the National Woman Suffrage Association and the American Woman Suffrage Association in the nineteenth century. The National had always supported the Anthony amendment, while the American had campaigned at the state level.[59]

Still, the Congressional Committee had several practical reasons to believe the Shafroth-Palmer bill would succeed. It would shift the ultimate responsibility from congressmen to people in the states; therefore, politicians in Washington should be more willing to support it. The Democrats had gone on record in favor of initiative and referendum, but not woman suffrage. And it answered the argument about states' rights.

Ruth and her colleagues felt "physically used up" after the struggle in the Senate, but their "fighting blood [was] still boiling" as they turned to consider how to introduce the amendment in the House. A resolution to permit women to vote for President, Vice-President, and congressmen was introduced in the House and was reported out of committee, neither favorably nor unfavorably, to the dismay of members wishing to avoid commitment before the election. The Shafroth Amendment was introduced by Representative A. Mitchell Palmer of Pennsylvania, although Ruth had been hoping to get a Southerner to sponsor the measure and vindicate her tactics.[60]

The Congressional Union was planning their big demonstration for May 2, and Ruth proposed that the NAWSA cooperate with them fully in the vain hope that "we could call them off on the Legislative proposition entirely and leave that field to us." But even in her own state Ruth could not prevent the demonstration from becoming another battle-ground between the Union and her own committee over their preferred amendments. Demonstration plans in Chicago were being handled by Grace Wilbur Trout, who had worked with Ruth the year before on the Illinois suffrage bill. The plan was to parade down Michigan Avenue, then meet to pass a resolution in favor of woman suffrage. The meeting was to be nonpartisan and to include men. However, by mid-April, Chicago suffrage leaders had received letters from both Ruth McCormick and Alice Paul, each asking for an endorsement of their respective amend-ments at the May 2 meeting.[61]

While Ruth McCormick was out West, the state board voted to endorse no resolutions at all. Ruth was furious. Before leaving, she had talked with Trout about adopting the NAWSA resolution, and Trout had told her not to worry. When Ruth returned, she demanded a special board meeting to reconsider whether the state association would subscribe to the National party line.

"I don't deny that I slammed doors and pounded desks and possibly shook my fist," she admitted. "I was excited and I was angry." The *New York Times* was inclined to view the split as between Republicans and Progressives, which Ruth hotly denied. She insisted the issue was whether auxiliary state associations should be loyal to the National.

There were other problems stemming from the vote. The state board's rejection was particularly embarrassing to Jane Addams, the National's acting president while Dr. Anna Howard Shaw was in Europe, and to Louise Bowen, who was also a National board member. When it was rumored that Jane Addams might not march in the Parade, Trout re-marked, "I don't care whether Jane Addams marches or not. I guess nobody will feel bad if she [doesn't]." Trout claimed she was protesting Shaw's "policy of annihilation" toward any person or organization that did not agree with her, and that her opposition was simply a reflection of the larger fight between the Congressional Committee and the Congressional Union. Antoinette Funk believed that Trout wanted to be national president herself, but that above all she wanted to "eliminate" Ruth McCormick, because she regarded her as "dangerous." The more experienced Grace Trout might well have been bitter because Ruth, a newcomer to suffrage politics, had been elevated over herself.[62]

Jane Addams suddenly developed a sick relative in Cedarville and left town. Mrs. Bowen declined to march "for purely official reasons," as did the members of her Chicago Equal Suffrage Society and Harriet Vittum and the members of her Women's City Club. The women were not the only ones to succumb to factional fevers; Progressive chairman Harold Ickes announced that male Progressives would not march because the Republican Hamilton Club had been invited to trudge ahead of them. Ruth McCormick marched, heading the Progressive division, which included two companies of uniformed nurses, a company of women physicians, and two companies of black women. The leader of the African-American women, Mrs. Irene Gaines, marched as one of Ruth's aides. It was ideal marching weather, with crisp air to encourage brisk walking. An estimated seven thousand people marched before two hundred thousand spectators. Unlike the previous year in Washington, the crowds were friendly and there was ample police protection. "There were many cheers for Mrs. Trout and many more for Mrs. McCormick," reported the *Chicago Tribune*. When the Progressive brigade passed Mrs. Trout in the march, Mrs. McCormick ordered, "Salute your president and commander, ladies," and they did.[63]

At the meeting after the parade Ruth was pleased that the Illinois Equal Suffrage Association's committee adopted a message for Congress almost identical to that recommended by NAWSA. The next day Addams, Bowen, and Trout even stated publicly that the rift was over. But Ruth could not agree. When asked "Is everything peaceful within the ranks?" she bluntly answered, "No," adding, "The war is not over by any means."[64] One bright spot, however, was the endorsement of woman suffrage by the General Federation of Women's Clubs at their biannual convention held in Chicago that June. This large and traditional group finally had overcome their suspicion that voting would corrupt their feminine nature, when they realized it would help them achieve their reform goals. When the vote came, all restraint was cast aside, and Ruth was delighted to see dignified women, middle-aged and elderly, mount their seats and throw their handkerchiefs into their air.[65]

Ruth McCormick had been receiving a great deal of publicity, not only in Illinois, but nationally, as she traveled through the South, up to Boston and New York, and out to Kansas City. Suffrage was an important issue everywhere, and Ruth was at the forefront of it.[66]

Her husband Medill, buried in the state legislature in Springfield, may have felt upstaged. But there was one thing outranking suffrage in "Washington importance," and that was the volatile Mexican situation. In mid-April, Medill suddenly left for Mexico, following a two-week speaking tour through the West. The President of Mexico had been assassinated, and his unrecognized successor, Victoriano Huerta, had refused to apologize for an insult to the American flag. Arrested twice, once as a spy,

Medill got a banner headline and a story that covered most of the front page of the *New York Times*. He wrote two articles for *Harper's Weekly*, defending the U.S. decision not to recognize Huerta.[67]

Medill may have been characteristically looking for dangerous adventures again. Or he may have been trying for equal billing with his suddenly illustrious wife. The *Chicago American* pointed out, however, that "the little war which interests us is petty in comparison with the war women have been waging for justice through so many years."[68]

The Senate adjourned the first week of June 1914 without considering the Shafroth-Palmer resolution, so the next suffrage project was to influence the fall elections. NAWSA proposed to raise fifty thousand dollars. Ruth proposed a "self-sacrifice" day on August 15, when women would forego some expense to make a donation, and a Suffrage Shop in the downtown Chicago "loop" to raise money and increase interest. (Ida Husted Harper inquired, "Can anybody recall any special sacrifice to earn the right that has been made by men who are now voting in the United States?") The shop sold baked goods ("We are going to show that women haven't lost their skill in housewifely arts"), white elephants, and produce.

A popular item in the Suffrage Shop was a postcard of Ruth McCormick with baby Triny, taken the year before. Hundreds were sold in the opening week, and thousands more had been made to be sold throughout the country. One day Medill happened to visit the shop; he hadn't known the cards were being offered for sale. Outraged, he insisted the item be withdrawn at once, sending similar orders to New York, Washington, Boston, and other cities where the picture was popular. He may have supported Ruth's political activities but apparently drew the line at marketing his family life.[69]

The next month, the congressional campaign got under way, and by August 15 more than twenty-five thousand had been raised. Unfortunately, the campaign afforded new grounds for Grace Wilbur Trout to attack Ruth McCormick. The Congressional Committee had published a "blacklist" of nine senators and nine congressmen. The Illinois Equal Suffrage Association, led by Trout, objected to the militancy of the blacklist and refused to circulate it in Illinois. They preferred, said Trout, to "work for good candidates and let the bad sink into oblivion." She objected once again to the National's power, complaining that the "suffrage trust" controlled all positions in suffrage organizations, dictated policies, outlined work, and opposed new ideas. The Republican Woman's League vowed to oppose Ruth's campaign activities, and the *Ex-*

aminer predicted it would be "the most picturesque fight since the woman's movement became a feature of politics."[70]

Ruth rejoined that the National merely wished to make public the records of certain congressmen so women could make up their own minds about them. Catharine McCulloch, Harriet Vittum, and other Illinois suffrage leaders approved of the idea. But there was controversy within the NAWSA Board itself over what was considered partisan politics.[71]

Typical of the controversy was the case of blacklisted House Minority Leader James R. Mann of Illinois. Mann had become notorious after the 1913 suffrage march in Washington. A woman in his district had called him after the march to protest that her daughter had been assaulted, to which Mann had replied that her daughter should have stayed at home. He became known thereafter as "Stay At Home" Mann. Ruth threatened to campaign against him personally. "If I never do another thing I intend to take a soapbox and raise my voice to defeat James R. Mann," she announced. By the end of the month Mann had written to Trout, declaring his support for the franchise for women. Ruth believed the threat of publicity about his record had brought him around, but Trout attributed his change of heart to her kindness instead.[72] Each woman was sure she was right.

The fracas led to speculation that Ruth McCormick would be a candidate to replace Grace Trout as state president in October, but Ruth declared she would not run, and that, in fact, she planned to retire from the state board. However, she couldn't resist remarking, "The time has passed when charm of personality and an easy going smothering of vital questions will suffice to hold an important office such as this one . . ." A rumor started that she was planning to withdraw from suffrage work altogether. The *Tribune* even ran the controversial mother-and-child photo, saying, "Mrs. Medill McCormick, suffragist, has succumbed to Mrs. Medill McCormick, wife and mother," adding, "Mr. McCormick does not want his wife to continue her suffrage work, which has kept her away from home almost continuously."[73] Ruth promptly denied plans to retire.

> Suffrage activities do not interfere with the home life. This year . . .
> convinced me more than ever that the charge of the "antis" that suffrage
> activities interfere with home life is without foundation.

Triny was tended by an old nurse who had reared an earlier generation of Hanna children. Ruth customarily had breakfast with her little girl, came home for lunch, and often took the child for a drive in the afternoon. Returning to Chicago from a trip, she protested, "I'll talk suffrage after I've found out how my baby is." Still, she tried to work an eight-hour day, and attended dinners and late afternoon receptions almost daily. But her husband, she said, not only had urged her to accept the leadership of the Congressional Committee, "he strongly desires that I continue my suffrage activities." She insisted that she had planned from the outset to spend just one year building the new congressional district organization.[74]

The McCormick-Trout breach widened at the convention of the Illinois Equal Suffrage Association October 29–31, 1914. Ruth had been limited by President Trout to a fifteen-minute discussion of the Shafroth-Palmer amendment, but when a cancellation left extra time in the program, an outcry arose for an expanded McCormick report, and about 100 of the 350 delegates stayed to hear Ruth explain the blacklist and NAWSA's opposition to the Congressional Union's anti-Democratic policy. Petty skirmishes continued throughout the convention. On the last day, Ruth McCormick, business-like in a dark skirt and white blouse, a large dark cartwheel hat tilted forward over her eyes, rose to a point of personal privilege. When Trout attempted to stop her, she insisted, "I have the floor . . . and I am going to read my statement so you might as well listen to it." Most of the delegates burst into laughter, including Mrs. Trout. Ruth accused the Illinois Equal Suffrage Association officers of suppressing the Congressional Committee bulletins. "They have concealed facts from you. I will not say they are prompted by personal motives, but I am not justified in saying they are not." The split in the suffrage ranks in Illinois shows that the coalition formed in 1913 had been a shaky one. But while Trout's backing of the Congressional Union and her criticism of the NAWSA alienated the Illinois Equal Suffrage Association from the national organization, Illinois did not join the Union. The problems between Trout and other suffragists were primarily ones of personality.[75]

The national election followed closely, on November 3. Women were particularly interested in two issues. The first, of course, was suffrage. Seven states had a suffrage question on the ballot: Montana, Nevada, Nebraska, Missouri, Ohio, and North and South Dakota. Of these, only two passed it, Montana and Nevada. Jeannette Rankin, leader of the Montana suffrage forces and later the first female congressman, was congratulated for her organizing ability by Chairman McCormick, who advised her to hire a lawyer immediately to guarantee the authenticity of the Montana returns.[76]

Ruth realized that big interests, especially the liquor interest, had been instrumental in defeating suffrage elsewhere. In North Dakota alone they had spent over forty thousand dollars, more than the women had been able to raise for all seven states. This realization may have made it easier for her finally to abandon the Shafroth-Palmer amendment and to concentrate on a federal one. Jane Addams bitterly blamed the defeat of suffrage on the war that had broken out in Europe:

> Today mankind is like it was in primeval days, when tribes were about to start forth on war missions. The women are sent to the rear and not allowed to participate in tribal councils.[77]

The other concern of the election was the success or failure of the Congressional Union's campaign against Democrats. Ruth judged their policy a failure because "democratic candidates whom they have attacked have been returned to Congress." The Congressional Union nevertheless claimed victory; in forty-three elections in woman suffrage states, only twenty Democrats were elected. But it was hard to determine how much attrition was due to the normal mid-term swing against the party in power. NAWSA and the Congressional Union remained staunch rivals throughout the suffrage campaign and into the next decade.[78]

Ruth also had a personal interest in the campaign. She had campaigned for her husband, and Medill was one of only two Progressives returned to the Illinois legislature. He had refused an offer to return to the *Tribune* in July and was now committed to a life in politics. But he would soon start a movement back to the Republican Party, a move that Harold Ickes condemned. "Medill had a good deal of ability, and so did his wife," he conceded, but he never forgave them for bolting.[79]

The NAWSA held its national convention in Nashville, Tennessee, a week after the election. Two of the main issues were the Congressional Committee's blacklist and the Shafroth-Palmer amendment. A lively debate arose over the blacklist when Ruth made the Congressional Committee report on the first day. A delegate from Massachusetts complained that the inclusion of Senator Henry Cabot Lodge on the list had cost them a suffrage plank in the Republican platform. But Rebecca Felton, chairman of the state legislative committee for Georgia, who in 1920 would be given an honorary appointment as the first woman senator, supported Ruth's position. She had fought for women's rights for many years. Her grey hair was covered by an old-fashioned poke bonnet, but she had lost none of her spirit. "I want to thank the Congressional Committee," she said, "for giving me the truth. I understand that is what it is for. Do I have to pet the lion when he is crushing me to death?" Ruth McCormick answered questions from the high rostrum in the state capitol hall for hours. At the end of the day, the convention decided to continue collecting information at Washington such as that on which the famous blacklist was based.[80] A long and complicated debate then ensued over the two amendments. Ruth supported the Bristow amendment, and described the Shafroth-Palmer amendment as merely a means to achieve it. Finally, both amendments were approved by the convention. Ruth McCormick was again appointed chairman of the Congressional Committee, but she was not active the following year; Antoinette Funk was placed in active charge, and the Chicago office was to be phased out. Ruth was also given a minor position on the board.[81]

Immediately after the convention Ruth and Antoinette Funk returned to Washington to lobby for both suffrage amendments during the final session of the Sixty-third Congress. The House Rules Committee, controlled by Democrats, voted the Bristow-Mondell amendment out of committee. The Congressional Union policy of threatening the Democrats might well have influenced this move. Ruth, however, claimed that their favorable report was due to work done in the home districts of the committee members opposed to suffrage. She was eager to know the attitude of "those Southern democrats who have explained their opposition to suffrage . . . as due to their views of state rights, yet voted 'yes' on the prohibition bill." She added cynically, "I wonder what excuse will be their next?" The first House vote on a suffrage measure was taken on January 12, 1915. It was rejected 174 to 204, 16 short of a majority, 78 short of the necessary two-thirds. The NAWSA announced it would continue to work for the Shafroth-Palmer amendment, because those who opposed it based their argument on states rights. The following day, Ruth called on President Wilson, who reiterated that it was a state, not a federal issue.[82]

Ruth McCormick withdrew from the NAWSA Committee at this point, although she would continue from time to time to lobby for suffrage in a limited way. What had her achievements been? When she took over the Congressional Committee from Alice Paul, NAWSA was badly divided, and she helped hold on to the large conservative membership who might have been alienated by someone like Alice Paul. She also kept the Congressional Committee on a political, rather than merely educational course, which was vitally important. She claimed that the Senate debate and vote, and the House debate and vote had come as a result of her six months of work along political lines.[83]

The success of Ruth's particular tactics was mixed. The blacklist of congressmen who blocked suffrage legislation held politicians accountable in a fairer and more effective manner than the Congressional Unionists.

Yet it caused much dissention in NAWSA. Very important was Ruth's ability to get publicity, albeit sometimes unwisely, which kept NAWSA firmly in the forefront of the federal amendment campaign. Also, her instinct for compromise was a good one, which served well most of the women who became successful politicians. (Frances Perkins, later FDR's Secretary of Labor, was called by a close friend "a half-loaf girl"; the same might have applied to Ruth.) On the other hand, her push for the Shafroth-Palmer amendment was widely thought to have been a mistake. The division over the two amendments worsened the split with the Congressional Union and even alienated a number of women who had remained with the NAWSA. Moreover, the Shafroth plan was unworkable if the NAWSA's goal of universal female suffrage regardless of color was to be met in the South.[84] Ruth's willingness to make concessions, which had helped pass the Illinois suffrage bill, was not enough in this situation, largely because the Southern "states righters" were not wholly candid about their real objections.

Ruth had learned a great deal from the experience. Suffrage, in her opinion, was "the greatest political victory ever won in the history of this country." The cause was opposed by both of the leading political parties and had a great deal of public opinion against it. She and her colleagues had needed to hone their organizational skills to combat fierce opposition and public indifference. The suffrage issue had shaped the attitudes of many women about women's roles in public life.

In this campaign, Ruth broadened her network of politically active women like those she had met in Chicago reform groups; many of the women she worked with in the suffrage fight were important role models and advisors during her later campaigns. Without their support she would not have had the strength she needed to meet men on equal terms, the secret of her success in the 1920s. The campaign also helped her to realize that her idealism and energy could find its best expression through political activity.

The reluctance of many suffragists to enter partisan politics after the vote was won has been explained by suggesting that women all worked together for suffrage, and that opposition did not come easily to them. Ruth McCormick's experience shows, however, that women were no strangers to opposition. Even with a clear-cut issue like woman suffrage, tactics and personal style still counted for a great deal, and Ruth had learned something about the uses and limits of each. But having become so experienced, why then did she withdraw from the heat of the fray?

Could it have been that leading an active political life was undermining her relationship with her husband and her young daughter? Or that she feared it might? This seems unlikely, because she always claimed that Medill supported her political activities. Was it because of the difficulties she got into with the Congressional Committee? Antoinette Funk was not an easy person to work with, and Ruth also may have become disillusioned with the infighting of the women and the opportunism of the politicians. Then, too, she may have wanted to distance herself from the failure of the Shafroth-Palmer amendment.

A critic might add that her abrupt departure from the project mirrored her transient interest in many ventures. Apart from the farm she had just bought in Byron, Illinois, where she established a dairy operation, and a newspaper she owned from 1928 until her death, she rarely pursued any interest more than a few years. Though it must be said that many activities benefitted from her brief, intense enthusiasm, she would likely be better known today if she had committed herself to one course for her entire lifetime. But in a sense, she did; all her activities were helping to make her into what she eventually began to call herself, a "professional politician."

4

The Irreconcilables: 1915–1919

"TANTRUMS ON THE HILL"

Whatever the primary reason for Ruth McCormick's reduced involvement with the national suffrage scene, her private life at this time was part of the problem. Medill's drinking had become so bad that for a time she lived apart from him, in an apartment in Chicago or with her brother in Ohio, while Medill stayed in Springfield. But she opposed Medill's brother, Bert, who wanted him institutionalized. Finally, Medill appeared one day and announced, "I'm not telling you this time, I'm telling myself in your presence, I'm never going to touch another drink." He may have stopped drinking, but he probably continued to experiment with drugs to control his depression.[1] Some of Ruth's drive to have a career and a life of her own could have come from her need to keep some distance from Medill's disturbing problems.

Despite their domestic problems, Ruth and Medill were still active in politics, though Ruth was somewhat less active than she had been the year before. In fact, for the next ten years, Ruth worked as hard for Medill's career as for her own, and soon his career eclipsed hers. The whole time, however, she gained experience and valuable contacts with his campaigns. Meanwhile, she began to position herself in the Republican Party so that when suffrage was won, she easily moved from the limited sphere of suffrage politics, in which she had already made quite a name for herself, into the wider world of state politics, on a nearly equal footing with her male colleagues.

Ruth also continued to work for suffrage. In January she accompanied the NAWSA president, Dr. Anna Howard Shaw, to call on President Wilson. They did not attempt to change Wilson's view that suffrage was a state issue rather than a national one, but they did try to enlist his support for suffrage in his own state of New Jersey. The president expressed great interest but confessed he had been so absorbed in national affairs he had not kept in touch with the suffrage situation. Then, two weeks before a special election in October, Wilson announced he would vote for the woman suffrage amendment in New Jersey. New York, Massachusetts, and Pennsylvania were also voting on the issue.* Ruth believed that the President's statement would help the cause.

> The fact that the President has announced his personal conviction . . . as a private citizen will give us a moral support far stronger than if he had made it a political move as the leader of his party, [but] . . . [w]e earnestly wish that the President had been able to extend his endorsement to the Federal amendment.[2]

The president refused to meet with representatives from Ruth's old rivals, the Congressional Union, and as the president was leaving the dining room of his hotel one day, two women tried to toss a note to him. When the Congressional Union announced they would pursue a policy of heckling the president, Ruth countered that she would lead opposition to such militant methods. Things came to a head when the National American Woman Suffrage Association held a conference in June to decide whether to condone or condemn the Congressional Union's militant stance against the president and the Democratic Party. An acrimonious debate led by Ruth and Antoinette Funk raged from nine in the morning until nearly midnight. Several delegations, including Grace Trout's Illinois affiliate, approved the tactics of the Congressional Union, but the main stream prevailed, and NAWSA adopted resolutions against the Union.[3]

During her tenure at the Congressional Committee, Ruth McCormick had organized congressional districts in forty-one states, and NAWSA planned campaign work at the district level to overshadow the militant methods of the Congressional Union. Ruth maintained that NAWSA need not send nonresident workers into a congressman's district to persuade him to vote for a Federal amendment.

> We can and do work through women in his own district . . . This is playing the game as American politicians understand it. As long as we

---

*According to one historian, Wilson's endorsement was calculated to improve public opinion of his surprising second marriage, slightly more than one year after the death of his first wife (Gould, *Reform and Regulation*, p. 196).

stick to plain, unsentimental methods which the American politician and respects, we can't lose. [4]

It was an indirect criticism of the Congressional Union methods borrowed from England.

Ruth had succeeded in having her campaign tactics approved by NAWSA, but she was losing support for the Shafroth Amendment. She angrily observed that seventy-two senators who voted against suffrage had just voted in favor of a national Prohibition amendment, a severe restriction of the states' rights they were supposed to be defending. In addition, a number of state affiliates were threatening to withdraw from the National unless support for the Shafroth Amendment were dropped. Always practical, by November Ruth herself was advising the Congressional Committee not to introduce the Shafroth-Palmer Resolution in the Sixty-fourth Congress. Carrie Chapman Catt was elected president of NAWSA a month later and tactfully moved an indefinite postponement of the bill. The conference voted the bill be dropped. [5]

Carrie Chapman Catt admired Ruth but thought her "young and undisciplined," and judged the Congressional Committee to be in "a pitiful condition." Ruth had only agreed to head the committee on the understanding that she have no real work, and Antoinette Funk had stopped work in June because of a disagreement with Ruth, who persuaded the NAWSA that it would be unwise to leave Funk in complete charge of the work in Washington. Finally, Antoinette Funk and Ruth both resigned. [6]

Ruth hardly needed to look far for other interests, especially women's labor groups, for which she continued to lobby and picket. In 1915 she represented the Illinois Consumers' League before the Illinois state legislature in behalf of a child labor bill. She also helped found a woman's section of the Navy League, dedicated to the Progressive proposition that greater preparedness would safeguard the peace. Ruth's abhorrence of war was strengthened by reports from Medill, who had visited Europe early in 1914. Even his adventuresome spirit was dampened by the trip, and he wrote:

> The prospect of being drawn into war is not agreeable to me, because I feel that I must go if we fight, and while, in Mexico, there might be adventure out of proportion to agony, in Europe, the agony outweighs the adventure. [7]

This new desire to remain detached from entanglements, foreign and domestic, turned the McCormicks to more pastoral enterprises. Though Ruth McCormick was primarily a politician, she had many other inter-

ests. Her childhood on her brother Dan's farm kindled a lifelong passion
for farming. Back in 1912 when Ruth and Medill were campaigning for
Roosevelt, they had found attractive farm land about one hundred miles
west of Chicago, near the town of Byron. At the time Triny was born,
no farm in Illinois produced certified milk; it had to be shipped from
Milwaukee. Uncertified milk was likely to be watered or adulterated,
sometimes with toxic substances. Ruth envisioned a model dairy farm,
to produce safe milk for the children of Chicago. The McCormicks
bought up several small farms—"the type of farm" she said,

> where you see shabby, rickety old sheds, unkempt meadows of poor
> hay, two dozen or so scrub cows nibbling their way through the tangle
> of underbrush, and four or five doubtful-looking cans of milk standing
> at the cross-roads waiting to be carted off to town.

The original Rock River Farm covered 900 acres, eventually expanded
to 2,200 acres by the late 1920s, and Ruth began raising Holstein cattle,
reputedly producers of the best milk for babies.[8]

High on a limestone bluff above the winding Rock River, the farm
was lush and flat with woodlands beyond, where Medill preserved a
tangled forest for pure pleasure. Medill had nothing to do with the cows,
and Ruth herself ran the dairy project.[9]

The pastoral scene was not always an idyllic one. At the beginning
of 1916 Ruth became pregnant again. Medill, who often suffered severe
hemorrhages from ulcers, was hospitalized, and Triny contracted whop-
ping cough. Ruth, overwhelmed, indulged in "a fit of nerves." In spite
of their medical problems, Ruth and Medill had plans for an ambitious
new campaign. Medill wanted to run for U.S. congressman-at-large as
a Republican.* The year before, he had begun to vote with the Republicans in the state legislature, declaring that the European war and industrial depression had destroyed the third party movement. As long as
she was able, Ruth worked hard for her husband's election.[10] Other
interests notwithstanding, the McCormicks were always thinking politics.

With an expanding family and continuing political interests, Ruth
needed an alter ego in the nursery. Miss Belle Samson joined the family

---

*In 1912 the number of Representatives was 435 and has remained at that number
since. Illinois had added two congressmen, but the state had not been redistricted, so
the two extras ran "at large," i.e. from the entire state.

as a much-needed governess for the headstrong Triny, who was becoming spoiled because her parents were often away. "Sam" was a trained nurse from Scotland, very strict in a loving way. She and Ruth shared the same values: they wanted the children to think of the lives of others less fortunate; good manners were simply kindness. Belle Samson's lifelong devotion to the McCormick children freed Ruth to pursue a career. But it never seemed to occur to Ruth that Sam should have time off, except the month of August. In her old age, Sam would complain that she never had a life of her own.[11]

By mid-July Ruth, in her eighth month, had to remain on the farm, well but uncomfortable, while Medill continued the campaign alone. She was, according to Medill, "not half as buoyant" as he was with the doctor's announcement that the baby would be a boy. The renowned Dr. Joseph De Lee was a pioneer in obstetrics, who crusaded to have babies delivered in hospitals, away from infection, and was one of the first to film obstetrical procedures. De Lee visited the McCormick farm every summer for his vacation, since he had no other life apart from his work. He always wore a light grey business suit that matched his goatee, and even on a visit to the country, he wore a stiff collar and white linen tie, wielding his movie camera at everything on the horizon. He neither read nor walked nor made small talk but would sit uneasily by the pool, camera in lap, clearing his throat from time to time, twitching one side of his face, crossing and recrossing his legs. When Ruth had become a prominent politician, he always referred to her as "The Gentleman from Illinois," clearing his throat when he proudly used this title. Ruth enjoyed having friends who were accomplished. "De Lee is brilliant," she would say. "A Portuguese Jew—a great pioneer in his field." In addition, she was devoted to him because she felt indebted to him for the successful delivery of her babies (the last when she was forty-one).[12] Dr. De Lee was proved correct; Ruth was delivered of a boy August 25, 1916. Named Medill McCormick, he was known in the family as "Johnny." Their little nesting period over, the family focus now returned to politics.

At the Republican Convention in Chicago in June 1916, a suffrage parade of five thousand had marched through a cold drenching rain more than one mile down Michigan Avenue to the Coliseum. Unmoved, the Republicans adopted a disappointing suffrage plank. They nominated Supreme Court Justice Charles Evans Hughes, however, who had kept aloof from both factions in 1912, and in July Hughes came out ahead of the platform in support of the Anthony Amendment. Medill campaigned against the Democrats for increased expenditures and for opposing the child labor bill; he criticized the tariffs; but most especially he criticized the lack of military preparedness. Roosevelt was impatient of Hughes's moderation on the preparedness issue and raised the issue of the war himself, which made the Republicans seem to support a war policy, despite Hughes's moderation. The Republicans had a campaign fund of more than nine hundred thousand dollars, but the McCormicks' friend Arthur Willert, the *London Times* correspondent, wrote, "No American campaign that I have seen has been worse managed than the Republican . . ." The Democrats had almost gone to war with Mexico over the Army's pursuit of Poncho Villa, and Wilson's Southern background worked to his disadvantage in the East. If the Republicans had not been so inept, they might well have won. As it was, the election was extremely close. For three days, the winner was in doubt. It was clear, however, that the Congressional Union's anti-Democratic policy had not been successful; Wilson won in ten out of the twelve woman suffrage states. Medill had his own reason to rejoice: "The Democrats barely retained their grip on the House," to which he had just been elected as a Republican congressman-at-large.[13] Ruth may have hoped that politics on the national stage would divert Medill from his dangerous depressions.

The McCormicks moved to Washington. Medill observed that

> in going from the House of Representatives in Springfield to the House of Representatives at Washington, I am conscious that I shall suffer the same sudden inconsequence that befalls a schoolboy when he becomes a freshman, or a splendid senior when he becomes a ten-dollar clerk.

But the concerns were anything but those of a school boy. Wilson had called a Special Session of Congress for April 2; it was clear that the situation with Germany had been worsening since the beginning of 1917. On January 31 Germany announced it would resume unrestricted submarine warfare. In early March three American boats were sunk by German U-boats. For a month, Washington was in a state of seething excitement, intensified by a city-wide street-car strike.[14]

Congress convened at noon on April 2, 1917. For the opening of Congress, Ruth McCormick was in the gallery to see her husband take his seat. Jeannette Rankin from Montana, who had worked under Ruth in the congressional elections in 1914, and was the first woman to be elected to Congress, was also joining the Sixty-fifth Congress. As Rankin walked onto the floor, the men of the House arose and applauded her entrance. Ruth was very conscious that she was witnessing history in the making. And there was more to come. Outside, the Capitol was engulfed by surging crowds as antiwar agitators mingled with sightseers. Evening came on with a soft spring rain, and the Capitol dome, illuminated for the first time, glowed against the dark, misty sky. Finally those within heard a clatter of horses' hoofs: the president had arrived.[15]

Members of both houses of Congress and members of the Supreme Court rustled to their feet. All the seats were full, and people were packed together on the floor of the House and in the galleries. A hushed silence fell over them as the president began to speak. When he said, "There is one choice we cannot make, we are incapable of making: we will not choose the path of submission," Chief Justice Edward D. White sprang to his feet, tears rolling down his face, his action a cue to the rest, who roared approval.[16]

The Senate approved the President's request to declare war, 82 to 86, on April 4. The next day the House began to vote. During the first roll-call, Jeannette Rankin, an ardent pacifist, did not answer, moving nervously in her seat. During the second roll-call, for any who had come in late, everyone turned to watch her. Finally the anguished woman rose and said, "I want to stand by my country but I cannot vote for war." Many thought the whole suffrage cause was discredited by Rankin's vote, and certainly the vote kept her from reelection for twenty-two years. At 3 A.M. April 6, the House acted 373 to 50 in favor of the declaration.[17] The two suffrage factions were split even more by the declaration of war. The Congressional Union began to picket the White House, challenging Wilson to apply his principles of democracy at home. In a spasm of wartime hysteria, the women were deemed security risks, and many were jailed. NAWSA, seeking support from Congress and the public at large, joined the war effort.

Immediately following the United States' declaration of war, Allied missions began arriving in Washington. The British arrived within two weeks, headed by H. J. Balfour, the British foreign secretary, followed soon by the French. Alice Longworth reported that the missions' arrival prompted a whirl of entertainments for the visitors—"such a round of gayety that one wondered how they stood it . . ." The McCormicks gave a dinner for Balfour to meet members of Congress. Correspondent Willert developed great admiration for Ruth's effectiveness as a hostess, especially in a town where important policy was often formulated over dinner. While not "intellectual like her husband," nor "particularly well-educated," Willert wrote, she "radiated vitality and was an adept at the chemistry of party giving." The Willerts made many social and political contacts at her heterogeneous gatherings. Alice Roosevelt Longworth, who regretted that her congressman husband Nick "had a habit of leaving politics at the office," admired the McCormicks, who "knew and had at their house everyone of every description—rather the way Father always did." Ruth McCormick's style was very casual, favoring Saturday night suppers, with artists, correspondents, ambassadors, and senators at small tables all over the house and no precedence. Men waited on themselves and on the ladies, buffet style. Menus featured corned-beef hash, salads, apple pie, and cheese. A new Italian ambassador once protested, "I'm an Ambassador." "Oh, no, you're just plain Mr. A—," she smiled. "Find yourself a charming lady and do like the others." Alice observed, "I think it pleased the Washington that went to and gave dinners to feel that entertaining the representatives of the Allies had a recognized part in 'winning the war.'"[18]

It is unclear precisely what role Ruth played in Medill's Congressional career, other than that of hostess. Medill McCormick's papers were lost when, with characteristic off-handed generosity, Ruth commissioned their good friend journalist Bill Hard to write an official biography of Medill after his death in 1925 and gave him all Medill's official papers. Hard never wrote the biography, and the papers were never seen again. Ruth had had her own office in 1914, and again in 1925, so there is no reason to suppose she did not work with Medill in Congress, perhaps in much the same capacity in which she had served her father, attending meetings, making notes, lobbying, attending to constituents. Certainly she would have been well-informed on every issue that interested Medill. She was also lobbying for the establishment of both a Children's Bureau and a Women's Bureau.[19]

As war preparations got under way, the streets of Washington began to swarm with khaki and blue. Congress remained in session during the long hot summer of 1917, as the legislators discussed war revenue and food control. A poor wheat crop, the second in a row, produced no surplus for the Allies. Speculators diverted eggs, poultry, and meat to cold storage, and prices soared. The government turned over unoccupied ground to any civilian who wanted to grow vegetables, and Potomac Drive, all the way to Hains Point, became one vast truck garden. "Wheat-less" and "meatless" days were instituted; "gasless" Sundays brought back the horse and buggy, and Washingtonians enjoyed the silent, empty streets. Citizens were even asked to save peach stones (they made charcoal used to filter gas).[20]

All noncombatants were urged "to do their bit." Back in Byron, Ruth taught at the Farm School of the Land Army. She trained a half-dozen young women, clerks and stenographers, to milk her one hundred cows and release the men from the farm. She milked cows herself, did her own housework to free servants for war work, and joined the ranks of

farm women knitting socks. The war came just when the feminist movement was surging, and it broadened the activities of women. They became
nurses, telegraph messengers, elevator operators, street car conductors.
They worked in munitions factories, railroad repair shops, on farms. The
Navy began to hire female clerks and stenos. Medill, in a speech at the
end of the year, noted, "Women everywhere have taken up the labor
which men lay [sic] down when they went to the front."[21]

Medill McCormick toured the battle fronts in France and Italy from
late August to mid-October 1917. He came under fire four times, which
must have satisfied to some degree his abiding thirst for adventure. At
a training camp in France where he was visiting the American Expedi-
tionary Force, he had a narrow escape from serious injury by a trench
bomb that exploded near him during practice maneuvers. It landed almost
at his feet, throwing stones and earth about him and scratching his face.
These details were reported by the *New York Times,* where Ruth may
have read them with who knows what palpitations. Medill was also under
fire at Chemin des Dames, then continued to the front line in Italy with
fellow Progressives William Allen White and Henry Allen. At breakfast,
Medill later reported to a group of veterans, they cavalierly discussed the
French language and translations that Paul Verlaine had made of Edgar
Allen Poe's verses, "and all the while the air roared and shivered from
the torture of the bombardment."[22] Ruth had wisely encouraged Medill
to go, and he missed her terribly:

> I would not have come on this journey I am afraid, but for your determining
> voice . . . I'm writing to give vent to the longing for you which is in my
> heart—in all of me . . . I feel as if my personality, my ego, myself were
> only half of it here on this splendid adventure.[23]

Her letters to him had gone astray; until they came, he wrote, "my heart
cracked." After they arrived he "began to cheer up, to whistle, to walk,"
as he read them over and over.

Medill returned to Washington to lobby for more munitions, and he
also called for bipartisan cooperation in Washington, "a council of men
who, irrespective of faction and party, represent . . . the energy and the
genius of America." The Republicans were feeling excluded from Wilson's
war plans, and indeed there were no Republicans in the Cabinet or
heading agencies such as those for munitions, food, or transportation.
In addition, Wilson had angered many Republicans by refusing to authorize Theodore Roosevelt to raise and lead a division of volunteers.
Medill, among others, had also criticized the president's proposal for an
"omnibus bill" on censorship, insisting the law should clearly define the

right of criticism, "more fearful the administration of the War and Navy Departments may break down [if their defects were not publicized] than that there will be publication of information useful to the enemy."[24] Medill was especially concerned with America's role in plans for closer military and political cooperation between European powers. He concluded, "I've learned a great deal about politics and the war. The politics will concern us all for a long time after it is over."[25]

But for now there were more immediate concerns. The winter of 1917–18 brought gloom to Washingtonians. They were depressed by news that the Allies had suffered reverses in the field. The season was one of the coldest on record; the fuel situation was desperate, the urban poor suffered greatly, and even the well-to-do were affected. Congress was incensed to learn that recruits were having to drill with broomsticks and to learn artillery on wooden cannons; Roosevelt and his allies in Congress made vigorous protests, while Wilson's secretary, Joseph Tumulty, deplored the "tantrums on the Hill."[26]

The GOP clearly needed to regroup. There was internal party dissension, and their criticism of the administration's war effort was unpopular. Theodore Roosevelt was hoping to mount a come-back, prompting the Longworths and the McCormicks to host a round of dinners in late December 1917 and early January 1918 for him to plan strategy. These social functions provided the opportunity for the Progressives and the Old Guard wing of the Republican Party to come together, united in their opposition to Wilson. One guest announced their impatience with administration policy "of utter exclusiveness, secrecy, and intolerance of Congressional participation . . ." But Roosevelt was hospitalized in February, the result of an infection contracted on a trip to Brazil. Afterward he never fully recovered.[27] The obvious leader was gone.

The McCormicks accordingly turned their attention to their own political future. Medill planned to run for the senate seat of James Hamilton Lewis, a Democrat who had managed to get himself elected in the Land of Lincoln during the Republican split in 1912. They knew a senatorial campaign would be expensive. Medill reflected,

> It happens that in my vocation, the harder I work, the more my labors are apt to cost. I have been to the front . . . I travel to make speeches almost invariably paying my fare and my lodging . . . I give four-fifths of my time or even more to public service, [and] something over and above the salary which I am paid.

Medill began to assemble his staff, a group that would remain intact to work with Ruth when she began campaigning ten years later. Helen

Bennett, who had met Ruth through suffrage work, and would work closely with her all through the twenties, was the manager of Medill's women's campaign committee.

Ruth also took part in Medill's campaign, so much so that a friend remarked to Gussie Hanna that she might yet become the mother not only of a senator but of a president. Mrs. Hanna smiled and said, No, she thought not; Medill was very much in earnest over his candidacy for the Senate but she felt sure he did not aspire to the presidency. "Perhaps not, but I wasn't thinking of Medill," the friend said. "I meant Ruth."[28] Once again, the money was on the mare.

Although Congress did not adjourn in July as usual, because of work connected with the war, by July 15 only a few committees remained in the Capital, and Medill's campaign could begin in earnest. For the second time since 1913, when the Seventeenth Amendment was ratified, the Illinois electorate would be voting directly for the U.S. Senator. Lewis was unopposed in the Democratic primary, but Medill was running against ex-Governor Charles S. Deneen and Chicago's mayor, William Hale Thompson. Thompson tried to exploit the pro-German sentiment in Illinois (Chicago was said to be the sixth German city in the world) but merely made himself offensive; the Chicago press referred to him as "Kaiser Bill" and "Wilhelm der Grosse." Thompson especially wanted to defeat McCormick in order to humiliate the *Tribune*, which often attacked him. In their first brush with Thompson's rough methods, Ruth emerged somewhat shaken, feeling

> about as discouraged as anyone can feel who has given up as many years as I have in active participation for good government. It did not look as if we had a chance to express directly to the voter the various complications of graft and dishonesty which confronted us on all sides.[29]

She would oppose Thompson herself a decade later and learn that he had not mellowed with time.

The primaries had more than the usual local interest because of the war. Wilson had tried to make the election of his candidates an "acid test" of patriotism, but the tactic backfired. Medill's platform was basically Roosevelt's—the Democrats' mismanagement of the war. He emphasized that, in contrast to Thompson, he was "loyal" on the war issue. The entry into the race of Representative George E. Foss had threatened to split the so-called loyal vote, and Medill had called on Roosevelt to speak for him at the Springfield State Fair in August. Roosevelt used the opportunity to pillory Wilson's "Fourteen Point" peace concept: "Professional internationalism stands toward patriotism exactly as free love stands toward a clean and honorable and duty-performing family life."[30]

In the senate primary September 12, McCormick beat Thompson by about sixty-three thousand votes. Outside of Cook County (Chicago) there was a landslide for McCormick, though Thompson led by over fifteen thousand in the city. A rainy day kept many voters away. The *New York Times* rejoiced, calling Thompson's defeat "salutary discipline for malignants."[31]

The Democratic incumbent was James Hamilton Lewis, a former congressman from the state of Washington who had moved to Illinois; the *Tribune* called him a "carpetbagger" who did the bidding of President Wilson. Medill McCormick defeated Lewis in November by fifty-three thousand votes. Lewis had not won a popular election in 1912; he had been chosen by the State Legislature. But Lewis, like Thompson, would return to oppose Ruth McCormick in later campaigns. Republicans won all over the country, gaining control of the Senate and the House. The stage was set for the fight over the peace plan and the League of Nations, a battle in which Medill McCormick would play a significant role, and which would shape Ruth McCormick's political philosophy for the rest of her life.[32]

The women were still fighting their own battle for the ballot. In January 1918 President Wilson endorsed the federal suffrage amendment, and the following day it passed the House by exactly the two-thirds needed. This was largely because the New York delegation had changed when New York State had adopted woman suffrage the year before, and three pro-suffrage men replaced three antis in Congress. State action, as Ruth McCormick had always claimed, helped win votes in Congress for the federal amendment. But in the Senate, the bill bogged down in committee, where it was voted on the next day and failed by two votes. On September 30 Wilson appeared before the Senate in person to ask for passage of the suffrage amendment as a war measure, possibly because he was eager to secure women's votes for his peace plan, which he expected them to support.[33]

Ruth, along with Daisy Harriman for the Democrats, energetically lobbied the Senate "nay-sayers." Harriman reported:

> A good many diplomatic migraines overtook . . . our lawmakers that
> spring . . . When we weren't gunning for Senators, the anti-suffragists
> were. They used to administer black looks when they came across our

suffrage groups in the Capitol elevator and bustled when they passed us
in the corridors.

Ruth also toured the country, speaking for the amendment and for candidates who favored it. [34]

Ruth was now certain that woman suffrage would soon be adopted and
began to move into party politics in anticipation of that event. She had
been named the Chairman of the Republican Women's National Executive Committee, a newly created branch of the Republican National
Committee, a position she later described as "my preparation for going
into professional politics on my own account . . . my first official service
with the Party." Ruth was bitter about Wilson's request that "politics
must be adjourned," largely because it seemed a masked attempt at pre-
venting women in volunteer work from participating in the campaign.
"So long as women will allow it," she said, the subtle discrimination
would continue:

> the Democrats will continue their policy of making all war workers feel
> that politics must be adjourned for those engaged in bandage-rolling or
> raising money on the Liberty Loan. Just stop and think for a moment how
> absurd this is. Why should the women give up their political activity any
> more than the men? The Democratic administration does not ask Mr. Insull
> to cease functioning as a Republican because he has accepted the chair-
> manship of the Council of Defense in the State of Illinois. Why am I less
> valuable as a speaker for the Liberty Loan because I happen to be
> chairman of this committee? [35]

The Republican Party, according to Ruth, felt there was no longer a
question of whether women would or should vote, merely when, and it
realized that the party needed to make preparations for additional voters.
They were desperate to win in 1920 and wanted as many women as
possible to register with the party. The National Republican Committee,
wrote Ruth, had finally "waked up to the fact that having lost every
suffrage state except Illinois in the last presidential election, it is advisable
for them to consider the woman's vote." Ruth believed strongly that
once the vote was won, women could best exercise the privilege of the
franchise by joining an established political party. In this she would differ
from many suffragists, who went on to form a Woman's Party and the
League of Women Voters. [36]

The war was over, but the peace was yet to be won. It would prove,
for Wilson, a struggle more intense and more frustrating than the war
itself. One of those who successfully opposed his peace plan, especially

his plan for a League of Nations, was Medill McCormick. Medill, in an article written for *Colliers* after his return from the front, opposed a Wilson-dictated peace plan and called for a bipartisan peace mission: "we must send, without regard to politics or past rancors, the best generals and diplomats we can find, to represent America in the councils which will sit in Paris."[37] But Wilson did not make Republicans part of his negotiating team, and many objected to the terms that Wilson approved, feeling that they compromised American sovereignty. Medill McCormick was among those who objected strenuously; so did Ruth McCormick, and, indeed, opposition to Wilsonian internationalism was the central plank on which she ran in 1928 and 1930.

In December 1918 William Borah of Idaho offered a resolution to permit the Senate to hold open sessions on the peace treaty. Open sessions of Congress had been held before only infrequently. Borah had been opposed to the idea of a League from the first time it was seriously considered in December 1916. He was concerned about who was to authorize the United States to declare war. At the same time, Henry Cabot Lodge reasserted that the Senate had an equal power with the president in treaty making. McCormick, Borah, and Lodge were the nucleus of a group opposed to the treaty and especially to the League. They became known as the "Irreconcilables"; tongue in cheek, they referred to themselves as "the Battalion of Death." They were joined by "peace progressives" such as Robert La Follette; "isolationists" like Hiram Johnson and Jim Reed (Borah, who was another one, preferred to call the title "anti-interventionists"); and a larger group who were "nationalist-minded but not isolationists," like McCormick. This latter included Philander Knox, Miles Poindexter, Frank Brandegee, and Lawrence Sherman, the other senator from Illinois. It must be said that while many may have been opposed to the principle of subsuming national sovereignty to an international group, they were protective of the Senate's power as well.[38]

Wilson sailed for Europe December 4, less than a month after the Armistice. He met with his counterparts at Versailles, until February 23, 1919, where they made the rough draft of a covenant for a League of Nations. During this time, a number of senators delivered speeches attacking the proposed League of Nations, the peace settlement, and, of course, Wilson's failure to name prominent Republican representatives or senators to the peace commission.[39] There were other smaller, even petty reasons, for their objections, some of them arising from a personal antipathy to Wilson. The McCormicks, for example, surely believed strongly in the principles they espoused but were no doubt affected by

Wilson's rejection and humiliation of their friend and mentor, Theodore Roosevelt, when he had offered his services during the war.

It is important to understand in its historical context the McCormicks' opposition to the League of Nations. The modern world is a smaller one than theirs was, and inevitably more international. Critics might pigeonhole all the opponents of the League as narrow isolationists. But many who opposed the League, including the McCormicks, objected to its apparent purpose of guaranteeing all the gains, including reparations, granted to the European victors of World War One. Medill wrote in 1923 to explain his position: "I am not an isolationist . . . No man has argued more insistently that American capital should be invested abroad." He also feared that an economic depression in the U.S. might result from Germany's having to pay indemnities, which would make her unable to buy American agricultural products.[40] In addition to the economic disadvantages, of course, Medill and Ruth believed it morally wrong, as well as politically unwise, for a peace treaty to reward the victors. The covenant of the League of Nations was published in the United States on February 14, while Wilson was still in France. Borah promptly objected that there was a conflict between the League and the Monroe doctrine. The British were also believed to have an undue advantage, since Article 7 provided for the "admission of all self-governing dominions and colonies"; England might control six votes. The week after the covenant was published Ruth and Alice Longworth spent long hours in the Senate gallery listening to the speeches against the League, and rejoiced when anti-League Jim Reed was applauded by the galleries "in an unprecedented manner," and in complete violation of the Senate rules. Wilson landed in Boston on February 23, where he warned that "any man who resists the present tides that run in the world will find himself upon a shore so high and barren that it will seem as if he had been separated from his human kind forever." But such hortatory talk just stiffened the resolve of the senators opposed to him, who were now doubly angry that he had made a public speech before addressing members of Congress. He further antagonized Congress by announcing that he would not call a Special Session of Congress (which would not ordinarily convene until December) until he returned from a second trip to Paris with the completed Treaty. A few days later, Arthur Willert, returning from the Peace Conference, dined at the McCormicks', and reported:

Borah was there . . . Both [he and Medill] were bitter about the President. They felt he'd betrayed his country in Paris and himself at home. He was mismanaging his visit to Washington as thoroughly as possible.

Medill showed Willert a copy of a letter he had sent to various Illinois organizations that were protesting his hostility to the League. He objected to giving England disproportionate voting power. Willert, despite his fondness for Medill, observed: "The Republicans are trying to re-awaken for their own ends in this mass of indifference not only the old instinct for isolation but the old distrust of the British." Medill was probably courting the Irish vote, which, in Chicago, was substantial.[41]

Medill also argued that the Treaty of Versailles would make "for war rather than for peace." He feared it would lead to a "new imperialism" that would engender future wars. Although he complained about Great Britain's possible undue influence and deplored the lack of a Home Rule clause for Ireland, Medill was wisely apprehensive about Imperial Japan:

> For thirty-five years Japan's foreign policy in Asia has been one of consistent perfidy and aggression . . . The wonderful material advance of Japan has been contemporaneous with that of modern Prussia and in close imitation of it.[42]

The night before Wilson left to return to Europe, he announced that he would "tell the people on the other side of the water that the over-whelming majority of the American people were in favor of the League of Nations." Alice Longworth and the McCormicks were furious. Medill made a statement to the press that "Europe must come to understand" that Wilson was acting in defiance of the wish of the people, expressed in the recent election. "It would be well," he told the *New York Times*, "if the President's pastor in Paris would preach Sunday on Matthew XXIII: 12."*[43]

A major difficulty now presented itself: after Congress adjourned op-ponents of the League had no forum. They feared if there were no further discussion, the country might accept whatever Wilson brought back. The Irreconcilables raised money and began to send speakers around the country. One of the most active was Medill McCormick, who, in the interests of victory, was not always above an appeal to prejudice; the League, he predicted, would promote a "superstate," with

> the efficient and economical Japanese operating our street railways . . . Hindoo janitors in our offices and apartments . . . Chinese craftsmen driving rivets, joining timbers, laying bricks in the construction of our buildings.

---

*"And whosoever shall exalt himself shall be abased; and he that humbleth himself shall be exalted."

Medill may have been a nationalist, but he was not a racist, at least, where African-Americans were concerned. During this time he was helping to organize an antilynching conference, admitting that his own state had been the scene of "lynching, mob murder, and of race rioting . . . Lynching . . . is no longer purely a Southern problem." Medill remained involved in racial issues throughout his Senate term. Ruth had made contacts among black women in Chicago and elsewhere during her suffrage campaigns, and she would later inherit Medill's network of black male educators and politicians.[44]

Medill McCormick was merely "doubtful" about the League at this time, although those who were fiercely opposed, like William Borah, Hiram Johnson, and Albert Beveridge, were trying to encourage his Irreconcilable tendencies. Borah was the spiritual leader of the group. Though he had a reputation for objecting to almost everything (Washingtonians marvelled that Borah, when he took his daily ride in Rock Creek Park, agreed to face the same direction as the horse), the sincerity of Borah's convictions was never questioned. He was a forceful speaker and a commanding presence: tall, muscular, with a noble head of black hair. With good reason the press called him the Lion of Idaho.[45]

The self-styled Battalion of Death met to confer not only on Capitol Hill, but in the sitting rooms of many Washington hostesses, chief among them Alice Longworth. Nick Longworth, who was in the House of Representatives, seems to have played no great part in the League fight, but Alice, carrying her father's torch, was an active participant throughout and recorded many of the goings-on. She and Ruth watched the proceedings from the Senate gallery and discussed the smallest points of strategy with Medill, Bill Borah, and the others. It is hard to tell how much of their stand against the League came from pure principle, how much from political considerations (Beveridge thought the Irreconcilables would become increasingly popular politically), and how much from fury at Wilson for having beaten Roosevelt and then spurned him.[46]

Wilson, by making concessions in Europe, had gotten a revised covenant accepted there by the end of April and called a special session of Congress for May 19. The Republicans, who now had a slim majority, proceeded to "pack" the Foreign Relations Committee with Irreconcilables, including Medill McCormick. With regard to the packing, Medill answered the Democrats' criticism by saying that the Republicans were only taking a page from the president's book; Wilson had "stacked" the Peace Commission. Wilson further nettled the senators by refusing to release a copy of the treaty, insisting he had promised to keep the conference decisions secret until official disclosure. But a *Chicago Tribune* foreign correspondent was able to smuggle out a copy of the final text, and on June 9 Borah marched into the Senate with the manuscript in hand. The treaty was signed at Versailles June 28, and less than two weeks later Wilson formally presented the Treaty to the Senate. Ruth and Alice gleefully noted, "There was scattered applause on his appearance, the Republican side in stern silence. McCormick and Knox remained seated."[47] A bitter battle was in the offing.

Willert recalled that at first it had seemed as if the president might have the League if he would compromise.

> He cast off the cloak of arrogant aloofness worn in March, he visited the Senate and conferred with groups of its members . . . Compromise was in the air. [But] it was soon clear that the President's new amiability was not to facilitate bargaining but to induce the Senate to accept the Covenant as it stood.

The battle was joined. The president, though wearied by the heat of a Washington August, undertook a tour in September through the country to generate support for the League. Johnson, Borah, Poindexter, Reed, and Medill McCormick, accompanied by Ruth, took to the hustings themselves. In Chicago, McCormick, Borah, and Johnson spoke to a wildly cheering overflow audience. In this contest of wills, Wilson's tour proved too strenuous for him. He had planned to visit twenty-three states, covering eight thousand miles. But three weeks after he set out, Wilson collapsed on September 25. His train rushed back to Washington; less than a week later, a thrombosis paralyzed his left side. He was shielded by his wife and doctor, who screened his callers, and gave out no word on the President's condition. Meanwhile, the debate in the Senate continued.[48]

Ruth herself fell ill in September. A week after the Chicago rally, she was reported to have been operated on for appendicitis. "Appendicitis" may have been a euphemism. Sometime between mid-1917 and mid-1919, Ruth miscarried a boy baby. Even though the pregnancy was already far advanced, she remained at home, tended by Sam. Almost twenty years later, Ruth wrote in her diary about

> the little boy I lost before he was born. What an impression it made on my life. The miscarriage appeared to be such a failure on my part. I always have a sense of guilt about it and yet I did nothing knowingly to disturb the fulfillment of his life . . . [49]

Ruth was an intensely maternal woman who felt that no woman was completely fulfilled who had not given birth. She also had an ovary removed at some point before conceiving her third child in June 1920.[50] It may be that the "appendectomy" was really an "ovariectomy." If not, the appendicitis would have occurred within eighteen months of another major operation, and following a miscarriage at almost full-term. These events must have been quite debilitating to the thirty-nine-year-old Ruth.

Notwithstanding her illness, she was able to return to Washington six weeks later, much to the satisfaction of Alice Longworth, who had been haunting the Senate gallery, committee rooms, and offices discussing the progress of the battle with Medill and Brandegee. On Ruth's return, "we again hunted as a pair," said Alice. "Pleasant it was to have someone to associate with who felt as keenly about the League fight as I did." Sometimes the hunting was almost literal, as when the two crouched in the electric car of Senator Frederick Hale, spying on a secret meeting at the house of Henry Cabot Lodge.[51] Alice and Ruth shared an intense love of mischief as well as loftier political ideals.

The Senate soon advanced several "reservations" to the League covenant, ostensibly to ensure American rights if the United States joined. These were supported variously by "mild reservationists" and "strict reservationists." The true Irreconcilables became known as "bitter-enders." Voting on the reservations proceeded from November 7 to November 18, 1919, on which day the Senate remained in session from 10 A.M. until 10:20 P.M. The next day, the Senate voted on the Resolution of Ratification. Ruth and Alice went up together to see the finish. Alice wrote, "It was the greatest crowd I have ever seen there. Speech followed speech—we wormed our way out of the galleries to get a hasty dinner"— and no doubt to have a cigarette; Ruth, like Alice, was an avid smoker— going up again about eight. The parliamentary procedure and tactics "were intricate to follow," even for two such experienced gallery-goers. But the upshot was that Wilson refused to let his followers vote for the treaty with the Lodge reservations. So an unconditional resolution of ratification was defeated. Jubilant, Ruth and Alice left the Capitol around 11:00 P.M., taking Bill Borah with them. The Irreconcilables gathered at the Longworth house for a hasty supper of scrambled eggs cooked by Mrs. Warren G. Harding.[52]

Although the League of Nations fight was possibly the most glamorous part of Medill's Senate career, he had many other concerns as a legislator. His first interest, after the League of Nations, was in establishing a Bureau of the Budget. In June, shortly after Congress convened, he introduced a bill for such a bureau. He had begun work on the bill while in the House and modelled it somewhat after the Illinois budget system that he had helped put through. Medill was given credit for his legislative strategy when the final bill was passed by both houses in May 1921. Medill was a good legislator, intelligent, well-informed, and energetic. He may even have entertained greater ambitions. Writing to his fellow Progressive, editor William Allen White, that fall, he joked, "When you have elected me President in '24, I am going to send you to London if they will send [J.M.]Barrie or [John] Buchan to Washington."[53]

The political relationship between Ruth and Medill in 1919 was now the reverse of what it had been in 1914. His political career had taken off, while hers was in eclipse. This was at least partly due to her ill-health for much of three years, but it also was because she was entering the larger male-dominated political arena, moving out of the suffrage fight. Also, she had devoted a great deal of time and energy furthering her husband's political career in recent years.

All of which is not to say that she lacked her own sphere of influence. In 1918 Republicans had named Ruth Chairman of the National Women's Executive Committee. At once, she outlined to the men of the Republican National Committee her thoughts on the newly created position. The party should be organized so that "Women . . . shall work not independently, but in association with men and under the leaders of the party." She pointed out that "cooperation between the sexes has increased the efficiency of the war administration here at home." The party's most important task was to recruit women, who, being "less bound by habitual party lines than men, . . . will more readily affiliate with the party which will bring current ideals of human happiness into practical application in homes." In other words, a Progressive platform would best attract these new voters. She especially wanted to recruit women who had been leaders in the suffrage and club movements.[54] When she spoke in New York to the State Women's Executive Committee in September 1919, she urged them to get out a big Republican vote in 1920: "It will be the work of women to get out not only the women but the men." She thought women could be even more effective than men.

> Most men are working for their families. They have no time to think of politics. It is up to the women, if they are to be good wives, mothers, and citizens, to inform themselves about political issues.

In addition to trying to persuade Republican women to get out the vote and trying to persuade Republican men to accept the women, Ruth's agenda included recruiting more newly enfranchised women into the party. "As far as I personally am concerned," she wrote, "suffrage is no longer an issue." She even had three "antis" on her committee. She did not approve of the Woman's Party, which had grown out of Alice Paul's Congressional Union:

> I believe that being enfranchised we ought to affiliate ourselves with a party and work within its ranks . . . not as women apart but as citizens. I am working to assist in perfecting the party organization which is composed of both men and women, for the purpose of electing a Republican President in 1920 . . .[55]

The suffrage amendment had finally passed the Senate June 4, a full eighteen months after passing the House. It would take another fourteen months for two-thirds of the states to ratify it, the last in August 1920, just in time for the election. To prepare for the campaign, the women within the Republican Party also reorganized in June. There would be a Women's Division headed by Ruth to "amplify" the work of the Republican National Committee among women. A separate Republican Women's Executive Committee would "aid in organizational and publicity work among women, speakers bureaus, Americanization work, etc." It is unclear why such a division was proposed or who proposed it. Back in January Ruth had said, "Our plan is to organize women within the party and not to maintain any separate Republican clubs for women." Perhaps she had found herself doing more traditional "women's work," which would now be delegated to the new Executive Committee, leaving her free to work within the National Committee on women's policy concerns. Not surprisingly, there is some evidence that Ruth was not happy with this new arrangement. Ruth's colleagues were certainly not happy. A worker in the state of Washington who claimed to have spoken with many Republican women during the last year, both in the Northwest and in other parts of the country, wanted Ruth to remain as head of both groups, to give Republican women a sense of unity. "Your name has become a household word from the Atlantic to the Pacific," she assured Ruth.[56]

After her illness in the fall of 1919, Ruth continued working until the end of the year, but she asked Will Hays, the Republican National Chairman, to name another head of the women's division. At first he was reluctant to give her up, but finally agreed not "to insist further in view of what you tell me the doctors have said." Ruth may have had a relapse, or she may have been pulling back from a situation she no longer wanted any part of. She wrote Winnifred Dobyns, warning Dobyns from becoming her successor,

> You know . . . the difficulties which surrounded my position as National Chairman, its disappointments and its stumbling blocks. My successor will

have a very much more difficult time than I had, and will have no power at all.[57]

This sounds as if Ruth had been frustrated in her ambition to place the women on an equal footing with the men. During the next two years, Ruth went on to organize a network of Republican Women's Clubs in Illinois. Although she had hoped that separate clubs would be unnecessary after women became full citizens, once again her idealism gave way to practicality.

Nevertheless, she was far from finished with her fight to see women fully integrated into the Republican Party. During their National Committee meeting in December, she felt compelled to make a short speech; still weak, she wrote out her remarks and condensed them to five minutes. Although she also "wanted to impress that particular body of men that the Progressive spirit was still alive," since "it was because of this Progressive spirit that the GOP has a chance to win in 1920," her strongest message was to caution the men not to dismiss the women's vote as uninformed or unreliable:

Men and women [in 1916] in the same proportion repelled or were deceived by the shabby slogan, the sham promises of peace by which the Democrats elected a President . . . We are none of us going to be hoodwinked again.

Her remarks were enthusiastically received, and observers remarked that she seemed restored to complete health. It was just in time. Women would soon have the vote. The day for women's groups and honorary posts was over. As the new decade dawned, Ruth McCormick, in the prime of her life at forty, was ready to practice what she would call "actual politics."[58]

5
Women Voters:
1920–1924

APPRENTICESHIP IN THE REPUBLICAN PARTY

"Politics Never Is a Game of Solitaire"

Ruth McCormick, at forty, had at last begun the career she believed she was born to, electoral politics. Women had the ballot, and the Republican Party was eager to secure their votes in order to make a comeback. Ruth had had eight years of training in addition to what she had learned from her father. She had worked in a presidential campaign, had learned to lobby in Springfield and on Capitol Hill, had dealt with the press and with unfriendly factions during the suffrage campaign, and had learned about Congressional politics as the helpmeet of a U.S. representative and senator. She was now ready to put all this experience to work in active campaigning.

There were plenty of political issues. The main ones that concerned Ruth were Prohibition and the League of Nations. The Volstead Act to enforce Prohibition had been passed in January of 1919. The idea of Prohibition was linked with patriotism during the war, when the Volstead Act was regarded by many who favored it as something of a war measure to help save food and manpower. Because of Medill's struggle with alcoholism, Ruth was personally a Dry. The law went into effect in January 1920.[1]

The League of Nations had finally been rejected, but strangely enough, American opposition to it grew even stronger after the issue was settled. The League of Nations, and its affiliate, the World Court, would figure in many of the Illinois campaigns during the next decade, and Ruth was credited with a share in the strategy of that contest.[2]

The political situation in 1920 was in a state of confusion in both parties. Wilson, following his stroke on September 25, 1919, remained severely incapacitated throughout 1920. On the Republican side, Theodore Roosevelt had died after a year's illness in January 1919, and his followers remained divided. Will Hays, the Chairman of the Republican National Committee, had supported Roosevelt in 1912, and late in 1919 he began to try to reconcile the old guard Republicans and the politically orphaned Progressives. He wanted a "harmony" platform committee to meet before the 1920 Convention and agree on principles acceptable to both groups. A number of former Progressives were invited to join, including both Medill and Ruth McCormick. They declined, however. As Medill put it to Harold Ickes, he did not believe the committee would "do any harm, or anything else."[3]

Nevertheless, all Republicans, including the McCormicks, were working hard to come together and win, after eight years in the political wilderness. Although Medill did not join Hays's committee, he made a peace-making speaking tour while Congress recessed during February and March, not only in Illinois, but in New York and Connecticut as well. Sometimes Ruth went with him when he travelled, but she was also speaking on her own, trying to reassure men that women would not immediately be seeking public office. At the same time, she wanted the men to realize that women should gradually win party endorsement. Typically, she began by mocking her male listeners: "Men have sometimes found it hard to believe that other women had the steadfastness and courage which they readily saw in their wives and sisters." Then she upbraided them: "This is our country, no less than yours. We have sacrificed as you have, in its defense . . . You must know, sirs, that like you we are citizens, we are Republicans, we are Americans."[4]

Republicans and Progressives could make a common argument that postwar problems had worsened because of Wilson's lack of leadership. The cost of living had risen sharply, and business prosperity was off. Unemployment increased, as did bitterness between capital and labor. There were strikes in the coal and steel industries. But the united Republicans, while they could exploit the weakness of the Democrats, still needed a leader of their own. During the spring, the McCormicks were working to broker the convention, and to that end Medill introduced his fellow Irreconcilable, Philander Knox, to Boise Penrose, a powerful member of the Old Guard Republicans. Will Hays and Herbert Hoover were also "acceptant-minded," as Alice Longworth put it, but the McCormicks finally decided to support the ex-governor of Illinois, Frank O. Lowden, as a favorite son candidate, and introduced him to Knox at their house in Washington. On June 4 a loaded train left Washington for the convention in Chicago. On board with the McCormicks were the Longworths, their old friend *London Times* correspondent Arthur Willert, Irreconcilables Cabot Lodge and Frank Brandegee, and Senator Warren Gameliel Harding, whom Penrose had considered and rejected the year before.[5]

In Chicago Republican women met at the Auditorium Hotel two days before the convention opened, to debate their strategy for getting positions of power, not merely honorary ones, within the party. The women were again divided on strategy. One group, led by Mary Garrett Hay of New York, wanted an organization of women parallel to that of men. Ruth McCormick, representing the other group, thought women should stop drawing the sex line now that they had suffrage. She believed the women should go into the parties on an equal footing with men, taking their chances for chairmanships of committees as individuals. If women insisted on parallel or equal representation, she argued, they might find themselves segregated and without real power. She thought they should merely ask for "adequate" representation.[6]

A compromise plan was adopted: The vice-chairman and assistant secretary would be women, and the Executive Committee would be enlarged by an "adequate" number of women. Ruth was made chairman of the Women's Committee and given the responsibility of guiding their resolution to the Rules Committee. She was reluctant to join the Executive Committee once it was formed, possibly realizing how little power she would actually have, but Harding urged her to accept it, and she finally agreed to be one of the two Progressives. Women in both parties adopted a two-part strategy. Since their ultimate goal was to have an equal status with men in the party structure, they supported measures that would increase women's representation in the party. At the same time they continued political activity within separate women's divisions.[7]

The first women delegates to the Republican Convention were thrilled with their new position. One exclaimed that only eight years before, her husband was "horrified" when she suggested she "should accompany him to the National Convention. It was no place for a woman, he assured me. Four years ago he let me go along to stay in his room and answer the telephone. This year I am a delegate-at-large, and he accompanies me."

One reporter observed that women delegates gave the convention the air of a prewar reception, formal, proper, and dignified, no small feat in the barn-like Chicago Coliseum where the convention opened on June 8, 1920. Although the Rules Committee was headed by the arch-conservative Senator James Watson, nonetheless a few Progressives, including Medill, Bill Borah, and Will White managed to get five demands of the National League of Women Voters on the platform.[8]

Once the platform had been written, the balloting for the presidential nominee began. By the second day the convention was deadlocked over Lowden and General Leonard Wood, Theodore Roosevelt's colonel at San Juan Hill. Wood was a "big, well-set-up man, approachable, and with a fine presence," according to Harold Ickes, but he "talked too much." Lowden's position, in turn, had been undermined by an investigation into his campaign expenditures. Medill met with Hays, Brandegee, and other Senate leaders in the Blackstone Hotel to discuss the nomination. Warren Harding was not their unanimous or even majority choice. Nevertheless, they favored Harding because he could be controlled. Under Roosevelt and Wilson, the president had taken over, and the Senate had been losing its preeminence. Harding would enable legislators to regain lost ground, they believed. Alice Longworth and Ruth were waiting outside the room where the men were meeting, and they eagerly followed the deliberations. Alice was frankly appalled: If the senators were strong enough to have influence, why not use it for someone worthier, such as Knox?[9]

The thermometer rose in the stuffy auditorium to 102 degrees as Harding slowly gained momentum. Demonstrations broke out, marching and cheering through the aisles, and the galleries responded with shrieks and the clatter of noise-makers. Finally Harding was nominated on the tenth ballot. The nominee, who liked to compare himself to McKinley, was the opposite of Woodrow Wilson in almost every way: friendly, relaxed, probusiness, an isolationist, and comfortable with the Senate, though even his friends admitted he was mediocre. Progressive editor William Allen White concluded sadly that the country was "tired of issues . . . and weary of being noble."[10]

The Democrats met in San Francisco later in the summer. The Democratic women were able to get more of their planks in the platform, perhaps because they had resolved the question of women's representation in the National Committee, opting for a woman representative for every man representative. But the rest of the agenda was less easily settled, and it took forty-four ballots before the delegates resigned themselves to James Cox, the diligent but drab governor of Ohio. His running mate was Franklin Delano Roosevelt. When Ruth campaigned in Illinois later that summer, she made a point of attacking Roosevelt's support of the League of Nations and sarcastically questioned his claim to understand the voters, particularly the women voters, of the West.[11]

Though ratification of the suffrage amendment was completed August

18, 1920, there was still a great deal of work to be done before women could be fully integrated into the political process. Frederick Lewis Allen, in *Only Yesterday*, observed that "few of the younger women had even a passing interest in politics; they thought it sordid and futile," but Ruth McCormick would challenge this attitude throughout the decade. One of her greatest contributions to the political life of her times was to show that politics were a respectable activity for women. She was very active in the fall campaign, organizing the women's vote for the Republicans, and Harding himself wrote to her humbly, "I do not feel qualified to criticize your plans, which appear to me to be admirable. You know very much more about this matter than I do, and especially of the psychology involved."

The Democrats campaigned for the League, while Harding tried to sidestep the issue. But mostly due to the American voters' desire to return to "normalcy," Harding won sixteen million votes to Cox-and-Roosevelt's nine million. Ruth gave Harding little credit for the victory. "He doesn't like a fight," she said.

> If it had not been for Mrs. Harding and [his manager Harry] Daugherty, he would have withdrawn before the . . . Convention. Discontent was expressed everywhere. [The American people] rushed to express their dislike, even hatred, of Wilson by electing Harding and giving him a tremendous vote.

Henry Cabot Lodge gloated to Medill McCormick, "We have won the fight. We have destroyed Mr. Wilson's League of Nations, and what is quite as important, we have torn up Wilsonism by the roots . . ." He believed the Irreconcilables were "thoroughly vindicated" by the election. Ruth may have drawn the same conclusion, because in her own campaigns at the end of the decade, she would turn again and again to this issue.[12]

In November Medill travelled to Europe. As usual, he felt desperately lonely without Ruth, and wrote: "I have no one here—or in the world no one else—[to whom] day by day I can open my mind and my heart. I begin to think that if we once were joined now we have fused . . . Think of me as kissing every surface you would have touched by my lips."[13]

For the third time in a row, Ruth was expecting a baby in a presidential inauguration year. After the ovary had been removed, she was surprised to become pregnant again. Three days after Harding's inauguration, on March 7, 1921, Ruth was delivered of another girl. The child was named Ruth after her mother, but nicknamed "Bazy" from an early effort to call

herself "Baby." Ruth was soon up and about, and shortly after the Inauguration she helped Alice Longworth in the awkward task of having
to call on Mrs. Harding. Alice had never liked the Hardings, and it must
have galled her to visit them in the White House. Ruth provided moral
support. They found Mrs. Harding a nervous, excitable woman with a
strident, high-pitched voice, and they escaped as soon as they decently
could.[14]

Reservations about the First Family notwithstanding, the Harding
administration began promisingly. The president's first official act was to
open the White House gates, which had been locked for four years, and
permit sightseers to enter. A peace with Germany was finally signed on
July 2. The Budget Act, on which Medill had been working for years,
had passed Congress in the last half of Wilson's second term, but Wilson
had vetoed it. On June 10 Harding signed it and made the McCormicks'
friend Charles Gates Dawes Director of the Budget. Dawes had first
entered politics in his twenties, running McKinley's campaign for Mark
Hanna in Illinois in 1896, and remained a close friend and political
mentor of Ruth's all her life. But Harding disappointed women voters
by ignoring virtually all of their issues in his first message to Congress.
One of Ruth's Republican colleagues tartly remarked, "All the women
realize that the men have no interest in the women voters now that the
election is over, and our immediate usefulness to the party fulfilled."[15]
It was a lesson learned.

In early March the Republican women organized according to the plan
they had decided upon before the convention. The twenty-one-member
Executive Committee of the Republican Party now included eight women.
Harriet Taylor Upton, an Ohio suffragist who was the daughter of a
congressman, was vice-chairman of the committee, and six others headed
regional divisions. Upton expected opposition from machine politicians,
especially in states where the Republican Party was divided into factions:
"[E]ach . . . is so afraid that the other faction will gain the women's vote
so that they would rather keep the women out," she warned her committee. Ruth was in charge of the Central Division, Wisconsin to West
Virginia, an area that Upton admitted was sadly disorganized. The eastern
states were already well organized, but Ruth was determined to outdo
them. She planned to speak in Wisconsin after June 1 and to hold a
section conference in mid-June, because by that time she would feel able
to leave her baby. Long-term plans called for a second conference in
Chicago in the early fall to prepare for the congressional campaigns in
1922. Since the congressional election came first, she wanted to use the
congressional district as the organizational unit, as they had in the suffrage

campaign. She was beginning to build the grass-roots support she would use when she became a candidate herself.[16]

Another role Ruth saw for herself was interpreting men and women to each other. Speaking to the men, she would say,

> I doubt sometimes if you quite realize how experienced we are both in organization and in politics . . . you will forgive us then, if we smile at times today when on occasions our men colleagues on the party Committees serving with us whisper that in time we will learn the political game, but we must have patience! I wonder, if they think at all, how they think we became enfranchised.[17]

She pointed out that men had never "governed cities or nations without the help of women. The only difference now is that the help is direct and openly recognized instead of indirect and unknown." Typically, she urged the women to learn to work with men, observing that "Politics never is a game of solitaire."

> Having ridden out of the West into full suffrage rights . . . women did not see that it was necessary to seek advice and learn the ways of politics from experienced politicians . . . if women will bring their fresh enthusiasms, their distinctive viewpoints, and their quick instincts into cooperation with men's longer experience, they can form a powerful partnership.

She goaded them: "The men think . . . that it is a fad with us and our interest will wear out."[18]

While the women may not have voted to the extent that Ruth McCormick and others hoped they would, it should be remembered that voter turnout all over the country was declining. Throughout the 1920s in presidential election years, the mean national voter participation was just over 50 percent, compared to almost 80 percent in the late nineteenth century. Feminist Suzanne La Follette wrote in 1926 that it was a misfortune for the woman's movement to have succeeded in securing political rights for women at the "very period" when those rights were worth less than they had been at any time since the eighteenth century. Jane Addams, asked if woman suffrage was failing, responded that the question should have been "Is suffrage failing?"[19]

Postsuffrage politics fell into three categories. The largest and best organized group were the women who sought to expand the reforms of the Progressive era. The smallest and most militant group was Alice Paul's National Woman's Party, which had been organized to lobby for the Equal Rights Amendment. And a few like Ruth Hanna McCormick were trying to use the political party and the vote as the most practical way to reform the system. Ruth believed that women's political influence was undermined by nonpartisan groups like the General Federation of Women's Clubs, the Woman's Party, or the League of Women Voters, which had grown out of NAWSA. She thought they were ineffective because they were as dependent upon the political parties to make necessary laws as the suffragists had been. Still, Ruth and the other women on the Republican Executive Committee did not want Republicans rejected over the issue of the ERA, and they planned to attend the conventions of women's groups to prevent their having a "terribly Democratic slant." They also joined many women's groups to lobby for the Sheppard-Towner Maternity Bill, the first major federal welfare measure, which passed in 1921.[20]

Although Ruth McCormick was intensely interested in women's participation in the electoral process, her political life was never completely divorced from Medill's. She was a senator's wife, and politics were inevitably part of the social scene in Washington. But socially, as well as in other ways, Ruth remained a bit of a maverick. She fulfilled her social obligations: Tuesdays were senators' "at home" days, on which she kept open house. But on Wednesdays (Cabinet days), Thursdays (Congressmen's days), and Fridays (Diplomats' days), she did not sally forth with a card case to make calls but went instead to the Senate gallery and listened to debates.[21]

Medill was at the peak of his career during the next three years. His main interests were in the Child Labor Amendment,[*] in restoring civil government to the Protectorates of Haiti and Santo Domingo, and in an antilynching bill. He was also concerned with the Irish problem, the creation of Czechoslovakia, and forest conservation. But as is often the case in politics, in 1922 Ruth and Medill McCormick were mostly concerned with the upcoming congressional election. Medill was made Chairman of the Senate Committee for the 1922 campaign, an important position for a freshman senator. As such he was in charge of the speaking campaign and was speaking a great deal himself. Fortunately, he was a witty and exuberant speaker. During one typical early speech, he skewered the former Democratic presidential nominee, who was stumping for the Democrats.

A fortnight ago, there emerged from the political limbo of lost souls, the

---

[*]The Child Labor Bill had been declared unconstitutional by the Supreme Court. Samuel Gompers selected Medill McCormick to try to put through a Child Labor Amendment in the Senate.

individual whom the Democratic Captains, in emulation of P.T. Barnum and Mark Twain, gaily nominated for the Presidency to afford the American people some measure of relaxation after the boredom and irritation gendered by the expiring administration. An analysis of the two thousand words delivered by Governor Cox on January 25 teaches us that he has forgotten nothing and has learned nothing since the people last retired him from public view. [22]

Ruth was also busy making speeches, such as one she gave in New England in the early spring of 1922. Though she always seemed self-assured, she wrote in her diary of her attempts to overcome stage fright. "My speech in Maine hangs over my head and I so dislike to speak at such a meeting. I enjoy talking to the women but these dinners frighten me and I know I am not good at it." She had other obligations as well, including the organizing of a Woman's Day Rally in Washington D.C. in early May. [23] That summer, Ruth retreated to the Rock River Farm with her children, but even in this bucolic setting she was hard at work reorganizing the Republican women throughout the state of Illinois. The Republicans had been in the White House two years, and there were criticisms of their shortcomings. Ruth wanted to uphold the administration by returning a Republican majority to Congress. The Cook County Republicans had asked her to organize a campaign committee, and she hoped to recruit four or five hundred women "as a signal to the men leaders that women mean business politically." She also wanted the women to be in a position to negotiate with the men for a good candidate to run against William Hale Thompson for mayor. [24]

It was not an easy task. Many women were out of town for the summer, some were too busy, some were nonpartisan, and some disapproved of members of the ticket. She had to wheedle and bully prominent women into allowing their names to go on the masthead. "It is important to us full-time politicians," she wrote one woman, "to have the support of women leaders devoting the bulk of your time to the betterment of mankind." To another, she thundered: "I absolutely decline to release you from serving on the executive committee. Will you not let me be the judge as to whether or not you will be useful . . ." Sometimes she would get carried away. "I really feel guilty," she wrote her old friend Louise Bowen, "for having persecuted you as I did in regard to the chairmanship of the Illinois Republican women. I apologize and want you to realize how hard it is for us to give you up." She also involved black women leaders Blanche Gilmer, widely known for social and welfare work, Helen Sayre of the Urban League, and Irene Gaines, the president of the Illinois Federation of Colored Women's Clubs. The black population of Chicago had grown 150 percent in one decade, and Ruth was eager to have them represented on her board.[25]

Ruth began to assemble a personal staff, as well, and hired as her assistant Anne Forsyth, intelligent, keen and "most agreeable to work with," a colleague from her suffrage days. Anne was distinguished looking, with a stern, strong face, and short grey hair. Ruth's other main associates were Helen Bennett, who also knew Ruth from the suffrage days, and her sister Estelline. Helen, like Anne Forsyth, dressed in tailored suits and sensible walking shoes. She was intelligent, widely-read, and very earnest, a trait underscored by her large tortoise-shell pince-nez. Her older sister Estelline was a secret rebel, not really interested in politics or feminism, who tagged along behind the other two at political gatherings and was often engaged by Ruth for publicity work.[26] Miss Forsyth and the Misses Bennett spent little time in the McCormick house when Medill was alive; he preferred chic society and was not interested in women who wore ground-gripper shoes. But Ruth liked them immensely, and after Medill's death the four of them formed a close working relationship.

Ruth had two types of women friends. There were many, like Forsyth and the Bennetts, for whom Ruth was a dazzling personality. Perhaps Ruth attracted these intellectual women because she possessed a glamour they lacked, with her fashionable clothes and dainty imported slippers. They also admired her spirit of adventure. Another friend of this sort was Martha Connole, a lawyer from the notoriously tough Illinois town of East St. Louis. Ruth appreciated Connole as a woman of force and intelligence, and Connole became a warm and loyal supporter. Ruth, like other politicians, notably Franklin Roosevelt, sometimes made use of a flirtatious manner with members of her own sex, to bring them even closer, and once wrote Martha Connole, "Now that you have a country estate of your own, perhaps the farm will not look so attractive to you, but I am still as attractive as ever."[27]

Ruth's other friends were more her social equals. Alice Longworth was one, of course. While Alice could advise Ruth on political matters, she also inspired her to great heights of silliness, especially after they had consumed vast amounts of iced coffee. They loved to do a monkey act, crouching on the arms of chairs and making faces, uttering cries, and gleefully pretending to pick lice off each other's bodies. Another close friend of Ruth's was Margaret Cobb Ailshie, a newspaperwoman from Boise, Idaho. The three were great talkers; Ruth's younger daughter Bazy sometimes wondered "who would have stayed quiet enough for the other to talk?" Margaret Ailshie shared many interests with Ruth, not just

politics, but when Ruth bought a newspaper in 1928, the world of publishing. She, too, had a sense of the ridiculous, although more subtle
than Alice's. Margaret, like Ruth, was very hard-working and had a
deeply ingrained sense of duty. She was also more likely to be on hand,
especially during family crises; in the late thirties she would write, "This
is the 17th house in which I have visited Ruth . . ."[28]

These two, and perhaps Margaret Blake from the *Chicago Tribune* days,
were Ruth's closest women friends. She had many male friends as well,
especially Dr. De Lee and a Catholic priest, Father Wilbur, who were
practically fixtures in her house. With other male friends Ruth could be
quite coquettish. "She wanted to be the greatest woman in a man's world,"
Ruth's daughter Triny concluded.[29]

Although she had begun early to collect a staff and perfect her organization, Ruth was opposed to a long campaign. "An off-year campaign
is dull," she thought. The best thing to do was to have "a short and
snappy campaign." Beginning in late September she and her Illinois
committee began to register women voters and to help with publicity.
By October 150 women were attending the weekly meetings, but Ruth
was still dissatisfied. When she complained that the registration was not
what it should have been, she was told that ". . . women who do their
own housework and take care of their own children and do their own
baking are busiest on Saturday." Ruth responded:

> That may be true but . . . no excuses will go after the second day of
> registration next Tuesday. The women have been given an equal share
> in Republican party matters and it is up to us to deliver, so buck up!

A male colleague was reminded of a football coach addressing the team
between halves. Most women, however, spent over fifty hours a week at
their domestic chores; only 5 percent of families in the mid-twenties
employed domestic servants.[30] Ruth, who had inherited a substantial
fortune from her father at a young age, seems not to have understood
the constraints on other women's time. She understood some things
better than Medill, but she still had much to learn.

Ruth was getting a crash course in economics. Harding had signed the
Fordney-McCumber Act creating new tariff rates, the highest ever known,
on September 21, 1922. American farmers, who needed to export, and
could only sell to the extent other countries were able to buy, were hurt
by this tariff. Ruth was very much opposed to it, and felt it was responsible
for a strong backlash against the Republican administration in the election. She believed that if the incumbent Republican majority had not
been so large, the off-year election would have given the Democrats

control of Congress. She was convinced that the country was essentially progressive, and against tariffs, and hoped the progressive element could control the party to prevent Harding's renomination. Harding could be expected to resist, but Ruth believed his decision would depend on his wife's health: if she were too ill to take an active part, he might tire of the struggle within his own party and be willing to step down. Always a realist, she ruled out Borah, Johnson, and others of the "extreme wing."[31] Harding, of course, died in office, and was succeeded by his Vice-President, Calvin Coolidge.

In order to study the economic situation in Europe at first hand, Ruth and Medill left in mid-November 1922 for a two-month fact-finding tour in France, Germany, and England. Curiously, Ruth disliked Paris, wondering "why Americans want to live in Paris to associate with the sort of Americans we try to avoid at home." She thought the clothes were no better than her dressmaker Jacques Potts could give her at home. In the nightclubs, "The songs were bad, the music poor, and the air unbearable . . . it is evident you must be a little intoxicated to enjoy it all." Her general discontent intensified when Medill left her alone for several days to accompany his mother to Nice.[32]

Medill McCormick was primarily interested in meeting financial experts to discuss proposals to reschedule foreign loans and German war reparations, and Ruth was prepared to help him in his diplomatic mission. "The French still refuse to face the fact that Germany can not pay unless she can get credit," Ruth observed, adding that it was "all complicated and interesting." She tried to communicate her point of view to the wife of an important French banker at lunch one day, and ended up in "a heated discussion," but hoped the Frenchwoman had taken home to her husband "some facts which will help clear his mind in relation to our foreign policies." Of course Ruth was also interested in women's issues and discovered that the French women's suffrage bill was not expected to pass the Senate. She found it appalling that "no French woman today can deposit or draw out any money from a bank without her husband's signature."[33]

Ruth used her time in Paris well but was relieved when they left Paris and traveled by car to Trier and Coblenz, where they endured frontier delays, poor food, and cold rooms, then proceeded by train from Frankfurt to Berlin. In Germany they were immediately struck by the hardships they saw there. Ruth had particular sympathy for middle class intellectuals who might be able to buy food and clothes but no books, theater, or concert tickets, and was told by one such lady at tea that "when you met your friends and acquaintances selling [matches] on the street you mustn't speak to them or refer to it when you exchanged visits." Although the physical appearance of Germany had improved since Medill's last visit in 1920, the mark was 8,254 to the dollar and falling rapidly. Ruth could see the writing on the wall:

> there is no denying the fact that the state of mind in Europe today is breeding war every day . . . unless the next conference settles something to relieve the situation, Germany will blow up.[34]

Their trip ended in London, where Lady Nancy Astor gave Ruth a luncheon with many of the political and "uplift" women. She was delighted to find that they all agreed with her arguments against the League of Women Voters and said "they had gone through that stage in England."[35] It was a encouraging note on which to end a trip that had been otherwise very depressing.

The McCormicks had a rough trip sailing home, pitching steadily in a hard wind for ten days, and arriving two days late. They caught the first train to Washington, arriving at the square red-brick house on Eighteenth and F Streets after midnight on December 24. The night they arrived, Bazy, almost two years old, woke up and came downstairs. "She nearly broke my heart," Ruth mourned in her diary:

> by looking at me as if she had never seen me before. When I asked her where Mom was she said, "All gone," and in reply to who I was said, "Nice lady"! But before she went to bed she smiled and said "Mom" so my heart was mended . . . Oh, the delight of once more holding them in my arms! They were so pleased to see us and so unusually affectionate that I think I made a resolve not to go so far away again until they are well grown. They do need their parents, and these parents do need each other, so the family must try to remain together as much as possible.

But the day after Christmas, Ruth was "back to the early morning details of housekeeping, back to the pile of letters" on her desk every morning, back to the telephone calls and the "endless interviews from people who want you to do something for them—help political or financial or both."[36] It seemed unlikely she would be able to keep her resolution.

REPUBLICAN NATIONAL COMMITTEEWOMAN

"We've Carried Water for the Elephants Long Enough"

All during the spring of 1923, as Medill McCormick began to plan his reelection campaign, Ruth struggled to work out her own role. She knew she could not be happy as a mere political wife. Lunching at the Congressional Club in early February and at tea with senators' wives afterward, she mused, "I had quite a nice time seeing the Congressional world and some society, but how can they do it year after year and day after day!" Nor was she really content to work at home. Johnny, then five-and-a-half, had had a private teacher, who had now left to raise her own family. At first Ruth was taken with the idea of tutoring him herself: "I am delighted with his progress . . . Each day I realize more and more that it is only by spending time with them that I learn to know the children and to gain their confidences." But four days later she gave up and enrolled him in a private school, reasoning, "It is better for him to know other boys and get group discipline."[37]

Because of her early training, Ruth had come to love political work. But like other politically-minded women of her generation—Eleanor Roosevelt, Frances Perkins, Belle Moscowitz—she had been reared in the Victorian tradition of serving men, and she easily made her husband's career her own. In early March the two of them took a long walk to lay plans for his reelection. Ruth was in favor of a hard summer campaign: "[I]t is always the early campaign which counts. A man's first reelection is the test. After that it is comparatively easy." Their strategy would be "going around and meeting people face to face." Ruth was in charge of organizing the newly enfranchised women to support her husband. She made a three-week trip, speaking in different Illinois towns, usually to groups of five hundred or more. Her self-confidence grew with her increased public activity. After speaking on the Child Labor Amendment to an audience of six hundred women in Harrisburg, Illinois, she positively glowed, "They were particularly nice to me and under their enthusiasm I made a good impression. It does please me so much to please them." And when she went on to Lincoln, she found that, though the roads were nearly impassable, the women and men who did come nearly filled the Court House. She returned late at night on the train with her supper in a paper bag, very much stimulated by campaigning.

> It is such a joy to work with these girls [Forsyth and the Bennetts] who are so intelligent and so ready to enjoy the game of life, and at the same time they do such an efficient job seriously.[38]

Ruth McCormick was less successful at writing articles. In April she spent a whole week with Estelline Bennett grinding out an article on the status of women in politics but conceded, "If I had any idea of how difficult it was going to be I should not have attempted it." She tried another article on the League of Women Voters that was rejected as too controversial; Ruth was contemptuous of the league because she believed very strongly that women should affiliate with a party in order to be effective politically. She could not conceal her glee in learning that representatives at the league's annual convention had dropped from 1300 delegates to 260. "I give them two more conventions," she gloated. It can be argued that many of the most gifted suffragist women may have had their political strength diluted by going into the league instead of participating in elective politics. Many politicians assumed that women were not really interested in politics, as the term was then understood, but rather in "reform," which was quite different.[39]

Much as she enjoyed her work, Ruth often felt pulled in two by family obligations.

> [D]uring all these days when I was most anxious to put the best I had in me into this work, Mrs. McCormick required hours of my time each day and so I worked nights to make up.[40]

Ruth's own mother, Gussie Hanna, had gone into retirement after Mark Hanna's death, and seems to have played almost no part in Ruth's adult life. She died in November 1921, shortly after the untimely death of her son Dan.

Although Ruth had her own work, Medill remained at the hub of her emotional and professional life, and she still saw herself as primarily an ally to Medill. Back in Washington when Congress reconvened, Ruth spent an uneventful few weeks cleaning out and rearranging Medill's files. Medill had just returned from another trip and she rejoiced: "I am too absurdly lonely without him and life is not quite so amusing or interesting when he is not here . . ." Three days later, however, her mother-in-law claimed to be so feeble that Medill decided to take her over and settle her in Paris. Bitterly disappointed, Ruth tried to convince herself "it is best for him to be away."[41]

The day before he left they took another long walk and planned trips they could take if he were defeated for the Senate—a long yachting trip, a hunting trip for big game, or projects on the farm. Ruth told herself firmly:

> Medill's career is very dear to us but if he is not returned to the Senate our life goes on in another channel quite joyously. We recognize no defeat. We have each other.

When he had gone, she wrote,

> Life is so different when he is away. The incentive for activity is reduced

and I feel lost without him . . . It is only the feeling that I must carry on
for him that keeps me going.[42]

When the McCormicks returned to Chicago to finish the campaign,
Ruth at first felt disoriented:

> It seems so queer to again be living in Chicago . . . I haven't time to be
> social and keep up the pace of my work, but . . . if I don't meet people
> I will not again get in touch with the life of the town . . . After this
> campaign I must give up an office job and pay more attention to the
> social side of life.

But at the same time, she couldn't help assessing the social scene for its
political value:

> The time seemed ripe to interest the rich and influential women. The Illinois
> Republican Women's Club Federation gave a wonderfully successful lunch
> . . . I followed it up the next day with a lunch where we organized a
> Ways and Means Committee . . . to raise a budget of $100,000 . . .
> The money came in not as fast as we hoped but faster than I expected
> and enabled us to go ahead with our downstate work.[43]

Ruth left Chicago to make a tour of the Twenty-Third Congressional
District with Anne Forsyth. "Everywhere we found interest among the
women and curiosity among the men," she noted. They were not speaking
on behalf of any candidate, nor even against Governor Lennington Small,
then under federal indictment, whom Ruth was determined to unseat.
They were simply trying to organize the women and get them to affiliate
with the party. "The old politicians saw something formidable and for
the most part are glad to take us into camp," she chortled and made
plans to hold a convention of the Republican Women's Clubs in early
November. These clubs would become her power base when she campaigned herself five years later.[44]

She began by calling together the Congressional District leaders, women
who had worked in the 1920 presidential campaign. These women made
up the first state board of the clubs and each one started the work of
organizing clubs in the counties and towns of her respective district.
Anne Forsyth recognized it as "up-hill work":

> Women were afraid of politics, they thought all politicians were crooked,
> and they did not know the give and take so necessary to party success.
> Ruth wanted to convince the women that the party had to be reformed
> from within.

But women responded to Ruth's sincerity and magnetism, and the clubs
became active and strong. They were able to tap into energies released

after the suffrage campaign and were successor organizations to the old NAWSA as much as the League of Women Voters was.[45]

Ruth McCormick wanted to concentrate on getting women into politics, and some accused her of ignoring other problems. Forsyth explained: "All the many issues the women espoused pounded at her for attention and some of the enthusiasts involved thought her less than honest because she did not saddle herself with their cause." Ruth did lobby vigorously for other women in some cases, such as Mary Barthelme, a lawyer running for judge of the children's court. Ruth wanted women, in turn, to work for the whole ticket, so that they could earn support from the men. She planned for her women to play a significant part not only in Medill's election, but in other races as well. She wanted "to stamp out Smallism throughout the state" as they had succeeded in "stamping out Thompsonism in Cook County." She added, "We are going to do it, and the women are going to play a very important role."[46]

Medill felt his campaign was doing well. "[I]t's not going to be easy for other people to organize formidable opposition to my renomination," he said smugly. But as his colleague Senator William McKinley observed, McCormick was "not a good campaigner for himself." Similarly, Harriet Taylor Upton, Vice-Chairman of the Republican National Executive Committee, wrote Ruth that she had for some months been very anxious about Medill's campaign. She had learned that the uncompromising stand Ruth had openly taken against the League of Women Voters was having a negative effect on Medill's campaign and urged her not to make more enemies at such a crucial time by pressing too strongly for the equal representation of women on the National Committee.[47]

In spite of such growing anxiety about the campaign, Ruth still had to make time for the children. "It is so easy to allow one's own fatigue to interfere with the children's pleasure," she noted in her diary. With her post-Paris resolution in mind, she said,

> I don't want to make the effort of going out [to the farm] tomorrow but I can't disappoint them. After all, they must have the best I can give them in companionship and pleasant times together. Every time I fail them is a black mark for me.

And yet she felt torn:

> Medill is here so little and I am so selfish about wanting to be with him that it is hard to know just how to divide myself. I suppose every woman has this problem . . . so much depends upon me to make it mean to each and every one what it ought to mean . . .

She seemed to dislike her occasional bouts of domesticity. Arriving at the farm, she described her housework as "not so pleasant," and complained that she had

> unpacked, put away clothes, scrubbed closets, bureau drawers, and washed china and unpacked linen until time to cook supper. I didn't know that carrots took so much longer than Brussels sprouts to cook . . .[48]

Ruth McCormick preferred to be in the line of battle. Medill McCormick and his opponent for the Republican nomination, Charles Deneen, opened their campaign officially on January 24, 1924. Deneen attacked McCormick for having voted to seat Senator Truman H. Newberry, who was ultimately denied a seat because of excessive campaign expenditures. McCormick, for his part, tried to associate Deneen, twice Governor of Illinois, with the notorious Governor Len Small.

Fortunately, Medill's work in the Senate at this time was attracting favorable attention. When the Child Labor Law passed by Congress was declared unconstitutional by the Supreme Court, labor leaders decided to press for a constitutional amendment. Samuel Gompers, president of the American Federation of Labor, had chosen Medill to introduce the amendment in the Senate. Gompers had met Medill through Ruth, whom he had known from the time when he worked with Hanna on the National Civic Federation.* McCormick had also done good work on the budget and in international affairs. He had taken Warren Harding's seat on the Foreign Relations Committee, the youngest man ever seated by that body, and he had done a great deal of useful work on Haiti. Although the country as a whole had regained a measure of prosperity, Midwestern farmers were still in the economic doldrums, between high land prices and low produce prices. The president of the Midwest Dairyman's Cooperative warned Medill of the "discontent and desire to whack somebody that existed among farmers." A third candidate, Newton Jenkins, entered the fray, running on a Progressive ticket to appeal to the malcontent farmers.[49]

Just as the primary campaign was winding up, Medill was called to Washington and left Ruth to make a radio speech (still quite a novelty) in his stead. "I do not want you to read a speech of mine for me," he wrote her, "but I am happy to think that you yourself can speak for me."

---

*The child labor amendment passed both houses of Congress easily in 1924, only to have its ratification blocked within a year by the business interests that by then were firmly in control of American politics. Flexner, *Woman's Rights Movement*, note 391.6.

None of his colleagues knew his positions so well, no one else in Illinois understood the compromises that a senator was forced to make in order to be effective.[50] Ruth and Medill had complementary political styles. He loved ideas and used his eloquence to persuade people to adopt them. She loved people and used political ideas to relate to them. Even though they were not campaigning full-time, it should have been enough.

In spite of having been endorsed by all the influential papers in Chicago, McCormick lost the primary to Deneen by less than six thousand votes out of more than eight hundred thousand polled. For several days the results of the election were in doubt, and afterwards McCormick considered calling for a recount. Finally, however, he decided it could not be accomplished within the time limit set for one. It had been a bitter fight. Medill summed up:

> I was opposed by the La Follette people, by the prodigal and corrupt state machine, by the KKK, and by a lot of good church people who fought me in order to punish Bert [McCormick] and Joe [Patterson] because the Tribune fought the Eighteenth Amendment for which I had voted.

Although Jenkins had polled 125,000 votes, enough to have ensured McCormick's victory over Deneen, Medill did not attribute his defeat to Jenkins. "I do not think we underestimated the widespread and well-grounded dissatisfaction among the farmers, or the amount that Jenkins would draw." Instead he blamed "the tremendous campaign fund" that had been raised by assessing state employees who depended on patronage for their jobs; this fund was used to hire workers, according to Medill, at polling places not only in Chicago, but throughout the state. Medill concluded, "I could not spend any such sum."[51] Ruth McCormick, in her own campaign five years later, would come to a different conclusion.

Ruth's analysis was that he had lost for several reasons: overconfidence on the part of his supporters, his absence from the active conduct of the campaign, not following his own judgment rather than the advice of his workers (she admitted she was one of his advisors), lack of strength in his personal organization, his honesty in limiting his expenditures to those permitted by "the letter of the law." Finally, he was "counted out in Chicago . . ."

> It was a great disappointment to us both to lose such a campaign and to lose it the way it was lost. In thinking it over it was so unnecessary . . . but of course it is always easy to win the battle on paper after it has been fought.

Her future campaigns would never suffer from lack of effort; if anything, they would suffer from her excessive zeal.[52]

Medill in public was philosophical. He wrote one friend:

> Mark Sullivan says I have had three careers, one as a newspaper man,
> one as a colonial organizer, and one as a politician and Senator but
> unless there be a recount to my advantage, my present career has come
> to a temporary check, at least.

"Of course, I am not going to give up politics," he wrote another friend.
But to Ruth, he suggested, "We must plan to take up our private lives
again, eschewing public activity in politics. I am going to do my level
best to be a farmer . . ." He took a trip to Cuba and Haiti to recuperate
from the rigors of the campaign, but wrote Ruth "I am disappointed in
my slow recovery. My dreams show a desire to escape reality."[53]

Ruth McCormick had a campaign of her own under way at this time.
As early as June 1922, Harriet Taylor Upton had written the other women
on the Republican Executive Committee that "Republicans will not get
anywhere until women are on the National Committee . . . The Executive Committee is simply a servant of the National," and the women
had no voting rights. Ruth herself had become dissatisfied with this
situation. She wrote of a woman who wanted to be on the Committee:
"she imagines in her innocence that those of us who enjoy the honor
have something to say and do!" She concluded the women were "really
nothing but window dressing and not very vivid decoration at that."
Meanwhile, the Democrats had elected women to the National Committee, where they voted and were as fully empowered as the men were.[54]

Back in spring 1923 Ruth had begun to lobby for equal participation
of women in the councils of the Republican Party, enlisting the help of
her friend Senator George Wharton Pepper of Pennsylvania, who called
for a special session of the Executive Committee. But Harriet Upton
wrote Ruth in November 1923 to caution her not to push for a conference
of women preceding the National Committee meeting. Upton argued
that the Chairman of the Republican National Committee, John T.
Adams, had already decided a year before to support equal representation
of men and women on the National Committee. He had only proceeded
very slowly because "there was opposition on the Committee, strong
opposition, too." Upton was convinced that Adams's gradual approach
would win over the members "unless something is done to stir them up."
She begged Ruth to "be patient" with her and take her advice "just a
little while longer." Ruth secretly considered Upton "well-meaning but
ineffective" and may not have taken her caution seriously.[55]

Despite their differences, Upton approved of one of Ruth's strategies,
developed during the Illinois suffrage fight:

Your suggestion in regard to the men on the National Committee who
are opposed to the 50/50 rule is very good . . . When the vote comes
in and we know which men are against it, we can pressure "refractory
members." It will be fine as you say to have a unanimous vote and men,
I have noticed, are apt to conform to the inevitable.

A resolution was subsequently passed by the Republican National Committee directing its members in each state to appoint immediately women associate members and recommending that the Rules Committee at the convention of 1924 add one woman for each state. A friend in California wrote Ruth gleefully, "When I heard that the National Committee had decided to recognize women as associate committeemen I knew that your fine Italian hand was still at work."[56]

Immediately after the primary election in April, Ruth telegraphed Louise Bowen: "I understand you are not a candidate to succeed yourself as National Committeewoman. I am therefore canvassing situation as candidate myself. Will withdraw if you've changed your mind." "Ideal if you'll become candidate," Bowen responded.[57]

Ruth then wrote the old Irreconcilable from Illinois, Lawrence Y. Sherman, for advice. She needed an outside perspective because Medill, whether for personal or strategic reasons, had "some apprehension" about her accepting the position. Ruth believed it would help her in her campaign to unseat Governor Small, not because the national committeewoman had any "authority," but because she could attend more meetings, make more speeches, and be more effective.[58]

Ruth wanted to coordinate the Republican women's effort with that of their Democratic sisters. She contacted Emily Newell Blair on the Democratic National Committee about a combined policy to insist that the League of Women Voters and other women's groups submit proposed planks to the party women to forward to their respective resolutions committees. Blair agreed, noting that Eleanor Roosevelt was the chairman for their subcommittee for planks submitted by other organizations. Ruth often worked with Mrs. George Bass, the Democratic National Chairwoman, sometimes speaking from the same platform, urging women to join a party and be active in party affairs.[59]

The Republican Convention met in Cleveland in early June, and Ruth was in a fighting mood: "We've carried water for the elephants long enough. Now we want to get in on the real show."[60] The day before the convention opened the Illinois delegation caucused and chose Ruth McCormick as Republican National Committeewoman for the same nonvoting, nonactive office that her predecessors had held. Nothing more could be done at that time, since the resolution providing for the change had not yet been submitted. But in fact, the chairman of the delegation, Frank L. Smith of Dwight, Illinois, was not friendly to the McCormicks. He hoped to bury Ruth in the old office, and then, after the resolution providing for the change in office had been carried, to reconvene the delegation and elect one of his own women. He was counting on the women delegates from Illinois not recognizing this second move.

The Illinois caucus was held after dinner. It was breathlessly hot, as Cleveland so often is in early summer, and the men were tired but pleased. The women were eager. When the introduction of new business was called for, Frank Smith in the chair and several of his supporters were mildly surprised, but unworried when Emily Dean, with smooth white hair and gentle blue eyes, arose. Hesitantly, she asked to put a motion to have Ruth Hanna McCormick declared the delegation's choice for National Committeewoman once the National Convention had granted women equal status with committeemen.

The crafty chairman eyed her indulgently. "Thank you, Mrs. Dean, but that motion is really unnecessary," he said evenly. "We elected Mrs. McCormick at the caucus." He waited for her to sit down, but she did not. "I'm sorry to disagree with you Mr. Smith," her soft voice purred, "but that vote this morning didn't take care of it. It only provided for her election under the old terms—made no provision for the new ones."

Smith remained outwardly self-assured. "Oh, that's all right Mrs. Dean," he replied. "That really took care of it. It's all the same thing you know."

Mrs. Dean began to flush, and people who knew her recognized her fighting blood. "Mr. Chairman," she said, "It is not the same thing, and I have made a motion."

"We don't seem to agree do we?" he bandied.

"Mr. Chairman," repeated Mrs. Dean. "I have made a motion and I would like to have it put to the house."

Smith began to be a little flustered.

"But suppose," he countered, "that I refuse to put the motion," not realizing that all these women knew their parliamentary procedure better than he.

"Then Mr. Chairman," smiled Mrs. Dean, "I shall have to appeal the decision of the chair." Everybody laughed. Smith sank back into his seat.

The motion was put and carried. Ruth McCormick was elected, subject to the passage of the motion the following day, to be the Republican National Committeewoman from Illinois, with all the rights and appurtenances of the office as enjoyed by the men. President Calvin Coolidge expressed his gratification at her election to an important position.

Ruth saw her new role as a liaison officer between national and state affairs. She went into every congressional district and every county to explain the national situation as it developed, and to give advice about local organization and consideration of local issues.[61] It was a victory for her and for the women.

But apart from her success at the Illinois caucus, Ruth found the Cleveland Convention "the dullest I have ever attended." She blamed much of it on William Butler, whom Coolidge had chosen as Chairman for the National Committee: "Not knowing the game, he does startling things." He put Borah up as a nominee for Vice-President without ascertaining that Borah was not interested. "No one is inspired by such a Chairman," was Ruth's cutting assessment. "The Convention ran away from him then and the majority wanted Lowden so they nominated him and he declined it . . . They went to [Charles] Dawes because they didn't know anyone else by name."[62] So Ruth's old friend became the vice-presidential nominee of the Republican Party.

After the convention the McCormicks hoped to enjoy their first peaceful summer together on the farm, but Medill could not, in the end, stay with them. His mother, as usual, cabled from France that she was not well and required her son's company. Then, just as he was about to leave, the McCormicks received a kidnap threat against their children. An unsigned letter demanded they put fifty thousand dollars in a nearby culvert on the night of July 3. Medill left as planned and Ruth had to cope with the crisis.

"We didn't take it very seriously," she wrote nonchalantly. She hired guards from a detective agency, who arrested two men when they came for the money. Afterwards, she continued to see men with lights in the woods, so she kept the detectives to watch the children. Triny, then eleven years old, and Johnny, seven, thought them stupid and indolent. "Fear was looked down upon in our family. We were not afraid of anything as vague as kidnappers," said Triny. The children made a game of eluding the detectives, running off into the woods when the men fell asleep under a tree. Finally, Ruth herself caught the detectives napping and dismissed them, laughing, "It was better than a play to see them jump when faced by my light."[63]

Ruth did, however, curtail her work in Chicago, eliciting a note from Sallie Hert, Vice-Chairman of the Republican National Committee: "I know you would not have a moment's peace in trying to stay away from them for any length of time. Just know we want you at headquarters and need you."

Ruth's husband finally returned in September. "I can't remember when

I have been so eager to see Medill," said Ruth, in New York to meet him off the boat:

> When he came back home during the war I was tremendously excited but no more so than today. Mother-in-law was not feeling well enough to leave her room so I had Medill all to myself all day and for dinner and a play.

They did take the time to go to Washington and dined alone with the Coolidges at the White House, but had no special luck in drawing out the taciturn President.

> It was rather difficult keeping up a conversation because apparently the President was not interested or did not wish to discuss any of the issues of the day. He did not want to converse with Medill who has just returned from Europe about even the general situation in Europe . . . He thinks mostly of our domestic affairs and is concerned just now with the matters of the campaign. This is quite natural but he also did not wish to discuss them in such a way as to get any information.

Ruth concluded that Coolidge was "not a man of vision or of very lively intellectual interest, but he is a good conscientious American citizen."[64]

Even that modest endorsement was enough to enrage their former Progressive colleagues. In the 1924 election Coolidge was being opposed by Bob La Follette, who was running as a Progressive for president, although there would be no Progressive tickets in the states. Harold Ickes was supporting La Follette and criticized "the limping heroes of Armageddon, [who], some openly and others by their silence, chose to support a proven corrupt administration." He felt that the McCormicks had betrayed the Progressive cause, and grew increasingly hostile, especially to Ruth, during the next twenty years. Both La Follette and the Democratic nominee John W. Davis were handicapped by the country's prosperity more than by any desertions. "I am beginning to believe," Ruth wrote in October, "that the high price of wheat will save us from La Follette."[65]

Ruth McCormick was surprised and pleased to be asked by the Republican National Headquarters to make speeches for Calvin Coolidge. She made her first national campaign speech to a packed hall of nearly two hundred. "It was not as good as it ought to be but was the best I could do on such short notice and to a group of women who are learning about politics," she decided. Senator McKinley reported to Medill that "The Pres't . . . spoke in the highest terms of Mrs. McCormick—in very complimentary terms." Medill, too, was speaking around the Middle West, but found it a joyless task. "Poor Medill is depressed and until after the election it seems difficult to alter his state of mind," Ruth said ruefully. "What this turn of events will mean for him is hard to forecast." Adding to his depression was the suicide of their friend and fellow Bitter-ender Senator Frank Brandegee. Ruth, when she learned of it, spent a long day trying to reach Medill, campaigning in Iowa. "I wanted to tell him myself and to say how I sympathized . . . He will feel it keenly, dear Medill . . ."[66]

Added to all her other troubles, the Borden Milk company discontinued their contract with her dairy farm. "It does seem as if almost everything had conspired to hit us," Ruth wrote disconsolately in her diary.

> It will mean a dreadful disappointment to me if we are obliged to give up the Dairy . . . It seems at times as if something will break in me if everything fails. I don't care for myself because I will substitute something else in life but Medill's illness will take time and I can't substitute until he can solve his problem. The ways of the Powers are strange. I wish I had a faith of some kind.[67]

At least the Republicans were still in power. Although La Follete polled the largest third party vote in U.S. history, aside from that of Theodore Roosevelt, Coolidge won easily. Medill, writing to the editor of the *London Times*, observed that the increase in the price of wheat had checked for a time the agrarian discontent, leaving La Follette's radicalism and even Davis's internationalism seemingly out of place. "I spoke from South Dakota to Pennsylvania," reported Medill, "and found that nothing aroused the crowd to real enthusiasms except a denunciation of the League of Nations and its American supporters."[68] Ruth took note of this fact for the future.

Medill McCormick had no more obligations to fulfill and felt himself worthless. Ruth lamented, "One so able must find his place again but the period of waiting is very hard for one of his temperament. I have faith in him. If only I could do something for him."[69]

6
On Her Own:
1925–1927

Ruth McCormick was concerned about her husband, casting about for what he might do after his Senate term expired in March 1925. Some of the old Progressives hoped to see him in the Coolidge cabinet. Arthur Brisbane, publisher for William Randolph Hearst, wanted Medill to take over the *Washington Herald.* But the most widely discussed possibility was that he be named ambassador to London. For this he had wide support, including that of Bill Borah, who, as Chairman of the Foreign Relations Committee, was anxious that the American representative in London be someone who would not be unduly influenced by the British. Coolidge did not appoint him, but instead of rejecting him outright, he let an announcement be made that the U.S. ambassador to Germany would be transferred to England. In her diary Ruth deplored the president's lack of frankness, but hesitated to speculate on what a second disappointment might mean to Medill.[1]

Although she was uneasy about her husband, Ruth pushed ahead with her own work. For two months she had been working on a Woman's World's Fair in Chicago. The project had started on a dreary afternoon in November 1924, during a meeting with Helen Bennett. Ruth had been pacing up and down, troubled by the financial state of the Illinois Republican Women's Clubs. The clubs had campaigned all summer for Coolidge and Dawes, but when Ruth appealed to William Butler, the chairman of the National Committee, to reimburse them for the seventeen thousand dollars they had spent, he turned them down. She stopped pacing for a moment, lifted one eyebrow, and said fretfully,

"Don't sit there feeling sorry for me, Helen. Tell me some way in which we can make money for these Clubs."

Helen Bennett then revealed a long-cherished plan to put on a great show, "of the women, for the women, by the women." Bennett had been the manager of the Chicago Collegiate Bureau of Occupations and had observed that college girls seemed to lack purpose in life. The fair would showcase careers open to them. She believed that "Happy women are those who do congenial work and do it well, whether it be taking care of a baby, singing in grand opera, measuring timber in a forest, making candy, writing books, or bossing a gang of workmen." She wanted to bring obscure as well as prominent women workers into the limelight. Ruth walked over to a window and stood with her back to Helen for a moment, then turned around and exclaimed: "There's just one thing wrong about all this. You should have told me all this four years ago. Now let's get busy."[2]

Although it was to be a women's project, Ruth typically first sought the opinions of three shrewd Chicago businessmen, William Wrigley, Jr., Samuel Insull, and S. P. Gerson, a public relations expert; all three encouraged her to go on. Next, she needed a good board: prominent, well-known women, preferably with social connections, but also able to do a good job. She didn't want just big names, she wanted workers. Louise Bowen was chosen as president. The board also included Edith Rockefeller McCormick who, with Louise Bowen and Ruth McCormick, was probably one of the three wealthiest women in Chicago. Ruth became the General Executive and Helen the Managing Director.

But time for preparation was short. They wanted to hold the fair in April and needed to sell sixty thousand dollars' worth of space in a few weeks, to say nothing of tickets. Ruth called on President Coolidge in early February to enlist his support. She had prepared a five-minute talk and rushed through it, afraid of being cut short by the next visitor. But Coolidge, in an uncharacteristic burst of enthusiasm, told her to take all the time she wanted. She spoke for over half an hour, and a way was found to finance participation by all branches of government in which women were involved. The president also agreed to give a fifteen-minute address on the radio—still uncommon—just before the opening; Grace Coolidge was to press a button to open the doors.[3] Buoyed, Ruth returned to Chicago to be with Alice Longworth who, at the age of forty-one, was expecting her first child. Ruth had persuaded Alice to see her own obstetrician, Dr. Joseph De Lee.

Medill McCormick went down to Washington the last week of February to wind up his Senate affairs, while Ruth remained in Chicago with

Alice and her new baby Paulina. Medill was staying in a room at the Hotel Hamilton, and on February 23 Ruth telephoned him. He sounded tired, but not ill, and he told her not to call him the next morning, as he planned to attend an all-night session of the Senate and wanted to sleep late. Ruth awoke on the morning of the twenty-forth with an overwhelming premonition of disaster.[4]

Their journalist friend Bill Hard had an appointment with Medill and phoned him at 9 A.M.; receiving no answer, he went around to the hotel in person. When his knock was not answered, he summoned the hotel carpenter to take down the door from its hinges. Medill was in bed; he was dead, presumably from an overdose of barbiturates.[5] Hard telephoned Ruth with the news.

Their daughter Triny, then thirteen years old, later said, "He obviously knew he was going to kill himself when he went back to Washington. He said 'good-bye' to me . . ." When Triny was reading in bed the night he left, her father came in and sat beside her. "He was extremely affectionate with me . . . He kept referring to his great love for me, how talented I was. Sort of a farewell speech."

Ruth took the train to Washington, with her close friends Margaret Blake and George Porter. Medill's cousin Joe Patterson escorted her to the station, then stayed behind with the children. President Coolidge sent a message to her on the train. Medill's mother wired: "I am crushed. The light of my life is gone. Don't be in such a hurry to bury him."[6]

When Ruth arrived at Medill's hotel room, she opened his trunk and found it contained several empty vials. She believed this was his way of letting her know what he'd done; he knew no one else would be able to open the trunk because he had arranged an elaborate set of keys for each of them. The hotel doctor gave the cause of death as gastric hemorrhage; Medill had suffered badly from ulcers. The coroner's report listed "Myocarditis."[7] Ruth kept his suicide a well-guarded secret for years.

Medill's body was removed to Cissy Patterson's house on Dupont Circle, where a funeral service was held the following day. Congress adjourned. The Coolidges, Chief Justice and Mrs. William Howard Taft, Secretary of State and Mrs. Charles Evans Hughes, Secretary of Commerce Herbert Hoover, Speaker of the House Nicholas Longworth, generals and admirals, foreign diplomats, congressmen, Bull Moose associates were all in attendance. The *New York Times* wrote a restrained eulogy to the forty-seven-year-old man, beginning: "If Medill McCormick's undoubted talents had been steadied by a sounder judgment and greater tenacity of purpose, he might, if he had lived longer, gone far in public life," and concluding, "he was yet a man who had made himself felt in various ways, who seemed still to have promise of a future of note . . ."[8]

Ruth took a special train back to Chicago with the body, and Triny was brought down to meet her. People in black streamed off, and finally the girl was permitted to get aboard alone. She found her mother waiting, swathed in black crepe, a widow's veil thrown back from her ashen, haggard face, so distracted that she had forgotten to fasten the straps of her shoes. She dropped to her knees and enveloped Triny in her arms.[9]

Condolences poured in. Most were unintentionally ironic complaints that so young a man had been snatched away too soon. Even Carl Jung, who had known about Medill's self-destructive tendencies for more than fifteen years, was surprised.

> When I read the news of the sudden and most unexpected death of Medill McCormick in the papers I could hardly believe it, since I had seen him not so very long ago in an apparently much better state of health than several years ago when he was on his great trip through Europe . . . The more I have been struck by his sudden end . . .[10]

Ruth McCormick had lost her husband, but more than that she had lost her closest friend. Whatever her difficulties with Medill—and they were many and serious—life with him had always been exciting and companionable. Also, apart from her feelings of loss as his wife and the mother of his three children, Medill's death left an emptiness of purpose. For years, his causes had been hers; it is likely that, had he lived, Ruth's life would have more closely paralleled that of other prominent women who achieved their political agenda through working with the men they helped elect to office: Belle Moskowitz, Molly Dewson, and Eleanor Roosevelt. Now it would remain to be seen what this woman, with all her experience, could achieve on her own.

The Woman's World's Fair was the first project demanding her attention. It was scheduled to open on April 18, just six weeks after Medill's funeral. "It was a difficult time for Ruth," Helen Bennett remarked.

> She did not quite know where to go, but in the midst of personal problems, she did not forget her obligations. She had started the Woman's World's Fair. She would see it through to a successful conclusion.

The day was raw and cold, but a large crowd had assembled outside the Furniture Mart. Coolidge, on his nation-wide radio hook-up, embarrassed Ruth considerably when he drawled, "I'm not sure what I'm supposed to be doing here except to ballyhoo Ruthie McCormick's cows." Mrs. Coolidge may have pushed her button, but the doors actually were opened by the doorkeepers. The public entered through a long narrow entrance-way. Originally, the board had been upset to learn that this important location was going to be dominated by the Moody Bible Institute; they had wanted an organization they could count on to provide an attractive, colorful exhibit to set the tone for the entire fair. But the Moody people, instead of the drably earnest endeavor the board was anticipating, provided women and men dressed in costumes of the various countries where the institute sent missionaries. A reed organ and costumed singers provided excellent gospel music, and drew a large crowd.[11]

Opportunities for women in the work force had increased greatly during World War One, and expansion into male-dominated occupations continued into the twenties. By 1922 only a third of women college graduates planned careers in teaching, compared with three-quarters a generation earlier. Well-educated daughters of the middle-class now wanted careers in business, social sciences, and the professions.[12]

At the fair two hundred exhibits represented more than seventy occupations in which women were engaged. Railroads, department stores, and other large corporations demonstrated the share women had had in establishing them. Women inventors, farmers, and physicians were represented, as well as numerous trades, businesses, welfare associations, and clubs. Women artists displayed their work in a gallery. A period costume pageant was staged, strolling musicians and jugglers wandered down the aisles, activities ranged from a lip reading demonstration to a fashion show.

Ruth herself had taken a small space in the back part of the hall, where she exhibited one of her prize Holsteins. The cow drew a surprising crowd of children, and a social worker remarked that while city kids could see wild animals in the zoo or at a circus, many had never seen a cow. Meanwhile, a Famous Women's Lunch was held to honor women like Jane Addams, Governor Nellie Ross of Wyoming, Cyrena van Gordon of the Chicago Civic Opera, and Fannie Ferber Fox, cookbook author. Ruth, as Executive Director, introduced them and made the startling claim, "I, too, have something to boast of. I am the largest milk producer of any woman in America." When shouts of laughter interrupted her, she was puzzled, but only for a moment.[13] The light note was welcome in what, for her, were dark times.

The eight-day exposition cleared more than fifty thousand dollars. People rushed to attend; papers put out special editions. The fair drew attention to the increased opportunities for women all around the country. The largest part of the profit was put into a fund to sponsor the fair on an annual basis, and the remainder went to help finance the Illinois

Women's Republican Clubs and the Women's Roosevelt Republican Club of Chicago. The fair's board members had all been members of the Illinois Women's Republican Club, and the club had put up the money to start the fair, but Helen Bennett insisted the fair itself was non-partisan and pointed to the diverse political backgrounds of honorees at the Famous Women's Luncheon. The Woman's World's Fair was held annually for four years. In 1926 forty foreign countries were represented. In 1927 the fair was held at the Coliseum, with 280 booths, representing more than 100 different occupations, and took in $160,000. Helen Bennett continued as Managing Director and Ruth as General Executive, even though the other directorships rotated.[14] Their enterprising idea had proven a success, but more than that, it had helped Ruth get quickly back to the work that would always be her best solace.

Ruth McCormick was in a unique position. She was forty-five years old and independently wealthy, with a yearly income of $185,000 at a time when the average annual salary was just over $2000. She had served a political apprenticeship of twenty-five years. While Medill was alive she had never really considered a separate political career. Before the war most women assumed that satisfying, important work was not really compatible with domestic happiness. During and after the war women began moving into the labor force in greater numbers, and by 1925 about one-fourth of these women were married with children. But there was still the assumption that a woman's home life was her primary responsibility. Although Ruth could afford plenty of household help, Medill was occasionally ambivalent about her career: "I hope you are going to give up speaking and politics and look after yourself and the farm," he had written her in the late teens.[15] He may have been concerned about his family, and he may also have feared her competition. Now, suddenly, she was alone and faced the need to rethink her future.

Even before Medill's death, in October 1924, Ruth had been asked to consider running as congressman-at-large in 1926. She was assured that she would have the support of Senator William McKinley. Ruth had seen this as a ploy to win her support for others: "They are so amusing," she wrote in her diary. "They can't imagine I don't want something and they imagine I will fall for the first job that is offered me and then they can get me in line for [Governor] Small now and the ticket." Instead, in the summer of 1925, Ruth opened an office in Washington, ostensibly to tidy up Medill's affairs. Rumors began to fly that she was preparing to take up her husband's fight against the proposed World Court. Ruth issued a formal statement saying that she believed

Coolidge wanted the Court separate from the League, but she did not believe proposed "reservations" would accomplish the separation. She also repeated the argument that England through its dominions and possessions would cast seven votes to America's one, and she objected to the Court giving the League advisory opinions about issues not specifically subjected for judgment. Her statement merely increased controversy and speculation about her plans. Carrie Chapman Catt formally contested Ruth McCormick's remarks point for point. Irish voters in Chicago applauded her "work in fighting John Bull's sinister machinations." She was characterized in news reports in highly political terms, as "an astute politician," "a clever public speaker," "an indefatigable worker."[16]

Ruth was not completely indefatigable. That summer, needing rest and a change, Ruth took her family out to the Turpin Ranch in Jackson Hole, Wyoming, where there was no running water and, mercifully, no phone. Milk was kept in a "milk house" over a cold stream, and Coleman stoves were used for cooking. Lost in her thoughts, Ruth rode through the beautiful hills by the hour. "It is as near to heaven as I ever expect to be," she wrote. "I can't even think of leaving without wanting to burst into real tears." But it was an illusion to think that even in the Rocky Mountains, Ruth could leave politics behind. A dreadful dirt road, nearly impassable, ran from the ranch to Jackson. Cut off from communication with the outside, Ruth rode into town one day, to discover that everyone there had learned she had been offered a nomination, before she herself had even seen the telegram.[17]

Throughout that "peaceful" summer, she was besieged with friendly suggestions about what she should do with her life. A vacancy appeared in the Civil Service Commission, and Coolidge announced he planned to appoint a woman. Ruth was "boomed" for the vacancy by many different groups, even by the National Woman's Party with which she had so often been at odds. She was urged to run as congressman-at-large, or even as a senator: "Why do you not take up the work left off by your late husband?" she was asked. Some wanted her to run for governor. "I can't see any point in wasting you on Congressman-at-Large," wrote one staunch friend, "Illinois needs you more than the nation does."[18]

By the end of the summer Ruth began slowly to increase her political activity, campaigning against U.S. membership in the World Court. Her old friend Senator Bill Borah stopped off in Chicago on his way to Washington to confer with Ruth and plan a campaign against the Court, which the Senate would consider when it convened in December. The next week she made her first public speech following her husband's death. She still wore mourning: loose black garments, described in the press as "draperies," with long black sleeves, and a black veil hung from the back of her hat. The somber clothes made her seem taller and slimmer, her face paler, her dark eyes more intense. Speaking to the DuPage County Republican Women's Clubs, she denied that she was a candidate for elective office. She pointed to her audience, and declared, "I'm going to stay right here and organize you," adding, "No state in the Union needs her women as our poor state needs hers."[19]

For all the snide remarks in the press about the "social lobby," women's influence was seen as critical in the debate over whether to join the World Court. Through the Women's Roosevelt Republican Club of Chicago, Ruth organized a large rally at the Auditorium Theater on October 20, where Borah denounced the Court as the "handmaid of the League," and the "agent and tool of the imperialists and militarists of Europe." On successive weeks the club invited as speakers Senator George Pepper, "a World Courter with strict reservations"; Nick Longworth, Speaker of the House; and George Wickersham, Taft's Attorney General and an ardent advocate of the Court. Ruth argued that, "A campaign of education on the subject will defeat the World Court rather than a . . . general harangue against the proposition."[20] She was that sure of the rightness of her position.

For the rest of the autumn Ruth kept up a brisk campaign throughout Illinois, urging her listeners to consider well the implications of joining the Court. In Elgin where two hundred men and women had turned out on a miserably wet night, she advised them against "the danger of swallowing propaganda whole" because it promised peace. People were reluctant to "dig any further." They just signed their names on the dotted line, and resolutions went back to Congress. Ruth deplored such careless "group resoluting," claiming that people did not understand half the resolutions they sent to Congress. She called for more study and discussion.

In taking a position against the World Court, Ruth placed herself in opposition to nearly every women's group in America: the National League of Women Voters, the General Federation of Women's Clubs, the American Association of University Women, the American Federation of Teachers, the National Council of Women, and legions of smaller civic societies, as well as the other women members of the Republican National Committee. However, Alice Longworth and Mrs. James W. Wadsworth, daughter of John Hay and wife of the New York senator, were said to be supporting her. The Democratic women were intrigued by this first real split in the ranks of Republican women since the suffrage amendment had been ratified. Ruth's opposition to administration policy was unusual for a Republican National Committeeman (as she called herself). Administration partisans tried to confine her to Chicago but failed. Ruth's speaking tours took her as far afield as Pennsylvania and Maine.[21]

The real agenda behind all this activity is not entirely clear. In fact, Ruth seemed ambivalent about her political goals. On the one hand, her political instincts led her to oppose American participation in the Court ("My father would turn over in his grave" at the thought of a Republican administration supporting a World Court measure introduced by a Democratic senator, she said.) On the other hand, when the Senate passed the resolution in favor of adherence to the World Court on January 27 by a substantial margin, Ruth balked at Senator Borah's call for a campaign to defeat in the primaries those who had supported the bill. In Illinois it was clear that if Senator William McKinley, as a loyal Republican, came out for the Court, his opponent, Frank Smith, would take an anti-Court stand to defeat him.[22]

Ruth disapproved of Borah's plan to defeat McKinley and other League opponents because she did not believe it was for the good of the country to defeat men "on this issue alone." In fact, she tried to defend McKinley on the World Court issue, saying the senator had received many resolutions from women's societies, carried away by a "false idea of peace," which asked him to vote for the World Court. She claimed McKinley did not approve of the Court, but felt compelled to respect his constituents' desires. In Washington, the pundits thought McKinley's political days were numbered, and considered it "remarkable that Mrs. McCormick is still for him." The women's vote had been tremendously important to McKinley in 1920. That year, the first in which women voted, women's and men's votes had been counted separately, and it could be seen that the women's votes had barely offset the majority the men had given Smith. Ruth may have thought she could deliver enough women's votes to tip the balance again. She argued that McKinley was the worthier candidate: "The thing for us to do is to clean house; to purge ourselves of the stigma that has been placed in Illinois . . . Look up these men's records," she told her listeners, implying that Smith's record would not stand close scrutiny. Some suggested she was endorsing McKinley because she expected his support in a run for senator or congressman-at-large. Or it may have been the other way around; McKinley had supported her for National Committeewoman at Cleveland the year before, when Smith's supporters had tried to maneuver her out of that position. Although she called the World Court issue a "smokescreen," and said it should not be made an issue in the Illinois primaries, two years later she would take the opposite position in her own campaign.[23] It could be argued that Ruth was campaigning for the sheer pleasure it gave her to exercise her skill.

In any case, she was not able to finish the campaign. She came down with flu at the end of March, and immediately afterward Triny contracted measles while they were in Washington. Her quarantine prevented Ruth from returning to Illinois at all before the primaries. Ruth's sister Mabel, whose husband had died, fell ill, too, and Ruth went to New York to arrange to have her taken care of. "It is most difficult . . . I don't seem to be able to work it out both for her happiness and safety . . . I fear it is only a question of time before it will be necessary to commit her." When Mabel died in the early 1930s, twelve-year-old Bazy was amazed to learn of her existence: "I didn't know she had a sister at all."

On top of everything, Medill's mother was having constant "attacks," and Ruth, trapped in Washington, felt obligated to visit her nearly every day. Finally, on May 6 she rejoiced, "Nice to be back at work again. Work is good for me and I really enjoy it."[24]

McKinley had been defeated by Frank Smith in the Illinois primaries. Ironically, Ruth was credited by some for having defeated him, by making the World Court an issue that Smith then appropriated. Most people realized, however, that Medill McCormick, defeated two years before as an anti-Court candidate, and McKinley, defeated as a pro-Court candidate, had both been opposed by the Len Small machine. But Smith had spent such enormous sums of money in the primary campaign, that the Senate refused to let him take the seat to which he was elected in November.[25]

Ruth's six-month speaking tour, though focusing on the issues of the World Court and the Illinois primaries, had given her many opportunities to speak on general issues, and to become more of a public figure herself. Her technique as a speaker was improving with time. A local columnist recalled Ruth campaigning in the Bull Moose days: "One minute the chill and haughty society leader, the next all aflame with ardent partisanship." But by 1926 "the chill seems to have been deleted." In its place she now saw "a blithe and sunny gaiety." Another reporter commented on her voice, "low in register, vibrant with life, frank and crisp in accent."[26]

Apart from opposing the World Court, Ruth's principal cause was the need for women to involve themselves much more deeply in elective politics. In 1924 only 46 percent of eligible Illinois women had voted, compared to 74 percent of men. Ruth created a sensation speaking at the Convention of the League of Women Voters in November when she announced, "I do not like the League," and advised women to quit the League and join a political party. "This government is a party government," she said. "If women want to help run it they must belong to parties.":

> I have been taken to task for criticizing the League. I am not criticizing the League. It has its functions. Those functions are educational . . . The League may start you off, but you cannot continue [your work] by reclining in the League . . . you have to join a good party.

She realized, however, "It's hard to get a woman to be partisan. She has spent so much time to secure the enfranchisements of women that she hasn't had time to find out the advantages of belonging to a certain party."[27]

Unless women participated they could not criticize the government, Ruth insisted. If there was crime in Chicago, it was because the woman voter was "too busy running from tea to tea—from club to club—to cast a vote" for people who would enforce the laws. She stressed that women had a special responsibility:

> We are not 100% American Citizens until we discharge our duties to government as faithfully as we discharge our duties to the home and church . . . The responsibility of women in forming public opinion is doubled because we influence both home and the business world.

On one hand, Ruth McCormick recognized the achievements of women in politics, especially in Illinois, and singled out Judge Mary Barthelme, Mable Reineke, State Representatives Katherine Good, Rena Elrod, and Lottie O'Neill, and State Senator Florence Bohrer; but on the other, she feared that women as a whole were basically not yet interested in politics. And until they were they would have no power. She dismissed the fact that there were "a few Congresswomen and a couple of women Governors" as not meaning a thing, "because nearly every woman elected to office so far has sentiment or some unnatural political condition to thank for her supposed success."[28] Most of these women were widows who had been appointed or elected in a gesture of compassion to fill out their deceased husbands' terms; as Alice Longworth rather morbidly put it, "They used their husbands' coffins as springboards." Ruth had learned her lesson about women in honorary posts. She wanted real power for women—and for herself.

Not surprisingly, rumors continued to grow about Ruth McCormick's political plans. "What is she in politics for?" speculated a columnist writing from Washington, D.C. "One doesn't have an organization of 200,000 women just for the sake of having it." Remarked another: "She is the first woman to have [such] an organization." "One imagines the politicians of Illinois would feel much more peaceful if she would declare a desire for a definite office," a third reporter concluded.

In May 1926 she was asked to consider running for governor. One member of the state Central Committee said he thought Ruth was the only person in the state who could beat her old nemesis Small. In her diary Ruth confessed she was flattered: "[I]t means the men are thinking of me in terms of regular jobs," she gloated. She considered the proposition carefully, but she felt torn by her two roles. "If it were not for the children I would see what support I could get," she admitted, but she still believed her real happiness lay "in making good first as a mother." There was no harm, however, in having recognition that she had won her "spurs in the political world to that extent."[29]

All through the fall she continued to be mentioned for the governor's job. Notwithstanding her diary account, her reluctance to run may have stemmed less from her qualms of conscience as a mother than from her uncertainty about the political wisdom of running. She admitted as much in November:

> It is difficult to know just how to most effectively play our political power . . . The women are determined to launch me as candidate for Governor but I am rather reluctant to allow them to do it because . . . I am stronger as a leader of our organization . . . I should like being a candidate and enjoy campaigning but I can't believe that much would be accomplished by such a move as I can't be nominated.

Instead, she envisioned the women's bloc as the balance of power in negotiations over the gubernatorial slate. She sat up late with Mabel Reineke one night, and concluded that it was advisable to let the men think she was going to run for Governor "in order to have something to trade."[30]

Ruth McCormick was also being considered for the Senate. Less than two months before the election, she had received a wire while vacationing in Jackson Hole, asking her to run as an Independent as a protest against Smith. "This I declined," she wrote, "as an Independent would have no chance." She was impressed by the initiative, however. "The Non-Partisan Voters League of the state offered to run me and finance my campaign. I had letters from men all over the state asking me to run." In spite of her lofty remarks about the importance of motherhood, she said frankly, "If the campaign had been started early in the summer it might have made more of a difference but no man can campaign the state in thirty days." Senator McKinley died suddenly on December 7, and there was some talk of her being appointed to serve the remaining three months of his term. She was even approached by Coolidge's personal secretary, Bascom Slemp. She refused to get excited by the prospect, but admitted, "it is amusing that the politicians even consider me in trying to smooth out the Illinois situation." In any case, she felt there was "no chance" of being chosen.[31]

As 1926 drew to a close, Ruth had still not decided what office to seek, but she was enlarging her political role in several directions. Since June she had been working with ex-Governor Frank O. Lowden on his plan to run for president in 1928. Crops were poor in the region, due to excessive rain, and she believed Lowden's position on farm issues would make him a stronger candidate than Coolidge. Lowden had asked her to be one of his national campaign managers and she accepted. "I am anxious to do it as it is the job I know best how to do. I like campaigning for the 'other fellow' best," she insisted, and began to do groundwork on precinct committeemen and members of the state delegation. She was also frequently in Washington, in part to lobby Coolidge to appoint a friend of hers to a federal judgeship in Southern Illinois. It was the first time she had ever had anything to say on patronage and she was interested to see if the politicians would recognize or consider that she had any "political strength." It transpired, however, that Senator Deneen was backing a different candidate and Ruth believed Coolidge was reluctant "to push Deneen too far."[32] She had not won, but she was learning.

Ruth McCormick was quiet throughout the spring of 1927, so much so that a Chicago reporter described her in May as a "woman of wealth and political capacity who follows the footsteps of Cincinnatus. Of course, Mrs. McCormick has her hand on a stanchion and not on a plow." But by June she was again considering the governorship. Following a meeting with Coolidge at the White House to discuss the political situation in Illinois, she declared to the press that there would be "no harmony among Illinois politicians until Governor Len Small has been defeated—but Governor Small will be defeated in the primaries—you can quote me." She was quickly asked if she were going to be a candidate for the governorship, to which she replied that it was a question she was considering. She was antagonistic toward Small who had backed Deneen against

Medill in 1924, but, more importantly, she opposed a man who had been convicted of using illegally one million dollars of the state's money. "He has got to get out," she said, "if I have to throw him out myself," and many people again encouraged her to run. A school principal wrote, "About the only good thing I have seen in the papers since Lindbergh landed in Paris is the report that you might be Governor of Illinois . . . I'm not strong for women governors but . . . I think you are the man for the job." She asked male friends to sound out their business colleagues on the subject of her candidacy. She was "particularly anxious" to know reasons why men would be unwilling to support her, other than because of her "handicap of being a woman." She wrote Alice Longworth that the politicians were "flustered" by her persistence and complained that a speech of hers in front of four hundred women in Champaign had been reported on the society pages. She begged Alice to come for a visit: "I need your advice as you will see things more clearly than I."[33]

Ultimately Ruth was deterred, not because she was a woman, but because Small was backed by the powerful Mayor William Hale Thompson, yclept "Big Bill the Builder." Thompson, defeated by Medill in the 1918 Senate primary, had been elected mayor of Chicago in April 1927, prompting this from *Time* magazine:

> The majority who voted for Thompson are not intelligent, free, self-governing citizens of a republic. They are suckers. They are not the only suckers in the land, but at the moment they are the most conspicuous ones.

In September, when it became clear that Thompson was supporting Small, Ruth concluded that "It would be nothing short of slaughter" to run as governor against the two of them. "I know how discouraging this must sound," she wrote one supporter, "and you will well believe it is as discouraging to me as to anyone else. But I know the practical side of politics, and I appreciate its futility." She was asked to consider a run for the Senate but felt the time was not yet come for a woman, especially for one who would "step from the ranks of plain citizens."[34] Both the governorship and the Senate were beyond her reach.

Ruth finally decided she would have the best chance against the Thompson-Small combination as a candidate for representative-at-large for Congress. One of the incumbents, Henry Rathbone, was considered vulnerable because he had supported another candidate against Thompson for mayor. Ruth admitted:

> I am getting support not because I am so popular as a candidate but because no one wants to be Congressman-at-Large, and everyone thinks

Rathbone a rather limp citizen. So I am not allowing my head to be turned about my popularity, but I think this is a good chance for me to break in. [35]

She intended to announce her decision in mid-October. In September, she went to Washington to put the children in school and settle her mother-in-law for the winter, after which she planned to return to Chicago to give her candidacy more serious consideration. The first night in Washington, however, a good friend who was a reporter for the New York *Herald Tribune* called to say he had already heard she was running and his paper wanted an interview.

"Confidentially," she told him, "the rumor has some foundation in fact, but for publication, I am not at home." He informed her that he would have to print the story because the *Washington Post* had it, and he didn't want to give them a scoop. So she agreed that if he would wait twenty-four hours, she would make a statement. "I sat down to write a statement," she later said.

I have written a great many statements for other candidates, and could think of many reasons why those candidates should run, but after chewing off the end of my pencil and pondering long and hard I could not think of any reason why I should run for office, or why anyone should vote for me . . . In the small hours of the night I gave it up and went to bed and slept, and I had an awful nightmare. When I waked up in the morning I decided that nothing on earth would induce me to do it. But as soon as I had drunk a cup of coffee, there were reporters, and I decided quite definitely to take the plunge, because I recognized, as an old hack Politician—having run the publicity department of many campaigns— suffrage and actual politics—that I could no longer be rumored about. I had more or less become a perennial candidate for all offices that happened to be vacant at the moment. It had been rumored that I aspired to everything from dog-catcher to Governor of Illinois.

She had worked for years, she realized, preparing herself to be of "some greater service" and whether she had prepared herself to be of greater service or not, "the people of Illinois" would decide for her in April. [36]

In her announcement Ruth declared "I choose to run," parodying Coolidge's succinct speech of the month before when he announced he did not chose to run again as president. She was running for the Republican nomination for congressman-at-large from Illinois in the April primary of 1928, in which there were two at-large seats from Illinois. The nomination would go to the two aspirants having the largest number of votes, and at the least, she would be running against the incumbents,

Rathbone and Richard Yates. The primary contest, according to the *New York Times*, promised to be "the liveliest kind of a three-cornered race," since Republican nominations for seats-at-large were, as a rule in Illinois, equivalent to election.[37]

Although she planned to be her own campaign manager, Ruth put Jim Snyder in charge of the "men's division." This was a pretty reversal of the usual practice for a male candidate to have a women's division. In fact, Ruth had never had a man on her political staff before this time. But she had her stalwarts as well; Anne Forsyth, Helen Bennett, and Katharine ("Sis") Hamill were part of a small group who immediately went to work preparing a mailing list, the largest political mailing list ever to have been assembled in Illinois. When the time came for county chairmen to be appointed, there were more than two hundred thousand names, and the chairmen were amazed to be presented with a list of several hundred people—in some cases a thousand or more—in their counties who were willing to go to work. In the absence of reliable polls, Ruth sent out stamped, self-addressed envelopes with her first mailing, to ask for reactions to her candidacy. Many were against her; typical was the response: "Public sentiment in this city is against women holding office." A few criticized her for campaigning too early in a "country community," where, at that season of the year, people were too busy for "political talk." The farmer, she was told, only "talks when he is idle." Ruth answered many of the letters personally, believing that a personal letter campaign was more effective than broadcasting pamphlets and literature.[38]

Ruth looked for support wherever she could. Somewhat surprisingly, Mayor Thompson came out for her; it was thought he was trying to mend his political fences by seeking the backing of the "better element" she represented. To those who wrote to criticize her on this issue, she responded that she had not sought Thompson's endorsement, and she was politically free. She quickly pointed out that the popular Vice-President Charles Dawes was also supporting her. She told Small supporters that voting for Small was no reason not to vote for her, and she told Rathbone supporters that they could vote for both of them, since two at-large representatives were to be elected.[39]

The next order of business was to undertake a speaking tour, the first ever on her own behalf. Before each speech, she mailed letters to people in the area, stating that she would be holding a meeting at a certain time and place to talk about her candidacy, adding to each letter: "Mrs. McCormick hopes you will be present, as she would like to discuss her candidacy with you." All went well for the first few meetings. Then one day a rugged-looking gentleman approached her after an overflow meeting, introduced himself, and announced: "You said you wanted to discuss your candidacy with me. Just what did you want to say?" Nonplussed for only a moment, Ruth quickly replied that she was very glad to talk to him, because she understood that his precinct had not made a good showing in the last election. He assured her the situation would be remedied. After he left, Ruth turned to Jim Snyder standing beside her and said, "Jim, we'll have to take that sentence out of those letters. I'll surely slip up some time." But it was not taken out. Afterward she was prepared.[40]

As she had anticipated in her diary, her political activity did not come without a price. When Ruth began her campaign in the fall of 1927, Bazy, six, and Johnny, eleven, were left in school in Washington, while fourteen-year-old Triny had gone to boarding school in Aiken, South Carolina. As Ruth became an important national political figure, her family felt the consequences. Bazy, as the youngest, was the most affected, and had mixed feelings about her mother's career:

> In spite of her tremendous dedication to politics—and she was a prodigious workhorse, paid a lot of attention to detail, which means a lot of time—she was very cognizant of the one-to-one relationship with her children, and being with them . . . I never had the feeling I was nanny-raised. Of course, with Father dying so young, I kind of grew up with Sam as a mother and Mother as a father. It was more that kind of relationship.

Such a relationship had its drawbacks: "I was low-man on the totem pole. [I saw her so little] I was almost afraid of her. I didn't feel comfortable with her until I was about twelve."[41] Ruth had been less busy when Triny was little, leaving her with little sense of competition from Ruth's career, but now Triny was fourteen and rebellious. One afternoon she and her mother were having a passionate argument in the library. Triny stormed out, and her mother called her "a most unsatisfactory child!" After Triny had run upstairs, Bazy crept into the library and found her mother sitting at the desk with her face in her hands. The little girl crawled into her mother's lap, patted her cheek, and said, "I am your satisfactory child."[42] Of course, Ruth was touched, and often called Bazy the "Satisfactory Child," which did nothing to improve the tensions between children competing for an increasingly small amount of their mother's time.

Johnny, at eleven, an age when he needed neither cuddling nor guid-
ance, was probably least affected. He seems to have been rather detached
and amused. "There goes Mother, talking politics and cows," he observed
to a visitor at the farm. On another occasion, he allowed little Bazy to
drag him indoors to wash and change, when she complained that his
appearance would lose their mother votes. On the other hand, he wistfully signed his letters to his mother, "I love you more than you love
me." Ruth had known that she might face criticism for having a career
while she had young children at home, but she always maintained that
"any intelligent and healthy woman who will plan properly and work
hard" could manage. She claimed to "spend more actual time with my
children than any other mother I know does with hers."[43] She did not
know the phrase "quality time," but she certainly understood the concept.

In general, Ruth was a permissive mother. "I have no time to nag
them. When we're together we enjoy each other," she said. "We were
allowed to do almost anything," said Triny. "I had to invent rules to tell
the other girls, so they wouldn't know how much freedom I had." Ruth
put up with an amazing number of pranks, particularly from Johnny. The
one thing Ruth would not tolerate was boredom. If a child complained
there was nothing to do, she was sternly sent off to meditate. Ruth might
leave a child "meditating" two or three hours.[44]

Young people found Ruth irresistible. One of Triny's friends, Janet
White, often dropped by for afternoon tea: "She made it a real ritual,
those slender hands spooning tea into the pot, adding water." Moreover,
she had a personal touch:

"She really gave you her attention. It doesn't sound like anything, but
it is, particularly from a busy woman . . . She was always saying, 'What
are you planning to do? What are your real interests?' I would say, 'I
don't know what I'm going to do. I'm going to try everything.' And she
would say, 'No, don't do that. Get your mind set, prepare yourself edu-
cationally. Realize you don't have as much time as you think you do. Be
serious about your life,' . . . Not many adults took sixteen-year-old girls
seriously. My stepfather, whom I adored, told me firmly, 'The best thing
a woman can do is marry an interesting, attractive man.'"[45]

Ruth McCormick did not merely tell such young people to dedicate
themselves to a calling, she showed them how it was done. She believed
that her whole life up to that point had been an apprenticeship preparing
her to be a politician and began to talk of following in her father's
footsteps. Ruth supported issues such as freedom from entangling alliances
and progressive reforms for the working conditions of women and chil-

dren, but it can be argued that they were less important to her than the art of politics. Her main goal was to bring women into the political process, both by organizing them into groups that would have political power and by motivating them to use it. And of course she hoped that her example as an ambitious, practical politician would inspire others to enter politics themselves.

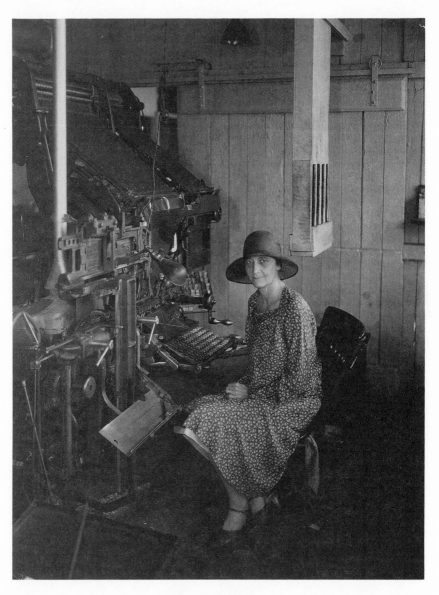

Ruth McCormick at *Rockford Register-Republic*.

Ruth McCormick (right of center) with Irene McCoy Gaines to her right, 1929. Courtesy of the Chicago Historical Society.

Martha Connole, 1925.

Charles Gates
Dawes, 1920s.

Ruth McCormick at Rock River Farm, 1920s.

Ruth with Johnny, Bazy, and Triny, Union Station, Washington, D.C., April 1930.

Ruth McCormick at Nye Hearing, 1930.

Conceding defeat: Ruth McCormick with Jim Snyder, November 1930.

Ruth McCormick and Albert Simms at their wedding, 1932.

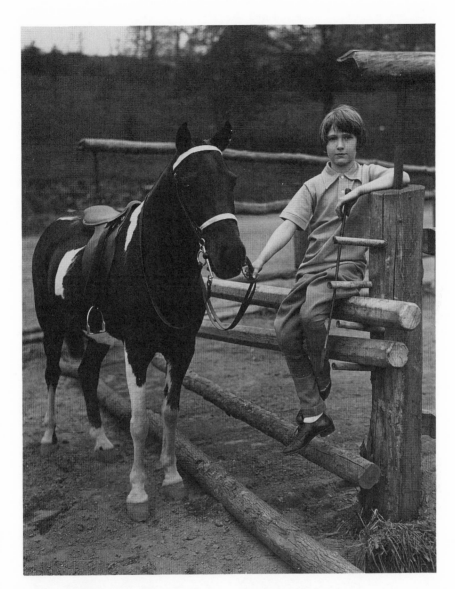

Bazy, c. 1929.

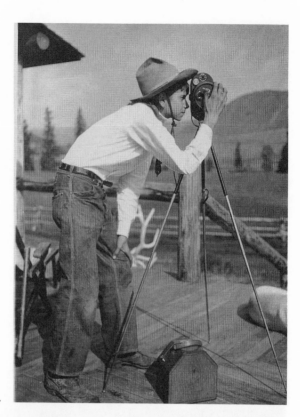

Johnny, c. 1930.

Triny (l.) and Bazy with Sam, 1930s.

Sandia School. Laura Gilpin photograph from Sandia School catalog.

Ruth Simms and
Alice Longworth,
Republican
Convention, 1936.

Johnny.

Ruth at Dewey Headquarters, 1940.

(l. to r.) Triny, Ruth, Bazy. Bazy's wedding to Peter Miller, 1941.

Courtie Barnes, Ruth, Peter Miller.

Ruth and Charlie Dawes, 1940s.

Ruth Hanna McCormick Simms.

7
Congresswoman-at-Large: 1928–1929

"NOBODY ASKED ME TO RUN"

Ruth McCormick opened her campaign in January 1928 with a unique statement:

> Usually when a candidate announces his candidacy, we read in the paper that owing to the demand of his constituency and the pressure of his friends, he has reluctantly agreed to make this great sacrifice and run for office. In all candor and honesty I must say that nobody asked me to run. I have had no demand upon me from constituents, friends, enemies, neighbors and family, and, as far as I know, nobody wants me to run. But I hope at the end of the campaign that I am going to find a sufficient number of people who think I ought to run.

As always, she emphasized her training and experience. "I served as a daughter of a United States Senator for four years. I served as the wife of a United States Senator for six years, as the wife of a Congressman two years: [I] worked in the office and read mail." She was under no illusions as to the nature of the job: "In my husband's term of six years we received jointly about 250 letters of commendation, and all the rest of the mail, which averaged anywhere from 200 to 700 letters a day, was criticism, condemnation or appeals for jobs."[1]

Ruth began her campaign with an intensive downstate tour. ("Downstate" in Illinois meant, and still means, anything beyond Chicago and its immediate environs.) In a little over two months she planned to visit all 102 counties in Illinois. This meant making half a dozen speeches a day in half a dozen different towns and spending each night in a new hotel. "When I first started in campaigning I thought it was hard work," she admitted, "but now that I have learned . . . that every train in southern Illinois either stops or starts at four o'clock in the morning, the rest seems easy." She always sprang out of her automobile, never waiting to be handed out with dignity.[2]

When Ruth arrived in a town, she usually took a few minutes to rest. She still had a tendency to get nervous, and she needed to focus on what she wanted to say. It was a rule with her never to dine or stay with friends, lest people think her snobbish or playing favorites. As a speaker, she had good rapport with her audience. She never talked down to them, but she never pretended to be other than who she was. She would wear plain clothes but also her best string of pearls or her diamond brooch in the poorest mining town. She was pleased when she learned of a remark made by a housewife after a small-town meeting downstate: "She's wonderful. We were all a little afraid to meet her. We thought that with her position and her money she would act important. But she was just as common as the rest of us."[3]

When friends complained of the crowds calling her "Ruth," she responded, "It did not cheapen me but brought me closer to the people I proposed to serve." Some even called her "Babe" Ruth. She was popular with the farmers, not only because she understood farming and could milk a cow, but also because she knew their humor. "They are a hard bunch to get a laugh out of," said Bazy, who became a cattle rancher herself, yet she recalled that her mother could "keep them laughing for ten minutes straight." On the other hand, unlike most politicians, Ruth never could remember anyone's name, and developed a technique of mumbling to cover up. She had tried using word-association to improve her memory but quit after the disastrous occasion when she called Mrs. Potts, her dressmaker, Mrs. Chambers. Ruth's personality, her big grin and hearty laugh, her facility for quick conversation won over people so that they failed to notice whether she learned their name or not.

While Ruth was touring downstate with Sis Hamill, Jim Snyder, back at headquarters, was in charge of a growing number of women. "I have had one ———— of a time with the coeds," he moaned to a friend. "I am sure that you appreciate the proposition that I have been up against in this campaign with 16 women in this office and no one to swear at!"[4] It was an unconventional campaign all around.

Ruth's main issues were aid for agriculture, support of Prohibition, a belief that war could be outlawed by treaty, but support for "preparedness." As a farmer, she supported the McNary-Haugen Bill, designed to achieve parity for the farmers with other industries protected by a tariff. Farm products had brought high prices during the war, causing land prices to rise accordingly, and many farms were mortgaged. During the 1920s, however, surplus grain and other commodities led to depressed prices; the farmers were caught in the bind between high mortgages and low prices. The bill would create a public corporation to buy wheat at a fixed cost before selling it overseas at the low world price. Whatever the bill's merits, however, the farmers' organizations were fragmented, businessmen were opposed, and everyone else was uninterested. The bill had failed to pass the House in 1924. Ruth made a special study of the farm issue, and was asked by other candidates, not only in Illinois, but also in Wisconsin, Indiana, and Minnesota, to speak on the problem.[5]

Prohibition, she believed, was a mistake, but it was the law, and the government "either ought to enforce it or repeal it." Personally, she was a Dry; after life with Medill, she did not drink at all. Yet she was constantly forced to defend her position, more so, she thought, than her male opponents. "I wonder why women are so much harder on another woman . . . ?" she mused. International affairs continued to be an important issue. By 1928 Germany had pulled out of the League of Nations and begun secretly to rearm. The League of Nations was dissolving, as Japan and Italy also withdrew when their expansionist plans were condemned.[6] Ruth supported a proposed treaty to outlaw war, which later that year became the Kellogg-Briand Peace Pact. Neither it nor the League proved of much use.

Although she made her views known on a variety of topics, Ruth's was essentially a personal campaign. She deliberately downplayed the issues, since the new Congress ordinarily would not convene until December 1929, two years after her campaign opened, and she believed the issues were bound to change over a two-year period. Ruth's main support came from the many local women's Republican clubs she had helped to organize in almost every county. Ruth was still their leader. Helen Bennett admired her "ineffable quality of leadership . . . what kept them working on even in between campaigns and in dull days . . ." Many people would work for her who wouldn't work for anyone else, and different sorts of people would work together for her sake.[7]

However, Ruth relied not only on the issues and on her personality to carry the campaign, but on meticulous organization. As a woman candidate, she knew she could leave no stone unturned. Her contacts cut across many strata: she was a dirt farmer and a society leader, in contact simultaneously with labor and business leaders. Anne Forsyth added to these contacts by organizing an extensive volunteer organization. Whenever a woman joined, she was sent three new pledge cards to recruit more volunteers. (Ruth's staff were dismayed to discover that if they mailed a letter to a woman addressing her by her Christian name instead of by her husband's name—Mrs. Mary Smith instead of Mrs. Otis Smith—the post office would not deliver the mail.) In three months they had built up a formidable machine. Ruth was sometimes criticized for using outmoded techniques learned from her father, but she didn't take such criticism seriously, believing that delegates and votes were still necessary for success.[8]

Helen Bennett reported that during the campaign Ruth kept office hours as rigidly as any employee. She enlisted people in whom she had confidence, then paid them the compliment of leaving them alone. One politician told Medill's cousin, Joe Patterson, by then in New York as publisher of the *Daily News*, "Ruth McCormick is working like mad to win an election she couldn't lose if she tried." Perhaps her appetite for all this activity sprang from feeling she had come into her own at last: "For thirty years I've been campaigning, but it's the first time I've carried the political football down the field and could look over my shoulder to see anything but a vacant field."[9]

And she wanted to win in her own right; she did not want to run as a "woman's candidate." "I am not a feminist," she wrote in an article. "It would be just as ridiculous for me to appeal to the voters of my state on the ground that I am a woman as on the ground that I have dark eyes . . ." In the twenties Ruth was part of the middle generation of women; older suffragists tended to be strident and bitter toward men, while the younger women were bored with the whole issue and took their political rights for granted. Women like Ruth and Elizabeth Fraser, a delegate to the 1920 Republican Convention, wanted to work with, instead of against, the men and were "not afraid to be charming."[10]

Ruth also believed it was politically unwise for women to be "single issue" oriented; politics were more complex. She did, however, want to inspire women to greater participation, as voters and as candidates. She deplored the failure of women to exercise the right of franchise (only 40 percent had used the ballot in the last election). But she and her staff were realistic about what they could expect women to do. "I find women are still afraid of doing any actual political work," Anne Forsyth wrote in January, "but they can all talk, and all we need in the end is enough people on election day . . . I believe a word of mouth campaign is of utmost value, and all that is necessary in this case."[11] Ruth wanted to achieve two things as a woman candidate. She believed it would impress people if a woman were elected to a statewide office, and that more women would thereby be encouraged to run. And she believed men politicians would be impressed by the strength of the women's votes and

could be influenced to reform. She placed responsibility for their participation squarely on the women:

> The presence of so few women in active politics is due not so much to
> men's great reluctance to admit them as to women's great indifference
> to being admitted. Too many women mouth the phrase 'going into politics'
> as if it were either dangerous or corrupt. Yet women cannot separate
> politics from civic life and expect to advance that civic life.

Theoretically, she believed that women were "better politicians than
men," but in "practice and experience" they were far behind due to the
short time women had been enfranchised. She concluded that "if the
theory of women and the experience of men could be amalgamated into
one great working force, there is nothing that could not be accomplished
toward better political conditions." She thought the main thing women
had to learn was that:

> they have to support others in order to get support for their own candidate.
> [Women] seem to think they should get everything for nothing, and do
> not realize politics is just as human as any other social relationship and
> operates in very much the same way. [12]

Ruth McCormick was surprised by the vehemence of resistance to her
candidacy because she was a woman. A typical letter ran: "I would not
think of voting for a woman for Congressman-at-Large any more than
to vote for one of my cows for such a responsible office." Ruth noted
that even her "very best friends were reluctant to back a woman candidate
. . . on the grounds that 'she hadn't a chance in this state.'" The Democratic National Committeeman, George E. Brennan, stated flatly, "Men
won't vote for a woman." Ruth tried to reassure them, "Party leaders and
outstanding businessmen have agreed women . . . haven't used all their
efforts to help the status of women to the neglect of the other sex, as
many had predicted."

She was able to persuade a number of men to endorse her, however.
Her old friend Charlie Dawes, now Vice-President, had come out for
her in November 1927. Although Ruth's rival, Rathbone, had a good
record on labor, by January labor leaders had come out for her on the
strength of the work she had done with Medill for the Child Labor
Amendment, and in February Ruth called at the White House to draw
attention to bad conditions among miners in the soft coal fields. She
continued to remind the voters they would vote for two representatives-
at-large. Ruth, like Medill, was always popular among the African-American voters on the South Side of Chicago, so much so that at the

beginning of her campaign, an imposter was arrested for using the name of Ruth Hanna McCormick to collect money fraudulently from women residents of his district. Foreign language newspaper editors endorsed her unanimously, the first time they had ever agreed on a candidate.[13]

Her old Progressive associate, Harold Ickes, however, refused to endorse her, not because she was a woman, but because he believed she was no longer progressive. He wrote, "On account of old associations and for personal reasons I sincerely wish that I might be able to do so." But he said he had found her "either eloquently silent" or "actively supporting" candidates that in her heart she must have known she should not have supported. He particularly criticized her for not having spoken out against Thompson:

> The fair assumption is that not only Mayor Thompson, but his political allies, including Governor Len Small, are behind you . . . I commend to your prayerful consideration the parable of the man with the three talents.[14]

Ickes was making reference to the main feature of the 1928 Illinois primary, which had little to do with Ruth McCormick's candidacy. The two main factions of the Republican Party were each intent on gaining control of the state machine. In power was the Thompson-Small-Crowe organization. Mayor William Hale "Big Bill" Thompson was not running that year, but wanted to keep power as the Republican leader through the election of key ward committeemen in Chicago. Governor Len Small, whom Ruth had fought for years, was being opposed by the Illinois Secretary of State, Lou Emmerson, a big, capable, and immensely popular man. State's Attorney Robert E. Crowe was opposed by Circuit Court Judge John A. Swanson, who accused Crowe of having been unable or unwilling to control organized crime, to which Crowe cynically replied, "When there was nobody on earth except Adam and Eve and Cain and Abel, the murder rate was higher than now." Frank Smith was running for the Senate once again, opposed by State Senator Otis F. Glenn. Senator Charles Deneen, who had tried with no effect to get the Senate to seat Smith two years earlier, was now opposed to Smith and the Thompson-Small machine that was supporting him. These Byzantine Republican alliances were constantly shifting, and Thompson, Small, Crowe, and Smith had been on opposite sides from each other, and in various combinations, on other occasions.[15] It is important to remember that Ruth McCormick was not just breaking into politics but was breaking into Illinois politics, notorious for being the roughest in the country.

As the election approached, different political organizations each printed specimen ballots that were distributed throughout the state. This "advance ballot" marking provided some interesting insights into the tangled web of Republican politics. Thompson, though supporting Small (who opposed and was opposed by Ruth McCormick), had declared for Ruth at the beginning of the campaign. Just before the election, however, his organization distributed sample ballots on which her name was not marked. Bobby Crowe, the most controversial figure in the campaign, although supported by the Thompson organization, nevertheless marked his sample ballot for the woman candidate. Small also marked his sample ballots for her, apparently believing he would need her help in November if he were to win the nomination. His opponent, Emmerson, also had her name marked on his ballots but, to everyone's surprise, Senator Deneen did not. Apparently neither the Thompson nor the Deneen faction felt comfortable with Mrs. McCormick's "anti-machine" politics. It was also said that Deneen's opposition was due to his fear that if she were elected to Congress she would try to take the nomination for the Senate from Senator Deneen in 1930 (which, in fact, she did). Adding to the confusion, the law had just been changed to permit a voter to call for either party ballot without losing his standing in his own party. Many Democrats were being urged to vote for Ruth McCormick.[16]

True to the cinema stereotype, politics in Chicago were often marked by violence. Two weeks before the primary election, on March 26, 1928, bombs exploded in the homes of Senator Deneen, then absent in Washington, and of Judge Swanson, who narrowly escaped injury or death. On the same night, a Republican candidate for ward committeeman, said to belong to the same faction, was assassinated with sawed-off shotguns, and a witness was murdered in his bedroom the following night. One of Ruth's supporters, Mrs. Eleanor Whiting, received threats that her home would be blown up next if she did not cease her political activities. Harold Gosnell, analyzing the Chicago political scene of this period, called it the "Pineapple Primary," in reference to the grenades. Violence produced a strong public reaction that aided the efforts of the Deneen-Emmerson-Swanson-Glenn faction, including Ruth. Heavy increases in voter registration, due to concern over crime and terrorism, were reported.[17]

Meanwhile, Ruth McCormick had finished her marathon sixteen thousand-mile downstate tour. Her male colleagues had been impressed with her physical stamina. At late night downstate mass-meetings, gubernatorial candidate Lou Emmerson would remark to the audience that the hour was late and the speakers all tired out. Glancing at the woman candidate, sitting demurely on the speaker's platform, he was fond of adding: "You'd be fagged out too, if you had been trying to keep up with Ruth all day." Her reporter friend Bill Hard wrote, "She sometimes seems thin and worn; but the flame inside her is always burning at top intensity."

Ruth was hitting her stride as a speaker. She would stand up on the platform, hands shoved into the pockets of her coat, lean forward eagerly, and speak without notes. "You cannot make a political speech until you get on your feet before an audience," she explained. "I have never prepared a speech, but I am always preparing an infinite number of speeches." Women and men came to hear her speak in roughly equal numbers. Humorist Will Rogers observed: "She is not like other women who go into politics, and who get up and tell you about the 'woman's angle.' She tells you about the people's angle."

The day before the election, she predicted:

> I'm going to be elected. I know I am. I am confident because of large crowds that have been coming here and because so many that came, came back again and brought others with them. That means something—and I think it means election.[18]

April 10, Election Day, was not without bloodshed. A black attorney opposing the Thompson-Crowe candidate for committeeman was machine-gunned to death in the "bloody Twentieth" ward. There were also alleged kidnappings of election officials and beatings of party workers, despite eight thousand special watchers appointed to supplement five thousand police guarding the polls. After voting in Byron, Ruth McCormick drove back to Chicago to meet Triny and Alice Longworth, who were arriving together from Washington. Alice and Ruth had a long tradition, going back to the Bull Moose campaign of 1912, of waiting up together to hear election returns. Alice shunned elective office herself, insisting, "Ruth is an important public woman of affairs, and I am nothing but an onlooker," to which Ruth replied:

> Alice is a statesman and I am a politician . . . She has no patience for the drudgery of details, but she has wonderful intuition as to where this or that tendency in politics is going to carry us, has an uncanny certainty in predicting results, and she dearly loves a fight.

Ruth claimed that she

> wouldn't think of making any decision without first getting [Alice's] judgment . . . When Senator McCormick died my thought was to give up politics myself. Alice knew what I needed better than I did. She told me . . . that I must not get out of politics even temporarily, not even for a day. She was right about it.[19]

Ruth may have wanted to show she had support for her unusually ambitious decision, and Alice Longworth's political judgment was reputed to be nearly as sharp as her tongue.

By 1 A.M. April 11 unofficial returns showed Ruth McCormick running ahead of Henry Rathbone, the runner-up, in 100 out of 102 counties. Eventually, she polled 805,776 votes, leading Rathbone by 92,670. (Shortly after he was nominated, Congressman Rathbone died, and the Republican State Committee put Richard Yates, who had finished third, back on the ticket.) Ruth, splendid in a black brocade and velvet gown, a small black velvet hat, and shoulder bouquet, struggled valiantly to shake hands with hundreds of eager people. She was delighted with her victory and credited the women of the state who had worked so hard for six months, saying that her election marked "the greatest step forward by women politically that has yet been achieved . . ." But she was "particularly pleased" to have had the help of "large numbers of men political leaders who have supported my candidacy not because I am a woman but because they recognize my work for the party and state."[20]

The highest percentage of votes ever cast in a Republican primary had brought victory not only to Ruth but to the Deneen machine. Deneen had emphasized the respectable note in politics, and the questionable Small-Smith-Thompson-Crowe combination had suffered. Mayor Thompson was even defeated for ward committeeman, which would curb his ability to distribute patronage. Swanson, Emmerson, and Glenn won their offices, and Deneen gained sway over a big majority of the Illinois delegates to the Republican National Convention and was even mentioned as a "dark horse" presidential possibility in case of deadlock.[21]

Smiling radiantly, Ruth Hanna McCormick was featured on the cover of *Time* magazine the week of April 23, the first and only female politician to appear there until 1959, when Margaret Chase Smith and her opponent shared a cover celebrating the fortieth anniversary of the suffrage amendment. The report emphasized Ruth McCormick's knowledge of power politics; the caption under her photo read "She learned the law of the jungle." She was characterized as "a high-strung person of taste and refinement," who nevertheless had learned party regularity from her father: "When the pack can help you hunt, do not be squeamish about the pack."[22] Ruth McCormick would accept endorsements from the Cook County politicians, but she drew the line at endorsing them herself. Nevertheless, suggestions that she was beholden to them continued to plague her unfairly for years.

Ruth next turned to presidential politics and the Republican Convention in June. Ex-Governor Frank Lowden had specifically asked her to help him with his presidential campaign, but he remained ambivalent about his desire to seek the office. Early in 1927 he had encouraged his friend Clarence Buck to open a Chicago office to coordinate volunteer efforts for a campaign. The inexperienced Buck was hampered by a shortage of funds and the vagueness of his commission. Herbert Hoover, President Coolidge's Secretary of Commerce, had not declared his candidacy, either, but he had a large organization, a campaign fund, and a great deal of patronage to distribute. In Illinois Lowden had been a popular governor and was supported not only by the farmers but by business groups as well. So he was surprised that he was unable to get Eastern businessmen and professionals to support him. An attempt by Ruth McCormick to persuade Pennsylvania "boss" William S. Vare of Philadelphia to support Lowden came to naught. The McNary-Haugen farm bill had twice passed Congress, but had been vetoed both times by Coolidge, who denounced it as preferential class legislation. The Republicans wanted to run on the Coolidge record, but Lowden would only accept a platform that endorsed the farm bill or other farm relief. Ruth thought the farm issue a vital one and believed that Lowden would somehow be accommodated by the platform committee. She was planning to second his nomination.[23]

Ruth McCormick arrived early in Kansas City, where she and Alice Longworth shared a rented house. She worked tirelessly as Lowden's publicity director, buttonholing dozens of unpledged delegates, trying to persuade them that Lowden could attract more votes than his rivals. She was up night after night, calling all over the country, soliciting proxies and trying to corral all the anti-Hoover forces. Bill Hard, as a journalist, was grateful that she had put life into the dying anti-Hoover cause,

> by spreading across the tops of the front pages of all the newspapers her famous model statement of assertive triumph in the midst of imminent defeat 'HOOVER IS STOPPED.' She went down with verve which lost her nothing.[24]

Hoover's strength proved overwhelming; almost all of the contested delegates went to him. When the convention voted down a minority attempt to place the McNary-Haugen plank in the platform, Lowden abruptly withdrew. This hurt Ruth, who had turned down a place on the Credentials Committee because she had planned to make a seconding speech for Lowden and had felt that one position was all she was entitled to.[25]

Fortunately, Ruth had other interests at the convention besides Lowden. One was the election of a Republican National Committeewoman to fill the vacancy created by her own departure. Bertha Baur was Ruth's candidate, endorsed by the Women's Republican Clubs. Mrs. Baur was opposed by Lottie Holman O'Neill, a Deneen candidate. Ruth was able to compromise with Deneen, agreeing to support his candidate, Roy West, for National Committeeman in exchange for Deneen's support for Baur. Ruth was not the only woman active in the 1928 Convention. The Credentials Committee was headed by a woman, Mabel Walker Willebrandt of California, and two other women were scheduled to give seconding speeches. In addition, the Chairman of the National Council of the National Woman's Party was to go before the Resolutions Committee to ask for planks in favor of the Equal Rights Amendment.[26]

That summer, while Ruth was resting with her children at the Rock River Farm in Byron, she received a surprise visit from the editor of the nearby *Rockford Daily Republic*, T. B. "Barney" Thompson. Thompson had come to her for advice. The paper was nearly bankrupt and was about to be sold to a combination and disbanded. Ruth promptly offered to buy the paper (and was immediately on the phone to Alice Longworth, exclaiming: "What do you think I've done?"). The purchase of the paper was a typical impulsive and generous gesture, but as usual, she pursued the enterprise aggressively. The *Republic* was consolidated with the *Register Gazette and Morning Star* in 1930, and circulation increased by over 50 percent. In the early 1930s she added a radio station to the company. Ruth always insisted that the paper was independent, not an organ for her political views. And despite her inherited wealth, it always pleased her to be able to make money on her own.[27]

In the fall Ruth McCormick was back on the campaign trail, promoting Hoover by attacking his opponent, Governor Al Smith of New York. "As a potential friend of the farmer he has an unfortunate environment," she said with mock sympathy. "His associates know so little about Mid-West farm conditions, they think corn comes only in cans and bottles." In point of fact, Prohibition and Governor Smith's Roman Catholic religious preference far outweighed the farm problem as campaign issues. Ruth toured southern Illinois on her own behalf somewhat less extensively during her fall campaign, but altogether she covered more than thirty-four thousand miles, averaging two to three hundred miles a day, usually by automobile, "in all kinds of weather, mostly bad."[28]

On November 6 there was a voter turnout of nearly 70 percent, due to the intensity of the issues. Ruth won an impressive victory, with a total of 1,711,651 votes. Only Hoover received more votes in the state of Illinois. She had been elected by the largest constituency ever rep-

resented by a woman and was the first woman congressman from Illinois.
But in her victory statement she insisted she was not going to Washington
as a woman's candidate.

> No doubt it was the women who gave me my chance in the primary . . .
> Once I began campaigning and men learned I could discuss the McNary-
> Haugen Bill and such legislation I was amazed and gratified at the support
> I received from them. Don't please refer to me as a woman's candidate.
> I am going to Congress as a Representative-at-Large from Illinois. In that
> capacity I represent all the people—industrial, manufacturing, agricul-
> tural and all. [29]

The day after her election, instead of resting after the strenuous campaign, Ruth prepared to leave for the Capitol because she had "so much
to learn":

> Monday morning I am opening my office in downtown Washington D.C.
> The procedure in the Senate is as familiar to me as to any Senator on
> the floor. I was there with my father and after for six years with Medill.
> But the House rules are all new to me. I must learn them in anticipation
> of the special session which will undoubtedly be called March 4. I want
> to be up to my job.

She rented an office suite of three rooms in the Labor Building and
immediately began attending to constituent requests. She mailed out ten
thousand Christmas cards, including even the Small workers on her list.
Already she was receiving queries about her intention to run for the
Senate. [30] For the first woman elected state-wide to a national office, this
was a real possibility.

"NO FAVORS AND NO BUNK"

Ruth McCormick was first, last, and always a politician. Her two years
as a legislator were less an occasion to make laws than an opportunity
to do what she did best—campaign. This was a fortuitous talent; for even
before she was called to a special session of the Seventy-First Congress
in April 1929, Ruth was challenged by a rival woman politician, Lottie
Holman O'Neill from the Chicago suburb of Downer's Grove. O'Neill
had been the first woman State Representative in Illinois, who by 1929
was serving her fourth term. O'Neill stridently issued a call to the "rank
and file of Republican women" to rally against the "bossism" of Mark
Hanna's daughter and dramatically resigned in protest from her position

as vice-president of the Illinois Republican Women's Clubs, which by then boasted about 350,000 members.

Her resentment of Ruth McCormick first arose when the speaker of the Illinois legislature, David E. Shanahan, had refused to name O'Neill Chairman of the House Committee on Education, offering her instead one of three lesser chairmanships. In what was meant to be a conciliatory gesture, newly elected Governor Lou Emmerson obtained for her the Chairmanship of the Waterways Committee. But she was not to be mollified. "I'll take no chairmanship at all," she told Shanahan and Emmerson.

> The hand of Ruth Hanna McCormick has balked me at every possible turn. Not only me but every other woman in the Party with leadership possibilities. Her personal ambition for power brooks no interference. She has no personal feeling against me, but she is Mark Hanna's daughter, with his desire to be boss.

Bill Hard defended Ruth McCormick from the charge of "bossism," observing that a woman with any organization at all was open to that charge: "Women have been expected to belong to no settled system . . . or to be faithful . . . members of machines [bossed by men]."[31]

O'Neill's original grievance seems to have been at Ruth's support of Bertha Baur as National Republican Committeewoman at the Republican Convention in Kansas City. Lottie O'Neill apparently had wanted the office herself; publicly, she objected to Baur on the grounds that the "Committee was dry and Mrs. Baur had campaigned on a beer wagon." Baur, in turn, insisted, "No wet and dry issue was involved. Mrs. O'Neill was my only opponent in the race . . ."

O'Neill accused Ruth McCormick of sending one of her deputies into Du Page County with a "promised list of patronage," in order to have her way. Ruth denied she had tried to prevent O'Neill's appointment as Chairman of the Education Committee. Ruth at that time was in Battle Creek, Michigan, for ten days, probably at the Kellogg Foundation where she occasionally went to rest and recuperate on their high-energy diet, and from there she issued a statement saying that she was unaware that O'Neill had sought the chairmanship.

> I regret that she was not appointed. I believe she would ably meet the requirements. I have no lieutenants working in Du Page County with a 'promised list of patronage.' As a congressman-elect, I have no patronage to offer. After I take my seat as congressman, I'll have no patronage to offer. I believe that Mrs. O'Neill is misinformed on all points raised in the interviews except the accusation that I am Mark Hanna's daughter.

Speaker Shanahan, in turn, was miffed by the implication that he could have been influenced in his decision:

> I have served in the House more than thirty-four years, have been elected Speaker at five sessions, and this is the first time I was ever accused in the press by any member of having been influenced by any public official to deprive a member of a chairmanship. [32]

In resigning, O'Neill claimed the Women's Republican Clubs had become an instrument for "carrying out the political aims of Mrs. Ruth Hanna McCormick" instead of working for "women's advancement generally." She had not informed the president of the Illinois Republican Women's Clubs, Emily Dean, of her resignation; Dean had learned about it in the press. Dean suggested that O'Neill had been "incited" by "some man or men . . . merely to create ill feeling among women legislators, and thus prevent them functioning as smoothly in their office as men." She also remarked that the "Deneen faction" of the club had always caused "a certain amount of friction," even though O'Neill had earlier denied any connection with Deneen. Finally, President Dean downplayed the importance of O'Neill's action, saying that it seemed as if Mrs. O'Neill was "having a nice little fight all to herself." But Lottie Holman O'Neill had made one point which Ruth ignored to her peril:

> The large sums of money expended by Mrs. McCormick in the recent campaign . . . [constitute] a barrier to representative government . . . it tends to eliminate from the field of candidates those men and women who have not large means at their disposal . . .

By June, she had chartered the "Lottie Holman O'Neill Association." Her fight against Ruth Hanna McCormick was far from over. [33]

Herbert Hoover was inaugurated on March 4, 1929, and declared that the gravest danger facing the American people was "disregard and disobedience of the law." He also hoped a way could be found for America to take her place on the World Court. Little emphasis was given to the issue of the economy, which was already spinning upward, out of control. In what, in retrospect, is a masterpiece of understatement, he did see a need to "establish more firmly the stability and security of business and employment." He then called for Congress to meet on April 15, primarily to consider the farm problem and to revise the tariff. [34]

There were three new women in the Seventy-First Congress, all, coincidentally, named Ruth. Ruth Baker Pratt from New York City, another Republican, was a member of the New York City Board of Aldermen, who had defeated a powerful rival in the primary. Ruth Bryan Owen, whose father, William Jennings Bryan, had opposed William McKinley in Mark Hanna's day, was selected from Florida as a Democrat. The *New York Times Magazine* observed that Ruth Hanna McCormick, whose "popularity is exceeded, if at all, only by that of Ruth Bryan Owen," entered the House "arm-in-arm" with Owen to be sworn in. Seven of the eight women in Congress were present on April 15, opening day (Ruth Baker Pratt was absent on account of illness), and they attracted a great deal of notice from the galleries. [35]

The three "Ruths" joined four other Congresswomen who had been re-elected: Mrs. Edith Nourse Rogers (R-MA); Mrs. Florence P. Kahn (R-CA); Mrs. Katherine Langley (R-KY); and Mrs. Mary T. Norton (D-NJ). All but Norton were widows of former congressmen. Mrs. Pearl Peden Oldfield (D-AR) had been elected in January 1929 to succeed her husband, who had suddenly died. However, she soon declared that "under no circumstances" would she return to Congress after her term expired, but wished to go back "to the sphere in which she believe[d] woman belongs—her home." Ruth McCormick was the only woman elected to represent an entire state; Illinois at that time had a population of over seven million. 1928 was the high point of women's representation in congress. The seven elected congresswomen were joined on the state level by 119 elected representatives and 12 state senators. [36]

A year later, the editorial correspondent of the *New York Times* wrote: "[The women in Congress] attend their duties in a practical way and never take part in debate unless that have something worthwhile to say." Ruth McCormick was an extreme example of that: she never spoke on the floor of the House at all, perhaps following the example of her father who had kept a very low profile during the first year or two he was in the Senate. Congressman McCormick was assigned to the Committee on Naval Affairs, of which an Illinois colleague, Fred Britten, was chairman. This was an important committee assignment, so she was not eligible for appointment to any other committee. The chairman informed her she would be known simply as "McCormick," to make her "one of us," and he appointed her to the subcommittee on "yards and books and the Naval Academy," with the provision that she "not appoint any girls to the Academy." She coolly responded, "You certainly are having a lot of fun with me, aren't you?" [37]

Jim Snyder reported to the Rockford newspaper publisher Barney Thompson, "Mrs. McCormick made a fine impression on her first day as Congressman. I expect the routine and the regular schedule of hours will irk her before long, but she is all enthusiasm right now." It was a

good thing, for Speaker Longworth was impatient to get legislation moving. After two weeks, Ruth remarked:

> In all the years that I sat in the gallery of the House, and as familiar as
> I thought I was with its proceedings, I have learned more in my first two
> weeks on the floor than I learned in all those years in the gallery. This
> proves our point, that if women could get on the inside, we could con-
> tribute something to the efficiency of government. [38]

On her first day in the House of Representatives, Ruth McCormick met
a colleague from New Mexico, Albert Gallatin Simms. The son of a
Confederate soldier from Arkansas, Simms had been a Southern Democrat until 1928, when he became a Republican to support Hoover against
Smith. (When he returned to Arkansas with a Congressional delegation,
his mother begged him, "Please, son, don't tell them you're a Republican,
they won't understand.") Simms had procured one of the highly desirable
aisle seats before Congress had opened. Representative McCormick was
seated next to him. On her other side was a gentleman who chewed
tobacco, constantly leaning over Ruth and Albert to use the spittoon.
Albert gallantly gave up his aisle seat to the tobacco-chewer, sparing
Ruth much inconvenience. [39] In addition, Albert was handsome and
charming, and Ruth found herself attracted to him.

Primarily, though, she was there to work. The House passed a bill
creating a Farm Board to aid the farmers' own cooperative associations.
These organizations would help farmers avoid overproducing certain commodities and help them hold surpluses until prices could rise. The day
after the bill had passed in the House, Ruth McCormick was in Chicago,
speaking before the Illinois Republican Women's Club, and arguing, "The
thing to do now is not only to pass a farm bill but to enact a measure
the President will sign . . . Admitting it is experimental, let us pass it
and use it as the basis for further amendment, if found necessary." This
speech was inserted in the Congressional Record on the same day by her
colleague, Congresswoman Kahn. It is the only signal contribution Ruth
McCormick ever made to the deliberations of the House. The act was
finally signed in June and a Federal Farm Board was created. But the bill
ultimately failed in its purpose, as there were not enough incentives for
farmers to cut production, the only sure way to raise prices. The tariff
revision was also passed rather rapidly in the House but died in the
Senate. [40]

Among other issues dealt with in the special session was Hoover's
request for the repeal of the National Origins clause of the Immigration
Act of 1924. In 1927 over sixty-five thousand Irish had been admitted

but only five thousand Italians. Ruth, in an attempt to secure labor votes, at first professed to support restriction of immigration "along humane lines," but in fact she was opposed to any restriction of immigration: "I feel that many of the races limited in immigration by the National Origins Act make valuable citizens."[41] Such a view hardly needs defending today, but it was risky in 1929.

Although the legislature was limited in its special session to consideration of the farm problem, tariff revision, and the National Origins problem, Ruth was at her best working for individuals, handling requests for pensions and pension increases for veterans and their dependents, and helping expedite matters before various federal departments and bureaus. Her constituents were mostly veterans of the Spanish-American war, though there were some from the "Indian Wars" and even some from the Civil War. She also supported a proposal to provide a branch library building in Washington (the D.C. government was administered by Congress) and sponsored a petition to make Armistice Day (November 11) a legal holiday.[42]

Less than a month after Ruth McCormick took her seat in the House of Representatives, word got out that she was planning to run for the Senate in the following year. As early as December 1928, just after her election to the House of Representatives, she was being urged to run for the Senate. At first she insisted she was "anxious to work out a more harmonious party feeling in the state rather than further any personal ambition for the senatorship." But it grew increasingly evident that after the 1930 census was completed, the state legislature would redistrict the state and eliminate her position of congressman-at-large. By April she was denying rumors that she would not be a candidate for the Senate. Ruth had written confidentially to a friend on May 3, 1929: "The rumor . . . that I had withdrawn from the Senatorial race [is] entirely without foundation. I am a candidate for U.S. Senator and will start organizing at an early date." The friend indiscreetly released the letter to the press. Ruth professed to be embarrassed by the publication of a letter written in confidence but denied nothing.[43]

The news, wrote the New York Times, "fell like a bombshell among the politicians" of Illinois. Governor Lou Emmerson's attitude was a matter for much speculation. Would he back Charles Deneen or Ruth McCormick, both of whom had endorsed him in the last election? There were grave doubts that Deneen could easily defeat her, "even among the Senator's associates, who recalled she polled a larger vote than any [sic] candidate on the State ticket in November." Although she had not chosen the timing, Ruth, always eager to look on the bright side, privately speculated, ". . . perhaps after all it is a good thing to have it settled."[44]

The campaign promised to be a hard one, forcing Ruth's team into action at once. As early as January she had asked her congressional aide, O. M. Farr, to make lists of social workers, farm advisors, newspaper editors, nurses, teachers, and railroad workers to receive government pamphlets. She urged him to send agricultural documents to voters in country districts where she had made a poor showing in the 1928 election. By mid-May Jim Snyder was already working so hard he could not take off on Saturday afternoons. He was predicting "a whale of a campaign" and suggesting that "Federal judges, states attorneys, and every agency at the disposal of Mr. Deneen is apparently being put into action." A lawyer in McLeansboro informed Ruth that Deneen was indirectly trying "to get certain men and women to run for the Senate" in order to weaken her by "dividing the opposition." "It is going to be a very bitter fight," Ruth agreed, adding, "I hope my friends will be more reasonable and not lose their sense of humor."

At that time, public opinion polls, such as those published by the Hearst newspapers and the *Literary Digest*, were less reliable than today's, and Ruth depended on "circular letters" (form letters) to assess support for her candidacy. In June her office mailed six thousand letters to committeewomen and men "to ask if you feel you can support me for the U.S. Senate in the coming April primary." She also asked each one for the names of five prominent voters in their precincts. Snyder reported an astonishing 70 percent response by the end of July.[45]

Congress suspended June 19, 1929, and Ruth returned with her family to the farm in Byron, from which she commuted to Chicago two or three times a week until August. Then she went to Wyoming for a couple of weeks to brace for a race that would "require all the physical vigor" she could store up. It was less a vacation than a chance to rest and prepare her speeches for the coming campaign. By the end of the summer Ruth was ready for a public announcement of her intentions. On September 1 a delegation from the Young People's Republican Club presented her a petition with twenty thousand signatures. Greeting them with a picnic lunch at her farm, she responded,

> If I followed the ordinary political formula, I would say, "This is so sudden." But I have never been accustomed to follow old rules . . . This isn't sudden. The question . . . has been discussed throughout the state. I am hesitating. I will make a definite statement within ten days . . . No one knows better than I that the coming primary will be the bitterest ever fought in the State. It will involve much added worry to my duties in

Washington. I am used to hard work. I like it. But I've been going as hard as I can in the last few months. [46]

Ruth McCormick announced her candidacy for the U.S. Senate on September 22, promising she would be "free from any direct or indirect obligation except only the fundamental obligation of integrity in public service." Or, as it later came to read: "No favors and no bunk." In addition to the campaign themes of Farm Relief and the Tariff Revision, Ruth would again emphasize her opposition to the World Court. The real issues of the 1930 senatorial campaign would not surface for some time.

In September she was still defensive about the imperfect Farm Bill she had supported in the House. The tariff schedule had passed the House of Representatives May 28 and was revised by the Senate in August. Ruth did not give it unqualified support:

It is good business to make the tariff wall high enough to protect the nation's industries, but it is not good to make it any higher than necessary in view of the country's position as the leading creditor nation in the world . . . If we demand that Europe pay war debts, and raise the tariff wall, we deny that possibility.

Her caution was justified by political realities. Congressmen from farm districts were concerned that the new tariff would not significantly protect farm prices but would contribute to higher prices on manufactured goods that the farmer had to buy. The special session of Congress adjourned November 23 without having reached an agreement. Also, the formula proposed by Secretary of State Elihu Root modifying Senate reservations about the World Court had been recently reinterpreted, nullifying the most important American reservations. It was predicted the World Court issue would be present in all nineteen senatorial contests, nowhere more so than in Illinois. [47]

The principal feature of Ruth McCormick's campaign, though, was that it was the first creditable attempt made by a woman to run for the Senate. Rebecca Felton of Georgia, active in politics since the middle of the nineteenth century, had received a complimentary appointment to the Senate by the governor of her state in 1922. She had served two days before she was succeeded by a duly-elected senator. Other women had run as Independents or had been beaten in the primary. In Ruth's case, she would have to run against a popular incumbent, Charles Deneen, for the nomination, but she may well have relished the idea of taking revenge on Deneen for beating her husband, as well as the possibility of becoming the first woman senator. Ruth stood a good chance of winning, because as congressman-at-large she represented the same electorate senators did. But there was more opposition to her campaign for the Senate. "People won't vote for a skirt," it was said. Ruth brushed that issue aside:

> I realize . . . the handicap of being a woman seeking so high an office but this was true when I first spoke on a public platform in 1906 and it has been true in every political step I have taken since that date.

In fact, there was very real opposition downstate, and it began to be rumored she would withdraw from the race. Acknowledging that the reports did "credit to the industry of the propaganda factory sending them out," she denied them flatly. Her supporters pointed out she had led the ticket in the last election, and that she was not the type to retire from the field. In fact, she was the only candidate to have declared by mid-November, although Deneen had begun to canvass for renomination back in June. It was also reported that a judge, a clerk of a federal court, and a U.S. marshal were all campaigning for Deneen, and that Deneen's men were letting it be known they would have thirty thousand census jobs to distribute. It was said that Deneen was using the prestige of federal offices to intimidate the foreign-born into supporting him. She decided to face these challenges head on.[48]

Ruth had to divide her time between Illinois, where she was beginning to campaign, and Washington, where she attended to her Congressional duties. A sample of her mail gives an idea of the variety of requests she was called upon to answer: a doctor asking her to introduce legislation legalizing abortion, which she declined as "manifestly out of place" for her; a bill affecting Spanish-American war veterans and their widows, which, her aide noted, had occasioned "more propaganda" in her office than all other bills combined; Ruth's assurance to a concerned woman that she would do anything she could to protect the canary breeders if only she had "a little more detail to work on."[49]

Meanwhile, Black Friday, the stock market crash of October 29, 1929, came and went to surprisingly little effect at first. People had been writing her for jobs and even for old clothes; now they began to ask for money as well. By the end of November she wrote a minister, "I have only a stated income and give away almost two-thirds of it each year, and I think if I had responded to all of the requests made of me this year it would have taken well over $1 million cash." Jim Snyder, who, like nearly everybody else, had been dabbling in the stock market for a couple of years, wrote his friend Judge William Radliff,

> Do you remember one day at Springfield during the State Fair that you bet me $100 that [Sedgie Survis] stock would reach 100 before Standard

Oil of Indiana. I hope that I shall be able to collect this $100 before Christmas as the family is very much in need of funds owing to miscalculations of stock market.[50]

The Depression had begun. They did not recognize it at the time, but for Ruth McCormick and many of her Republican colleagues, it was to be the most significant fact of their political careers.

8
The Senate Campaign: 1930

Ruth McCormick opened her historic campaign on January 13, 1930, a mere ten years after women had won the vote. Even so, it had the look of a modern campaign. During the fall she had been building a coalition that included not only her regular power base among the Republican women of the state, but labor and, in Cook County, black voters as well. On Labor Day she spoke to a crowd of six thousand, recalling the days of her youth when the first unions were struggling to organize. A large number of trade unions came out in her support. The African-American community in Chicago was strong for Ruth; in fact, Congressman Oscar de Priest, Illinois' first black congressman and a long-time ally, was the only member of the Illinois congressional delegation to support Ruth against the incumbent Charles Deneen. She also had the support of Irene McCoy Gaines, a prominent organizer among the black women in Chicago. In late November 1929 Gaines made a passionate speech condemning Senator Deneen and endorsing Ruth McCormick. "We should support Mrs. McCormick for the Senate because we have nobody there," she said. She criticized Deneen's record as state's attorney and as governor, claiming he had been slow to act against the rioters in Springfield who had set fire to black homes, killing the children inside. She also criticized Deneen's record as senator. When Mrs. Hoover had entertained Mrs. Oscar de Priest along with other Congressional wives at the White House, and a "disgraceful speech" was made by Senator Cole Blease of South Carolina, "against Negro womanhood," Deneen had remained silent, and it remained for Senator Hiram Bingham from Connecticut to rise to their defense. Deneen, Gaines concluded, had the body of a

Senator but the mind of a "common ward heeler"; Ruth, on the other hand, was "always on the right side." Irene Gaines, along with Mary Church Terrell, another prominent black woman, made a number of such speeches in Ruth's behalf.[1]

Ruth's campaign opened in Shelbyville, Mattoon, and Charleston, "the buckle of the corn belt." Listeners came through fog, over ice-coated roads and sidewalks to hear—or to gawk at her.

> I am aware that perhaps the chief opposition to my nomination and election is the fact that I am a woman. I realize . . . I shall be regarded as something of a pioneer, as I was in the days when we were making the campaign for women's suffrage . . . I hope nobody will vote for me simply because I am a woman, or vote against me solely because I am a woman.

Still, though she did not campaign as a woman, it would be expected that she was naturally sensitive to women's problems. In November she had met with Secretary of the Treasury Andrew Mellon to urge an increase of the income tax exemption for unmarried persons from $1500 to $3500:

> The present exemption . . . is unjust, both to men and women but especially to women. The present law works to the disadvantage of unmarried persons who, without being heads of families in a legal sense, actually are supporting . . . others than themselves.

She also buried old differences with the National Woman's Party to join them in opposing the nationality convention of the world code, which held that a woman could lose her nationality if married to a citizen of another country. This had even happened to her colleague in Congress, Ruth Bryan Owen, who had had to reapply for U.S. citizenship when she returned to America.[2] There was a long agenda of women's causes to address.

Although Ruth McCormick insisted that she was "not running as a woman, but as one who desires to serve," she encountered considerable opposition to the idea of a woman nominee for the Senate in her downstate speaking tour. Even a senior staff writer for the *Chicago Daily News*, Paul R. Leach, felt free to write that "Her career up to 1924 was merged in that of her husband, which proves, if nothing else does, the high degree of her intelligence, for any woman has sense who can waive a career for herself to see that her husband is a success." Part of this resistance may have come from Ruth's frankness about her ambition. Eleanor Roosevelt, Molly Dewson, and Belle Moscowitz, other politically active women of her time, all worked behind the scenes to promote their programs. Even Frances Perkins, the secretary of labor in the Franklin Roosevelt administration a few years later, felt compelled to protest, "I never, never dreamed of being Secretary of Labor . . . I never had any notions in my mind—never, never, so help me, God. I'm not a different kind of woman than most of the women in this country." In spite of such views, Ruth predicted women would control the Congress within twenty-five years.[3]

Having attempted to put aside the "woman question," Ruth went on to discuss other issues: her experience, her alliances, the farm and tariff bills, and the World Court. She was experienced enough to run for the Senate, she said, because as congressman-at-large, her constituency had been "identical with that of a U.S. Senator." She denied any compromising alliances, and argued that individual candidates should run without factional slate making, in the original spirit of the primary law. And she defended the work Congress had done on the farm marketing bill and the tariff. Up until the day before she began her speaking tour, her staff was preparing briefing papers to show Deneen's vulnerable areas, concluding that he had voted correctly on the farm bill, and that it would be unwise to criticize his attitude on immigration. It was felt that she would be on firmer ground attacking the World Court, and she could denounce it as the "back porch" leading to the League of Nations. She need not even mention Deneen by name, but he had voted for the World Court in 1926. So had Senator William B. McKinley, and it had led to his defeat by Frank Smith.[4]

Her speechwriter Fred Smith reported to her Congressional aide O. M. Farr after the first three days, "The crowds are really remarkably large . . . There are more men than women—her candidacy is being taken very seriously." And he noticed that sentiment against the World Court was "pronounced." By the second week, Smith wrote Farr that he would be surprised "at the way the World Court issue has taken hold in Illinois." It was a good issue. Ruth was perfectly sincere about wanting to avoid foreign entanglements; it was a position she defended for forty-five years. But she was a practiced politician, and she was going to make full use of this issue to win. Her speeches began to emphasize her opposition to the Court: "It has been said the League Court is not an issue in the campaign, but I want to say now I am making it an issue." Among her objections to the League was that its authority was predicated on the use of force to guarantee the spoils of victory. "The League was organized to enforce the Treaty of Versailles, to enable the victors in the Great War to maintain their territorial advantages." Predictably, the *Christian Science Monitor* accused her of being opposed to peace; she replied that she believed involvement with the League would draw the United States into European wars. She pointed out she had supported the Kellogg plan to outlaw war and the current disarmament conferences.[5] She was interested in finding the best means to peace.

In addition to attacking Deneen in his most vulnerable area, Ruth wanted to mobilize her grass roots supporters, especially the women, to get out and vote on primary day. "Many women say, 'Oh, I can't have anything to do with politics because it's so corrupt. I'm going to see who they put up.'" The primary law was not bad, she insisted, but it would not work unless people took advantage of it. This was an understandable concern. In 1928 over three million people had voted for president, but less than a third of them had voted in the primary. "I am not asking them to go to the polls and vote for me, necessarily," said Ruth, "but I am asking them to vote." She knew that turnout in an off-year primary was even lower than in a presidential election year. Another problem she foresaw was that the established machine had a "deliverable vote," which she knew would "in a great many cases" be delivered against her.[6]

Ruth hoped to buck the odds with extensive organization. Before a speech, she sent out hundreds of personal letters inviting people to come hear her. "We have found," Snyder wrote one down-state worker, "that her personal letters have brought larger crowds than any other sort of advertising." By the end of February, when she had spoken in eighty-five counties, the night meetings were drawing close to one thousand people. Ruth's enthusiastic workers labored in two shifts, day and night, on correspondence. One woman wrote of waiting in her car in the train station in Lincoln, when an express train hurtled in and screeched to a halt. The engineer jumped out, raced over, handed her the McCormick literature and asked her to vote for his candidate. Natalie H. Pegram, the president of the Illinois Federated Women's Clubs, was willing to do almost anything; she took care of babies while mothers went downtown, and even planted four rows of onion sets for a farm woman who wanted to register.[7]

Even great enthusiasm, however, was not always enough in such a new endeavor, and well-coordinated work was not always easily achieved. Irene Gaines reported that the African-American women of Danville refused to work under the direction of the white chairwoman of Vermilion City. There was even dissension within the ranks of her black colleagues. Leroy M. Hardin, in charge of the campaign among black men, objected that Mary Church Terrell was catering to the "silk stocking" class. Terrell defended herself to Jim Snyder, and cited a visit to a man called John Brown who kept a "place" in Peoria. As she was explaining her mission to his assistant, she heard men talking in the back room, and asked to be allowed to speak to them:

> The men were playing cards (maybe they were gambling, but that was none of my business) and I talked to them about Mrs. McCormick. Some women were also present (maybe they were not saints. I didn't stop to inquire.) But they all listened to me attentively and respectfully. I invited them to come to my meeting the following Sunday afternoon. They applauded me loudly and the first man I spied when I entered the hall was one of the men I saw in John Brown's place . . .

She concluded, "I am using every ounce of my strength trying to win votes for Mrs. McCormick. Sometimes I work sixteen hours a day . . ." Complaints were made that Deneen was spending more on the black

voters than Ruth was. "Special meetings are held for the ladies on Friday
night," wrote a worker in a black Chicago neighborhood:

> Last Friday night, the women were presented with bath towels, at another
> time with nice creton [sic] aprons . . . I live in the Second Ward and
> many people there have lately come from the South and they do not
> know what it is all about and it is not surprising that they are so easily
> led by a small gift.

Another black worker, Jenny E. Lawrence, reported that Deneen was
hiring black women to canvass door to door, adding plaintively, ". . . it
is making it hard for our [volunteer] workers . . . an effort should be
made to put them on the books." But already by the end of February
1930, Farr reported that there were rumors around Washington as to the
sum of money Ruth McCormick had spent. Sis Hamill cautioned a
worker, "As you undoubtedly know, we are being watched very carefully
as to our expenses . . ."[8]

On February 9 former Senator James Hamilton Lewis formally announced his candidacy for the Democratic nomination for U.S. Senator.
The *New York Times* rejoiced that Illinois would have "one more chance
to repent for retiring the courtliest and most musical personality of the
Wilsonian age." It had been Medill McCormick who had retired him in
1918. Ruth McCormick and Charles Deneen were said to be feeling
secure with their one hundred thousand-member Republican majority,
but, the *Times* concluded hopefully, "strange things happen in politics."[9]

In between trips to Washington to vote on important legislation, Ruth
continued to make an energetic downstate campaign, even though her
efforts to organize in the rural areas were hampered by the condition of
the roads, many of them still unpaved in 1930. She spiked a story that
she had hired a railroad handcar to make a speaking engagement when
the roads were impassable, by telling a story hardly more credible:

> I went in a caboose. The automobile road was washed out and I hadn't
> time to drive the long way around, so I jumped into the caboose on a
> freight train. They had ordered a handcar but it was − 18° and the
> railroad people thought the trip might be pretty hard on the men.

Ruth managed to imply that, nearly fifty, she herself would have been
equal to the trip. Such self-assurance was typical of the mature Ruth
McCormick, now an experienced speaker. She would start quietly, usually
with an anecdote, her hands clasped behind her. As she worked to the
climax, she would gesture sparingly with the slim forefinger of her left
hand. Although she took pains to choose attractive clothes, she would

soon forget them, and was likely to toss her coat onto an unswept platform, and pull off her hat without the aid of a mirror. She never read
her speeches, except on the radio, where she needed to make every
minute count. It was a mark of her professionalism that she no longer
took even radio speeches too seriously. Once when she and Ruth Bryan
Owen were to open a Washington radio program together, they panicked
the manager of the program by pretending to fight over which of them
would speak first.[10]

While Ruth, and even her stand-ins like Helen Bennett, were drawing
large crowds, Deneen was not faring as well. A worker in Lincoln reported
he had talked there "to 88 persons . . . Of this number I counted 14
Democrats, 22 straight-out McCormick voters and about 10–12 of the
paid workers they have hired. This number included most all of the
present office holders in the Court House." Deneen was hardly campaigning at all; he remained in Chicago, "to build up his own political
fences and to burrow under Ruth's," according to one analyst. The fine
reputation he had built supporting the winners in the clean sweep of the
1928 primaries was beginning to tarnish. Bill Hard speculated that Deneen was hampered by having been too indulgent of certain local politicians in Chicago. Another columnist criticized Deneen as the head of
the Republican Party in Illinois for allowing cliques to develop within
the party. Deneen had also alienated the Better Government Association
by refusing to endorse their ticket for the Cook County Board of Com-
missioners. Although they were furious with Deneen, saying the senator,
faced with a choice "between righteousness and the devil," had chosen
the latter, they did not particularly wish to support Ruth McCormick,
whose anti–World Court stance bothered them. Ruth defended herself
from charges that anyone against the Court must be in favor of war by
saying solemnly:

> I remember one cruelly long night I spent crumpled up in a big arm chair
> in the East Room of the White House watching [McKinley and Hanna]
> pace up and down . . . Never were there two more devoted friends but
> the country was about to go to war with Spain and [they] held different
> views.

She liked to emphasize her "Quaker stock."[11]

There were other issues clamoring for attention. The president of the
Women's Christian Temperance Union (WCTU), Miss Helen Hood,
thought it would be unwise to retire Deneen from the Senate, as he had
always supported Prohibition. Ruth's staff quickly protested. Deneen, in
the last judicial election, had combined with Tony Cermak, who ran on

a Wet ticket with a bottle opener as a campaign emblem. Moreover, it was pointed out that the WCTU was not supposed to endorse candidates. One of the membership wrote to Hood that Deneen appointed the Prohibition officers who were failing to enforce the laws: "If WCTU officials and members, of which I am one, cannot see this, I think they should pray for light." Although Ruth was a Dry, she refused to make any pledges whatsoever about legislation concerned with the Eighteenth Amendment.[12]

The farm question was all but forgotten. Charles Deneen and Ruth McCormick, as Republicans, were hardly going to make an issue of the deepening depression under Hoover. After two months of strenuous campaigning, Ruth seemed to have left behind the problem of being a woman. Downstate, the candidates battled over the World Court, while up in Cook County, the issue became their political alliances. Deneen defended his support of the World Court as the Republican Party position. Ruth disagreed, claiming that the only Republican platform that had endorsed the Court was that of 1924. By 1930 the Senate's reservations about adherence to the Court had been addressed by Secretary of State Elihu Root, working with the British foreign secretary, and his proposal was due to be voted on by the Senate. Ruth, however, was bitterly opposed to the "Root formula," claiming that it would give the League the right to ask the Court for an advisory opinion on any issue in which America claimed an interest. She challenged Deneen to state publicly whether he would vote for the Root proposal. Deneen pointed out that the formula might be rewritten in the Foreign Affairs Committee and refused to commit himself to a vote. It was a touchy issue. Under fire from women's groups because of her stand, Ruth said she supported a World Court not associated with the League. She could not understand why the Hague Tribunal, officially known as the Permanent Court of Arbitration, then in use for almost a quarter of a century, could not continue to be used to arbitrate international disputes. Ethnic groups like the Poles and the Yugoslavs were in sympathy with her position and endorsed her candidacy. She was also supported by a large number of veterans of World War I.[13]

Politics being what it is, high-minded discussion of the topics of the day frequently degenerated into purple passages.

> The Senator has a mental picture of . . . a cowering Europe [threatened with being driven] out into the storm, but the rescuer is near. The Senator is rushing into Chicago. He will arrive in the nick of time, hoarse and breathless and will exclaim, "Let that lady go. Here are the papers." [Producing the Root formula] he will . . . turn to lay a soothing ice cold hand on the brow of Europe.[14]

Ruth's arduous downstate campaign drew to a close. She had traveled thousands of miles throughout Illinois' 101 downstate counties, discussing agricultural and manufacturing interests, the issues of cities and villages, the problems of southern cotton and northern wheat. Like Mark Hanna, she had carried her campaign directly to the voters; like his, her campaign expenditures had been enormous. She had become an efficient campaigner. One telling report was of her boarding a train at Rock Island and being asked by the porter what time she wished to be called for the 6:59 arrival. "Quarter to seven, please," she answered.

"But that leaves you only fourteen minutes to dress."

"I can do it in ten," she boasted.[15]

Ruth McCormick liked to boast of her hardiness, too. "I've noticed," she was quoted as saying, "that as the weather got colder, the more insistent some of the workers were that it would be a great deal better for me to have them precede me by train rather than ride with me in an open car." Heaters in cars were just beginning to appear, but Ruth did not approve of them. She claimed her vitality was due to rest and good food:

> I sleep like a log whenever, wherever I can. Fifteen minutes' sleep in a car will relieve fatigue. Twenty minutes is too much, will make me feel groggy . . . I try to live largely on dairy products . . . and avoid coffee as much as possible.

She attributed her emotional hardiness to her women's rights background: "I've been heckled [before]. That's where suffragists have the advantage over men. They know how to take heckling, or they should." One time, a voice from the crowd bellowed that she was "a rotten campaigner." Ruth replied, "I agree with you, my friend, but how little you and I count in the face of such opposite opinion."[16]

Feeling fit and on a roll, Ruth McCormick opened her Chicago campaign on March 10 at headquarters on East Monroe Street. On hand was a Mr. George Goodrum, who had once stood by to open Mark Hanna's carriage door, again dressed in the brass-buttoned coat, tall silk hat, and other garments of the gay '90s. Her Cook County manager was W. R. James, an aide of Governor Emmerson. His position in her campaign amounted to a tacit endorsement from the governor. The men supporting her had been organized as the Voters Progress Club by Lucius Wilson, who remarked, "When Mrs. McCormick launched her candidacy, no one, or nearly no one believed she had a Chinaman's chance. I can speak of that feelingly because my own friends kidded the life out of me for tying myself to what they insisted was a dead end."[17]

Ruth McCormick shocked her supporters with her opening speech, a bare-knuckled attack on Deneen's political irregularities and his peculiar friendship with a local gangster known as "Diamond Joe" Esposito. Esposito had been indicted back in 1908 for the murder of a man who was shot in a barber chair. Eight months later the case was "nolle prossed." In 1923 Esposito's cafe was closed by the police for one year for violation of Prohibition. Yet in 1926 Esposito ran for County Commissioner on the Deneen ticket, and Ruth claimed that Deneen had also attended various banquets given by Esposito, some in Deneen's honor. At the end of the 1928 campaign, Esposito was shot down in his car in a typical gangland murder. Ruth speculated that Esposito had sought campaign contributions from bootleggers for Deneen, but the bootleggers may have assumed it was protection money and, disappointed, may have taken revenge. In any case, Deneen attended Esposito's funeral, explaining, "I went . . . because he fell in the common cause." (Deneen's house, and that of Judge John A. Swanson, candidate for State's Attorney General, had been bombed a few days later.) Esposito's funeral had been extraordinarily gaudy, even by gangland standards; ten thousand dollars' worth of roses had been strewn over the ten miles between the church and Mt. Carmel Cemetery. Ruth "talked roses" at every opportunity.[18]

Politically, Congressman McCormick accused Senator Deneen of being "100% regular in Washington but 60% Democratic in Cook County" where he had made election deals with Tony Cermak, a "dripping wet" Democrat who had run for the U.S. Senate in 1928 on a "fluid platform." Allegedly, he was very quiet about these associations when campaigning downstate. Deneen responded that Ruth McCormick had bolted the Republican Party in 1912; Ruth then criticized Deneen for excessive party loyalty: "He votes the way the party wants him to, without regard for his own opinions. There comes a time, occasionally, when a senator must make a decision for himself." She went so far as to criticize Deneen's association with State's Attorney Swanson, the "clean" candidate who had beaten the notorious Bobby Crowe two years before, because Ruth claimed Swanson had obtained only 695 guilty verdicts out of 3,990 grand jury indictments, and there was still a "general feeling of insecurity." Deneen, in turn, accused Ruth of unsavory associations because she had been endorsed by Crowe, exclaiming: "We shall not be surprised if we are informed that Ali Baba and the forty other gentlemen composing his organization have also declared for the lady." Ruth reiterated that she had made no pledges or deals with any leaders or factions, even though other Cook County politicians were beginning to endorse her. "Endorsements from anti-Deneen groups appear to indicate that everybody likes to be a winner," she told her audience in Joliet.[19]

The *New York Times* reported Congressman McCormick walking a fine line, not going out of her way to welcome but not repudiating, the support of Snow, Barrett, and the City Hall faction, either:

> City Hall support does not carry . . . any high recommendation of its recipient, but it has organization and voting value . . . In a primary which seldom polls more than half the available vote, help is particularly effective.

Ruth herself made a distinction between accepting support and forming an alliance. "As a candidate I am not running for the exercise. I want votes," she said bluntly. Deneen claimed the Crowe-Snow-City Hall crowd were using her money for their own campaigns:

> Large sums of money are being expended . . . Those who usually favor the cause with the largest funds are active in her support. In my judgment there has not been an Illinois campaign so expensive as the one she is conducting.

At the very least, the Cook County endorsements allowed her to save some money, which she reinvested downstate.[20]

As the pace of the campaign became horrific, Ruth compared herself to the Duchess in *Alice in Wonderland,* running just to keep from falling behind. "If I'm ten minutes late at the noon meeting, I'll be twenty minutes late at the next, and will lose an hour by the end of the day. So I insist upon keeping going everlastingly." A week before election day, she was making seven speeches a day, beginning with a mass meeting at the Apollo Theater at noon, and including an address to a Women's Republican Club, a radio talk, and four speeches in suburban communities, ending close to midnight. Her storied stamina notwithstanding, she was beginning to look tired and worn.[21]

The campaign was attracting national attention for many reasons. Ruth McCormick was coming to be regarded as the leading woman in American politics, though hers was not specifically a feminist campaign. In fact, both candidates were prominent. Deneen had been in politics since his election to the state legislature in 1892. He had been governor twice and was the incumbent senator. Ruth had been active in politics since 1896 and was associated with Mark Hanna and Medill McCormick, as well as having achieved distinction as the first female congressman-at-large. Finally, the World Court was a national issue, and many were watching the outcome of the election for that reason alone.

Primary Election Day, April 8, was bright and sunshiny and an unusually high turnout was predicted. After voting in Byron, Ruth returned to Chicago to meet Alice Longworth and Triny, back from boarding school. (Johnny, thirteen, and Bazy, nine, had remained in school in Washington throughout the campaign.) Surrounded by friends and family, Ruth remarked: "I don't get excited in my own campaign until election night at about 7 o'clock. When the phones begin to jingle, then I know what real excitement is." After a "hideout dinner," she returned to her headquarters at the Palmer House hotel. At one end of the room was a huge white and gold cake in honor of her recent fiftieth birthday. A crowd milled around hoping for a glimpse of her. Ruth talked with the precinct workers, exclaiming, "Isn't it grand?" or "Thank you very much—don't you feel proud of yourself?" At one point Triny interrupted: "Cicero (Al Capone's stronghold) has gone for you two to one." "I don't believe it!" laughed Ruth. To questions about possible defeat she answered, "I'll still be in Congress and still happy." Governor Emmerson called in the middle of the evening to predict she would win by 175,000. "Oh, I just can't stand it!" shouted Alice Longworth. But Ruth still wanted to know about particular counties and precincts. One reporter speculated that "she'd worked so hard in the soil of politics for six months, she couldn't lift her mind to victory."[22]

Ruth was reluctant to claim success prematurely:

> I am not going to be too sure. I know I am probably nominated and all that but I have been through many campaigns, I know my downstate precincts, and I'll just wait awhile. Besides, I am carrying a big load. Women all over this country are watching this election. I intend to be careful for their sakes.

Nevertheless, she was glowing with happiness, and her deep and hearty laugh rose often throughout the evening. Early results showed her ahead by almost two hundred thousand votes, the state's largest plurality in an off-year election, and this against a man who had been undefeated in thirty-eight years of public service. Ruth finally issued a statement late that night:

> I would be less than human if I were not highly pleased with the result . . . Any man, and particularly any woman would be grateful . . . I am grateful to all the voters, both men and women, who made this victory possible . . . [In the fall] I shall make as vigorous a campaign as I have made for the nomination.

It had been the heaviest primary vote in years and included a large

"The Female of the Species"   *By* **Morri**

turnout in the rural areas, in spite of the fact that it had been a warm, sunny day ideal for farm work.[23]

Medill's cousin, Joe Patterson, publisher of the tabloid *New York Daily News*, cabled her enthusiastically: "Attaboy, girl!"[24]

The *New York Times* admitted with chagrin that their forecasters had been wrong. They found it difficult to believe the World Court issue could be "dramatized" into a two hundred thousand-vote majority:

Of course, Mrs. McCormick had a special appeal for women voters . . .

> The liquor question did not . . . figure . . . Their machine alliances were almost equally unsavory, although here Mrs. McCormick had the advantage of being merely the placid beneficiary . . . rather than, as Mr. Deneen is, a political ancestor of present-day Chicago conditions.

Their conclusion was less dismissive: "Whatever the reasons, the result is astonishingly plain: Mrs. McCormick is the first woman ever to be nominated for the Senate by a great political party." Jeannette Rankin of Montana, the first woman in Congress, had run for the Republican Senate nomination in 1918. After her defeat, she ran a losing campaign on an Independent ticket. Other women had appeared as nominees of the Socialist and Prohibition parties, but Congressman Ruth McCormick was the first woman nominee of a major party. Also important was the significance of her win for the World Court issue. The *Times* rejected the conclusion that the World Court, which they called "an article of Republican faith," could be "swept away" by one Senate primary in Illinois. It criticized Hoover, saying if he

> had early and vigorously taken the lead in the matter and identified his Administration with the policy of joining the World Court, Mrs. McCormick [would not] have ventured to campaign in open defiance of his authority as head of her party.[25]

The *Chicago Tribune* reported gleefully that "18 Senators who voted for the World Court in 1926 have not been reelected in primaries or elections, and 11 others have retired or died." Senator Glenn judged that "Mrs. McCormick's victory over an opponent with high character and standards" must have been due to her stand on the World Court. Other factors were also considered to explain her victory. Paul Leach of the *Chicago Daily News* pointed out that Deneen had felt so certain of his power, he had neglected the campaign until it was too late. Ruth, on the other hand, was characterized by David Lawrence, the future founder of *U.S. News and World Report*, as "a master political strategist." He praised her tactics: formidable alliances, business as well as welfare issues, good organization, and an aggressive campaign. Ruth, however, was quick to credit her success to women voters. The League of Women Voters later found that, although the number of voters had declined from that of 1928, men had declined by 13 percent and women by only 7 percent, giving women greater proportional strength.[26]

Mayor Thompson's support was harder to measure. His organization had once again won control of local organizations, forty-three of forty-five ward committeeships and all the major offices of Cook County, causing Thompson to gloat that "Truth crushed to earth shall rise again."

THE FIGHTIN' SPIRIT OF A FIGHTIN' SON OF OHIO.

Ruth, however, felt that the mayor's forces had jumped on her band-wagon, and she pointed out that her slate led Thompson's by 176,000, enough to have elected her without his assistance. It was thought that Bill Thompson had been working less for Ruth McCormick than against Charles Deneen, and that he was likely to desert her on the Prohibition question.[27]

And Prohibition was on her mind. James Hamilton Lewis, whose nomination as the Democratic candidate was practically uncontested, was expected to make Prohibition the main issue in the fall campaign.

Ruth McCormick had revenge on Deneen for her husband's defeat, but Lewis might well savor revenge on her for his own defeat at the hands of her husband in 1918. However, the Democrats had been defeated in every senatorial election in Illinois since 1892, except the divided 1912 Bull Moose election, and Ruth's election was widely accepted as assured. A *Wall Street Journal* reporter ridiculed the prospect of a Lewis victory:

> Washington would welcome "Jim Ham" and find some use for him. What use? Well, what use is the parsley with which the cook garnishes the new potatoes? Of what use is the paper frill on a lamb chop? Of what use is the frost on a well-made glass of mint-julep?[28]

The day after the election, Ruth slept until mid-day and spent the early afternoon receiving congratulations of friends and feminist leaders all over the nation. She paused as she left her headquarters at the Palmer House to thank the hotel personnel for their help. Making her way to the train which was to take her back to Washington at 4 P.M., she posed for photos and talked for "talkies" while the Pennsylvania Railroad officials delayed the train's departure one half-hour to wait for her.[29]

Ruth was met at Union Station the next day by Johnny and Bazy, and by Ruth Owen and Florence Kahn, who presented her with a bouquet of roses and said: "All women of America feel your victory as a step forward for womanhood, the biggest thing for women since the passage of the suffrage amendment." Ruth refused to discuss the primary. "It's all over now and I am back for work. I'll be back at the House tomorrow for the remainder of the session." When she appeared on the floor of the House of Representatives the next day, as a message from the Senate was being read, Florence Kahn spotted her and led the applause in which many Democrats joined the Republicans. Ruth laughed a little self-consciously as members crowded to shake hands before she took her seat between Kahn and Ruth Pratt. That afternoon, she met for an hour with President Hoover at the White House, then told the Press:

> Naturally I refrained from seeing the President during the primary fight, but now we will be in very close touch. We are all anxious to have our state platform coincide with that of the Administration and I am anxious to go over every detail with the President.

They had "agreed to disagree" on the World Court question. Questioned about her stand on Prohibition, she said she approved the president's law-enforcement policy: "I have always been a dry and you've never known me to switch around." On Monday she returned to the House where Speaker Nick Longworth invited her to take his chair and preside with the gavel. Fred Smith reported to Jim Snyder that she was "having the time of her life."[30]

The prospect of a woman senator pleased some and alarmed others. Humorist Will Rogers wrote approvingly:

> I like her. She is not continually yapping about the 'woman's angle.' We want a woman that will help out us men. We can't get a man there to do it. Ruth won't feel at home there in the Senate. She's too young. There is 40 old ladies there now . . .[31]

Ruth was able to savor her victory only a short time. She had won the nomination, but she still had, Snyder warned, "a terrific fight" ahead of her. It was by no means certain that the Senate, the "most exclusive men's club in the world" was ready to accept a female colleague. Even Theodore Roosevelt's 1912 running-mate, the erstwhile Progressive Hiram Johnson, Ruth's cohort at Armageddon, wrote of her victory in the primary:

> Some of us consider it a punch in the eye to the Senate, because it means the admission of the first woman. It is quite true that the Senate may not have lived up to its traditions of late years, but its thorough breakdown and demoralization, in my opinion, will come with the admission of the other sex.

It seems surprising that with eight women in Congress there should still have been so much resistance to a woman in the Senate. However, there were 435 members in the House and only 96 in the Senate.[32]

And there would be other opposition as well. In the same election, Lottie Holman O'Neill, running for the nomination as State Senator, lost to incumbent Richard Barr. She had been in the lower house for four terms. Now she would be unoccupied, freer than ever to contest Ruth McCormick. Back in Illinois, the Democrats adopted their platform. Ruth's gleeful comment was:

> I have not had time to read the Democratic platform . . . , but I understand I am a whole plank in it, all by myself. I am enormously flattered. There are so many things that a normal Democratic platform usually views with alarm and points to with pride, that I could not reasonably have hoped for any attention whatever; much less a whole big plankful of shivers and horror. Perhaps it is to be explained by the fact that the Illinois Democrats had so little platform material to work with.

The platform also opposed the League of Nations and the World Court and called for the repeal of the Eighteenth Amendment and the Volstead Act. Candidate Lewis, Wilson's whip in the Senate when Wilson had first proposed the League of Nations, now claimed that he had publicly rejected the League many years before. He planned to sidestep the World Court issue by focusing on Prohibition.[33]

Prohibition was not popular in Illinois. A referendum in 1922 on the manufacture of light wines and beers had showed the state to be Wet by more than four hundred thousand votes, although the Drys insisted their full strength had not voted. Ruth had been supported in the primary by many voters of foreign birth or descent who were opposed to the League of Nations, but such voters also tended to be anti-Prohibition. At the end of April an old friend and political advisor, Judge Charles H. Miller of the circuit court in Boston, wrote, "I think I was interested more in your success than you as it has been the friendship of the years." He then proposed a novel solution to the Prohibition problem: "Why could you not take this position: I am dry but in the event of a referendum and the people of the state of Illinois vote otherwise I am a representative of my state and will comply with the will of the people."[34]

So on June 4 the Republican Central Committee of Cook County, ostensibly without consulting Ruth McCormick, petitioned to put three questions on the ballot in November:

- repealing the Eighteenth Amendment;
- granting states the right to determine which beverages should be considered "intoxicating";
- repealing the Illinois Prohibition law, the "search and seizure act."

Ruth McCormick did not comment, claiming to think other issues more important.[35]

A more troubling issue was the matter of her campaign expenditures. All through the spring, Deneen and other Republican opponents had made caustic references to the amount of money she was spending. Their comments attracted the attention of Senator Gerald P. Nye, a Republican from South Dakota, who headed the Senate Campaign Fund Investigating Committee.* On April 22 Nye announced that he was sending special investigators to Illinois, as well as to Pennsylvania, to inquire into complaints of excessive expenditure. However, "excessive expenditure" had never been defined. When Truman H. Newberry of Michigan spent $195,000 on his 1922 campaign, the Senate considered this amount

---

*Nye was later described by columnist Joseph Alsop as an "unappetizing man" who became "Adolf Hitler's strongest defender in the Senate." Joseph Alsop, *F. D. R., A Centenary Remembrance, 1882–1944* (New York: Washington Square Press, 1982) pp. 109–10.

"too large" and Newberry was "rebuked" by the Senate, resigning before his term ended. William S. Vare of Pennsylvania had spent $780,000 and was denied his seat altogether, while Frank L. Smith of Illinois had spent $450,000 in 1926, more than $200,000 of which was donated by public utilities magnate Samuel Insull. Smith was also denied his seat. Senator Robert La Follette, Jr. had proposed a ceiling of one cent per voter, but his proposal was never acted upon. To this day, campaign financing remains an unresolved and thorny issue. Ruth's former friend Harold Ickes promptly wrote Nye, offering "leads" to his investigators.

Ruth informed the Nye Committee on May 2 that she had spent a not-unprecedented $252,572. She pointed out the critical distinction that it had been her own money, leaving her beholden to no one. But she professed to welcome the investigation: "I regard this inquiry as extremely important . . . It offers a basis for legislation which will provide specific regulations of expenditures in primary campaigns." She warned, however, that new laws should take into account the need to balance money expenditures against the "patronage influence," especially canvassing by the incumbent's "payrollers." Deneen had reported spending $24,495.22.[36]

Nye could find no evidence that either candidate had spent more money than had been reported but thought it likely that money spent on their behalf had not been included. He was also puzzled by the discrepancy between the $6,000 Ruth McCormick spent in Cook County, which produced nearly half the votes, and nearly $250,000 spent downstate. He suggested she must have received help from Mayor Thompson.

Ruth was forced to publicly defend her expenditures. "My campaign was essentially an anti-machine campaign," she wrote in a letter to the editor of the *New York Times,* responding to a hostile editorial on June 14. Large expenditures were necessary to

> overcome the organized machines, and . . . to combat the indifference of non-machine voters . . . It is the non-machine vote which a candidate who has no machine must work for, and which necessitates expenditure of money for literature, halls, advertising, traveling, radio, banners, canvassers, pledge cards, sample ballots, and many incidentals.

The Democrats were hoping the "excessive expenditure" issue would work to their advantage, especially as unemployment and social unrest continued to grow and the effects of the depression were increasingly apparent. In May her assistant Jim Snyder protested:

> I am gradually going mad. This office has averaged 15–20 people a day in search of jobs or work, and an equal number of letters for help

> in the way of clothes. I have practically used all the old clothes and shoes
> on the Gold Coast during the last campaign.

A month later, Snyder wrote Ruth:

> We have had 200 requests for jobs during the past month. Have taken
> care of approximately 40 . . . at Marshall Field, Merchandise Mart,
> various other places, among your friends and mine.[37]

These conditions were gradually infiltrating the campaign.

As soon as Congress adjourned in mid-July, Gerald Nye went to Chicago to begin hearings. Ruth McCormick asked to be the first witness herself. Before a capacity crowd in the court room of the Federal Building, she appeared for nearly four hours. She was alone, without counsel. The other senators on the committee were absent, so Nye was also alone. It was a dramatic confrontation, and newspapers gave the hearings ample coverage. Nye questioned her closely about her associations, trying to establish whether the "vast sums expended by the Thompson machine in Cook County" should be counted among her campaign expenditures, since Ruth's expenditures in Cook County had been much smaller than for her downstate campaign. She began to chafe at Nye's assumption of an alliance with the Thompson machine.

"The Chairman may be wrong," Nye said at one point, "but you must have had some assurances of strong support in Cook County."

She retorted:

> You are wrong. You are entirely wrong . . . I know the situation in
> Chicago. I knew the factions opposing Deneen would spend time and
> energy in the county contest here. Deneen was running for two offices—
> U.S. Senator and for what you might call County leader. To beat him
> for County leader, opposing factions had to beat him for the Senate.

Ruth defended her spending as necessary to offset Deneen's use of patronage: he could appoint postmasters, census enumerators, and marshals, and a Federal judge had conducted Deneen's campaign in his district.[38] She pointed out that she had run from 50,000 to 150,000 votes ahead of local politicians in Chicago. She reminded Nye that she had testified under oath she'd had no alliances with any organization, "and that was the truth, whether he believed it or not." The Chairman of the Republican Cook County Central Committee, B. F. Snow, testified to explain Cook County's support:

> When there was an apparent wave of sympathy for Mrs. McCormick, I
> assumed the responsibility of marking sample ballots for her in all wards

where the Committeemen did not object. I thought it would help our ticket
and I believed it worked both ways.

He confirmed that she had not asked for his support. [39]

"This is the most miserable job ever wished on a man," Nye complained. After three days of hearings, he adjourned until August, disappointed to have found that he had been misled by reports that she
had spent more than she claimed having spent herself plus $67,000 spent
by others on her behalf. A provocative syndicated column appeared that
same day, noting that Ruth McCormick had frankly told the Committee
she had spent $250,000 of her own money, and that

This bid certain members of the Committee pause. What be, if women
were permitted to spend their money like that? Certainly there would be
no political sanctuary for men if such carryings on were allowed . . . .[40]

It looked as though the problem would diminish into insignificance,
and with some relief Ruth wrote a supporter that she had "had a good
deal of amusement out of it." But suddenly, events took a bizarre turn
when Ruth announced that her offices at the farm in Byron had been
broken into. It turned out that her correspondence had been gone over,
although nothing had been taken. Nye's only comment was a hope the
perpetrators would be caught and punished. Meanwhile, the Nye Committee's chief investigator, William Hunter Baldwin, identified by both
the New York Times and the Chicago Tribune as the former chief of the
Ku-Klux Klan secret service, had vanished and had not been seen for
some time. [41]

Furious, Ruth reacted with characteristic vigor and impulsiveness. On
August 30 while Nye was back in his home town of Fargo, North Dakota,
a Chicago detective turned up there, allegedly compiling a biography of
Mr. Nye. At first, Ruth refused to comment, but soon admitted hiring
him. "I wanted to find out who was shadowing and robbing me," she
explained. She protested that her statement of expenses was the most
complete ever submitted by a candidate, yet

prosecution became persecution. My offices were broken into . . . Spies
had invaded my living quarters [some time earlier she had discovered a
strange woman in the closet of her room in the Drake Hotel] . . . My
. . . telephone wires were tapped . . . In making my own investigation
of the Nye investigators I have acted in self-defense.

She added defiantly, "What is Senator Nye going to do about it?"[42]

Nye was absorbing Ruth's attention and energy at a crucial point in
the campaign. A New York Times editorial quipped, "Were it not for an

occasional dispatch giving the gist of a calm, effective speech made by Mr. Lewis at some point . . . the impression would be that Mrs. McCormick is running against Senator Nye of North Dakota." Nye held further hearings in September, "to learn why Ruth McCormick had hired detectives to shadow him." She offered to present evidence that committee investigators had tapped her wires, but Nye refused to allow it. The crowded galleries were rewarded with a dramatic scene when Barney Thompson, publisher of her Rockford papers, gave testimony. Suddenly he produced photographs showing in detail how the telephone wires to her house were connected by a wire leading to a deserted house two miles away.

"Do you imply that this was done by the Committee or on its orders?" asked Chairman Nye.

"It doesn't require any great stretch of imagination to think that," Thompson replied.

"The Committee will not further permit itself to be drawn away from the purpose for which it is here, unless you are prepared to state the Committee is definitely connected with this wiretapping incident," said Nye.

"Just as man to man," said Thompson, "you ought to give Mrs. McCormick a chance to clinch this and prove to you, all the way from the Committee right up to the deserted house, that it is under the direction of the Committee."[43]

Illinois Attorney General Oscar Carlstrom also came to Ruth's defense. "If we let a lot of whippersnappers . . . say who may or may not sit in the Senate, we lose our right of representation," he said. He released to the press the testimony Nye refused to hear, including an affidavit from a private detective admitting that a committee investigator had introduced him to the former telephone company employee who had wiretapped the apartment of Ruth's private detective. Nye issued a denial of the committee's involvement and adjourned the inquiry the following day, September 18, until after the election; he was not required to make a report until the December session of Congress.

It is difficult to assess the full impact of the hearings, but they were certainly harmful. It underscored Ruth's large expenditures, which were seen as objectionable during the depression. Then, too, some regarded her behavior as undignified—"She Snoops To Conquer" was the caption of one political cartoon when the counterspy story came out. On the other hand, many people felt that she had been unfairly attacked; they called the Nye Committee the "Spy Committee" and characterized Nye and like-minded radical Republicans as "assistant Democrats." Nye's decision to suspend the inquiry raised even more questions about his motives.[44]

With the investigation out of the way, Ruth McCormick still had to face the Democratic candidate Lewis and the Prohibition issue. She had always considered herself a Dry, while Lewis had come out in favor of state control of Prohibition, which amounted to its repeal. With the referendum on the question scheduled to go on the ballot, Ruth McCormick announced that she would agree to be bound by the results of the triple referendum. The *New York Times* remarked:

> Mrs. McCormick was a good Dry in the Spring when she was nominated for Senator. She is now an *ad interim* Dry, subject to the will of the people. The Republicans took refuge in the triple referendum. Thus, it is hoped to take the wind out of Democratic sails. Mr. Lewis has the advantage of straightforward and courageous convictions. The forced conditional 'flop' of Republicans is not engaging from the outside, but the Illinois Republicans can stand a good deal.[45]

They chose to overlook Lewis's own "flop" on the World Court question.

The Drys made an immediate outcry. "For the purpose of winning Wet votes . . . Mrs. McCormick is ready to abandon her convictions under the pressure of political expediency," said the superintendent of the Illinois Anti-Saloon League. He announced that the league would support any worthy candidate for the Senate who would uphold the Dry cause. Ruth McCormick's old antagonist Lottie Holman O'Neill sprang forward and was promptly endorsed by the league as an Independent candidate. The *Chicago Tribune* observed that as O'Neill was "known to be a bitter political enemy of Ruth McCormick, it will be charged her candidacy is a spite campaign rather than a dry campaign," and speculated that by splitting the Drys, O'Neill would help insure a Lewis victory. Ruth sweepingly accused the Anti-Saloon League of attacking popular government, the Bill of Rights, and the tradition of majority rule "going back 700 years to Magna Carta." Throughout the campaign, she insisted that hers was the only possible position:

> I am as dry as when I wrote my platform for Congressman-at-Large two years ago, but I don't believe . . . I have any right . . . to vote contrary to opinion expressed in a legal and orderly way by the people . . . My distinguished and gallant opponent said, "I'm going to vote Wet no matter what the people of Illinois say." He can't do what he says he is going to do . . . All he can do is submit an appeal for repeal of the amendment to the states.

No Time for a Parasol, Mrs. M'Cormick

A month later, warming to her theme, she said, "Ham Lewis wants you to believe when you put a cross by his name and then run home, froth will still be on the beer which has mysteriously appeared on your table." Lewis responded by holding up a Bible and reciting, "Thou art neither hot nor cold nor cold nor hot. Therefore repent ye for Thou art a fraud to Thyself." Such rhetoric aside, Ruth McCormick's position no doubt cost her a good portion of the women's vote that she must have been counting on.[46]

Colorful though the debate on Prohibition may have been, it was not the decisive issue in the campaign. The election of 1930 came almost exactly a year after the stock market crash of October 29, 1929. The depression became the crucial topic, although neither candidate singled it out as a dominant theme until the campaign was nearly over. Ruth bravely sought to dismiss the Democrats' talk of "hard times" as mere "calamity howling," saying that postwar conditions had produced a "back-wash" all over the world, everywhere worse than in the United States. Blaming Hoover for these conditions was like blaming him for "the drought and the floods and the spots on the sun," as another Republican candidate phrased it. She pointed out that Republicans had already taken action with a new tariff to protect wages and jobs and stabilization corporations to help farmers. A Democratic Congress, she warned, would only deadlock with the White House and stall the "business revival." By the end of the campaign, with the crisis deepening, however, she was admitting that "the question is not whether everybody gets a bottle of beer but whether everybody gets a job." Chicago was especially hard hit by the depression. Over half of the employees of the electrical industries plus a large proportion of the furniture, packing, clothing, printing, and transportation industries were out on the streets. The best Ruth could do was to cite the similar breadlines and soup kitchens of 1893 and argue that electing Democrats in a Depression would be progressing from the frying pan to the fire.[47]

While Ruth was trying to hold fast against her Democratic opponent, she was having real problems with members of her own party. The primary fight had left a number of disgruntled Deneen supporters. In some districts that had held meetings of five or six thousand Republicans before the primary, Snyder was hard put to find a "corporal's guard" to support her in the fall. It was uphill work to build new organizations from scratch. The victory of a woman had caught some of her supporters by surprise. A campaign worker from Ottawa reported:

> There was a quiet backcurrent among some of the leaders, including the

> Governor . . . who outwardly gave loyalties to the nominees, but many
> men around him were just a little disturbed about the possibility of ex-
> tending petticoat rule . . ."

The governor was warned that if Ruth McCormick were elected, they
would soon have a woman governor. "So jealousy moved in to affect the
vote," her friend concluded. A lawyer in McHenry County summed up,
"There is an immense Republican vote that is not for you today." Martha
Connole fumed:

> A group in Illinois took charge of her campaign in order to double-cross
> her . . . I suffered the tortures of the damned . . . standing by and
> watching people stab her in the back.[48]

Lottie Holman O'Neill was also on the attack, claiming a vote for
Ruth McCormick would be a wasted, since she wouldn't be seated by the
Senate. She cleverly reminded an audience in Mattoon that Medill
McCormick had voted to unseat a Senate colleague for spending only
half of what Medill's own widow had now spent. "Thus Senator Mc-
Cormick rises up to condemn Ruth McCormick," O'Neill concluded
ghoulishly. She also threw in the idea that a vote for Ruth McCormick
would be a vote "for the vicious city hall gang."[49]

Then, from an unexpected quarter, Ruth was finally cleared of long-
standing accusations of her ties to Big Bill Thompson. Two weeks before
the election, Thompson printed and circulated a pamphlet urging African-American voters to vote for Lewis. He claimed the *Chicago Tribune*
and Medill McCormick had been guilty of racist statements. Fifty thousand of these circulars were distributed to black churches in Chicago by
police officers. Oscar de Priest, a black congressman from Chicago, was
appalled. "No sane man," he said, ". . . would ask the colored people
to vote for a Democrat." Ruth McCormick deplored the "malicious and
unjustifiable attack on my late husband" but was pleased that she would
now be believed about her association with Thompson. Lewis remarked
that "The Mayor left the lady waiting at the altar," but thought the furor
of her reaction was merely to distract attention from the fact that she
had "not one word to say about overcoming the poverty and misery" of
the unemployed. J. Ham Lewis always referred to his opponent as "the
lady," a polite gesture that complemented his spats and the fresh red rose
he wore in his buttonhole. But in the final days of the campaign he
removed the kid gloves. He said of her campaign expenditures:

> When a woman dishonors the State of Illinois far beyond the corruption
> attempted by any man, no appeal of sex will save her from just judgment

> . . . Cook County will cast a big vote against a woman whose inherited
> riches were wrung from the poor.[50]

It was an effective tactic which played particularly well in such desperate
times.

Ruth campaigned hard until voting day, insisting bravely that there
were "always more Democrats before an election." But as the first returns
came in Election night, they were from the outset overwhelmingly against
her. Characteristically, she took it well. "Oh, Lord," she laughed, "we're
just swamped." Lewis had a projected plurality of 685,000. He'd won
three to one in the city of Chicago and carried 89 of 102 counties.
Compared to Hoover's plurality of 455,000 in 1928, it was a swing of
over a million votes. In Chicago Lewis won forty-seven wards out of
fifty. Ruth carried the predominantly black second, third, and fourth,
showing that Thompson's attempts to alienate black voters had been in
vain. When asked to what she attributed her defeat, Ruth quipped,
"[S]omebody else got more votes."[51] But she was not blind to the real
reasons.

The 1930 returns gave Democrats their largest majority, even greater
than it would be in the presidential election of 1932 with Franklin Delano
Roosevelt. Democrats had won all over the country, gaining eight seats
in the Senate and fifty-one in the House. Ruth McCormick was buried
in the Democratic landslide. "From the beginning her campaign has been
lighted by an unlucky star," admitted the *New York Times*. She had been
saddled not only with Hoover's unpopularity, but also with the Prohibition question. The Wet vote on the referendum was much higher than
for previous referenda, especially on the question of repeal of the Eighteenth Amendment. The new Congress would have thirty more Wets
than Drys. Then, as if the depression and Prohibition were not enough,
there was also Thompson's opposition, the opposition of other rival
Republican groups smarting after the primary defeat, and, of course, the
fact that she was a woman.[52]

Apart from these disadvantages, it must also be said that she had made
serious mistakes. "Flushed with her brilliant primary victory," said a
contemporary analyst, she had become careless:

> McCormick failed to notice the change in sentiment [caused by the Depres-
> sion]. She incurred the enmity of Thompson's organization by boldly
> slighting its contribution to her cause. The conspicuous display of her
> wealth before the Senate Committee . . . injured her cause.

She had had no real campaign manager who could have warned her of
these dangers; she claimed she liked to get directly in touch with indi-

vidual voters. This may have caused her to become too involved with the Nye feud and to waste energy that might have improved her position in the race. However, since she lost by more than 744,000 votes, there was probably little she could have done to change the outcome. In the last analysis, however, there had been something of a victory, too. Helen Bennett believed that her greatest contribution had been to prove "that women, a completely feminine woman, could be a great force in politics."[53]

Ruth McCormick was not one to look back in regret. Triny observed, "I saw her through many triumphs and defeats, and you could hardly tell the difference." Election night, Ruth telegraphed congratulations to Jim Ham Lewis and, back at her hotel with Triny, was preparing to go to bed. Suddenly her face lit up with an impulsive thought.

"I think I'll call Albert Simms," she said.[54]

9
New Mexico:
1931–1939

"THE DUCHESS OF ALBUQUERQUE"

During the twenties it had seemed that Ruth Hanna McCormick was in the vanguard of women moving into the political arena. But as it turned out, her victory over an established male politician in the 1930 primary was the crest of the wave. Ruth McCormick was one of the first women brought down by a depression that saw immense retreat everywhere from the gains women had made during the 1910s and 1920s.[1] Her loss to Lewis in the general election ended any further attempts on her part to win national office, but it did not put an end to her career in politics. For the moment, though, she was eager for new experiences.

Two days after the election, Jim Snyder observed: "The battle is over and we have had a good trimming. Mrs. McCormick is in perfectly wonderful humor and I think is having more fun out of it than anyone else." She was busy writing friends and supporters:

> It is a little early to tell what general effect on the state and nation will result from the tidal wave which swept over the country. It undoubtedly means something more than most of us are able to analyze now . . .

She claimed to be "delighted" to be able to attend to her newspaper and farm and went so far as to claim, "I am sure I can be of greater influence and greater service as a private citizen than I could be as a Senator." However, to her old mentor, ex-Senator Lawrence Sherman, one of the Irreconcilables, she confided: "I am sorry I could not have done more to help the party and the state. Confidentially, the party and state will need more than one individual to pull it out of its present factionalism . . ."

She wondered whether the tensions were due to the primary law, "with persistence of factional strife after the primary is over?"[2]

The one bright note had been the Women on Juries Referendum, which had passed. Up to this point, there had been resistance to women on juries, because of the fear that they might be harmed by "listening to shocking testimony which they would then have to discuss with strange men behind locked doors through the night." The League of Women Voters thanked Ruth for her "significant part" in the campaign for its passage, especially "for securing action of the Republican party at their State Convention."[3]

Ruth returned to Washington for the closing session of Congress, and at the end of December she gave a debutante party for seventeen-year-old Katrina. Prohibition was still in effect, however, and Ruth, especially vigilant because of her bad experience with Medill, never allowed any alcohol in the house during Prohibition. "I was sunk at the prospect of a dry party," Triny recalled. "But my great flame at the moment, Eddie Burling, whose father was a friend of hers, said, 'Don't worry, my father and I will fill our cars absolutely full and park them in the alley next to where the party will be.'" Ruth was innocently unaware of all the clandestine drinking. After the party, she and Albert Simms went down to the Potomac River to watch the sunrise, and Triny slipped off with Eddie. Triny crept home about eight A.M., expecting her mother to be frantic with worry. She tiptoed up to her mother's room and found no one there. Her mother was still out with Albert.[4] It was a last, lighthearted fling in the Capital.

Congressman Ruth McCormick paid a final call on President Hoover before Congress adjourned in early March, bringing him maps of the election results "to show him the state of mind Illinois is in." As she left office, Ruth firmly declared, "Nothing could induce me to get into the next race." In Chicago on her way to Rockford, she waved off reporters, saying that she was no longer news and spoke of her forthcoming career as a newspaper publisher. According to her daughter Bazy, Ruth left politics with no real regrets. "She wasn't disappointed about the election. She was too savvy a politician to think she had a chance." Bazy also believed Ruth was perfectly honest in saying she looked forward to getting out of politics. "She'd eaten that apple," Bazy said flatly.[5] It was time for new interests.

Albert Simms was waiting in the wings. Albert, two years younger than Ruth, had gone west at the age of twenty-four to recover from tuberculosis of the lungs, settling in Albuquerque by 1920. He was largely self-educated and a great reader. In 1914 he married Katherine Mather, who was also a tuberculosis patient. She died a few years later, leaving him a millionaire. In short order, he became the president of an Albuquerque Bank, and served in the New Mexico legislature as a Democrat. He joined the Republican Party and won election to Congress in the Hoover victory of 1928. In 1930 he was defeated through the efforts of Bronson Cutting, a powerful, independent-minded New Mexico Republican, who was supporting the Democrats that year. After leaving Congress in March 1931, Simms directed a finance company.[6]

After Ruth McCormick's defeat, Albert had invited her to visit the West, and soon rumors of a romance were flying. Ruth dismissed the gossip as "screamingly funny," and due solely to the fact that she was "the only Congressional widow and Mr. Simms the only Congressional widower," but Albert was indeed courting her. Ruth, however, refused to be rushed, and Albert's impatience grew as the year wore on. He wrote her almost daily.

"I need to talk to you today," he says in a typical letter:

> my spirits are low. I've let a spell of bronchitis seize me and in my anxiety to get over it before I see you I get panicky because I've always possessed the complex that my hearts [sic] desire in life is not for me . . . try so hard to fight it off when I see you at the end of the road waiting for me—loving me—believing in me . . . My secret lover, don't let me get into the dumps, laugh me out of it, love me forever Sweet as I shall do you . . . Be my lover, be my lover.[7]

His entreaties eventually convinced her. In July Albert visited Ruth in Byron, where she tried to evade reporters by driving down to Streator the night before he arrived. She stayed with a friend who kept a tea room, telling her, "I'm going to meet my fiancé tomorrow," happily making her own sodas at the shop in the "carefree spirit of a young girl."

Ruth and Bazy spent the winter in Colorado Springs, where Johnny was in boarding school. The Fountain Valley School had been founded in 1929, one of the first boys' boarding schools in the West. It was, of course, instantly affected by the depression. When Johnny enrolled two years later, Ruth lent her support through her spirited participation on the board and up to eighty thousand dollars a year until the school had stabilized, and she was always regarded as one of the school's founders. Johnny, at fifteen, was, according to his roommate Bobby Dietz, "a great big guy with no meat on him. He walked kind of crooked, never walked straight to you. Shy." But he was not shy around Bobby, and they got into plenty of mischief; Johnny was intrigued with explosives and used them for many pranks. Johnny was also interested in photography, not a particularly common interest in 1931. "He was interested in all kinds of things," concluded Bobby.[8]

Ruth visited Albuquerque from time to time, and the prospect of a "Simms-McCormick alliance" alarmed Simms's rival, Bronson Cutting. Nevertheless, he invited them to lunch and afterwards confessed to his mother that Ruth had "made herself agreeable." He was perplexed about their relationship: "I can't help thinking there must be something to the Simms affair, although it seems to remain in status quo for a long time."[9] Cutting's concern about Ruth proved justified later.

At last, in the spring of 1932 Ruth Hanna McCormick and Albert Gallatin Simms were married at noon on March 9, in a brief, simple service in Ruth's rented house in Colorado Springs. Ruth was attended by her old friend Margaret Ailshie, and the Isleta Indians of New Mexico, special constituents of Albert's, presented the bride with a matate grinding stone. The Simmses did not go on a honeymoon and were quite startled early the next morning when ten-year-old Bazy marched into the bedroom before they were up, as was her custom. Bazy was ambivalent about the marriage and intensely disliked her new stepfather. She felt "he was a phony . . . He was forever trying to butter me up . . ." But Bazy was pleased to see her mother so happy.

> I think she really loved him. I had never seen her so kittenish. He was full of charm, he romanced her, took her dancing all the time. He used to laugh gleefully afterwards about how she married him thinking they were going dancing every night and they'd never been dancing since.

After her difficulties with Medill, Ruth was apparently willing to settle for someone who was less a soul-mate, but more comfortable as a companion. However, after seven years of singlehood, after all the changes of the twenties, Ruth was not about to take second place to her husband. "She was like a reigning queen with a consort," one friend observed many years later.[10]

Alice Longworth was shocked by Ruth's decision. "Marry Albert Simms!" she hooted. "Sleep with him—one thing. But never marry him—how could she have done it!"[11] Although Albert was clever and handsome, Alice undoubtedly felt he lacked Medill McCormick's patrician air.

Ruth moved to Albuquerque, New Mexico (known as "Duke City" after the Duke of Alburquerque, Spain), into Albert's old stone house on Fourteenth Street. Soon after she arrived, she began to work with the architect John Gaw Meem, whom she'd known from his work at Fountain Valley, drawing up plans for a ranch house she would call "Los

Poblanos." Albuquerque at this time still had the character of a small town, with a population of about thirty-five thousand. "It was an un-sophisticated place, with no visual beauty at all, though the site of the town was good, between the parentheses of the mountains and the Rio Grande," novelist and historian Paul Horgan, a New Mexico resident from the age of twelve, recalled. But the town was in transition, "reaching out," said Horgan, "toward metropolitan activities."[12]

Ruth's first project was to organize a school that would be suitable for Bazy. The Sandia School, named for the Sandia Mountains on the eastern rim of Albuquerque, * was to prepare Bazy and a few of Ruth's friends' daughters for eastern prep schools. Ruth and Albert bought the old Commercial Club, later renamed the Simms Building, where they had a suite of offices, one on each side of a large waiting room on the second floor. Ruth quickly became busy with the school, local politics, and an increasing number of community activities. Albert, with his financial background, handled her business affairs. Albert also kept dairy cattle. When Ruth married him, she brought four carloads of her own stock out west. Albert was always startled and impressed when he came across her name in cattle magazines. "She went into the new life with gusto," according to Bazy, "learned all about New Mexico, flora and fauna and Indians. No going back to Washington to visit. She just closed that door."[13]

Ruth did remain in politics, but only to a modest degree. In 1932 she returned to Illinois for a meeting of the state's Republican Women's Club prior to the Republican Convention, where she spoke heatedly against renominating Hoover. She also scolded the women for having so few delegates at the convention and predicted they would never have more until they got to work "back home in their precincts and came on gradually but inevitably to adequate representation in national political gatherings." Fall brought the 1932 election. "No one out here has even a modest amount [of money] outside of Mrs. Simms," complained Bronson Cutting. "She is reported to have given the Republicans $200,000." He was bitter about her contributions and gleefully reported that during a radio talk on the eve of the election, she "broke down in the middle . . . lost the last half of her manuscript," started to appeal mistakenly to the voters of Illinois, and they "had to turn on a phonograph record to fill out her time." In spite of this poor beginning, Ruth kept her hand

---

*They are reddish in color when hit by the setting sun; *sandia* means watermelon in Spanish.

in politics throughout the thirties. "I'm glad you brought me out here, Albert," she once remarked. Politics in New Mexico was the same as in Chicago, "only they do it in two languages."[14]

In the off-year election of 1934 Ruth McCormick Simms made national headlines by bolting the party rather than support Senator Cutting who had by then returned to the Republican fold. She and Albert, who had succeeded Cutting as Republican National Committeeman, supported the Democratic nominee, Representative Dennis Chavez. The acerbic *Literary Digest* columnist "Diogenes" described the New Mexico political situation as a struggle between "two outlander baronies," which nevertheless had national significance. (Cutting was a rich New Yorker and Harvard graduate who, like Albert, had gone west for his health.) Albert had switched party lines in 1928, to support Hoover against Smith, while Cutting had supported Franklin Delano Roosevelt in 1932. "Diogenes" speculated that if Cutting, now a Republican again, were elected, he might lead the insurgent bloc in Congress and end by opposing Roosevelt for the presidency in 1936. "Diogenes" enjoyed the irony of imagining that Ruth Hanna McCormick Simms might indirectly be aiding Roosevelt, but concluded that, "The Simms barony realizes it must beat Cutting to hold any political prestige in the State." Ruth was starting to think that "Chicago politics look like a pink tea party compared to Bernalillo County politics." Though Cutting would win, he was killed soon afterwards when his small plane crashed flying him back to New Mexico. The Simmses' candidate Chavez was appointed to succeed him.[15]

By 1936 Ruth Simms saw the Republican nomination as a contest between ex-President Hoover and Governor Alf M. Landon of Kansas. Landon was a Theodore Roosevelt Progressive who had fought for the balanced budget and against the Ku-Klux Klan but was handicapped by an uninspired speaking delivery. At first Ruth was lukewarm about his prospects, but as time went by she became reconciled to Landon and developed some enthusiasm about his chances for winning. At the Republican Convention in Cleveland the first week of June, Ruth Simms was one of the seven people chosen to second Alf Landon's nomination.

Ruth was also still interested in the position of women at the party convention and announced that she hoped "to see a number of women named to important committees." She herself had been offered a place on the strategic Resolutions Committee but was eliminated when the New Mexico delegation made her chairman. During a radio interview with the celebrated journalist Dorothy Thompson, Ruth reminisced about early conventions: "women were not allowed in caucuses then because they liked to go out and tell what happened." Ruth insisted that "any intelligent woman" could find a political niche, but she was once again indignant over the lack of women delegates, feeling, as an old reform progressive, that women were particularly suited to supply solutions to the "social ills" plaguing the country.[16]

Among her old cohorts at the convention were Alice Roosevelt Long-worth, Corinne Alsop of Connecticut (Theodore Roosevelt's niece), Bertha Baur of Chicago, now a Republican nominee for Congress, and former Congresswoman Ruth Baker Pratt of New York. Pratt was campaigning for the repeal of Section 213 of the National Economy Act, which provided for the dismissal of either husband or wife when both were employed by the government, a campaign Ruth enthusiastically supported. In addition, she collaborated with Albert Mitchell, a New Mexico rancher and National Committeeman, to form a western caucus with which she worked closely for the rest of her political career. The *New York Times* characterized Ruth Hanna McCormick Simms "as one of the shrewdest minds among women interested in political matters," but her old nemesis Harold Ickes, grudging her the publicity, complained sourly that Ruth "was never one to hide her light under a bushel."[17]

Ruth Simms campaigned for Landon in seven middle-Western states that fall, contrasting him to Franklin Roosevelt by remarking that Landon was "completely and absolutely genuine . . . calm in the midst of excitement . . . [and] thrifty." One reporter observed, "The Party fathers respect her judgment, and the voters love to hear her talk." She was so well-received in Baraboo, Wisconsin, according to another account, that when she began to bring her speech to a close, "There burst forth from the audience an entirely spontaneous chorus of 'No, no,' and other notes of regret." Ruth called for volunteers to return to "old-fashioned soap box oratory. Forget formal meetings in halls, go out onto the streets to do some political button-holing," she advised.

None of it, of course, was going to be enough against Roosevelt. Ever the optimist, a week after the election Ruth wrote:

> The election was in many ways a good thing. It puts up the test of New Deal politics directly to Roosevelt and his advisors. Now that he has a free hand, we as a people can hold him responsible. If he fails, many interesting things may happen.

Herbert Hoover, apparently not offended that she had supported Landon against him, wrote, "I do want to see you . . . Surely this party needs some shaking up." Ruth was also pleased that her ex-brother-in-law, Colonel Robert McCormick, publisher of the *Chicago Tribune,* was "in such a panic about the future, it makes me laugh." There was no love lost between them. In the teens she had resented Bert's suggestion that Medill should be committed to an institution, and the *Tribune* had not supported her in her Senate campaign.[18]

Though Ruth's political activities caused some to speculate that she was hoping to succeed Bronson Cutting as the Republican state boss, most of her activity at this time lay outside the realm of politics. Part of Ruth's new life with Albert was travel and relaxation. They went to Europe shortly after they were married and toured the British Isles. Like many another politician of her day, Ruth had always claimed to be Irish. She liked to refer to her "Irish temper," or her "Irish love of a good fight." Estelline Bennett, in her publicity department, had written a flowery article comparing Ruth to a medieval Irish queen. So the Simmses' first stop was Ireland, where they made a fruitless search for the Hanna (or Hannay) ancestral home, Sorbie Castle. When the family went on to visit the children's governess, Belle ("Sam") Samson, in Sam's native Scotland, they discovered Sorbie Castle in Galloway, and Ruth had to foreswear her Irish pretensions. The Simmses also went to Bermuda one spring for six weeks, to escape the New Mexico winds. Bazy recalled:

> It was in the early happy days of their marriage and Mother was all decked out in flannels and sweater sets and playing golf—a life she had never tasted before . . . She had a new image of herself as a semi-retired suburban wife."[19]

Yet Ruth's children were pulling away from her, even though, with Sam on hand, they had never much constrained her activities. In 1935 Triny had married Courtlandt Barnes, a stockbroker with a passion for music, and was living her own life in the East. She had rejected her mother's brand of politics for socialism and stove to be accepted by her husband's intellectual friends in New York. When Ruth came to visit, she embarrassed Triny by making pronouncements to their friends on art and music, of which she knew little. Courtie, however, was unfazed. "Don't mind," he'd say to Triny, "I love your mother. She's one of the warmest people I know, and she has a great sense of humor, so just forget all this." But Triny felt humiliated. Johnny was trying to find himself; he wanted to leave college and to write. "Life is too short to fool around on the wrong track," he insisted. In 1937 he began a long trip through South America, vowing not to return until he had something to show for himself.[20] Fifteen-year-old Bazy was away in boarding school in the East.

On a trip to Bermuda, Ruth had written Paul Horgan that she had "at last outlived the desire for so much action, and I propose to rest my legs and use my head—it is so full of ideas and impressions it is ready to pop." But Ruth could never stay still for long. Soon after the 1936 election she reported:

> Today for the first time I have cleared my desk. I am working hard and fast on the new school building. The Little Theater opens the 24th. Our weather is so beautiful I hate being obliged to spend so much time indoors. After I get the school running I hope to have sense enough to stop promoting.

The following year, however, she was writing Alice Longworth:

> I am up to my neck in school, Trinchera Ranch, and all the civic activities I am engaged in here. Yes, why do I do it? I wish I had a little common sense but I can't keep out of them, and . . . I have such a good time doing them![21]

Her efforts were producing results. The Sandia School which Ruth had started in 1932 as a small tutoring group for Bazy and a handful of other girls had grown very quickly in five years. When a private primary school closed, Sandia was expanded in the midwinter term of 1935–36 to include lower grades, forty-four girls in grades one through ten. By the fall of 1936 enrollment was up to seventy-five, and the school added a small boarding department. Even though they had expanded from three buildings into five, space was still inadequate. Ruth bought 126 acres (for approximately sixty dollars an acre) in the Parkland Hills District, then barely within the Albuquerque city limits. She drew many local artists into the school expansion. John Gaw Meem, who had just finished Ruth's house, Los Poblanos, and an adjoining guest house, La Quinta ("The Villa"), designed the school buildings in New Mexican "territorial" style, low buildings with soft white walls and red tile roofs. In the dining and reception hall were murals by Olive Rush, a well-known modernist painter from Santa Fe, showing aspects of student life. In a garden of native cactus and shrubs, Ruth installed a sculpture by the realist Santa Fe artist Eugenie Shonnard.* Laura Gilpin's beautiful photographs illustrated a school catalogue.[22]

In addition to the ordinary prep school curriculum, the school offered current events seminars (often led by Ruth), field trips emphasizing local Indian and Spanish culture, horsemanship, the Very Little Theater, and sex education, an enormously progressive feature for the day. Ruth's ideas

---

*The statue was later transferred to the Socorro campus of the New Mexico Institute of Mining and Technology.

on education may have been influenced by her association with John Dewey, a founder and fellow board member of the Fountain Valley School. Legally, Sandia was a proprietary school (i.e., owned by Ruth Simms). In the late 1930s she was investing approximately thirty thousand dollars a year. But even more important than her money, she gave her time. Ruth confessed to her diary:

> Each day I realize more and more the difficulty of running a school . . . The detail of organization is complicated and bringing together in close relationship a group of women—unmarried women—creates an atmo-sphere charged with dynamite. It fascinates me, irritates me, discourages me, and at times wears me out, but I come back to it with renewed vigor because it intrigues me.

Unfortunately, she got little support from Albert who thought the head-mistress was a lesbian and that "all those women around her all the time" had a bad effect on Ruth. But Ruth felt that, although "The school takes up a lot of time . . . I believe it is the best job I have ever done."[23]

The Very Little Theater which Ruth started at the school was a con-tinuing example of her interest in dramatic arts. The original Little Theater of Albuquerque had been started in 1930, and its first play had been directed by Kathryn Kennedy O'Connor, a Broadway actress who had come west to treat her tuberculosis. O'Connor recognized that the depression was an unpropitious time to build a theater, and some of the directors even believed it was wrong to seek support for such a "frivolous" enterprise. When Ruth Simms joined the Little Theater, she, too, at first was opposed to building a theater, but changed her mind when William Keleher, a lawyer and historian, offered a large plot of land for the building. Through contacts in Washington, Ruth was instrumental in having the Little Theater project approved as the first WPA project for the city. She also helped raise a substantial part of the money in the community, by contacting all the merchants, bankers, and professional men and women and organizing civic-minded women for more fund-raising efforts. She persuaded the board to hire John Gaw Meem to design another "territorial" building, instead of the Indian adobe one originally planned.

At first, Kathryn O'Connor was afraid that Ruth would play "Lady Bountiful," paying for the theater and later controlling it. When Mrs. O'Connor told Ruth she was afraid the theater's independence would be compromised, Ruth looked surprised and calmly said, "But my dear woman, I've no intention of paying for the whole thing. I know how to deal with men like those you saw today," men who were dragging their feet in the hopes that Ruth would rescue the project. When she did not, building suppliers put liens on the building, and it was not until the community at large had raised half of the money due that Ruth made a gift of four thousand dollars to pay off the final debts. The Little Theater was re-organized in the summer of 1937, and Ruth was made president.[24] It was a notable achievement in such hard times.

By 1937 Albuquerque was seen as a mid-continent oasis. According to Paul Horgan, it was reaching out "tendrils to the sophisticated world," which Ruth was helping to foster. She became involved in the arts, he said, because "it was a role, the suitable thing to do . . . She did it superlatively well, with grace and generosity." Ruth had been involved in the arts in a small way in Illinois in the 1920s. She had helped found the Allied Arts Extension, a cooperative movement financed by local communities to share exhibits of painting, sculpture, and hand crafts. She was quoted to the effect that the real artistic impetus in America came from small communities not large cities. She had already worked with sculptor Jo Davidson on a trip to Paris and with John Gaw Meem in New Mexico. They were established artists whose work she appreci-ated. They did not need patronage; she wanted their work because it was good.[25] But there were a number of lesser-known artists whom she was able to help and encourage throughout the depression.

Ruth took an active interest in Paul Horgan's writing. Soon after Ruth met him on a visit to Roswell, Horgan became a frequent visitor at Los Poblanos, a welcome companion and a valuable source of insight into Ruth's character. "Her style was one of highly bred informality," he recalled:

> She was gracious and warm, but always on her own terms, with a sense of protocol involved. She was a great lady, rather consciously. Immensely focused on whoever she was talking to . . . she had a sense of command . . . but she was so charming, it never put anybody off.

Although she was not an avid reader of fiction ("most novelists fail to interest me because they have no psychological understanding"), she championed Horgan's novels. She even helped him place his sister, who needed psychiatric help, in the Menninger Foundation, insisting they take her even though they claimed there was no room. Horgan later said: "She wanted to help my sister because she said, 'A frustrated person will never be a happy or a useful one.' That captivated her view of what people are here for—to be useful." Horgan also admired her abundant sense of fun:

> One time I was there for a weekend when [Bazy] was home from school.

> There was a barn dance at Los Poblanos . . . The star of the party was
> Ruth Hanna McCormick Simms. She danced the best, the most, the fastest
> . . . she kept stimulating the young people, Bazy's friends, to have more
> fun, come on, clap hands.

Through Paul Horgan Ruth met a number of other young New Mexico artists. The New Mexico Art League had been founded in 1930, and there was a great deal of activity in the arts between the wars, especially a trend toward decorating public and business buildings with murals. Toward mid-century, New Mexico had more resident artists per capita than any other state in the Union. Artists in New Mexico could live quietly and inexpensively. They had light and scenery and the picturesque Spanish-American and western heritage for inspiration. But they were being badly hit by the depression.[26]

Ruth considered her addition to her ranchhouse, La Quinta, her "playhouse," and planned it to be a miniature culture center where art exhibits, readings, and musical events could take place. In fall 1935 Paul Horgan brought a close friend, Peter Hurd, a young painter married to another painter, Henriette Wyeth, to visit Ruth.[*] Peter was experimenting with various fresco techniques and had already been commissioned to do one mural. He persuaded Ruth to let him do a fresco on one wall at La Quinta. ". . . I'm shameless as far as modesty goes," he confessed to Paul Horgan, "but hell, you know I'm desperate when the matter of paintable wall spaces in New Mexico comes up." Paul and Peter visited again in August 1937 for Ruth to approve Peter's plan for a fresco of San Ysidro, and Peter wrote his wife Henriette, "I have grown to know Mrs. Simms much better and to respect her great shrewdness of observation and appraisal of people . . ." Ruth, on her part, enjoyed their company; after dinner when, as she said, "poor old Uncle Albert felt knocked out and went off to bed, the boys entertained me. We had good talk." They enjoyed her, too, for she was lively and still attractive. Henriette described Ruth:

> She had a wonderful firm chin. She was not sentimental, but had a cutting
> sense of fun. At the same time, she was quite feminine—she wore lovely
> dinner pajamas, which fell beautifully so you didn't realize they were
> pants. She was very feminine and she made Unc feel adorable.[27]

But it was Ruth's interest in their work that counted. At La Quinta she

---

[*]Henriette was a member of the family that included the artists N. C. Wyeth (her father) and Andrew (her brother).

employed a number of laborers, artisans, and artists. There was hand-made tile, hand-wrought iron, and carved wood. An older Santa Fe artist, Gus Baumann, supplied decorative features. Writer Horgan particularly admired the library she had built for Johnny:

> It was beautiful. The wood had a wonderful old-gold glow. I asked Mrs. Simms, "How on earth did you get that wonderful patina on the wood? What kind of wax?" It was not painted, but the natural wood, the grain and color with a beautiful kind of pearly glow. She made one of her wickedly amusing faces, lighted up with a little look of triumph, and she said, "I had workmen in here for months, rubbing the panels with the palms of their hands, the natural oil."

Horgan concluded, "that was Renaissance in its lavishness and grandeur." The Southwestern artists were glad to learn of Ruth's plans to hold exhibits in the gallery at La Quinta, although Bazy suspected that her mother was probably more interested in artists than in art. A lecture series was also sponsored at La Quinta, beginning in 1937, where Thornton Wilder, Rockwell Kent, and Elmer Rice were some of the speakers.[28]

Ruth's interest in the arts extended to music. In 1942 she and several others conceived the idea of a June music festival, eight chamber music concerts, the first of which was offered at La Quinta. These were very successful and were still continuing in the 1990s. Robert Mann, later one of the founders of the renowned Julliard String Quartet, met Ruth when he performed there during the first year. Although he was just twenty-one, he and Ruth felt an instant attraction for each other, and after Mann was drafted into the Army, they kept in touch by letter. Ruth planned to sponsor a string quartet for Mann at the University of New Mexico after the war.

"It was the tragedy of her death that sees me now at Julliard," Mann said in 1986. "What I might have fashioned with her help might have been even more wonderful for me." He admitted Ruth was not knowledgeable about music, but said she believed it was important and wanted to support it.[29]

Ruth acknowledged that La Quinta was an endeavor to help artists through the depression. But her very close friend Barbara J. Dietz noted that in many other projects, "palpably evident" attempts to help out were always spoken of as sound business decisions.

> It wasn't that Helen Ryan needed a job—Sandia School had to have a music teacher and wasn't it lucky that Helen was available. Irene Fisher didn't need to eat, but Ruth, just by chance at that particular time wanted some publicity work done. [Estelline and Helen Bennett] had to be per-

suaded to act as field representatives for the school. The candy maker in Colorado Springs [Fanny Robbins] where Ruth's Christmas list grew year by year . . .[30]

In her late fifties, Ruth had a constant struggle to keep from doing too much. "Just as I am trying to find fun time, I become involved in more and more work," she complained. Her 1937 summer schedule was hectic indeed. A glance at her diary shows:

June 14—Bazy arrives with Sam.
         Colorado Springs-Fountain Valley School Graduation. (Intro-
         duce Speaker; Trustee Meeting.)
June 17—Overnight train from Colorado Springs.
         Arrive 12:45 just in time to speak at Rotary Club about Sandia
         School.
         John Meem—color for new dorm.
June 18—Laura Gilpin—work on Sandia catalog
June 20—"Chief" to Rockford.
June 21—Meeting with Newspaper Guild
June 22—(Albuquerque) Gus Baumann to hang pictures
June 26—Little Theater Board
June 28—Olive Rush—drawings for mural Sandia School

In addition, people constantly sought her political advice. Typical was a Mrs. Cleveland, whom Ruth described as:

an earnest hard worker in the political life of California. I know the type so well—a nice human being, plain looking, not much money, may or may not have a husband in the "offing." Public issues the passion of her life . . . she came to ask advice . . . told the same story true of every state—the women are divided, what can be done to pull them together.[31]

When Ruth needed a break, she organized expeditions such as one to the old Turpin Ranch in Wyoming in June 1937 with Bazy, two of her girlfriends, and her step-cousins, Johnny and Albert Simms. The teen-agers seemed lethargic compared to Ruth, who went riding every day and at night read Aldous Huxley's *Point Counterpoint* and *Eyeless in Gaza*, exclaiming, "his books provoke the consideration and questioning of such a variety of subjects." Ruth was impatient with the indolence of the young and railed in her diary:

The boys want to fish. There are no fish so they sleep 10 hours and take 2 naps. They never read books or papers. There is no snap in them, no love of life, no enthusiasm, for anything. They walk slowly, drag them-selves around, slump into their chairs . . . At table they never volunteer a remark . . . They have no social sense, no thought of having accepted hospitality there is any obligation to do anything about it . . . unless I

break in every so often, the boys go to sleep and the girls giggle themselves
into a state of exhaustion . . . they are appealing but I want to shake
them all . . . particularly my own . . . I am failing terribly.[32]

Ruth was more hopeful about her son, who was due to return after ten
months in South America. Ruth went down to Albuquerque from the
ranch and spent three weeks cleaning her desk, to be ready to enjoy his
company. (She also admitted to herself, "It is always a joy to get back
in harness.") Johnny arrived just before his twenty-first birthday on August 25. Ruth had great plans for him. She proposed to buy a huge ranch,
the Trinchera Ranch, in southern Colorado, so that he would have an
occupation to sustain him while he was establishing himself as a writer.
Johnny, in fact, was cool to the project, but finally agreed that he would
"invest" in land to be operated by his mother and stepfather. Ruth was
pleased to have her boy back: "He gives me so much pleasure and companionship—such a sense of the joy of youth—his humor is delightful,
his taste so kin to mine it gives me constant response to my own feelings . . ." Later in the month she rejoiced further:

He is making an attempt to study and read. If he can discipline himself
and dig in he will accomplish something . . . For the first time he is
interested in our business affairs, in my campaigns, newspapers, etc . . .
Before he left for South America, he was so indifferent to business, politics,
and public affairs it worried me . . . Now he has become a living question
mark . . . I am more and more confident as to his future and the wisdom
of my having permitted it rather than to have insisted on college.[33]

Ruth was clearly delighted to have Johnny home, yet having him
home must have exacerbated the tensions in her marriage to Albert.
Albert himself described a somewhat combative relationship with his
wife:

Shortly after I married Ruth I found that she was quite a willful person
with the courage of a wildcat and the hitting power of an electric current.
She pushed me around all the time. And I loved her dearly. I found after
we married that I would have to adopt a cunning attitude in order to live
with her happily and for her to be happy with me. During most of the
year I would follow her along and let her push me around like a sheep.
About once a year I would catch her in some flagrant attitude toward
me that was crassly off-side and I would just raise hell about it, putting
very much more venom in it than it justified. She would look at me in a
hurt sort of a way, and perplexed, and then let me alone for a few
months.[34]

Living with Ruth may not have been easy. Ruth had arrived in Albuquerque "like royalty," according to a young friend of hers, George Byrnes. "Albert just faded into the wallpaper." "He would sit all evening and not say anything," recalled Betty Wood Seymour, another young friend of Ruth's. "He was distant and pompous," was journalist George Baldwin's less gentle assessment. Bazy summed it up: "Her friends didn't cotton to him." Ruth's children didn't cotton to him either. "We were brought up to believe it was vulgar to talk about food or money," said Triny, yet "Uncle Albert never talked about anything else." She teased him about the provinciality of New Mexico. Johnny and Albert were even less compatible. Contemporaries described Johnny as charming, shy and temperamental, though with a good sense of humor. Henriette Wyeth added, "He had a real feeling for the arts; he was one of us." As the only male in his mother's household for several years, Johnny might well have resented Albert's intrusion. On the other hand, Bazy speculated, the fact that "Johnny was very like Father in appearance . . . extremely engaging . . . casually aristocratic, must have been very difficult for a second husband." Johnny also teased his mother about retiring to the provinces, addressing letters to her at "Los Poblanos Truck Farm." Albert, for his part, belittled Johnny's interest in poetry, telling Ruth he was weak and incompetent and foolish for not wanting a career on the *Chicago Tribune*.[35]

One of Johnny's true passions was mountain climbing. The year before he'd gone to Lima, Peru, with a professor from Brown University to climb a particular peak for a good view of a lunar eclipse. Back in Albuquerque he often climbed the Sandia Mountains, within view of their house at Los Poblanos. On June 22, 1938, Johnny and his friend Dick Whitmer went on one such climb. The night before, Johnny and Dick, together with Bobby Dietz, Johnny's roommate at Fountain Valley, whose family lived near the Simmses, met at the home of another friend. They talked about the expedition Dick and Johnny were making the next day, to climb an outcropping known as the Shield. Bobby recalled, "We talked about how the last man to scale that surface up there, in 1903, had died. We all, like kids, said, 'That's not gonna happen to us.' We sat out on the lawn having a beer."[36]

The next night, Ruth and Bazy were playing backgammon after dinner. Uncle Albert had gone to bed early, as usual. It was odd that the boys had not returned by dinner, since they couldn't have climbed in the dark. But it was possible they'd stopped off somewhere to eat. Ruth began to fidget. Bazy saw no reason for concern: "Johnny was twenty-one. I don't know whether she had an intuition or she logically had more reasons to worry." She called Bobby Dietz, who volunteered to take her up the mountain. "Uncle Albert never got out of bed," Bazy recalled bitterly.

> By midnight, something was obviously wrong. He just sat there in bed with a concerned expression on his face while we were getting flashlights, organizing the search . . . We drove up the mountain road in a kind of futile way, I mean how are you going to find people in the middle of the night on a mountain, but we didn't know what else to do.[37]

Around 2 A.M. Ruth called Triny, who was living in Washington, five months pregnant with her first child. "Johnny is lost in the mountains," her mother said. "I didn't want you to read it in the newspapers." After she hung up, Triny began sleepily to think, "Why 2 A.M.? There are no newspapers at this hour." She called back.

"Do you want me to come out?"

"More than anything in the world," answered Ruth. That was why she had called, but she wouldn't have asked. Triny was not allowed to travel by plane in her condition, so she and Courtie took the *Super Chief* train. One of the conductors, a Mr. Kelly who knew Ruth and her family well, allowed Triny to get off during a water stop on the second day to call. It was against the rules, but by this time, the boys' disappearance had become national news, and there was a great surge of sympathy for the family.[38]

Ruth needed her daughters because she was getting little support from her husband. The morning after the boys' disappearance, Ruth met with the police. "She kept breaking down," Bazy said. "You would have thought her husband would be with her but he was not. He just went about his business during the whole thing." Later that morning, at the first press conference, Albert Simms "expressed no concern over the youths' safety," according to the New York Times. Bobby Dietz and several other men had met at dawn in the mouth of Juan Tabo Canyon to resume the search on horseback. "Albert didn't like Johnny," Bobby recalled. "That morning up there—he was telling Ruth how irresponsible Johnny was. I wanted to . . ." He made a clenched fist.[39]

Toward evening on the second day, June 24, Dick Whitmer's body was found at the base of the Sandia cliff. Ruth spent the following days at the Juan Tabo base camp, directing operations. Bazy rode through the mountains and Triny stayed in camp with her mother. Albert never went near the mountain after the first day.[40]

Ruth did not break down publicly, but at night she would retire to her bed with an eggnog. She slept little, feeling, she said, as if Johnny were in her womb again, reliving the labor pains at his birth. During the day, she tried to "control my fear and anguish, . . . to protect my Bazy, his old nurse, and my big girl who was carrying her first baby."[41]

Ruth enlisted help from all quarters: youth in the CCC camps; Governor Clyde Tingley; the National Guard, which provided rolling kitchens; Francis Froelicher, the headmaster of Fountain Valley, who was an experienced climber. She "clung steadily to the hope that her son was caught in some crevice and was still alive." By the end of the third day, nearly 350 men, including some of the finest mountain-climbing talent in the Rockies, were baffled. The *New York Times* reported the mother "was near the breaking point, her taut nerves controlled only by a powerful effort of her will." Then, a week after the search had begun, Isleta and Sandia Indians, searching the north side of the cliff, located the body in a nearly inaccessible spot, and Ruth finally went to bed "in a state of nervous and physical prostration."

It was assumed the Shield had been struck by lightning, knocking Dick off on one side and Johnny off on the other. Johnny had apparently been taking pictures of the storm. Later his camera was recovered; the film showed shots of the lightning.[42]

Paul Horgan wrote Ruth at once, and she replied,

> Triny, Courtie, Baze, Sam, Albert and I are huddled here together trying to face life again. I shall not pretend to you that it is easy. Johnnie was a rare human being. He never failed me. There are no dark spots—not one—as I have gone over and over his entire life. What I had not realized was how much I depended upon him . . . now I know that it was because of this sympathy and understanding that I was able to face my life with such courage as I was able. He was a great inspiration to me and if he had outlived me, he would have carried on for me. Now I must live without him but because of his confidence in me, I must carry on in memory of him. It is the hardest battle of life I have ever fought.

Because of the publicity, condolence letters poured in, many from people Ruth did not know. Slowly, she began answering the letters, determined to respond personally to every one. At first, she found, "Writing is most difficult. It hurts too much in spite of the weeks gone by." She may have deluded herself as to the nature of her relationship with Johnny when she wrote, "He meant to carry it on for me—Quinta, the school, this ranch, the paper, all . . ." but since she believed it, she now felt her life was without real purpose. She admitted, but only to a few, "I am tired out, utterly exhausted . . . I am doing my damnedest."

When Paul Horgan visited her, he observed:

> She was devastated. We were sitting there one time, looking out at the

mountain where Johnny was killed, she told me she was deliberately staring the mountain down. She said Albert had begged her to go away and come back with some edge taken off the pain. She said, "No, I said to him, if I go, I will not return. If I don't face it and conquer it now, my life here is over.

Horgan added, "I've thought about that many times in my own life, it's been a very powerful motivator."[43]

Finally, Ruth agreed to go up to Trinchera Ranch. Bazy and three girls went too and kept her riding long hours in the mountains every day. Ruth gained some comfort from exertion and exhaustion:

I am physically tired and for the first time I can feel relaxed enough to sleep. There is not much to remind me of Johnny here . . . The country is rough enough to make me figure out the way up and down the mountain which keeps me thinking . . . I can go for two or three days quite gayly with only a little sort of tug in my heart and then it comes over me like a wave and it rattles me—I feel as if I am on a sea in a fog and can't find my way out.

Nevertheless, she was determined to pull herself back into her "old joy of living attitude," and tried to extract amusement from the difficulty she had communicating with a new Chinese cook.[44]

Ruth travelled east with Bazy, who was beginning her senior year in boarding school, but afterwards, Ruth found it was hard to be alone. She wrote her younger daughter:

leaving you the other morning gave me a homesick feeling . . . I do want you to know how much you have meant to me always but particularly this summer. I know you don't like to be sentimental and I dislike it as much as you do but when I feel deeply I like to express my feelings . . .
45

Apparently, her relationship with Albert did little to ease her loneliness.

Returning to Albuquerque, she plunged into what she wanted to think was "a critical political campaign." Her friend, the rancher Albert Mitchell, was running as the Republican nominee for governor. The Democratic Party was unusually vulnerable, laboring under the handicap of the recent indictment of seventy-three of its members for WPA graft. The state machine was led by Senator Dennis Chavis, whose son-in-law, sister, nephew, and secretary were among those indicted. But on October 26 Ruth slipped on a rug in her bathroom, fell, and broke her hip. She had been scheduled to speak on the radio that night in behalf of the Republican state ticket. She kept her engagement, speaking into a microphone next to her hospital bed. "It will take more than a broken hip to silence me," she declared. In fact, she had broken the femur below the socket of the hip joint.[46]

She was "very much irritated" with herself. The leg was painful until the pins were in; after that there was little pain, but she was fairly immobilized. It was a month before she was able to hold a little bed desk in her lap and write. For once, she found talking to people "very tiring," but school officials, Little Theater Board meetings and the Republican women were still all being organized under her direction.[47] It was not enough, though, to distract her from her loss.

When Bazy came home at Christmas, for the first time in her life, she found her mother "unravelled." Although she believed her mother was "absolutely the strongest person I ever knew," Bazy was afraid her mother was breaking down.

> She and Uncle Albert were like strangers living together—no communication at all. UA would come in and kiss her on the forehead and they would have a glass of wine before dinner. But after dinner, he went straight to bed. Mother was a night owl, and with her bad hip it was hard for her to sleep. She had moved into a separate bedroom where she had a special bed. I realized there was nothing doing with UA at all.

Ruth, alone with her thoughts, brooded. She was in a wheelchair where she could see where Johnny fell. She'd left his cowboy hat on the chair in her room where he had left it the night before he went climbing. It seemed that her mother could talk of nothing else. Bazy was alarmed.

> She'd gotten to the point where she deified Johnny, deciding he'd been almost "too good to live." That was the first time I'd ever seen anything like that, she was a pragmatic, strong person.

Bazy made up stories, because Ruth loved hearing of pranks she never knew anything about. It was the only thing that could lift her spirits. Bazy also made up a story about poor health as an excuse to stay with her mother all spring, even though it meant she could not graduate from high school.

As Ruth gradually recovered, she tried to busy herself with more small projects, organizing the New Mexican Republican women, consulting about New Mexico's participation in the New York World's Fair, arranging art exhibits in the La Quinta gallery, serving on various community boards.[48] She even had a poker table made to fit over the wheel-chair. But it was not the same.

Said Triny:

There were many tragedies in her gallant life. She was so brave and so full of love for humanity that she appeared to her world to have risen above these ghastly blows . . . Most people did not even know how awful they were. My father's drinking . . . was an agony to her . . . Then a second bad marriage of another kind. I gave her my share of socks, but Johnny's death killed something in her forever.[49]

10
A Master of Politics:
1939–1944

THE DEWEY CAMPAIGN

"Politics Is a Capacity for Infinite Detail"

Raymond Moley, *Masters of Politics*

By the summer of 1939 Ruth had nearly recovered. Her leg had healed. So too had her spirit; if not completely, she had herself under control. She and Bazy headed for the Trinchera Ranch as soon as Bazy returned from school. Albert seldom visited the ranch, as he thought the altitude was a problem for his damaged lungs. * Bazy believed her mother preferred to live at the ranch because "she was not the sort of person who would have considered divorce, and yet she didn't particularly want to live at home."[1]

Ruth's life seemed empty though. Her enthusiasm for her many projects, especially the Trinchera Ranch, was much diminished now that Johnny was no longer there to share. While he had not actually participated much in her plans, she had made them with him in mind.

It was at this point that she discovered Thomas E. Dewey, a man young enough to be her son and a political novice who needed her vast expertise. And so Ruth Hanna McCormick Simms would become the first woman named to manage a preconvention presidential campaign. Indeed, there would not be another for nearly a half century.[2]

That summer Ruth had begun to think seriously about who could be run against Franklin Delano Roosevelt. She was afraid Roosevelt would try to push America into the looming European war. In 1938 following

---

* According to Bazy, "Albert was a tremendous hypochondriac, but Mother never paid any attention to it even when she liked him." Albert Simms outlived Ruth by more than twenty years.

the Munich conference and reports of escalating atrocities against Jews, the U.S. had withdrawn its ambassador to Germany. Although many Americans supported the move, it alarmed those who, like Ruth, agreed with Herbert Hoover that European tensions had "made a general war inevitable every 100 years since the Romans kept the peace." Preserving European democracy should be a European, not an American, problem, she thought. Ruth was not a Quaker pacifist, although she sometimes found it expedient to claim to be, but she had always believed it was against America's interests to be embroiled in European conflicts.[3] "I will never vote for war," she had said in her 1930 campaign, "unless it is to protect this country." Such a view may be criticized today in light of what we know about the Nazi death camps. But in 1939 a large number of people agreed with her. Even by 1941 polls conducted by the *Chicago Tribune, New York Daily News,* and the University of Chicago revealed that seven out of ten respondents were against American participation in the European war. It was not until Pearl Harbor that this acrimonious debate ended.[4]

1939 was an auspicious time for Ruth Simms to reenter the political scene. In 1938 the Republican Party began to rise from the tomb in which it had been interred since 1930. That year the Republicans won eighty-one seats in the House of Representatives, six in the Senate, and eleven governorships. Outside of the solid Democratic South, they won a majority of the votes cast that year, picking up eight to ten percentage points in important industrial states.[5] But there was as yet no leader adequate to challenge Franklin Delano Roosevelt. The principal Republican contenders seemed to be Senator Arthur Vandenberg of Michigan, an extreme isolationist with a probusiness record, and Senator Robert Taft of Ohio, cold and colorless, who nevertheless enjoyed long-standing party affiliations in the South.

It was at this time that Thomas E. Dewey burst on the scene, running a spectacularly close race for the governorship of New York at the end of 1938. Dewey had already made a name for himself as New York's crusading district attorney, warring on gangsters who, after Prohibition, had turned to numbers and protection rackets. Appointed special prosecutor by Mayor Fiorello La Guardia, Dewey had received so much publicity that when he ran for district attorney of New York County in 1937, some polling places in Brooklyn had to put up signs, "Dewey Not Running in this County." One of the first presidential candidates to gain national attention via the electronic media, Dewey's exploits were described in radio broadcasts and movie newsreels, culminating in a feature movie starring Humphrey Bogart.[6] It was a new kind of prominence, but prominence all the same.

In New York the 1936 Republican gubernatorial candidate had lost to the Democratic incumbent Governor Herbert H. Lehman by over five hundred thousand votes. In 1938 Dewey came within sixty-four thousand votes of winning a state with a million more registered Democrats than Republicans, demonstrating he could attract voters of both parties. The Communist Party, headed by Earl Browder, withdrew their own candidate to support Lehman. If they had not done so, analysts believed, Dewey would have been elected. A few weeks after the election, Dewey received even more publicity from a racketeering trial. A Gallup Poll revealed that 27 percent of Republicans sampled favored Dewey before the trial, but 50 percent of them favored him afterwards. Dewey had planned to run for the governorship again in 1942, but now he began to consider the Republican nomination for the presidency in 1940.[7]

Despite Dewey's liabilities—he had no national political standing, was not a governor, senator, or congressman, and, at thirty-seven, was barely above the constitutional age requirement—many felt it would take a vibrant figure like the fighting D.A. who had taken on Tammany Hall to beat Roosevelt. One commentator observed:

> The old wheel horses in Dewey's party realize . . . that he is still unripe for Presidential picking, but they know, too, that he is one of the best fruits in the meager GOP orchard . . . They know they haven't anyone around with one-tenth of his vote-catching glamour.[8]

Dewey needed an experienced political mentor, and in September 1939 she appeared. For the past year, Ruth had been following his career. Bedridden with the broken hip, she often listened to the radio, and she was impressed by his speeches during the governor's race in 1938. "I knew he had qualities," she remarked. "You must have cold objectivity judging a disembodied voice." Although her leg was still somewhat stiff, Ruth travelled east to meet Dewey. They met at lunch and became involved in a discussion that lasted until 6 P.M. Dewey showed her a great many letters he had received from all over the country and asked her to analyze them. She had been dubious but quickly realized they indicated great potential. Ruth already knew Vandenberg and Taft but did not think either was the man to beat Roosevelt. Dewey was that man.[9]

Triny speculated later that her mother, wanting to become active in politics as a distraction from grief, also could not have helped Taft the same way she helped Dewey, because Martha Bowers Taft was politically talented and very involved in her husband's campaign. Ruth told Triny that a campaign "was the only thing she could think of doing to get the throbbing wound of Johnny's death stilled, at least for a year." Ruth's relationship with Dewey, as it developed, gave her great satisfaction. Though many people found Dewey remote, Ruth got along well with him. She was very warm herself, which made up any deficiencies on his part. Ruth had the quality of empathy with people; much as people who can pick up accents, she could share the beliefs of another person.[10] Dewey was young enough to be her son, which may have given her the kind of interest in guiding his future she had taken in guiding Johnny's. She may also have liked to see herself as a successor to her father, McKinley's campaign manager.

Not everyone agreed that her motives were psychological. Ruth's assistant in the campaign, Irene Kuhn, believed that although Ruth may have been trying to forget about Johnny's death, she was primarily motivated by patriotic concern. This was an impression Ruth herself liked to foster, writing Bazy: "The war has so confused the political situation that I have decided to remain in the East . . . and help with the Dewey Campaign . . . these are serious times and we must do our bit."[11]

Ruth faced a formidable task. Political analyst Raymond Moley wrote, "It was amazing [Dewey] went so far with so little natural political endowment," and he gave Ruth Simms a great deal of the credit for Dewey's success on the national scene. Another analyst remarked, "[Dewey's] greatest handicap was his inability to project his very real concern for people as individuals." Irene Kuhn was more blunt: "Dewey never saw a human being. It was all faces he was addressing . . . People somehow know that." Wolcott Gibbs was even more critical: "His vanity is enormous, of which he is aware and even proud. He once refused to appoint an otherwise capable man, saying, 'He's as arrogant as I am.'" Dewey was also a perfectionist who demanded precise, thorough planning sessions and became legendary for rewriting his speeches again and again. This overcautious behavior irritated his state chairman, Ed Jaeckle:

> [We] would be arranging a trip . . . and we'd have to break up the train because a car wasn't on the right place. Here's a man running for President of the United States and he wants to decide whether a car is going to be 20 feet from here or 25 feet from there.[12]

But Dewey had assets, the greatest of which was a trained and effective speaking voice (he had reluctantly chosen law after a promising start on a singing career), and his stirring speeches and radio broadcasts appealed strongly to his audiences. This was especially important because politics had entered a new rhetorical age, that of the radio. Huey Long, Benito Mussolini, Adolph Hitler, and Franklin Roosevelt had all achieved prominence in part because of their ability to use the new medium. Ruth Simms herself was another great asset. She had the most national contacts of anyone on his staff. She had been in politics forty-four years (as she was fond of reminding reporters) and knew the West as well as the East. In addition, she was a vital, driving force, even at sixty, with superb organizational capabilities.[13]

Dewey wanted to announce his candidacy in early September 1939, but on September 1 Germany invaded Poland, and two days later, England and France declared war on Hitler's Reich. On September 13 Roosevelt called a special session of Congress to consider repealing the arms embargo and adopting a "cash and carry" plan favorable to the allies. Dewey was persuaded to postpone announcing until the front pages would have less war news. Republicans tended to view the war situation as one that Roosevelt was exploiting to draw attention away from what they believed were failures on the domestic scene, and Ruth in her diary even predicted "some sort of peace by New Years." Ruth believed the lifting of the embargo would be the first step into war, and she didn't want the United States to take even that step.[14]

Having opposed American entanglements in Europe at least since the League of Nations fight in 1919, it is not surprising that Ruth had firm convictions on the subject. Tom Dewey was far less firm in his convictions, and his vacillating, or at least, vague, pronouncements on the war situation made it harder for him to find support as conditions in Europe worsened all through the spring of 1940.[15]

At first Ruth worked behind the scenes, building the organization that would support Dewey's drive for the presidency. By early November, however, it was no longer any secret that she had become one of the big leaders in the Dewey movement. Characterized as the "Dean of American woman politicians," Ruth Simms was expected to become one of Dewey's "field marshals" as soon as his campaign was in the open. "She bears a name and has the political background that will give Dewey's cause instant and widespread prestige," said the Washington Star. Ruth was chafing at the bit. "It will be a relief when headquarters open and departments are running so we can move faster." Her impatience was palpable: "So few people learn how to organize their time and so they waste other people's time . . . Here are grown men and women—the men are worse than the women—who are earning their own living who waste their own and everyone else's time."[16] As the campaign organization coalesced, Ruth quickly became known for her tactful leadership; even the least important worker felt a keen sense of responsibility. She was just as likely to have a quick lunch with a stenographer, and question her with intense interest on her ideas about the campaign, as to confer with the obvious leaders. Ruth still swore by personal contact. When she was setting up the Dewey organization, the New York managers would shake their heads in horror at her long distance phone and telegraph bills. The long distance phone was not used nearly so casually then as today. Ruth told one of the budget-minded local staff in New York City that she had just called some unknown man in a small town in South Dakota for just that reason:

> That's probably the first time he has ever had a long distance phone call from New York, and the very fact that Dewey's manager thinks him important enough to call long distance from New York will make him a strong Dewey worker. He will be so proud he will tell everybody in town . . .

This proved to be a very effective technique, but her long distance phone bills were staggering.[17]

Ruth's ability to appreciate the importance of the radio and telephone demonstrated her flexibility. She may have been an ideological conservative, but she was personally innovative. She commented several times during the campaign on the differences between the campaign she was managing and the one her father had managed in 1896, when she was learning the art of politics:

> In those days, unless a man owned a double-breasted frock coat and a silk hat, then he was no statesman, except in the case of a favored few from the South and West who insisted upon wearing black sombreros instead . . . The chewing tobacco era was just dying. Most conference rooms had as many cuspidors in them as they had chairs . . . Some of the meeting places of politicians could not be dignified by the name conference room. Many a deal was pulled off in the back room of a cafe, over a whisky bottle. I am just trying to give you a picture of a time when women who wanted the vote were called crackpots, when candidates for Presidents conducted front-porch campaigns, when open pre-nomination activities were carried on almost exclusively by political managers, when the people themselves had nothing to say about selecting the men for whom they would vote.[18]

Ruth realized that with radio, movies, paved roads, and a wide distribution of newspapers, the selection process had changed, and she applauded that fact. Since 1912 she had pushed for the people to select their own candidates. Ironically, in 1940 the Republican presidential nominee would be a man who had not run in a single primary.

In addition to the routine organization work of recruiting personnel, arranging publicity and planning itineraries, Ruth had to school her young candidate in everything from the background of key individuals to the mechanics of the various primary processes. She clipped and annotated articles for Dewey and wrote him long detailed memoranda. She sorted his mail and explained the importance of what she forwarded. She met with delegates and with others who would be meeting delegates themselves.[19]

Especially important, however, was her role in making speeches and in helping Tom Dewey with his. Ruth Simms gave her first big speech on his behalf before the Massachusetts Women's Republican Club in Boston on November 24, 1939. "My hat's in the ring," she announced, echoing Theodore Roosevelt. "I'm declaring myself for Thomas E. Dewey." She addressed squarely the issue of Dewey's youth, citing framers of the Constitution who were not forty years of age at the time and several youthful contemporary governors, as well as the Massachusetts senator, young Henry Cabot Lodge. Her assistant Irene Kuhn was impressed.

> I'd never seen a woman address a group before. Women were not running around making speeches in those days . . . What made Ruth a good speaker was her complete sincerity, her feeling for people . . . She was on a level with every group she ever spoke to, without ever once forsaking what she was, herself . . . It was as if she had a map of what she going to be and do in her head. She was very clear about what she wanted to say, and . . . when she spoke [her thoughts] came out clearly, like drops of water that formed a little pool.

Ruth continued to improve as a speaker, but she was not one to rest on her laurels. When she spoke to the Fairfield County Republican Women's Club in Bridgeport Connecticut in November, she noted afterward, "I was not in good form. I need practice and preparation for speeches so I must get to work on it."[20] She wanted to be better.

Ruth Simms's position in the campaign was made public when Dewey formally announced his candidacy on December 1, 1939, and opened his headquarters at 100 East Forty-second Street "amid the usual fanfare of exploding photographic flashbulbs, the grinding of newsreel cameras, and the applause of the faithful who jammed [the room]." Ruth's old antagonist Harold Ickes, now Roosevelt's Secretary of the Interior, the self-styled curmudgeon and epigrammatist par excellence quipped that Dewey had "thrown his diaper into the ring." At first, newspapers an-

nounced that J. Russel Sprague was the campaign manager, and that Ruth Simms, as was customary, would be leading a women's division. The next day a correction appeared, "Sprague and Simms are co-managers," reported the *New York Times*. "For the first time since women obtained the vote they will participate on an equality with men in an important political movement." Although Belle Moscowitz had actually directed Al Smith's nomination campaign in 1928, she was never given the title of manager. Not until Susan Estrich was designated the manager of Michael Dukakis's presidential campaign in 1988, nearly fifty years later, was Ruth Simms's achievement surpassed.[21]

Sometimes Ruth Simms was described as Dewey's "Western campaign manager." "She was," said her daughter Bazy, "if the West starts in Ohio." Russ Sprague, her co-manager, was Dewey's chief money raiser and, as the Republican National Committeeman, entitled to a prominent position. He was also the Republican boss of Nassau County on Long Island, the wealthiest community, per capita, in the United States. Even those who religiously voted Democratic were registered Republicans in Nassau County; otherwise, it could be strangely difficult to get telephone wires or water connections passed by their homes. But Sprague's experience in national politics, like that of Dewey's other advisors, was limited, and Sprague depended on Ruth Simms to run the national organization. John Foster Dulles was Dewey's advisor on international affairs. Charles Sisson, Herbert Hoover's Assistant Attorney General, Theodore Roosevelt, Jr., and state chairman Ed Jaeckle were the other top Dewey advisors.[22]

Ruth was understandably pleased with her appointment and the recognition it gave her. It was not a token appointment, and she felt she had earned it. She hoped that more women would make a "profession of public service":

> But to do what I'm doing means that you have to serve for many years and work as I have worked. Don't let's talk of women as women. Let's make the honest point that we're equal with men. I used to go up and down the country, urging women to be active in politics, to consider it their duty as citizens. You don't have to do that any more. They are organized and alert everywhere.

She felt that she had demonstrated that the opportunities were finally there; it was now up to the women themselves to take advantage of them. She declared herself "thoroughly opposed to interjecting the sex question into politics. It is a dead issue." She did not have a feminist agenda, but she was quite eager to let women know that Dewey would be a good candidate for them, just as she wanted younger voters to believe the same. She was aware that she had special appeal for the women voters, and she used the old Progressive argument of women's special abilities and responsibilities. "Don't kid yourself," she told one women's group: "You know good and well that the men are not going to do any work. Men haven't the time to do this work and therefore it is our job. It is like the division of work we have in our homes."[23]

Ruth worked out of a small anonymous apartment at 447 East Fifty-seventh Street, with scarcely an object of her own, except the famous brown leather address book said to contain the name of everyone who was anyone in the Republican Party. If the weather was fair, she would walk briskly to the Dewey headquarters on Forty-second Street across from Grand Central Station, where she had a barnlike white office, empty except for a map, a conference table and chairs. Five secretaries would be flipping the morning mail into baskets. Irene Kuhn recalled her coming into headquarters,

> striding so purposefully. She always looked so well. She dressed in the appropriate manner, in beautifully tailored suits. She always wore a hat, and Belgian shoes. I said, "You look as if your clothes just fit themselves on you, you didn't actually put them on." She said, "I try not to be

extravagant. I keep my clothes allowance at $10,000 a year." I was
thinking—I didn't know what to think! To me, it was an enormous amount
of money.

Ruth was tall, and with her excellent posture, still gave the impression
of being slim. She had a small head, and her fine, grey hair was worn
in a flat bun, with the side marcelled in soft waves. Her crisply efficient
appearance was softened by her eager expression, dazzling grin, and lively
brown eyes. As she talked, she gestured frequently with her small hands.
Though she put in long hours, up to eighteen hours a day—"She worked
extremely hard, she went way beyond what anyone would have called
the limit," Kuhn insisted—"at the end of the day, she would look as
fresh as when she started."[24]

Immediately after announcing his candidacy, Dewey made a speech
in Minneapolis. Though his managers claimed that his first appearance
in the Midwest was all they had hoped for, and the audience had been
enthusiastic, Republican Party leaders were still reluctant to endorse him.
The main problem of the campaign, apart from the war issue, was to
turn Dewey's popularity with the rank and file Republican voters into
votes at the convention. Robert Taft, described by *Time* magazine as
"phenomenally dull, phenomenally serious, phenomenally popular at the
polls," was piling up delegations in the South; by mid-December he had
nearly three hundred delegates versus Dewey's ninety-two (which included the New York delegation, by no means a sure thing). On top of
that, a poll of 481 editors of daily newspapers found the majority still
saying in December that Vandenberg would be the Republican candidate.[25]

Complicating matters altogether was a new figure emerging on the
scene, Wendell Willkie, whom *New York Times* columnist Arthur Krock
called "the darkest horse in the stable." Willkie was a brilliant businessman, president of a utilities holding company at forty-one. But he was
a maverick who had espoused socialism in college, dressed unconven-
tionally, and still refused to own a watch, a fountain pen, or a car. He
had not even joined the Republican Party until November 1939.[26]

As Ruth Simms spoke around New York in January and February 1940,
her focus became clearer. Although she didn't acknowledge it in public,
she was beginning to worry about Willkie. Despite the carefully cultivated
rustic charm, Willkie knew his public relations; and his main campaign-
ers, although amateurs to politics, were energetic and resourceful. As
the spring went on, they organized chain letters and Willkie Clubs and

disseminated articles by and about Willkie. Harold Ickes aptly called Willkie a "simple, barefoot Wall Street lawyer." Ruth spoke for the election of instructed delegates to the convention, realizing that in the event of a deadlocked convention, someone who seemed to be fresh on the scene could step in and take over.[27] She responded further to the Willkie threat by organizing a 7,500 mile speaking tour for Dewey through thirteen western states in February.

It was a tedious and complex task. She had to plot his itinerary, decide where he would speak, where he would appear on the train platform, where he would receive the press. She also made suggestions about what Dewey might say in all of these places and circumstances. Throughout his tour, Ruth continued to monitor the situation: "An ardent but erratic Dewey supporter . . . must be handled carefully . . . Wants to board train before Oklahoma City in order to give Mr. Dewey situation throughout oil states . . ." was a typical wire. The crowds on his trip were "a campaign manager's dream"; his train was continuously being halted to get Dewey to come out to the rear platform. It was 0° at Olivia, Minnesota, when the train pulled in, but one hundred people were waiting for him there. There were five hundred at Miles City, Montana, when he came through at 1 A.M. Ruth kept revising his schedule, trying for a delicate balance between meeting demands from a public she wanted to interest and conserving her candidate's energy. She wired him once solicitously, "How are you coming?" Dewey gamely responded, "Yielding to local pressures worse than New Deal. Patient doing nicely, but treatment guaranteed to kill or cure." Dividing a candidate's time was important, and Mrs. Simms was said to know as much about the subject as Roosevelt's legendary campaign manager, Jim Farley. The *New Republic* claimed that Dewey was drawing most of the discontented Republicans who had voted for Roosevelt in 1932 and 1936, but were now ready "to return to the fold."[28]

In politics, it is good to have the right enemies. Ruth scored a triumph on March 26 when the new issue of *Look* magazine hit the newsstands. Her one-time colleague Ickes had launched a characteristically intemperate crusade against his former Bull Moose associate. Claiming he'd made a mistake in saying Dewey wore diapers, he said "rompers" was the correct term, because Dewey "has to have somebody to button him up behind. And by his buttoners-up-behind shall ye know him!" Switching metaphors, Ickes called Dewey a "photogenic, radiogenic Charlie McCarthy" and asked "who is the Edgar Bergen of his Charlie McCarthy?" He revealed that the "Headman of the Dewey Brain Trust" was Ruth Hanna McCormick Simms:

the daughter of the man who is still the symbol of making money talk in American politics . . . The voice may be the voice of Dewey but the hand is the hand of Mark Hanna . . . This is no time to have a singer of songs without words for President. This is no time to have a Mark Hanna for President—by proxy, by descent, or escheat or otherwise.

Of course, the same situation could be seen in a different light; Wolcott Gibbs called her "a President-maker by inheritance, and a Dewey cabinet member by inclination."[29]

By this time, Ruth was becoming swamped by work and was planning an intensive five-week speaking tour of her own. Therefore, Charles Sisson was promoted to "co-manager" with her, while J. Russel Sprague was designated "manager." Sprague was no manager at all, according to Jaeckle, and Charlie Sisson was placed in charge of New England because Ruth needed help. Albert, who had stayed in New Mexico throughout the campaign, except for their Christmas holiday in Charleston, S. C., was visiting New York, which only added to Ruth's responsibilities. She wrote Bazy:

U.A. is sick, and it takes a good deal of my time to keep him cheered up. It is rather lonely here all day by himself. I come home to lunch with him and spend the evenings, so you know how hard I work all day to keep up at the office.[30]

Nonetheless, Ruth made a whirlwind speaking tour in Wisconsin a week before the first crucial primary there on April 2. She gave six speeches in two days, claiming to "have the New Deal on the defensive." Visiting the Dewey Headquarters in Milwaukee, she glanced at the calendar on the wall and announced that she was almost sixty years old. It was a boast, not a lament. It enabled her to make the point that never since the days of Theodore Roosevelt had she seen crowds like the ones coming out for Dewey. "My first convention was in 1896. I mention [this] merely to show you I am a veteran and that you had better listen to the words of wisdom!" Four years older than Eleanor Roosevelt, Ruth had begun to enjoy a mild rivalry with her. When both passed through Denver in April, by coincidence, a New Mexico paper compared them:

Both are shrewd, forceful women, thoroughly schooled in the intricacies of politics by virtue of association since childhood with the keenest political minds . . . Both women are particularly adept at meeting the press. Veterans of scores of interviews, each easily skirts tricky questions . . .

Paul Horgan recalled a time when Ruth was going to counter Mrs. Roosevelt in some event:

> She got a wicked gleam of battle in her face and, grinning happily, said
> in effect she would dispose of E.R. "How?" I wondered. And she said,
> "Oh, I'm going to be so much gooder than Eleanor." As she said it, she
> gave a little snake-like flick of her tongue, left and right. And a smile,
> happily evil.

Writing Bazy, Ruth inquired, "Have you seen the buttons that say, 'We
don't want Eleanor either'?" [31]

The Wisconsin primary took place just as Ruth Simms was reaching
Cheyenne, the first stop on a tour of twenty cities in thirty days. All
twenty-four delegates had pledged to Dewey on the first ballot. The press
responded with amazement to Dewey's decisive victory. Before then, the
general attitude had been summed up by a writer for the *New York Times*,
who called Dewey "the Christian Science candidate . . . He thinks he
is running but he is not." Dewey's big win in Wisconsin made Ruth an
even bigger draw as she began her campaign tour: eleven cities in four
days through Washington and Oregon, one day in Denver, then on to
Albuquerque in time to meet Dewey on his own swing through the
Southwest to California. "From New York to Albuquerque in 12 days—
with three nights in a bed!" she lamented, then added with her characteristic optimism: "As a matter of fact, it is a real rest. I have Hazel
Henning [her secretary] along and have caught up on my mail and now
am writing speeches to deliver in Washington." [32]

Ruth Simms's leadership role in Dewey's campaign was widely recognized by this time. "She is the only real big-time politician in the
crowd," wrote columnist Raymond Clapper in the *Washington* [D.C.]
Daily News: "She is the political brains and carries the load in organizing
the campaign. Everywhere you go around Dewey headquarters in New
York you hear them saying, 'I'll have to ask Ruth.'" Trying to come to
terms with a woman in such a role, one reporter waggishly referred to
her as the "generalissima'am" of the New York candidate's armies. Another characterized her as "Mahout Simms," leading the G.O.P. elephant.

As always, her personal appearances were well received. She arrived
in Centralia, Washington, in a driving rain, and the *Centralia Chronicle*
almost gushed:

> It is not often that a distinguished woman, nationally known, who was
> born and bred in the atmosphere of politics, pays a visit to our city . . .
> Let Centralia show Mrs. Simms that we are a live and progressive city
> and are pleased with the courtesy of her visit.

In Aberdeen an editorial remarked that she "presented Dewey's claims
more logically than has been done either by anyone else or by the

candidate himself."[33] She was being accepted on her own merit, not as a woman or a Hanna.

Ruth continued to work for pledged delegates.

> It is an easy thing for political leaders to get in a smoke-filled hotel bedroom and decide whom they want for President. But it is another thing when they take that man out before the rank and file . . . Let us be certain the people want the man we choose to be our standard bearer at Philadelphia.

While Ruth was pleased by news of Dewey victories in the Illinois and Nebraska primaries, she was disappointed by the small vote cast: "It is disheartening to think that any man or woman would fail to vote in a preference primary any more than in a general election. We should not forget that we select as well as elect."[34]

When Ruth Simms left the state of Washington, she had visited every congressional district, averaging eight speeches a day. James M. Bailey, president of the Dewey for President Clubs in Washington, estimated that she addressed over ten thousand people in platform and radio talks. She campaigned for Dewey as she had campaigned for herself, using the strategy she had learned from her father: get information directly to the voters.[35]

By April 16 after brief visits in Portland and Denver, Ruth was back in Albuquerque to arrange for Dewey's visit there. A procession of 150 cars met him at the station and escorted him to Los Poblanos. *Luminarias*, traditional New Mexican lights made by placing candles in sand-filled cut-out paper bags, outlined the driveway and the residence. A Mexican string orchestra played New Mexican music as Dewey swung into the gates. The carnival spirit persisted as a crowd of four thousand packed the armory for his speech at noon the next day, and he addressed an overflow crowd at lunch at the Hilton Hotel. Ruth's festive arrangements had their serious purpose, however; Dewey was not doing especially well in New Mexico, where Republicans favored Vandenberg. They selected an uninstructed delegation. Even Albert Simms could not be elected a delegate, and only after a sharp fight, was he made an alternate.[36]

Ruth's own personal stock ran very high after the public exposure of a speaking tour. "The lady with the quadruple name," as the *Los Angeles Express* described her, was again said to rival James A. Farley, Roosevelt's wily campaign manager. She returned the compliment with a twinkle, calling Farley the "greatest political organizer the country has ever seen except one, Mark A. Hanna." The compliments did not cause her to allow the pace to slacken; instead she sent Dewey on a swing through the deep South—Texas, Alabama, North Carolina, and Charleston, West Virginia. Altogether Dewey travelled thirty-five thousand miles in seven months, making 110 recorded speeches and addresses.

In spite of all this effort, fewer than half of the one thousand Republican delegates were chosen in preferential primaries. Taft would still have considerable clout among the party hierarchy.[37] And, Ruth knew, Willkie was standing by.

Ruth's candidate had peaked, as it turned out. The "phony war" in Europe came to an end with Hitler's invasion of Norway, Denmark, the Netherlands, Belgium, and France. Ed Jaeckle sensed at once that the Dewey campaign was in jeopardy:

> The night we got word Hitler had entered the Lowlands, we held a meeting, as usual on the second floor of the Ritz Carlton. I said, "'Let's be honest about it, Tom. They'll never elect as President of the United States a 38-year-old kid in this kind of situation.' They almost threw me out of the window. But Ruth was not far off my thinking. Although she may not have said so publicly, she was disturbed about the picture at that time.[38]

However, the *New Republic* columnist "TRB" had a disturbing sexist theory about Dewey's waning popularity:

> The general dislike of Dewey by politicians . . . has many peculiar aspects . . . I have become convinced 99% rests on . . . the sex of Mr. Dewey's principal campaign manager, Ruth Hanna McCormick Simms. No major candidate has ever had a woman as a principal backer before. It is unorthodox, unprecedented, discomforting . . . [Mrs. Simms] is far more experienced and practical-minded than anyone . . . connected with the Taft or Vandenberg campaigns . . . If Mrs. Simms were a man . . . he would be a sure-thing bet for the nomination. Industrialists would tell themselves that maybe they didn't know much about Dewey but they'd worked with good old Simms these thirty years and that was enough for them.[39]

Ruth pretended to an optimism she did not feel. "We are running like mad and picking up delegates every day in spite of the War and because Taft and Willkie only 'muddies the stream'," she wrote her young friend Betty Wood. But a short week later she admitted to a colleague at the Dewey headquarters in Chicago that "All of Wall Street has gone starry-eyed about Willkie" and that "Fifth Avenue and Park Avenue are singing his praises."[40]

Although some Dewey aides were claiming the support of over 350 delegates, the Willkie boom, Dewey's youth and inexperience, his continuing and worsening problems with the New York politicians, and the resumption of the war in Europe, all began to undercut Dewey's strength. The war, of course, was the factor hardest to finesse. When speaking around New York state, Ruth insisted that U.S. participation in the war was not inevitable:

> Everywhere I hear people saying casually we are already in the war. We are not in the war. We are not going to be unless Congress takes us to war. And Congress won't if you will it so. It is the issue on which the national campaign is to be fought.

As the war situation worsened, Dewey's staff tried to shore up his position as the front runner. Staff headquarters even claimed that a poll by Emil Hurja, former statistician for the Democratic National Committee, showed Dewey's national percentage was 66.3, from 52.9 on the Eastern seaboard to 79.6 in the Rocky Mountains.[41]

On June 10 Italy entered the war on the side of the Axis powers, prompting Roosevelt to make an impassioned speech at his son's graduation from the University of Virginia Law School about an Italian "stab in the back." It has been said that Thomas E. Dewey was the first American casualty of World War II. In retrospect, it is hard to see how Dewey, or any Republican, could have fought successfully the war issue and the old adage, "Politics end at the border." Jaeckle and others from New York urged Dewey to use the occasion to push through changes in the New York political machine, so that he would be in control of the party for the 1942 gubernatorial election or even the presidential election in 1944. Early in June Dewey sympathizers in the state's convention delegates suddenly replaced Republican National Committeeman Kenneth Simpson, suspected of being an erratic Dewey supporter, with Russ Sprague. Apart from any consideration of the war issue, or Willkie's public relations tactics, this drastic move sabotaged Dewey's chances for nomination. Without Willkie, such a strategy might have succeeded in bringing the delegates into line. But it was only two weeks before the convention, and Willkie was ready to take advantage of Dewey's weakness.[42] In May Willkie had begun speaking to Republican audiences, first in New York, then in St. Paul, Indianapolis, and Des Moines. By midMay, Willkie began to appear in the Gallup polls and in just two weeks' time, had risen from 3 percent to 5 percent. Although he participated in no primaries in the 1940 campaign, Willkie was a write-in candidate in New Jersey. After a one-week campaign, he drew more than eighteen thousand write-in votes, which gave his candidacy a tremendous psychological boost. At this point, the Gallup poll was showing that most

Americans thought the U.S. would eventually enter the war. Although Willkie was not yet a declared interventionist, he was the only Republican taking the initiative on the war situation; his formula was to ensure peace through stronger defenses, which could best be achieved by freeing private enterprise for greater productivity.[43]

Furthermore, Willkie had his own brand of charm. Columnist Arthur Krock described Willkie's "intensely sparkling eyes under a bramble of black-brown hair, a face of unusual animation, large of stature, strong and resonant of voice, one long thick leg invariably draped over the arm of his chair." (Dewey privately referred to Willkie as "our fat friend.") Speaking in Topeka, Willkie announced, "I'm the cockiest fellow you ever saw. If you want to vote for me, fine. If you don't, go jump in the lake, I'm still for you." In Minnesota he tossed a dull speech into the air and exclaimed, "Some damn fool told me I had to read a speech to you. Now let me tell you what I really think." Although he claimed his support was a real "grass roots movement" ("Yes, it is," agreed Alice Longworth, "The grass roots of the country clubs of America"), his campaign was a carefully crafted job of public relations. As the head of a billion-dollar company in a very politically conscious branch of American industry, public utilities, Willkie and his colleagues knew how to organize local committees, generate letters to editors and legislators, and interest the press.[44] And, to Ruth's chagrin, it was working.

Willkie soon gained another advantage, although it was not then recognized. On May 16 the Committee on Arrangements for the Conventions had been meeting all day at the Bellevue-Stratford Hotel in Philadelphia, discussing the distribution of tickets to the public for seats in the gallery. Seventy-year-old Ralph E. Williams, heading the committee, suddenly collapsed and died. In his place was named Samuel F. Pryor, the National Committeeman of Connecticut and an ardent Willkie supporter. Pryor's appointment enabled Willkie supporters later to overwhelm the delegates with their partisan activities. Arriving in Philadelphia for the Convention, Willkie claimed he had "no campaign manager, no campaign fund, no campaign headquarters. All the headquarters I have are under my hat." However, when Dewey was asked to comment on what had already become a Willkie boom, he bitterly remarked, "I am still lost in admiration for the technical skill with which the job has been done."[45]

Dewey's campaign headquarters opened a full week before the opening session, scheduled for June 24. The *Philadelphia Enquirer* found it a "strange campaign headquarters. Not a political leader in sight. No cigar butts littering the floor. Just a soft-spoken woman." It was perhaps typical of the age that even national journalists were slow to accept that a "soft-spoken woman" could be a formidable political leader. At first, Dewey left the personal direction of his headquarters to Russ Sprague and Ruth Simms, although most of the other candidates were in Philadelphia. The Willkie onslaught finally forced him to put in an appearance two days before the official opening in order to talk personally with wavering delegates. Though Dewey appeared to have more delegates than any other candidate, they were still not enough for a first ballot nomination. Failure to win on an early ballot could mean a rush to Willkie by released delegates. The Dewey strategy became one of creating an impression of unstoppable support. Ruth had engaged seventy-eight rooms at the Walton Hotel, and delegates were lined up waiting in conference rooms. Dewey moved from one to another, consulting in fifteen-minute shifts. Spokesmen issued optimistic estimates of delegate support, circulated testimonials to his popularity, and staged press conferences. Arriving delegates found a Dewey poll, showing Dewey was preferred to Willkie seven to one among the 50 percent of the population earning $1200 or less. Dewey's publicity team argued that the Republican candidate must be able to draw Democratic voters in order to beat Roosevelt.[46]

Willkie's team was equally active at this time. His manager mobilized the "Associated Willkie Clubs of America" to bombard delegates with telegrams and letters. Telegrams by weekend were estimated to be close to one million. Though some were genuine, many were not. Alf Landon attempted to answer them all when he returned home, and eighteen sacks came back to him marked "addressee unknown."[47]

Eager for a story, the press was also fanning the Willkie flame. Headlines from the *New York Times* during this period included:

"Willkie is Called the Man to Beat"
"Effort is started to stop Willkie"
"Willkie Boom Hits New High . . ."
"Surge for Willkie at Philadelphia"
"Willkie Chief Fear of Dewey Backers"[48]

The Dewey managers' first plan had been to hold several "favorite son" delegations in reserve for the second ballot, to create an impression of growing strength. Now they were convinced they had to call in every vote on the first ballot, to encourage the convention to follow the leader. Interviewed on June 18, Ruth dutifully predicted Dewey would get four hundred votes on the first ballot and increase his strength on the second.[49]

The convention opened on Monday, June 24. There were fourteen thousand people in the Philadelphia Convention Hall, including one thousand delegates and one thousand alternates. Willkie partisan Sam Pryor was controlling access to thousands of gallery tickets and had the right to limit or exclude visitors on the convention floor. Ruth's daughter Bazy, a Dewey volunteer, was downstairs on the floor handing out buttons. She took quick notice of Pryor's work:

> I was aware of them packing the galleries . . . They reprinted tickets . . . the ushers had been bought off. When you came in with your legitimate ticket, you couldn't get in. They disrupted the Convention. No matter who got up to speak, the galleries would start chanting "We Want Willkie."

It was so overwhelming that Ruth, growing alarmed, told Dewey they were seeing "the fascist movement of America."[50]

The nomination procedure started nearly an hour before its appointed time. Dewey, the first to be nominated, was thereby deprived of some much-needed tub-thumping enthusiasm, because many of his supporters were still absent when his name was placed in nomination. When Representative Charles Halleck of Willkie's home state of Indiana placed Willkie's name in nomination, the galleries, as usual, were screaming "We Want Willkie," but whistles, boos, and heckling from delegates supporting other candidates showed there was increasing resentment at the tactics of the Willkie fans.[51]

The balloting began at 4:45 P.M. on Thursday, June 27. Nomination required 501 votes. On the first ballot, Dewey led with 360, ominously short of his anticipated 400. From the outset, however, Dewey had difficulty in holding even those delegates pledged to him as the result of popular referendums. Defections in his own badly divided state delegation, where he had lost a third of the New York delegates before the balloting even began, as well as losses in the New Jersey delegation, hurt him sorely. These defections may have then influenced uncommitted delegates to switch to Willkie. Such is the psychology of a nominating convention, that once a recession has begun, however slight, it is taken as a sign of weakness and is impossible to check. Willkie, who had been expected to poll only 40 or 50 votes on the first ballot, made a dramatic showing with 105. The second ballot confirmed what was happening on the first. Several states had been pledged only for the first ballot, so the switch was on. Dewey dropped from 360 to 338, while Willkie rose from 105 to 171. Taft made a modest gain, from 189 to 203 and, in fact, slowly gained momentum through five ballots. Many insiders predicted Taft would get the nomination at last.[52]

After the second ballot, the convention was adjourned, and the Dewey managers met with Taft's cousin and campaign manager, David Ingalls, to try to agree on a mutual plan to stop Willkie. Although the managers reached an agreement, Taft's people soon sent word that he had vetoed the idea. Taft leaders believed that continued balloting would eventually gain the nomination for their candidate. In turn, they urged Dewey to throw his support to Taft, but this he refused to do, still hoping to be the victor. His New York strategist Ed Jaeckle sarcastically observed:

> They were sure they could win. So was Dewey. They were each going to win. Dewey wouldn't let anyone manage . . . He wanted to be the candidate and the manager. You can't run a campaign with the candidate being manager. His personal dislikes, his ambitions enter into his judgment.

This inflexibility would be at the root of Dewey's split with both Jaeckle and Ruth Simms during the 1944 campaign.[53]

Willkie won by the end of the sixth ballot. Even in retrospect, the phenomenon of the Willkie nomination is hard to understand. It is important to realize, however, that it was not entirely the blitz it is usually pictured as being. The Mid-West, South, and West held out against him. As Dewey faded, Taft assumed leadership among the Midwest delegations. The western states, which had been Ruth Simms' special responsibility during the campaign, stayed with Dewey. Ironically, the East, which had stampeded for Willkie, later voted for Roosevelt, while the West remained loyally Republican. In part, Willkie was attractive because he had a fresh, apolitical image, appealing at a time when voters were fed up with corrupt big-city bosses, big government in Washington, and the European quagmire. While the American public was confused about the European situation, and the convention was divided in its opinion on foreign policy, Willkie's policy, similar to Roosevelt's, was perhaps in greater accord with the overall mood of the time. With France fallen and England threatened, Dewey's inexperience and Taft's isolationism were great liabilities. Willkie was also inexperienced, but not as young as Dewey, and no isolationist. Add to this the marquee factor: Taft was comparatively colorless, and Dewey's self-assurance often seemed arrogant, while Willkie's offbeat persona made wonderful copy.[54]

Dewey telephoned his congratulations to Willkie at 1:30 A.M. on Friday, June 28. Asked for an analysis of the balloting, he quipped, "I led on three ballots, but they were the wrong three." His curious cheerfulness was reflected in a remark to Alf Landon: "If we can't take it, we shouldn't be in politics, and I hope by now, I have learned to take it."

No doubt he was aware that he came out of the campaign with vastly increased prestige. His inner circle appeared more shaken than Dewey at the results. Ruth took the defeat badly. She was bitter because she felt an outside force was taking over the party, and that the convention had been hijacked. She was too loyal, however, to make a public protest. She wrote that although they all knew that there was "something to be investigated" at the Philadelphia convention, a Senate inquiry at that "particular point" would be "lamentable."[55]

Ruth was also suffering from fatigue. The following day, she postponed a visit to the Deweys at their farm, wiring, "Much as I want to see you both I'm much too sleepy to be articulate." To Triny, she seemed very vulnerable:

> I went to see her at the dreary flat. She looked haggard, frightened, as she had [after my father died]. Was it that the pain of Johnny's death had returned—the thought of returning to Uncle Albert—was it she thought she might be of no more use in the world? She was a doer; her life was now empty. Dewey's defeat was a sadness, but the real sadness was the void that immediately followed.[56]

She also may have feared that Dewey's loss meant certain American involvement in the war. Ruth returned to Albuquerque, and soon her personal secretary could say she had recovered:

> Mrs. Simms looks and feels fine, goes horseback riding every morning for a couple of hours and is feeling not the worse for the work she did during the campaign. Immediately on her return here she plunged into work at her school . . . I think that she just can't be idle one minute.[57]

Wendell Willkie named Ruth to his twelve-person advisory committee. Ruth apparently had reservations about accepting the position because Dewey himself wrote to urge her to take it:

> I think there is no way you could gracefully refuse even if you should desire to do so . . . it will not be an active or operative committee to such an extent that it would put any burden on you and it is a symbol of unity of the party in the major task, that of eliminating the New Deal.[58]

Ruth could not only promote party unity, she could serve two other important functions. She was popular with women, and Willkie, having run in no primaries, had been chosen by men at the convention. Ruth was also well-connected in the West, where Willkie was weakest. In fact, however, she played no part in Willkie's national campaign. Analysts like Raymond Moley assumed she would have been willing to help, given her long record of party loyalty, and that "surrounded by amateurs, [Willkie] apparently overlooked the opportunity to enlist a real veteran." Perhaps Willkie intentionally "overlooked" her because he disliked professional politicians and, on the strength of his success in Philadelphia, believed he and his amateurs would be enough. For her part, Ruth was reluctant to involve herself in the Willkie campaign; she did not approve of the national leadership: "the leadership of this campaign is identical to the leadership of the campaign four years ago . . . it was the worst managed campaign that the Republican Party has ever experienced."[59]

Ruth remained vitally interested in Dewey's career; he was speaking during the campaign, and she offered advice: "When the time comes for you to consider an itinerary I will be glad to cooperate with you in such states in which I believe you will have the most influence in my Western country." She went on to say, "We have had such a good time working together for ten months, it is my desire to work with you as closely in the future as in the past . . ."[60] Dewey answered ten days later:

> I do hope you are going to be able to make a speech or two at least. It does seem strange, our having been so close together for almost one uninterrupted year and then finding you continuously 2500 miles away.

As the summer progressed, Willkie's position on domestic and foreign affairs became clearer, and it must have disturbed Ruth to no small extent. He supported most of Roosevelt's foreign policy and was unable to control his own party in Congress, which routinely voted against the measures Willkie supported. He was out of touch with most of the Republican hierarchy and professional politicians. In addition, he managed to alienate women by announcing that the position of Secretary of Labor should be a "man's job," a direct blow at the incumbent secretary, Mrs. Frances Perkins.[61]

Through it all, Ruth strove to maintain her optimism, but it was not getting any easier. "The campaign looks sunk," she wrote to Bazy, "but I keep having the feeling that some way Willkie will nose ahead . . . I must admit Willkie has made every mistake known to man and I suppose reason points to a defeat." Finally, on election eve: ". . . I prophesy before the night is over we will have the laugh on the other fella. Have been working in my precinct all day and will be up all night as usual." But on November 6: "He laughs loudest who laughs last. I was 100 percent wrong . . . Still have my sense of humor and am looking forward to interesting old age."[62]

Fifty million people voted, the highest number until 1952. It was Roosevelt's narrowest victory to date. The Republicans' greatest gains were in the upper Midwest, the Rocky Mountains, and the Far West, where the Republican vote was 10–25 percentage points higher than it had been in 1936.[63] It is hard to escape the conclusion that Ruth Simms' efforts had not been without their effect.

THE WAR YEARS

Politics: "My Right and My Pleasure"

They might have made history together, Thomas E. Dewey and Ruth Hanna McCormick Simms. Dewey was well-positioned for the race in 1944, and Roosevelt's health was deteriorating. Ruth Simms was eager to take up the fight again almost as soon as the 1940 election was over. But it was not to be. Dewey was reluctant to declare himself too soon and wanted to concentrate his energies on the governorship. Then by the time he was ready to run, he had shifted politically, and the isolationist politics of Ruth Simms, acceptable until Pearl Harbor in December 1941, were a clear liability. Instead of confronting her with their differences, however, and making a clean break, Dewey led her on until the very end. Although it was to be a sad finish to her long, ground-breaking career, there were no hints of that bleak future in the winter of 1940.

By December polls were already showing that 60 percent of all Republicans again preferred Dewey; the Willkie aberration was a thing of the past. Ruth Simms wanted Dewey immediately to position himself as the front runner in 1944 and wrote him encouragingly:

> I haven't been able to get final figures but I believe it can be proven if you had been the candidate, the electoral college vote would have been very different . . . I have been having some difficulty with some of your ardent supporters in a few of the Northwest states, trying to prevent their starting organizations in support of your candidacy for '44. I don't want to dampen their spirits . . .

Taking the long view, she discussed possible candidates for Republican National Chairman: ". . . The Party ought to be well organized immediately in order to avoid . . . a pre-Convention fight four years from now." Dewey was keeping himself in the public eye, speaking out against Roosevelt's proposed Lend-Lease Act for giving the president authority that should have been reserved to the Congress. But he was adamant that he intended to run for governor and to serve for four years.[64]

Ruth Simms continued her interest in Dewey's career and wrote:

> The fire bell always stirs the blood of the retired fire horse, and as time

approaches for your campaigns, I am brimful of curiosity as to what is
going on in backroom caucuses . . . a few bits of information would be
of great benefit to my peace of mind.

She went on to give him more advice about restructuring the national
party organization, and Dewey seemed eager to have her support. In fact,
on a trip East in December 1941, Ruth had no sooner arrived in New
York than she received word that her cousin Lucia's husband, Malcomb
McBride, had just died in Cleveland, and Ruth promptly left to spend
Christmas with Lucia. Dewey complained:

> I am totally unable to understand why you couldn't spare time to write
> or telegram before you arrived. If you were busy, I could have ushered
> you off the train and ridden in a taxi to wherever you were going . . .
> In short, I am mad at you. But I have been mad at you before and you
> have been mad at me before and I suppose you will stay away for
> another couple of months now, and I shall be all over it. If you don't at
> least let me take you off the train next time you are coming I shall be
> thoroughly outraged . . .

It was a warm note, even for a politician, and especially one like Dewey.[65]

In February Ed Jaeckle advised Dewey to state publicly he would serve
out his term, because if he did not, he would lose the support of the
legislature and would not have a successful administration. "If you are
honestly drafted," he told Dewey, "that will permit you to excuse yourself
from your commitment." He, Russ Sprague, and Herb Brownell would
"dust up the bushes and create a draft." It seems that Dewey did not
advise Ruth that this would be his strategy.[66] It was a sign of things to
come.

It did not help that Ruth never reconciled herself to the war, even
after Pearl Harbor, and vainly hoped it might be an issue in the 1942
congressional elections. "When gas rationing hits the mountain states,
there is bound to be resentment . . . There is no way to raise sheep and
cattle without means of transportation. There are no railroads connecting
the ranches," she observed to Dewey. She thought rationing set an om-
inous precedent:

> It will not be long before the men in factories will be told where to work
> and for less pay and for longer hours and they will not be permitted to
> leave their place of employment without permission of the government.
> Americans don't like that sort of treatment and they will demand a change.
> There is only one change that can be made, stop the war!"[67]

Ruth had no real work in Dewey's gubernatorial campaign, and when, after Pearl Harbor on December 7, 1941, she had wired Roosevelt to ask how she could help in the war effort, she had received no reply. So she turned to the Trinchera Ranch, determined to raise meat. She planned eventually to run five million cattle and ten million sheep in the Colorado mountains. "During the last war I milked cows and now it looks as if I would ride fence," she remarked. Ruth went up to the ranch in mid-June 1942, explaining that as her men were being drafted, it was necessary for her, at age sixty-two, to "punch cattle." This prompted Dewey to respond: "Aren't there men to do men's work, at least as far as cow punching is concerned? There must still be work for brains and it is pretty hard to do brain work and punch cows at the same time." Ruth confessed to Dewey later in the summer: ". . . There are times when I am riding the mountains when I think of you all having a campaign without me and I have a pang. I love it and it is in my blood but my work is here."[68]

Ruth had ignored the ranch for several summers—Johnny's death, the broken hip, the Dewey campaign, and Bazy's wedding in the summer of 1941 to Peter Miller had distracted her. She decided Trinchera was being incompetently run, so in the fall of 1942 she fired the manager, and began to run it herself. Here she still had a lot to learn and was often frustrated. "I have never felt so silly about any business as I feel about this ranch," she wrote Bazy: "I have worked my head off and I have proved to be the world's worst rancher. No that isn't quite true. I am the world's worst steer speculator. The sheep have done well." But at the end of September she claimed: "By another year I will know how to do it myself. There is nothing difficult about it and I am learning very fast . . ." Coping with the problems of labor shortage and food rationing, she decided to butcher some of her oldest sheep herself: "The government will ask us not to eat much meat but we can not keep our sheep herders satisfied unless they get meat, and if we do not give it to them they will take it."[69]

Meanwhile, Dewey was elected governor of New York and moved to Albany. He wrote Ruth that his new home was "not the sprightliest of cities." The new governor had few friends and almost no intimates in Albany at this time, and his letters to Ruth were still very warm. When Ruth was sick with flu for three weeks in March 1943, Dewey wrote: "After all you and Albert have been through this winter, it seems to me you ought to realize you cannot win the whole war singlehanded . . . Come here for a change of atmosphere and rest." Ruth first had to get her "steers in the mountains and the lambs safely started up the canyon," then promised to come East, assuring her young protégé:

> I am following your administration step by step and day by day and am
> as vitally interested as you are in your accomplishments. It irritates me
> to receive letters now commenting on your work as governor in glowing
> terms from those unable to visualize your abilities two years ago.

As she saw it, the political situation was becoming serious and something
needed to be done about it and, "as usual," she would try to stir them
up and "then return to my cows."[70]

When Ruth finally did arrive in Albany, she and Dewey had an all-
evening and all-morning talk. He gave her the impression he did not
"want or intend to be a candidate for President," so she returned to the
ranch to battle drought and labor shortages, telling Bazy it was "[t]he
toughest job I have ever undertaken." They were shearing nine thousand
sheep to get eighty thousand pounds of wool, and running six thousand
head of steers to graze in the mountains. In spite of the drought, they
were farming three thousand acres of irrigated land and raising grain and
hay for winter feed. The feed situation was critical, and she was angry
that the government would not let the ranchers slaughter to reduce
surplus. Ruth believed that the American people would soon be tired of
government interference and predicted, "the Republican Party will elect
the next president." She again urged Dewey to consider running for the
presidency:

> The present political situation demands leadership . . . It is true we have
> a year . . . You know better than anyone how quickly time passes . . .
> The majority of Republicans in state legislatures and minor officers are
> for you. I remember very well everything you said in Albany . . . [but]
> there is a very distinct responsibility . . .[71]

In September 1943 Dewey and other Republican leaders met at Mackinac, in rural Michigan, to discuss postwar policy. The conference produced "The Declaration of Mackinac," a call for international disarmament
and an undefined "cooperative organization" of nations. This was an
abrupt departure from the platform on which Dewey had run in 1940,
and Bert McCormick's conservative *Chicago Tribune* protested: "Dewey
Goes Anti-American." They editorialized,

> In his anxiety to hold New York he has lost the nation . . . now he has
> finished the pilgrimage to Downing Street by way of Wall Street. He has
> bought and been bought by the prospect of millions for his campaign
> fund from New York Bankers.

The *Tribune* was surely guilty of overstatement, but according to Ed
Jaeckle, Dewey was in fact "fascinated, obsessed with money," which led

him to be influenced by Roger Strauss and other Wall Street bankers. Jaeckle also thought Dewey was reacting to suggestions by Harold Ickes and others that Ruth Simms had become a handicap. Even though her connections with the *Chicago Tribune* were more apparent than real, they existed in the mind of the public, and Dewey considered this a negative factor, writing his mother, "The *Tribune* is a terrific liability" in states outside of Illinois. In short, Dewey no longer wanted to be associated with Ruth Simms.[72]

Ruth, of course, had no inkling of his change of heart. All during the fall, she continued to write him long letters of advice, urging him to distinguish between those who had selfish reasons for wanting him to run, and those, like herself, who for patriotic reasons were urging him to run. Jaeckle saw it that way as well:

> Other people associated with Dewey were "yes-men." They were looking to the time when Dewey would be President, who was going to get what . . . Dulles wanted to be Secretary of State. Roger Strauss wanted to be Ambassador to England . . . So everybody would listen to what the great man thought. Or thought he thought.

Ruth Simms and Ed Jaeckle believed that Dewey should not change his 1940 image. There was a continuous debate in the Dewey camp as to whether Dewey should present himself as a "tough cop" or a "lofty intellectual." Jaeckle would say:

> Tom, you made your reputation as a D.A. If you want to be a Sunday school superintendent, it'll take a long time to establish that fact. You might be a good one but you can't sell it overnight. Why don't you get on the stump and talk like a D.A.![73]

In early November 1943 Ruth outlined for Dewey a strategy by which he could accept a draft. She had many arguments in favor of his declaring his candidacy. She believed people would "react strongly against anything that looks like political maneuvering, or insincerity on the part of the candidate." She doubted that the "average American citizen" could be persuaded "that Tom Dewey does not want to be a candidate for President in 1944," and she was convinced that the Republicans, eager for a winner, would go elsewhere if he did not declare soon. She was also concerned about the situation in which the "old Dewey leaders" were being placed. "The old leaders, of course, continue to write me and I have about run out of excuses and reasons for their neglect . . ." Finally, any holding back ran contrary to her instincts. She herself "did not reluctantly consent to become a candidate at the urgent solicitation of my friends. I went after it myself because I wanted it." She thought Dewey should do the same.[74]

Dewey reluctantly agreed to have a high level strategy meeting with Ruth in January 1944. Dewey answered her request for this meeting with an unusually short, cold letter; his letters from then on were conspicuously different from the warm, chatty ones of the previous three years. It warrants observation here that Dewey's reluctant strategy was perhaps the correct one. After all, he would win the nomination. In his biography of Dewey, Richard Norton Smith argued that although Dewey's pledge not to leave the governor's office may have hurt him some, it also helped him avoid the problems of peaking too early and freed him from the kind of demands being made on other candidates. As Dewey told Arthur Vandenberg: "The best way to campaign is by performing a public service that people know about." Nevertheless, he appears never to have engaged in an open debate on the subject with Ruth but to have kept her increasingly at arm's length.[75]

Ruth continued to write him long newsy letters, but she was becoming involved in New Mexico politics for the first time.

> They have never permitted me to be active politically in this state, and have always taken the attitude that the only reason I moved to New Mexico was because I thought I could more easily run for public office in this state. Now they are convinced of my sincerity and are eager for my help in reorganizing the party.

This had kept her from getting to New York until mid-February. After the Dewey meeting, she continued to act as if she was very much involved, and political leaders continued to visit her. In March, she wired Dewey she was "in almost hourly touch with the Oregon situation . . . [and] reporting daily to Mr. Brownell [Dewey's new campaign manager]." She telegraphed a friend: "May I remind you this is a campaign year with no time to rest. Just back from undertaking big pre-convention job which will keep me on the road and busy night and day." Ironically, Herb Brownell, a relatively inexperienced young man in his early thirties, often contacted her without Dewey's knowledge and relied heavily on her advice.[76]

President Roosevelt's visibly deteriorating health made the nomination of the Republican candidate an even more pressing issue. In April delegates pledged to, but unauthorized by, Dewey badly beat Wendell Willkie's in the Wisconsin primaries. Ruth wrote Tom Dewey a long analysis of the political situation and announced her willingness to serve: "I am making an effort to be prepared to give you worthwhile suggestions in regard to personnel for the national campaign, and ideas on the campaign itself." Still, she must have sensed his growing coolness and added: "I have periods of regretting the distance between Albany and Albuquerque during the last few weeks." Ruth continued to write Dewey long letters, but he seldom acknowledged them. Finally, on June 5, Ruth wrote an even longer letter, voicing her concerns:

> You are surrounded by a small group of very intelligent New York men . . . Your immediate advisors, however able, cannot inform you of the sentiment of the people as a whole because no one of them has ever lived away from the Atlantic seaboard . . . People throughout this country all the way out to the coast have remembered [your Western trip in 1940] and you, and they are still for you.
>
> To win the election you must be the same Tom Dewey they saw and knew in 1940. It is this factor that concerns me now. The impression we receive from your more recent speeches is of a change . . .
>
> You are not being true to yourself; you are not like the sort of speeches you are delivering now . . . I earnestly urge you to broaden your base of close advisors . . . I hope you receive this letter in the spirit in which it was written—sound advice from an old experienced campaigner.
>
> Love,
> affectionately, Ruth.

She apparently received no direct answer. But she soon received an indirect response which prompted the last letter she was to write him:

> Dear Tom,
>
> Today I have been shocked into a decision to write this letter to you now, rather than let the situation continue as I had thought was best policy on account of pressure during the campaign. The shock was administered by persistent rumors coming from New York headquarters, and again today a query to the local paper in Albuquerque by the AP to locate me to ask the cause of our split . . .
>
> My answer will be the truth. I am engaged in the active management of this ranch, doing the sort of work I have always done in assisting state organizations for the campaign . . . As long as I feel it necessary to write at all, I will continue. For you and me to have any misunderstandings seems ridiculous. If I had any idea of the cause which has created this situation, I could deal with it as I always deal with my personal relationships, with complete frankness and honesty. Why you have not been frank with me I am at a loss to know or understand.
>
> I am therefore forced to the conclusion that I have entirely misunderstood our political and personal friendship. As long as it remains between you and me it can be adjusted or dropped but if it becomes public property and rumors continue to spread it will enter the political campaign

and be interpreted to the disadvantage of all concerned . . . My position in the party and the part I propose to take in the campaign is as I planned it many months ago . . .

I do not want or would I be willing to accept any position within the party organization or out of it. I will always be active in party affairs, vitally interested in its success, and the promotion of its leadership in my state and in the nation. It is my inheritance and my conviction of my participation as a citizen. It is my right and my pleasure. Beyond that I have no ambition. My life is full of all sorts of other interesting activities and I am too selfishly happy at home to be willing to exchange it . . .

If I have misinterpreted our former relationship your continued silence will answer me. Under no circumstances will it interfere with my participation in the campaign in support of the national ticket this fall. If your silence continues it will leave me free from any personal obligations to you as an individual candidate to pursue my political beliefs which may or may not follow your political thinking . . . I am always sincerely yours,

Ruth Hanna Simms.

There is no indication that he answered this letter, or that they ever corresponded again.[77]

Ruth attended the Republican Convention in Chicago in mid-June, "supporting the national ticket." At her suite in the Blackstone Hotel, she told supporters that the New York governor had held on to his 1940 strength in the Mountain and Pacific states. "I personally expect to see Dewey nominated on the first ballot," she said. She had waived her "right" to be Chairman of the New Mexico delegation in order to go on the Resolutions Committee and spent her time before the convention seeing people to learn trends in the Mid-West before the committee met. The city was having the hottest June in thirty years, with temperatures past 100 degrees buckling the street car tracks. The Chicago stadium was bare as an indication of wartime austerity; twenty-five thousand crowded into a hall designed for twenty-one thousand to hear Dewey accept the nomination.[78]

Immediately following the convention, Ed Jaeckle became another victim of Dewey's new-found independence. He also received word indirectly, from a reporter, that he was being released. According to Jaeckle, "These things always came from him, but he used other people to do it, he planted these things." Commenting on Dewey's treatment of Ruth Simms, Jaeckle said,

Sure, it hurt her. It hurt me when he did the same thing to me. He wouldn't sit down with you and say, "Look, we have a very close relationship. I think certain things have happened . . . and this is my decision." He wouldn't do this, he'd have a third party do it. The fact that she told him some home truths had some bearing on it—he didn't like that.[79]

To save face, Ruth let it be widely known that ranch work left her no time for active campaigning: "The labor shortage is terrific. When I found out conditions I was obliged to make up my mind definitely to withdraw from the political campaign." In September she wrote Francis Froelicher: "I am not overworked really, and am feeling very fit physically . . . I know I give the impression of being fatigued when . . . I am not tired but desperately disturbed [by the Dewey campaign]." Then, in mid-October, while she was riding the range, her horse put a foot in a hole and fell. "There is nothing dramatic about my fall," she protested. "It is just ignominious and stupid . . . My shoulder hit a rock . . . I splintered a piece of bone off the top and broke the big bone . . . at the shoulder."[80]

Ruth was taken to the Billings Memorial Hospital in Chicago for the operation on her shoulder. Bazy and Peter Miller were also living in Chicago, expecting their first baby in early December. Ruth's principal regret seemed to be being "shut up during an election." Dewey relented and came to visit her in the hospital, but Ruth, though mildly pleased at the gesture, could not refrain from telling him that he was making the greatest mistake of his life and still had time to change.[81]

Ruth was not bedridden. She had Jacques Potts make suit coats to fit over her sling and continued to correspond and to take an active interest in the campaign. "We are going to win the election," she predicted, "by an eyelash or a landslide." After Dewey's defeat she expressed a professional's disappointment at a lost opportunity:

> The only real regret is not that we were beaten, but because we were able to pick up so large a popular vote and were beaten so badly in the electoral college. It smacks of being outsmarted in certain localities, which is always humiliating.

She must have thought it would have been otherwise if she had been involved.[82] It was a bitter thought after so many years of effort.

Shortly after the election, Ruth was able to leave the hospital and move into a hotel. But a few days later, she woke up in excruciating pain and went back to the hospital, where she was diagnosed with pancreatitis. The doctor delayed the operation, hoping to avoid one. On the afternoon of the following day, December 4, he did operate but was too late; the pancreas had ruptured. Albert, who had remained in Albuquerque until this point, came to Chicago. The doctor took Peter

Miller aside and told him Ruth would not have long to live. She amazed them all by surviving another three weeks.[83]

"None of us admitted Mother was dying," said Bazy. "She had a wonderful nurse, Miss Heinz, who came in at night and said not to be afraid. Mother answered, 'I was never afraid in my life.' She never was afraid, but it also bespeaks the frame of mind she was in, she didn't have a lot more to live for. She had a bad marriage, and no more work to do."[84]

Ruth was unconscious most of the last few days. But the night of December 30, when Triny went back to the hospital, she found her mother, "on fire with fever, but also all keyed up, feeling well." Ruth reached out and took her hand and told her that she had always wanted to do the sort of work Triny was doing, working for civil rights reforms. She had only left the stockyards settlement, she said, because Medill had not liked it there. Triny thought this little speech was typical of Ruth's extraordinary empathy. It was very cold in Chicago that night, and her mother then said, "Puss, open the window and put your hands out, freeze your hands and put them on my forehead." Triny did so, again and again.[85]

Early the next morning, the last day of December, Ruth died. Her daughters, their husbands, and Albert took her body back to Albuquerque on the train, the *Super Chief*, which Ruth had ridden so many times crisscrossing the country on campaigns and business jaunts. At sundown there was a tap on Triny's door. It was Mr. Kelly, the conductor who had tried to help and comfort her six years before, when she'd gone west at the time of Johnny's death. It was quite a coincidence; Chicago "Chiefs" crossed each other going to and from Los Angeles daily. But Kelly was there again. He sat down opposite Triny, looked at the floor a minute, then raised his head.

"I hauled her back and forth across the country over and over again," he said, "and now I'm taking her home for the last time."[86]

Epilogue

Since Ruth died when I was barely three weeks old, writing this book has been a voyage of discovery, not only of who she was, but of how I came to be myself.

It was not easy discovering who she was. Her daughters, two very dissimilar women, gave me widely different accounts of their mother. When Bazy read the first draft of the manuscript, she said of the parts where I had quoted Triny, "It makes me think we had different mothers." In a sense, of course, they did. Ruth was relatively inactive during Triny's childhood and very active during Bazy's. Their impressions of her relationship to their father, of her hopes in the 1930 Senate campaign, of her involvement in the Rockford newspapers, even of her brand of cigarette, vary greatly.

One thing they both agreed on, however, was Ruth's penchant for embroidering her stories. She was not one to dwell on the past, but if something made a good story, she liked to tell it.

"We would kid her about it," said Bazy, "and say to each other, 'Well, here comes Number 17.' She was a marvelous raconteur, and she never let the truth stand in the way of a good story." Triny said the same: "You have to be careful about believing her anecdotes. She would embroider them and make a wonderful story out of them. They were her way of attracting attention among intellectuals, because she could not talk about Joseph Conrad or the situation in the Middle East. But she could tell an amusing story, and she was daring and attractive, and the intellectuals would just die over this creature!"

In our family, most of us are story tellers, just as most of us are gregarious, like to laugh, and enjoy hard work. In this instance, I have tried to curb the excesses of the story telling tendency, and to confine myself to what I could verify. Although it has not always been easy to separate fact from fantasy, I think I do have a sense of what Ruth was like as a person. And I have come to realize that I owe at least two things to my grandmother.

One is my attitude toward problems, passed down to me through my mother. Triny told me a story typical of Ruth (a *true* story, she emphasized). One day Ruth was driving her horse, as she loved to do in Byron. She met a dejected-looking man on the road and stopped to ask if she could help. His situation was hopeless, he told her. He had no education, no training, and had become an alcoholic. He was sure his wife would leave him, taking their four children. Ruth immediately suggested he come to work as her herdsman. He learned all about cattle breeding and never took another drink. "She never, ever believed that there was nothing to be done about a situation," Triny concluded. "She believed that you could just move mountains."

Even in small matters, Ruth was exactly the same. Peter Miller, Bazy's husband, recalled the first time he met his prospective mother-in-law. Ruth had at first opposed the marriage on the grounds that the couple were too young, so Peter was nervous and very chagrined at being wracked by violent hiccups. Immediately Ruth urged him to try her favorite cure. "That was her whole attitude," he said. "'You've got a problem, I've got a solution.'" I'm like that myself, an inveterate meddler. I have come to believe that it was her itch to solve people's problems as well as her devotion to principles and thirst for competition that drove her career in politics.

I owe her something else as well. Five days after the operation on Ruth's pancreas, I was born to Bazy and Peter Miller. It was obvious that Ruth was dying, and there was tremendous pressure on the new parents to give their daughter her name. Peter had photographs taken and brought the enlargements to Ruth's room at Billings Hospital. From her bed, she called Bazy, who was in bed at the Lying-In Hospital.

"Give her her own name!" she insisted.

Barnie Thompson, the editor of the Rockford newspaper, refused to print my name for a week, hoping that Bazy and Peter would relent. They held out and named me Kristie.

Notes

CHAPTER 1

1. *Cincinnati Enquirer,* June 3, 1903, Ruth Hanna McCormick Scrapbook, McCormick family papers, held by Kristie Miller, hereafter cited as McCormick Collection.

2. Thomas E. Felt, "The Rise of Mark Hanna," Ph.D. diss., Michigan State University, 1961, p. 68; Herbert Croly, *Marcus Alonzo Hanna: His Life and Work* (Hamden: Archon Books, 1965), pp. 8, 14, 17; Mrs. Baldwin interview by James Morrow, Box 4, Hanna-McCormick Family Papers, Manuscript Division, Library of Congress, Washington, D.C.; Thomas Beer, *Hanna* (New York: Octagon Books), pp. 23–25.

3. Solon Lauer, *Mark Hanna: A Sketch From Life* (Cleveland, Ohio: Nike Publishing House, 1901), p. 66; Croly, *Marcus Alonzo Hanna,* pp. 46–48; Felt, "The Rise of Mark Hanna," p. 32; Michael E. McGerr, *The Decline of Popular Politics: The American North, 1865–1928* (New York: Oxford University Press, 1986) pp. 13, 21; Elizabeth Manchester, Notes, ms., Box 131, Hanna-McCormick Papers; Beer, *Hanna,* p. 26.

4. M. A. Hanna to C. A. Rhodes, July [31], [1864]; M. A. Hanna to C. A. Rhodes, June 16, [1864], McCormick Collection.

5. Croly, *Marcus Alonzo Hanna,* pp. 65, 85–86, 88–90, 94.

6. Ibid., pp. 65–97, passim.

7. Ruth Hanna McCormick to R. N. McLennan, May 7, 1928, Box 40, Hanna-McCormick Papers. Spelling and punctuation have been standardized in Ruth Hanna McCormick's letters. Ruth McCormick Tankersley [Bazy] to author, October 16, 1985; Croly, *Marcus Alonzo Hanna,* pp. 74–75; Felt, "The Rise of Mark Hanna," p. 65; Mary Phelps interview by James B. Morrow, May 18, 1905, Box 4, Hanna-McCormick Papers; C. A. R. Hanna to Will Rhodes,

November [11], 1880, McCormick Collection; Irene Kuhn, conversation with author, October 1984.

8. Kuhn, 1984.

9. Tankersley conversation with author, September 1987; Lucia McBride interview by Elizabeth Manchester, Box 131; M. A. Hanna to James Foraker, February 28, March 18, March 27, April 6, April 23, 1888, Box 2; Charles W. Holman, "Above All Else, A Farmer," *The Farmer's Wife*, February 1928, pp. 10 ff., clipping, Box 131; Helen Bennett, unpublished manuscript, Box 109, Hanna-McCormick Papers.

10. Eric Johannesen, *Cleveland Architecture 1876–1976* (Cleveland: Western Reserve Historical Society, 1979), p. 48; McBride interview by Manchester; Tankersley conversation with author, September 1984.

11. McBride interview by Manchester, Box 131, Hanna-McCormick Papers; Tankersley conversation with author, September 1984; Katrina McCormick Barnes [Triny] conversation with author, September 1984; on attitudes toward mental illness, see Susan Ware, *Partner and I: Molly Dewson, Feminism, and New Deal Politics* (New Haven: Yale University Press, 1987) pp. 41–42.

12. Estelline Bennett, unpublished article, [1929], Chicago Historical Society; Tankersley conversation with author, September 1924; Helen Steward Marlatt to Bazy Miller, November 14, 1950, Box 109; M. A. Hanna to Foraker, Box 2, Hanna-McCormick Papers.

13. Frances Parkinson Keyes, "Mark Hanna's Little Girl," *Delineator*, October 1930, pp. 14 ff.

14. Tom Hill conversation with author, June 1988; Thomasville Historical Society, *Thomasville, Georgia: A Place Apart* (Dallas: Taylor Publishing Company, [1985]); Keyes, "Mark Hanna's Little Girl."

15. Eleanor Patterson, *The Washington Herald*, August 19, 1930; Keyes, "Mark Hanna's Little Girl."

16. Tankersley conversation with author, October 1987; Irene McCoy Gaines, ms. of speech, November 25, 1929, Chicago Historical Society; Keyes, "Mark Hanna's Little Girl"; Gloria Gavert, archivist, Miss Porter's School, to author, February 1, 1989; McBride interview by Manchester; Ruth Hanna McCormick, ms. of "Politics: A Prescription for Every Citizen," Box 131; Helen Frances Warren to Elizabeth Manchester, April, 1951, Box 109, Hanna-McCormick Papers.

17. Lauer, *Mark Hanna*, p. 63.

18. Croly, *Marcus Alonzo Hanna*, pp. 110, 118, 124–26, 137, 161–62, 169; Felt, "The Rise of Mark Hanna," p. 71, 262; James Ford Rhodes, *The McKinley and Roosevelt Administrations, 1897–1909* (New York: Macmillan, 1922) p. 4; Margaret Leech, *In the Days of McKinley* (New York: Harper and Brothers, 1959), p. 483; H. Wayne Morgan, *From Hayes to McKinley: National Party Politics 1877–1896* (Syracuse: Syracuse University Press, 1969) pp. 482–83, 485–88; Barbara W. Tuchman, *The Proud Tower: A Portrait of the World Before the War, 1890–1914* (New York: Macmillan, 1966) p. 162.

19. Felt, "The Rise of Mark Hanna," pp. 256–58; William L. Shirer, *Twentieth Century Journey: A Memoir of a Life and the Times*, vol. 1, *The Start, 1904–1930* (New York: Bantam Books, 1985) p. 69.

20. Morgan, *From Hayes to McKinley*, p. 486, 490; Felt, "The Rise of Mark Hanna," p. 281, 284; Croly, *Marcus Alonzo Hanna*, pp. 175–76.

21. *New York Times*, December 13, 1903; Croly, *Marcus Alonzo Hanna*, p. 175; *Museum Echoes 2*, 1957, p. 14.

22. Unidentified interview by Morrow, Box 4; Ruth Hanna McCormick biographical material, Box 131, Hanna-McCormick Papers.

23. *Chicago Tribune*, April 6, 1930.

24. Morgan, *From Hayes to McKinley*, pp. 491–92; Beer, *Hanna*, p. 152–53, 254; Croly, *Marcus Alonzo Hanna*, p. 191, 207; Felt, "The Rise of Mark Hanna," pp. 291–92; Rhodes, *McKinley and Roosevelt*, p. 17; Mark Sullivan, *Our Times: The United States 1900–1925*, vol. 1, *The Turn of the Century* (New York: Charles Scribner's Sons, 1927) p. 293; McBride interview by Manchester, Box 131, Hanna-McCormick Papers; *New York Times*, July 29, 1896.

25. Michael E. McGerr, *Decline of Popular Politics* (New York: Oxford University Press, 1986) pp. 22, 29, 45–52 passim., 58, 64–65, 90–91, 104, 107, 140; Leech, *In the Days of McKinley*, p. 86–87; Lauer, *Mark Hanna*, pp. 50–55; Felt, "The Rise of Mark Hanna," pp. 252, 337, 339, 341–43; Sullivan, *Our Times*, vol. 1, p. 139; Rhodes, *McKinley and Roosevelt*, p. 26; Morgan, *From Hayes to McKinley*, p. 510; Charles Dick interview by Morrow, Box 4, Hanna-McCormick Papers.

26. Felt, "The Rise of Mark Hanna," pp. 342–43; Croly, *Marcus Alonzo Hanna*, p. 185; Lewis L. Gould, "The Republican Search for a National Majority," in H. Wayne Morgan, ed., *The Gilded Age* (Syracuse: Syracuse University Press, 1970) pp. 185–87; Morgan, *From Hayes to McKinley*, p. 509; Rhodes, *McKinley and Roosevelt*, p. 24; Myron T. Herrick, p. 64, quoted in Morgan, *From Hayes to McKinley*, p. 516.

27. Leech, *In the Days of McKinley*, p. 88–89; Croly, *Marcus Alonzo Hanna*, pp. 215–16; Felt, "The Rise of Mark Hanna," p. 336; "Politics," Box 131, Hanna-McCormick Papers.

28. McGerr, *Decline of Popular Politics*, p. 140; Leonard C. Hanna interview by Morrow, Box 4, Hanna-McCormick Papers; Croly, *Marcus Alonzo Hanna*, p. 206; Beer, *Hanna*, p. 140; Morgan, *From Hayes to McKinley*, p. 508; *New York Tribune*, August 2, 1896.

29. Morgan, *From Hayes to McKinley*, p. 486–87, 510; Leech, *In the Days of McKinley*, p. 76; H. H. Kohlsaat, *From McKinley to Harding, Personal Recollections of Our Presidents* (New York: Charles Scribner's Sons, 1923) pp. 30–31; William Allen White, *The Autobiography of William Allen White* (New York: Macmillan, 1946) p. 295.

30. Leech, *In the Days of McKinley*, p. 76; Foraker 91–92 in Morgan, *From Hayes to McKinley*, p. 510.

31. Leech, *In the Days of McKinley*, p. 69, 87, 96; Morgan, *From Hayes*

to McKinley, p. 519; Beer, Hanna, p. 165; McGerr, Decline of Popular Politics, pp. 6–7.

32. Chicago Tribune, April 6, 1930; Leech, In the Days of McKinley, p. 96; Lewis L. Gould, Reform and Regulation: American Politics from Roosevelt to Wilson, Second Edition (New York: Alfred A. Knopf, 1986) pp. 9–10; New York Times, November 12, 1896; Rhodes, McKinley and Roosevelt, p. 30, 123–24; Beer, Hanna, p. 175; Felt, "The Rise of Mark Hanna, p. 236.

33. Mark Hanna, His Book (Boston: Chapple Publishing Co., 1904) p. 74; McBride interview by Manchester, Box 131, Hanna-McCormick Papers; Leech, In the Days of McKinley, pp. 116–19; Alice Roosevelt Longworth, Crowded Hours (New York: Charles Scribner's Sons, 1933) p. 70.

34. Croly, Marcus Alonzo Hanna, pp. 272–80, passim.; New York Times, February 22, 1929.

35. Croly, Marcus Alonzo Hanna, pp. 240–41, 274; Rhodes, McKinley and Roosevelt, p. 36; Barnes conversation with author, September 1984; Grace Robinson, "Cutting Sex Out of Politics," Liberty Magazine, March 31, 1928, pp. 23–29.

36. Croly, Marcus Alonzo Hanna, pp. 272–80, passim.; New York Times, February 22, 1929; S. J. Woolf, "Dewey's Right Hand Woman," New York Times Magazine, February 18, 1940, p. 10; "Politics," Box 131, Hanna-McCormick Collection.

37. Will P. Frye interview by Morrow, Box 4, Hanna-McCormick Papers; Croly, Marcus Alonzo Hanna, pp. 412–13; Robinson, "Cutting Sex Out of Politics," pp. 23–29; Elmer Dover interview by Morrow; Charles F. Leach, interview by Morrow, Box 4, Hanna-McCormick Papers; Holman, "Above All Else," p. 11.

38. Croly, Marcus Alonzo Hanna, p. 459; Rhodes, McKinley and Roosevelt, p. 8; Augusta Hanna interview by Morrow, Box 4, Hanna-McCormick papers; Margaret B. Downing, Globe Democrat [February 17, 1914], McCormick Scrapbook; "Politics", biographical material, Box 131, Hanna-McCormick Papers.

39. Beer, Hanna, p. 206; Croly, Marcus Alonzo Hanna, p. 278; Arthur Wallace Dunn, Gridiron Nights (New York: Arno Press, 1974), quoted in Sullivan, Our Times, vol. 1, p. 74.

40. Tankersley conversation with author, June 1985, October 1987.

41. Sullivan, Our Times, vol. 1, p. 63; Leech, In the Days of McKinley, p. 529, 533–42; Rhodes, McKinley to Roosevelt, pp. 134–35; Croly, Marcus Alonzo Hanna, pp. 309–17.

42. Croly, Marcus Alonzo Hanna, p. 322, 328, 334–35; Leech, In the Days of McKinley, pp. 555–56; Harold L. Ickes, The Autobiography of a Curmudgeon (Chicago: Quadrangle Books, 1943) p. 50.

43. Rhodes, McKinley and Roosevelt, pp. 139–40; Charles G. Dawes, A Journal of the McKinley Years (Chicago: The Lakeside Press, R. R. Donnelly and Sons, 1950) pp. 249–52; New York Tribune, September 28–29, 1900, quoted in Leech, In the Days of McKinley, p. 557.

44. Marguerite Green, *The National Civic Federation and the American Labor Movement, 1900–1925* (Washington: Catholic University of America Press, 1956) pp. 4–6, 15–20.

45. Ibid. pp. 28–33, 29–42; Croly, *Marcus Alonzo Hanna*, pp. 395–96, 399–401, 410.

46. Croly, *Marcus Alonzo Hanna*, p. 355; Gould, *Reform and Regulation*, p. 31; Lauer, *Mark Hanna*, p. 116.

47. Leech, *In the Days of McKinley*, p. 560; Lauer, *Mark Hanna*; Croly, *Marcus Alonzo Hanna*, p. 361.

48. Theodore Roosevelt, April 17, 1906, Box 4, Hanna-McCormick Papers; Beer, *Hanna*, p. 148; Croly, *Marcus Alonzo Hanna*, pp. 360–61, 373, 375, 394.

49. Charles A. Selden, "The Father Complex of Alice Roosevelt Longworth and Ruth Hanna McCormick," *Ladies Home Journal*, March 1927, pp. 6 ff.

50. Biographical material, Box 131, Hanna-McCormick Papers; Leo E. McGivena et al., *The News: The First Fifty Years of New York's Picture Newspaper* (New York: News Syndicate, 1969) p. 10; Lloyd Wendt, *Chicago Tribune: The Rise of a Great American Newspaper* (Chicago: Rand McNally, 1979) p. 342, 350.

51. *Quincy* [IL] *Journal*, June 3, 1903; Medill McCormick to R. S. McCormick, [1902], Box 1, Hanna-McCormick Papers.

52. Medill McCormick to R. S. McCormick, December 24, 1901, Box 1, Hanna-McCormick Papers.

53. McBride interview by Manchester, Box 131, Hanna-McCormick Papers; Barnes conversation with author, September 1984; *New York Times*, June 17, 1902; Keyes, "Hanna's Little Girl," p. 58; Beer, *Hanna*, p. 129.

54. Keyes, "Hanna's Little Girl," p. 58; *New York Times*, September 30, 1902; Medill McCormick to R. S. McCormick [1902]; M. A. Hanna to R. S. McCormick, February 8, 1903, Box 1, Hanna-McCormick Papers.

55. Croly, *Marcus Alonzo Hanna*, pp. 423–27; *Buffalo News*, June 2, 1903.

56. Medill McCormick to Ruth Hanna, May 22, 1903, McCormick Collection; Medill McCormick to Mr. and Mrs. R. S. McCormick, March [1903], Box 1, Hanna-McCormick Papers.

57. Medill McCormick to Mr. and Mrs. R. S. McCormick [spring 1903], McCormick Collection; Keyes, "Hanna's Little Girl," p. 58; *Gainesville* [OH] *Daily Courier*, May 30, 1903; Medill McCormick to Ruth Hanna, May 14, 29, 31, 1903, McCormick Collection; *Columbus Press*, June 2, 1903.

58. Croly, *Marcus Alonzo Hanna*, p. 430; *Cleveland World*, June 9, 1903; *Cleveland Leader*, June 10, 1903; *Cleveland News Herald*, June 9–10, 1903; Northampton [MA] *Gazette*, June 10, 1903; *Chicago Inter Ocean*, June 10, 1903; Dunkirk [NY] *Herald*, June 10, 1903; *Cleveland Plain Dealer*, June 4, 11, 1903.

59. Beer, *Hanna*, p. 286; Meriden [CT] *Journal*, June 10, 1903; *Washington Post*, June 7, 1903; *Cleveland World*, June 10, 1903; *Cleveland Plain Dealer*, June

11, 1903; Longworth, *Crowded Hours,* p. 63; Selden, "The Father Complex"; Rhodes, *McKinley and Roosevelt,* p. 284.

60. *Cleveland World,* June 10, 1903; *Cincinnati Enquirer,* June 11, 1903; *Cleveland Leader,* June 11, 1903; *Chicago News,* June 10, 1903.

61. *Cleveland World,* June 10, 1903; *Cleveland Recorder,* June 10, 1903; *Cincinnati Enquirer,* June 7, 1903; *Chicago Chronicle,* June 10, 1903; *Chicago News,* June 10, 1903; Johnstown [NY] *Republican,* June 10, 1903; K. M. McCormick to Medill McCormick [undated] McCormick Collection.

62. Alice Lee Roosevelt Longworth Diary, June 10, 1904, Manuscript Reading Room, Library of Congress, Washington, D.C.; *Cleveland Plain Dealer,* June 11, 1903; *Cincinnati Enquirer,* June 11, 1903; *Buffalo Courier,* June 10, 1903; Beer, *Hanna,* p. 286.

63. *Cleveland Plain Dealer,* June 11, 1903; *Cleveland Press,* June 10, 1903.

64. Hon. Jas. R. Garfield interview by Morrow, February 14–May 6 Box 4, Hanna-McCormick Papers; Liberty.

CHAPTER 2

1. Woolf, "Dewey's Right Hand Woman," p. 19; Selden, "The Father Complex," pp. 6 ff.

2. Box 3, Hanna-McCormick Papers; Croly, *Marcus Alonzo Hanna,* pp. 420–21, 437; Rhodes, *McKinley and Roosevelt,* pp. 279–80, 285; M. A. Hanna to N. B. Scott, August 20, 1902, Hanna-McCormick Papers, quoted by Gould, *Reform and Regulation,* p. 52; Charles Dick to Elmer Dover, February 10, 1906, Box 4, Hanna-McCormick Papers.

3. Beer, *Hanna,* p. 267.

4. Selden, "The Father Complex," pp. 6 ff.; see also Gould, *Reform and Regulation,* p. 54.

5. Croly, *Marcus Alonzo Hanna,* p. 452.

6. Ibid., p. 454.

7. Woolf, "Dewey's Right Hand Woman," p. 19.

8. *New York Times,* February 15, 1904; Selden, "The Father Complex"; Longworth, *Crowded Hours,* p. 63.

9. Ruth McCormick to Medill McCormick, undated, McCormick Collection; financial records, Box 132, Hanna-McCormick Papers.

10. Robinson, "Cutting Sex Out," pp. 23–29.

11. Tankersley conversation with author, September 1984; Ruth Hanna McCormick Simms to Katrina McC. Barnes [Triny], [1942], McCormick Collection.

12. Shirer, *Twentieth Century Journey,* pp. 94–109; Sullivan, *Our Times,* vol. 3, p. 460; K. M. McCormick to Medill McCormick, [undated], McCormick Collection.

13. Medill McCormick to Ruth McCormick, May 14, 29, 22, [1903], McCormick Collection.

14. Holman, "Above All Else," p. 11; Keyes, "Hanna's Little Girl," p. 58; Ruth McCormick to Medill McCormick, February 4, 1909, McCormick Collection; McBride interview by Manchester, Box 131; Mary King Patterson to Ruth McCormick Miller [Bazy], November 2, 1950, Box 109, Hanna-McCormick Papers.

15. Karen Blair, *The Clubwoman as Feminist: True Womanhood Redefined, 1868–1914* (New York: Holmes & Meier, 1980) pp. 57, 69, 93, 105, 118–19; Elisabeth Israels Perry to author, October 1990.

16. Alice Kessler-Harris, *Out To Work: A History of Wage-Earning Women in the United States* (New York: Oxford University Press, 1982) p. 121.

17. Allen Freeman Davis, *Spearheads for Reform: The Social Settlements and the Progressive Movement, 1890–1914* (New York: Oxford University Press, 1967) pp. 30–32; F. Kelly, President, National Consumers League; J. Lathrop, first Director, Children's Bureau, U.S. Department of Labor; E. Lathrop, distinguished sociologist, Breckenridge, Dean of University of Chicago School of Social Work, Dr. A. Hamilton, pioneer in industrial hygiene and medicine. See Eleanor Flexner, *Century of Struggle: The Woman's Rights Movement in the United States*, rev. ed. (Cambridge: Belknap Press, 1975) p. 215.

18. Jane Addams, *Twenty Years At Hull House* (New York: Macmillan, 1910; Signet Edition, 1961) p. 136; Elsie Reif Ziegler, *Light a Little Lamp* (New York: John Day, 1961) pp. 185–91; *Mary McDowell and Municipal Housekeeping: A Symposium* (Chicago: University of Chicago Settlement League, 1938) p. 64–65, 122.

19. Davis, *Spearheads*, p. 117; Barnes conversation with author, September 1984.

20. *Mary McDowell and Municipal Housekeeping*, p. 127; Manchester notes, Box 131, Hanna-McCormick Papers; Irene McCoy Gaines ms. of speech, November 25, 1929, Chicago Historical Society; Keyes, "Hanna's Little Girl," p. 60; Ray Ginger, *Altgeld's America* (New York: M. Wiener, 1986) p. 23.

21. Howard E. Wilson, *Mary McDowell, Neighbor* (Chicago: University of Chicago Press, 1928) pp. 25–28. Wilson thanks Ruth Hanna McCormick in his Preface.

22. *Mary McDowell and Municipal Housekeeping*, pp. 79–82; Wilson, *Mary McDowell*, pp. 84, 60–66.

23. Tankersley to author, December, 1990; The Senator was Joseph M. Dixon of Montana. *Christian Science Monitor*, February 2, 1928; *National Civic Federation Review*, September, 1908, p. 22, Box 131, Hanna-McCormick Papers; *Christian Science Monitor*, op. cit.

24. David Morgan, *Suffragists and Democrats: The Politics of Woman Suffrage in America* (Ann Arbor: Michigan State University Press, 1972), pp. 25–26; Ware, *Partner and I*, p. 33; *Chicago Tribune*, February 24, 1904; Ginger, *Altgeld's America*, pp. 246–47; Kessler-Harris, *Out to Work*, pp. 152–53.

25. Maud Nathan, *Story of an Epoch-Making Movement* (New York, 1926) pp. 1–14, quoted in Flexner, p. 213; Ginger, *Altgeld's America*, pp. 244–45;

Olive Banks, *Faces of Feminism: A Study of Feminism as a Social Movement* (New York: St. Martin's Press, 1981) pp. 111–15; William Allen White, *The Old Order Changeth*, rev. ed. (Milwaukee: The Young Churchman, 1917) pp. 152–53.

26. Ginger, *Altgeld's America*, p. 11; *Mary McDowell and Municipal Housekeeping*, pp. 101–2; Adade Mitchell Wheeler and Marlene Stein Wortman, *The Roads They Made: Women in Illinois History* (Chicago: Charles H. Kerr, 1977) p. 73.

27. Florence Jaffray (Mrs. J. Borden) Harriman, *From Pinafores to Politics*, (New York: Henry Holt, 1923) p. 89; *National Civic Federation Review*, op. cit.

28. Unidentified clipping, March 11, 1908, Box 131, Hanna-McCormick Papers.

29. Steven M. Buechler, *The Transformation of the Woman Suffrage Movement: The Case of Illinois 1850–1920* (New Brunswick: Rutgers University Press, 1986) p. 169.

30. Green, *National Civic Federation*, p. 208; *National Civic Federation Review*, pp. 9–10.

31. *National Civic Federation Review*, pp. 12–16.

32. Green, *National Civic Federation*, p. 486.

33. Isabel Ross, *An American Family: The Tafts* (Cleveland: World Publishing, 1964) p. 197; Longworth, *Crowded Hours*, p. 149–51.

34. Longworth, *Crowded Hours*, p. 152; White, *Autobiography*, p. 402.

35. Manchester, Notes, Box 131, Hanna-McCormick Papers; Wendt, *Chicago Tribune*, pp. 360–61

36. K. M. McCormick to Medill McCormick [undated], McCormick Collection.

37. Wendt, *Chicago Tribune*, p. 361.

38. Ruth McCormick to Medill McCormick, [undated], McCormick Collection.

39. Ruth McCormick to K. M. McCormick, February 4, 1909, McCormick Collection; Wendt, *Chicago Tribune*, p. 374.

40. Medill McCormick to Ruth McCormick, March 10, 1909, McCormick Collection. Some of the correspondence between C. G. Jung and the McCormicks was previously published in *Spring 50* 1990:1–25.

41. C. Jung to Ruth McCormick, April 15, 1909, McCormick Collection.

42. Medill McCormick to Ruth McCormick, April 22, 1909, McCormick Collection; C. Jung to Ruth McCormick, July 9, 1909, McCormick Collection.

43. C. Jung to Medill McCormick, July 15, 1909, McCormick Collection.

44. C. Jung to R. McCormick, July 20, 1909, McCormick Collection.

45. Medill McCormick to Ruth McCormick, April 21, September 21, 1909; March 10, 1910, McCormick Collection.

46. Ruth McCormick to Katrina McC. Barnes [Triny], [1943], McCormick Collection.

47. Longworth, *Crowded Hours*, pp. 179–80; Barnes conversation with author, September 1984.

48. K. M. McCormick to Medill McCormick, July 14, October 29, [1910]; October 18, 1910, McCormick Collection.

49. K. M. McCormick to Medill McCormick, [undated] McCormick Collection.

50. Theodore Roosevelt to Medill McCormick, June 20, 28, 1908, Box 5, Hanna-McCormick Papers.

51. Gould, *Reform and Regulation*, 141, 84, 138; Archibald Willingham Butt, *Taft and Roosevelt* (Port Washington: Kennicat, 1971) p. 434; George Wickersham to Charles Nagel, July 3, 1910, Charles Nagel papers, Sterling Memorial Library, Yale, quoted by Gould, *Reform and Regulation*, p. 137.

52. Manchester, Notes, Box 131, Hanna-McCormick Papers; Robert M. La Follett, *La Follette's Autobiography: A Personal Narrative of Political Experiences* (Madison: Robert M. La Follette, 1913) p. 494, p. 507.

53. La Follett, *Autobiography*, p. 556; Keyes, "Mark Hanna's Little Girl"; *New York Times*, September 8, 1911.

54. *North American Review*, May 1911, pp. 691–93.

55. Theodore Roosevelt to Col. Cecil A. Lyon, December 21, 1911; similarly to Judge J. C. Pritchard and Pearl Wright, Box 5, Hanna-McCormick Papers; Gould, *Reform and Regulation*, pp. 146–47; La Follette, *Autobiography*, pp. 556–99.

56. Margaret B. Downing, *Globe Democrat*, February 7 [1914], McCormick Scrapbook; *National Civic Federation Review*, July 1, 1911, p. 20; *New York Times*, May 8, 1911.

57. *New York Times*, February 6, 1912.

58. Gould, *Reform and Regulation*, pp. 147–48; Longworth Diary, February 12, 13, 1912; Selden, "The Father Complex," pp. 6 ff.; *New York Times*, February 23, 1912.

59. *New York Times*, April 11, 1912; Belle Case La Follette and Fola La Follette, *Robert M. La Follette*, vol. 1 (New York: Macmillan, 1953) p. 434; *Seattle Times*, April 9, 1940.

60. Gould, *Reform and Regulation*, p. 155; Sullivan, *Our Times*, vol. 3, p. 71.

61. Harriman, *Pinafores to Politics*, p. 99; White, *Autobiography*, p. 457; Ickes, *Autobiography*, p. 160; Hermann Hagedorn, ed., *The National Edition of the Works of Theodore Roosevelt*, vol. 17 (New York: Charles Scribner's Sons, 1926) pp. 204–31, quoted in John Allen Gable, *The Bull Moose Years: Theodore Roosevelt and the Progressive Party* (Port Washington: Kennikat Press, 1978) p. 17.

62. Harriman, *Pinafores to Politics*, p. 99.

63. Longworth, *Crowded Hours*, pp. 196 ff.; Gable, *Bull Moose Years*, p. 15; Harriman, *Pinafores to Politics*, pp. 99–100.

64. Longworth, *Crowded Hours*, pp. 196–203, 201; Gable, *Bull Moose Years*, pp. 4, 5, 17; Kohlsaat, *McKinley to Harding*, p. 77.

65. Gable, *Bull Moose Years*, p. 19; Wendt, *Chicago Tribune*, p. 388; Her-

mann Hagedorn, *The Roosevelt Family of Sagamore Hill* (New York: Macmillan, 1954).

66. Mrs. Theodore Roosevelt, Jr. (Eleanor Butler), *Day Before Yesterday*, (Garden City: Doubleday, 1959), pp. 60–61.

67. Gable, *Bull Moose Years*, p. 75–76; White, *Autobiography*, p. 483; Harriet Taylor Upton, in *Roosevelt As We Knew Him: The Personal Recollections of 150 of His Friends and Associates* (Philadelphia: John C. Winston, 1927) pp. 163–64.

68. *New York Times*, August 5, 1912, quoted in Gable, *Bull Moose Years*, p. 58, pp. 40, 107; Davis, *Spearheads*, p. 198; Gable, *Bull Moose Years*, p. 81.

69. Ibid., pp. 28–29.

70. *New York Times*, July 15–16, 1912; Gable, *Bull Moose Years*, p. 145.

71. Gable, *Bull Moose Years*, pp. 58, 48; Wendt, *Chicago Tribune*, pp. 389–40.

72. Harriman, *Pinafores to Politics*, pp. 112, 114.

73. Medill McCormick to Theodore Roosevelt, November 18, 1912, Box 5, Hanna-McCormick Papers; Gable, *Bull Moose Years*, p. 148; Certificate, Box 133, Hanna-McCormick Papers.

74. Woolf, "Dewey's Right Hand Woman," p. 19; Theodore Roosevelt to Ruth McCormick, November 12, December 4, 1912, Box 13, Hanna-Mc-Cormick Papers.

75. Hagedorn, *Roosevelt Family*.

CHAPTER 3

1. Banks, *Faces of Feminism*, pp. 91–92.

2. Gable, *Bull Moose Years*, p. 167; Davis, *Spearheads*, pp. 202–5; A. Funk to A. H. Shaw, July 8, 1914, National American Woman Suffrage Association Papers, Reel 33, Manuscript Division, Library of Congress, Washington, D.C., hereafter cited as NAWSA Collection; White, *Autobiography*, p. 483; Cott, *Grounding of Feminism*, p. 29.

3. Flexner, *Woman's Rights Movement*, p. 256; Buechler, *Transformation of Woman Suffrage Movement*, p. 182–83, 186; Cott, *Grounding of Feminism*, p. 17–18; Estelline Bennett, "The Lady From Illinois," *Pictorial Review*, April 1928.

4. Anna Howard Shaw, *The Story of a Pioneer* (New York: Harper & Bros., 1915) p. 316; Morgan, *Suffragists and Democrats*, pp. 79–80.

5. Flexner, *Woman's Rights Movement*, p. 271; Woolf, "Dewey's Right Hand Woman"; Aileen S. Kraditor, *The Ideas of the Woman Suffrage Movement, 1890–1920* (New York: W. W. Norton, 1981) p. 72.

6. Inez Haynes Irwin, *The Story of the Woman's Party* (New York: Harcourt, Brace, 1921) p. 25; Andrew Sinclair, *The Better Half* (Westport: Greenwood Press, 1965) p. 302; Flexner, *Ideas of Woman Suffrage Movement*, pp. 272–73; Morgan, *Suffragists and Democrats*, p. 7.

7. Morgan, *Suffragists and Democrats*, p. 7; Sinclair, *Better Half*, p. 302; Flexner, *Ideas of Woman Suffrage Movement*, p. 273.

8. Box 13; Helen Bennett, "Women's Trade Union League," unpublished ms. Box 13, Hanna-McCormick Papers; Wheeler and Wortman, *Women in Illinois History*, p. 82.

9. Ruth McCormick to Theodore Roosevelt, April 24, 1913, Box 13, Hanna-McCormick Papers; Gable, *Bull Moose Years*, p. 186.

10. Ickes, *Autobiography*, p. 167.

11. Gable, *Bull Moose Years*, pp. 160–61; Ickes, *Autobiography*, p. 166.

12. Adade Mitchell Wheeler, "Conflict in the Illinois Suffrage Movement of 1913," *Journal of Illinois State Historical Society*, 76, no. 2 (Summer 1983): 103.

13. Buechler, *Transformation of Woman Suffrage Movement*, p. 149, 178; Arthur Wallace Dunn, "Who's Who in the Affairs of the Nation: Some National Figures, Seldom Heard Of, Who Are Doing Big Things," *New York Success*, April 1921, Clipping, Box 131, Hanna-McCormick Papers; George Fitch, "The Noiseless Suffragette," *Colliers*, August 9, 1913, pp. 5–6.

14. Fitch, "The Noiseless Suffragette."

15. Buechler, *Transformation of Woman Suffrage Movement*, pp. 177–78; Fitch, "The Noiseless Suffragette".

16. Gertrude Foster Brown, "The Opposition Breaks," from *Victory: How Women Won It, A Centennial Symposium, 1840–1940*, NAWSA (New York: HW Wilson, 1940); Wheeler, "Conflict in Illinois Suffrage Movement," p. 104; NAWSA Collection, Illinois Equal Suffrage Association Files, Reel 38.

17. Brown, "Opposition Breaks"; Brand Whitlock, *Her Infinite Variety* (Indianapolis: Bobbs-Merrill, 1904) pp. 90–92.

18. Brown, "Opposition Breaks"; Grace Wilbur Trout, "Sidelights on Illinois Suffrage History," *Illinois State Historical Journal*, 13, no. 2 (July 1920): 145–79; Wendt, *Chicago Tribune*, pp. 398–99.

19. Estelline Bennett, undated article, Chicago Historical Society; Buechler, *Transformation of Woman Suffrage Movement*.

20. Trout, "Illinois Suffrage History"; Brown, "Opposition Breaks."

21. Trout, "Illinois Suffrage History."

22. Wheeler and Wortman, *Women in Illinois History*, p. 107; Brown, "Opposition Breaks"; Fitch, "The Noiseless Suffragette."

23. Brown, "Opposition Breaks"; Wheeler, "Conflict in Illinois Suffrage Movement."

24. Wheeler, "Conflict in Illinois Suffrage Movement"; Fitch, "Noiseless Suffragette"; Trout, "Illinois Suffrage History."

25. Wheeler, "Conflict in Illinois Suffrage Movement," quoting *Chicago Daily Journal*, June 14, 1913; Trout, "Illinois Suffrage History"; Fitch, "Noiseless Suffragette."

26. Irwin, *Story of the Women's Party*, pp. 3–4; Buechler, *Transformation of Woman Suffrage Movement*, pp. 176, 196; Trout "Illinois Suffrage History"; Dunn, "Who's Who."

27. Helen Bennett, "Woman's Suffrage 1913," unpublished ms. Box 13, Hanna-McCormick Papers; Trout, "Illinois Suffrage History;" Robert Afton Holland, "The Suffragette," *Sewanee Review* 17 (July 1909): 272–88, quoted in Kraditor, *Ideas of Woman Suffrage Movement*, p. 36; Banks, *Faces of Feminism*, pp. 56, 246; Addams, *Hull House*, p. 237; Wheeler, "Conflict in Illinois Suffrage Movement," p. 105.

28. Buechler, *Transformation of Woman Suffrage Movement*, p. 186; Banks, *Faces of Feminism*, p. 93; Kraditor, *Ideas of Woman Suffrage Movement*, pp. 281–82; Ruth McCormick, ms. of speech, Box 111, Hanna-McCormick Papers.

29. Buechler, *Transformation of Woman Suffrage Movement*, p. 178, 148; McCormick speech, Box 111, Hanna-McCormick Papers.

30. Trout, "Illinois Suffrage History"; copy of letter from John P. Wilson and John J. Herrick to Governor Dunne, June 24, 1913, for R. H. McCormick, Box 13, Hanna-McCormick Papers; Trout, "Illinois Suffrage History;" Margaret Haley, ms. of speech to Chicago Teachers Federation, March 20, 1930, Chicago Historical Society; Wheeler, quoting *Chicago Tribune*, July 1, 1913; Addams to Ruth McCormick, July 14, 1913, Box 13, Hanna-McCormick Papers.

31. Irwin, *Story of Woman's Party*, pp. 14, 23–24.

32. Sinclair, *Better Half*, p. 301; Irwin, *Story of Woman's Party*, p. 3, 13; Sinclair, *Better Half*, p. 103.

33. Irwin, *Story of Woman's Party*, p. 13; Sinclair, *Better Half*, p. 103.

34. Morgan, *Suffragists and Democrats*, p. 2–3.

35. *Suffragist*, 1 (November 15, 1913), p. 3; Flexner, *Woman's Rights Movement*, p. 274–76; Banks, *Faces of Feminism*, p. 45; *New York Times*, January 5, 1914.

36. *New York Times*, December 3, 1913.

37. Flexner, *Woman's Rights Movement*, pp. 274–76; Sally Graham to author, January 14, 1986.

38. Mary Ware Dennett to Harriet Laidlaw, form letter, Dec. 19, 1913, Folder 113, Harriet Laidlaw Papers, Schlesinger Library Radcliffe College; Graham to author, February, 1986; *Boston Transcript*, January 29, 1914.

39. Banks, *Faces of Feminism*, p. 22; Kraditor, *Ideas of Woman Suffrage Movement*, pp. 221–22.

40. Banks, *Faces of Feminism*, p. 22; Kraditor, *Ideas of Woman Suffrage Movement*, pp. 221–22.

41. *Washington Herald*, January 14, 1914.

42. Ruth McCormick memo, [undated, c. April 1914] NAWSA Collection, Reel 33.

43. Graham to author, March 2, 1990.

44. *New York Times*, January 10, 1914; *Inter Ocean*, January 10, 1914.

45. *Globe-Democrat*, February 7, 1914; *Inter Ocean*, January 10, 1914.

46. *Chicago Tribune*, January 15, 1914.

47. *Inter Ocean*, January 31, 1914.

48. Ruth McCormick to A. H. Shaw, February 3, 1914, NAWSA Col-

lection, Reel 33; *Chicago Tribune*, February 11, 1914; *Record-Herald*, February 14, 1914; *Examiner*, February 12, 1914.

49. *American*, January 30, 1914; *Post*, January 7, 10, 1914, [unidentified clipping] McCormick Scrapbook; *Journal*, January 16, 1914; *Record-Herald*, January 13, 1914; *Inter Ocean*, January 3, 7, 14, 1914; *Examiner*, February 2, 1914; *Tribune*, February 4, 1914.

50. *Record-Herald*, February 9 , 16, 1914; A. Funk to A. H. Shaw, February 26, 1914, NAWSA Collection, Reel 33.

51. Morgan, *Suffragists and Democrats*, pp. 91–92; Flexner, *Woman's Rights Movement*, 276–77; Graham to author, March 2, 1990.

52. Ruth McCormick to A. H. Shaw, March 4, 1914, NAWSA Collection, Reel 33.

53. Ibid.

54. A. Funk to A. H. Shaw, op. cit.; Inez Haynes Irwin, *Angels and Amazons: A Hundred Years of American Women* (New York: Garden City, 1933) p. 392.

55. *Examiner*, March 8, 12, 1914; *Chicago Tribune*, March 11, 1914.

56. Ida Husted Harper, Special to the *Daily News*, April 18, 1914; *Inter Ocean*, March 9; *New York Times*, March 9, 1914.

57. Harper, *Daily News*, April 18, 1914; Ida Husted Harper, "The National Constitution Will Enfranchise Women," *North American Review*, May 1914, pp. 709–21; *Chicago Tribune*, March 20, 1914; *Record-Herald*, April 26, 1914.

58. Kraditor, *Ideas of the Woman Suffrage Movement*, p. 208.

59. Maud Wood Park, *Front Door Lobby*, ed. Edna Lamprey Stantial (Boston: Beacon Press, 1960) p. 24; *Record-Herald*, February 16, 1914; Harriot Stanton Blatch and Alma Lutz, *Challenging Years: The Memoirs of Harriot Stanton Blatch* (New York: Putnam, 1940) p. 246, quoted in Kraditor, *Ideas of Woman Suffrage Movement*, p. 208; Banks, *Faces of Feminism*, p. 136; Flexner, *Woman's Rights Movement*, p. 227.

60. *Chicago Tribune*, April 7, May 6, 1914; Ruth McCormick to A. H. Shaw, March 4, 1914, NAWSA Collection, Reel 33.

61. Ruth McCormick to A. H. Shaw, March 4, 1914, NAWSA Collection, Reel 33; *Record-Herald*, March 26, 1914; *Examiner*, April 14, 1914.

62. *Journal*, May 1, 1914; *Examiner*, May 1, 3, 6, 1914; *American*, May 1, 1914; *Tribune*, May 2, 1914; A. Funk to A. H. Shaw, April 29, 1914, NAWSA Collection, Reel 33.

63. *Examiner*, May 1, 3, 1914; *Chicago Tribune*, May 3, 1914.

64. *Record-Herald*, May 4, 1914; *Chicago Tribune*, May 3, 1914.

65. Blair, *Clubwoman as Feminist*, p. 4–5, 115; *Chicago News*, June 13, 1914.

66. *Post*, March 9, April 9, 1914; *Examiner*, March 30, 1914.

67. *Post*, March 9, 1914; *New York Times*, May 11, 14, 1914; Medill McCormick, "Just Out Of Jail," *Harper's Weekly*, May 30, 1914, pp. 6–7.

68. *Chicago American*, May 1, 1914.

69. *Record-Herald*, June 7, July 11, 1914; *Examiner*, July 23, 26, 1914; *Chicago Tribune*, August 7, 1914; Ida Husted Harper, *Suffrage Snapshots* (Washington D.C.: Leslie Judge Publishing, 1915) p. 82.

70. *Herald*, September 7, 1914; *Chicago Tribune*, September 13, 15, and October 27, 1914.

71. *Herald*, September 4, 7, 1914; *Examiner*, September 27, October 11, 1914.

72. *Herald*, September 13, 28, 30, 1914.

73. *News*, September 17, 1914; *Chicago Tribune*, September 24, 1914.

74. *American*, February 13, 1914; *Globe Democrat*, February 7, 1914; *Examiner*, September 25, 1914.

75. *Examiner*, October 30, 1914; [unidentified clipping, Oct. 29, 1914], McCormick Scrapbook; *American*, October 29, 30, 1914; *Herald*, October 31, 1914; *News*, October 31, 1914; Buechler, *Transformation of Woman Suffrage Movement*, pp. 181–82, 227.

76. *Chicago Tribune*, November 5, 7, 1914.

77. *Chicago Tribune*, November 5, 7, 1914.

78. *News*, November 4, 1914; Sinclair, *Better Half*, p. 326; Sara M. Evans, *Born for Liberty: A History of Women in America* (New York: The Free Press, 1989) p. 167.

79. Medill McCormick to Joseph Patterson, July 31, 1914, *Chicago Tribune* Archives.

80. *Herald*, November 14, 1914.

81. *Chicago Tribune*, November 12, 14, 16, 1914; *Examiner*, November 14, 18, 1914; *Herald*, November 16, 18, 1914.

82. *Examiner*, November 18, December 31, 1914; *Chicago Tribune*, January 13, 1915; *Post*, January 14, 1915; Sinclair, *Better Half*, p. 326.

83. Graham to author, January, 1986; Ruth McCormick, ms. of speech, Box 111, Hanna-McCormick Papers.

84. *Herald*, January 2, 1915; Ware, *Partner and I*, p. 210; Flexner, *Woman's Rights Movement*, pp. 276–77; Kraditor, *Ideas of Woman Suffrage Movement*, pp. 205–7; Graham to author, March 2, 1990, January 1986.

CHAPTER 4

1. Lucia McBride to Elizabeth Manchester, [1950] Box 131, Hanna-McCormick Papers; Barnes conversation with author, September, 1984, October 27, 1986.

2. W. Wilson, telegram, January 14, 1915, NAWSA Collection, Reel 13; *New York Times*, October 7, 1915.

3. *Herald*, May 23, June 8, 1915; *Chicago Tribune*, May 23, 1915.

4. *Examiner*, May 20, 1915; *Washington Times*, May 22, 1915.

5. Ethel M. Smith to Mrs. Stanley McCormick, May 22, 1915, NAWSA

Collection, Reel 33; *New York Tribune,* November 5, 1915; Morgan, *Suffragists and Democrats,* p. 98.

6. Carrie Catt to Maud Wood Park, January 18, 1916, Carrie Chapman Catt Papers, Microfilm ed., Reel 5, #000196, Manuscript Division, Library of Congress, Washington, D.C.

7. Edward T. James and Janet Wilson James, ed., *Notable American Women* (Cambridge: Harvard University Press, 1971) pp. 293–95; *New York Times,* October 16, 1915; Biographical booklet, Box 109, Hanna-McCormick Papers; *Everybody's Magazine,* 23, no. 3 (September 1915): 261; Medill McCormick to K. M. McCormick, [undated] McCormick Collection.

8. Katrina McCormick Barnes, "Rock River Farms," unpublished ms.; Rosalie Heller, "We Farm on the Desk, interview with Mrs. Medill McCormick," typescript, Box 15, Hanna-McCormick Papers; ms. description of Rock River Farms, Box 131, Hanna-McCormick Papers.

9. Barnes, "Rock River;" Holman, "Above All Else"; Barnes conversation with author, September 1984.

10. Medill McCormick to K. M. McCormick, March 27, 1916; *New York Times,* June 9, 1915.

11. Barnes conversation with author, April, 1985; Barnes, "Rock River."

12. Medill McCormick to K. M. McCormick, July 14, 1916, K. M. McCormick to Medill McCormick [May 1916?], McCormick Collection; Katrina McCormick Barnes, "Dr. De Lee and Father Wilbur," unpublished ms.

13. Flexner, *Woman's Rights Movement,* pp. 287–88; White, *Autobiography,* p. 528; Sinclair, *Better Half,* pp. 328–30; Medill McCormick, ms. of speech, July 4, [1916], Box 109, Hanna-McCormick Papers; [Sir] Arthur Willert to Geoffrey Robinson [Dawson], October 14, 1916, Archives of *Times,* London, quoted in Gould, *Reform and Regulation,* p. 203; Gould, *Reform and Regulation,* p. 193; Seward W. Livermore, *Politics Is Adjourned: Woodrow Wilson and the War Congress, 1916–1918* (Middletown: Wesleyan University Press, 1966) pp. 9–10; Medill McCormick to K. M. McCormick, Nov. 11, 1916, McCormick Collection.

14. Medill McCormick, ms. of speech, January 17, 1917, Box 109, Hanna-McCormick Papers; Sir Arthur Willert, *Washington and Other Memories* (Boston: Houghton-Mifflin, 1972) p. 96–97; Sullivan, *Our Times,* vol. 5, p. 272; Harriman, *Pinafores to Politics,* p. 213; Edith Bolling Wilson, *My Memoir* (Indianapolis: Bobbs, Merrill, 1938) p. 131.

15. Wilson, *Memoir,* pp. 132–33; Livermore, *Politics Is Adjourned,* pp. 13–14; Ruth McCormick, ms. of speech January 13, 1930, Box 111, Hanna-McCormick Papers; Willert, *Washington Memories,* p. 96–97; McAdoo, quoted by Sullivan, *Our Times,* vol. 5, pp. 272–73; Harriman, *Pinafores to Politics,* p. 213.

16. Wilson, *Memoir,* pp. 132–33; David Frankin Houston, *Eight Years in Wilson's Cabinet,* quoted by Sullivan, *Our Times,* vol. 5, pp. 273–74; Willert, *Washington Memories,* p. 96–97.

17. Sullivan, *Our Times*, vol. 5, p. 478; Sinclair, *Better Half*, p. 330; Wendt, *Chicago Tribune*, p. 425.

18. Longworth, *Crowded Hours*, pp. 248, 258–59, 278; *New York Times*, May 8, 1917; Willert, *Washington Memories*, p. 55; Robinson, "Cutting Sex Out," pp. 23–29.

19. Helen Bennett, ms. of radio speech, March 22, 1930, Box 80, Hanna-McCormick Papers.

20. Wilson, *Memoir*, p. 135–37, 167–68; Livermore, *Politics Is Adjourned*, p. 48; Sullivan, *Our Times*, vol. 5, p. 458.

21. *Christian Science Monitor*, February 2, 1928; Sullivan, *Our Times*, vol 5, p. 458; Manchester, Notes, Box 131; Medill McCormick, ms. of speech, Dec. 12, 1917, Box 109, Hanna-McCormick Papers.

22. Medill McCormick, ms. of speech to veterans' group [1920s], Box 109, Hanna-McCormick Papers; *New York Times*, August 25, 1917.

23. Medill McCormick to Ruth McCormick, [undated] Box 1, Hanna-McCormick Papers.

24. Livermore, *Politics Is Adjourned*, pp. 13–14, 17–28; *New York Times*, November 19; May 3, June 1, 1917.

25. Medill McCormick, ms. for *Colliers* [undated] Box 109, Hanna-McCormick Papers; speech, November 11, 1917, op. cit.; Medill McCormick to K. M. McCormick, October 15, 1917, McCormick Collection.

26. Livermore, *Politics Is Adjourned*, pp. 62–68, 79–80.

27. Livermore, *Politics Is Adjourned*, pp. 92, 94, 101, 104–5; Longworth, *Crowded Hours*, p. 264; *New York Times*, January 26, 1918.

28. Medill McCormick to Malcom McBride, January 17, [1918], and various other items, Box 6; Justus L. Johnson to Bazy Miller, November 4, 1950, Box 109; Nye Committee Hearings, Vol. I, p. 41, Box 113; Medill McCormick to Theodore Roosevelt, May 14, 1918, Box 6, Hanna-McCormick Papers; *New York Times Magazine*, June 9, 1929.

29. Livermore, *Politics Is Adjourned*, pp. 137, 123; *New York Times*, September 13, 1918; Wendt, *Chicago Tribune*, pp. 436–37; Ruth McCormick to Mable A. McLenahan, September 10, 1918, Box 13, Hanna-McCormick Papers.

30. Livermore, *Politics Is Adjourned*, pp. 115–21, 123, 212.

31. Livermore, *Politics Is Adjourned*, pp. 185–86; *New York Times*, September 13, 1918.

32. Wendt, *Chicago Tribune*, pp. 437–38; Livermore, *Politics Is Adjourned*, p. 244.

33. Flexner, *Woman's Rights Movement*, pp. 301–3; Sinclair, *Our Times*, p. 333; Livermore, *Politics Is Adjourned*, p. 183; Kraditor, *Ideas of Woman Suffrage Movement*, pp. 209–10; Banks, *Faces of Feminism*, p. 147.

34. Harriman, *Politics to Pinafores*, p. 274; Woolf, "Dewey's Right Hand Woman"; *New York Times*, January 15, 1928.

35. Wilson, *Memoir*, pp. 169–70; Ruth McCormick, ms. of speech "The Duty of Citizens," April 10, 1928; "Politics: A Prescription," Box 111; Ruth

McCormick to Mable McLenahan, September 10, 1918, Box 13, Hanna-McCormick Papers.

36. *New York Times*, April 13, 1930; Woolf, "Dewey's Right Hand Woman"; Flexner, *Woman's Rights Movement*, pp. 301–3.

37. Medill McCormick, ms. for *Colliers*, op. cit.

38. Ralph Stone, *The Irreconcilables: The Fight Against the League of Nations* (New York: W. W. Norton, 1973) pp. 15–20, 37–38, 41; Frederick Lewis Allen, *Only Yesterday: An Informal History of the 1920s* (New York: Harper & Row, 1931) p. 25.

39. Allen, *Only Yesterday*, pp. 20, 24–25, 55.

40. Medill McCormick to Lansing Ray, November 2, 1923, Box 12, Hanna-McCormick Papers; *New York Times*, February 25, 1920, quoted by Stone, *Irreconcilables*, p. 165.

41. Stone, *Irreconcilables*, p. 59; Willert, *Washington Memories*, pp. 126–27.

42. Medill McCormick to Mrs. Cyrus Hall McCormick, [undated] Box 6, Hanna-McCormick Papers; *New York Times*, August 21, 1919.

43. Longworth, *Crowded Hours*, p. 282; *New York Times*, March 16, 1919.

44. Stone, *Irreconcilables*, pp. 77–78, 81, 83–84; *New York Times*, March 6, 1919; Medill McCormick to Moorfield Storey, February 24, 1919, Hanna-McCormick Papers, Box 6; Wendt, *Chicago Tribune*, pp. 464–65.

45. Stone, *Irreconcilables*, pp. 27–31, 86–88, 115, 183; *Boston Evening Transcript*, May 1, 1919, quoted in Stone, p. 89.

46. Stone, *Irreconcilables*, pp. 27–31.

47. Stone, *Irreconcilables*, p. 98; Wendt, *Chicago Tribune*, pp. 441–42; Longworth, *Crowded Hours*, p. 286.

48. Willert, *Chicago Tribune*, pp. 131–32; *New York Times*, September 8, 1919; Stone, *Irreconcilables*, pp. 128–33, 131–32, 187.

49. *New York Times*, September 20, 1919; Tankersley conversation with author, September 1984; Ruth Hanna McCormick Diary, August 24, 1937, McCormick Collection.

50. Barnes conversation with author, September 1984; Elizabeth Wood Seymour conversation with author, September 1984.

51. Longworth, *Crowded Hours*, p. 289, 294.

52. Ibid. pp. 291–92.

53. Charles Wallace Collins, May 27, 1921, Box 7, Hanna-McCormick Papers; Medill McCormick to William Allen White, September 27, 1919, Box 6, Hanna-McCormick Papers.

54. Republican National Women's Executive Committee pamphlet, [January 10, 1919] Box 111, Hanna-McCormick Papers.

55. Ruth McCormick to Alice H. Wadsworth, [September 1919] Box 13, Hanna-McCormick Papers.

56. Will H. Hays, September 5, 1919, Box 13, Hanna-McCormick Papers;

Josephine C. Preston to Ruth McCormick, September 5, 1919, Box 13, Hanna-McCormick Papers.

57. Will Hays to Ruth McCormick, [September 20, 1919]; Ruth McCormick to Mrs. Fletcher Dobyns [undated], Box 13, Hanna-McCormick Papers.

58. Ruth McCormick, ms. of speech, Box 111, Hanna-McCormick Papers; *New York Times*, December 11, 1919.

CHAPTER 5

1. John D. Hicks, *Republican Ascendancy 1921–1933* (New York: Harper and Row, 1960) p. 178–79.

2. Joseph Gies, *The Colonel of Chicago* (New York: E. P. Dutton, 1979) p. 80; *New York Times*, April 9, 1930.

3. White, *Autobiography*, p. 581; Will Hays telegram to Medill McCormick, January 10, 1920, Box 6, Hanna-McCormick Papers; Medill McCormick to Harold Ickes, February 8, 1920, Box 36, Harold L. Ickes Papers, Manuscript Division, Library of Congress, Washington D.C.

4. Various items, Box 110, Hanna-McCormick Papers; Ruth McCormick, ms. of speech, Box 111, Hanna-McCormick Papers.

5. Allen, *Only Yesterday*, pp. 29–30; William Allen White, *A Puritan in Babylon: The Story of Calvin Coolidge* (Gloucester: Peter Smith, 1973) pp. 204–5; H. L. Williamson to Medill McCormick, March 11, 1920; Medill McCormick to David Shanahan, May 30, 1920, Box 6, Hanna-McCormick Papers; Longworth, *Crowded Hours*, pp. 306–7, 309–10.

6. Emily Newell Blair, "Women at the Conventions," *Current History* (New York Times Magazine) October 1920, clipping in Box 13, Hanna-McCormick Papers.

7. *Chicago Tribune*, June 7, 1920; Ruth McCormick to K. M. McCormick, July 2, 1920, McCormick Collection; Ware, *Partner and I*, p. 150.

8. Emily Blair, "Women at Conventions;" White, *Puritan*, p. 199; White, *Autobiography*, 582–85; Ickes, *Autobiography*, pp. 222–24.

9. Wendt, *Chicago Tribune*, pp. 465–67; Ickes, *Autobiography*, pp. 225–26; Kohlsaat, *McKinley to Harding*, p. 227; White, *Puritan*, p. 207; Longworth, *Crowded Hours*, pp. 310–12.

10. White, *Puritan*, pp. 209–12; White, *Autobiography*, p. 586; Allen, *Only Yesterday*, pp. 34–35; Hicks, *Republican Ascendancy*, p. 25; White, *Autobiography*, p. 597.

11. Emily Blair, "Women at Conventions;" Stone, *Irreconcilables*, p. 173; *Chicago Tribune*, August 31, 1920.

12. Allen, *Only Yesterday*, p. 79; W. G. Harding to Ruth McCormick, August 6, 1920, Box 13, Hanna-McCormick Papers; Stone, *Irreconcilables*, p. 176; McCormick Diary, November 1922; Henry Cabot Lodge to Medill McCormick, November 13, 1920, Box 6, Hanna-McCormick Papers.

13. Medill McCormick to Ruth McCormick, December 1, 1920, Box 1, Hanna-McCormick Papers.

14. Barnes conversation with author, September 1985; Seymour conversation with author, September 1985; Longworth, *Crowded Hours*, p. 323.

15. Allen, *Only Yesterday*, p. 104, 108; Hicks, *Republican Ascendancy*, pp. 51–52; Shirer, *Twentieth Century Journey*, p. 361; White, *Autobiography*, p. 597; Henrietta W. Livermore to Harriet Taylor Upton, [undated] Box 13, Hanna-McCormick Papers.

16. Harriet Taylor Upton, General Letter to Members of Committee, August 19, 1921 and Harriet Taylor Upton, General Letter to Members of Committee, December 31, 1921, Ruth McCormick to Mrs. Henry Youmans, April 30, 1921, various letters, Box 13, Hanna-McCormick Papers; Ruth McCormick, ms. of speech, February 13, 1920, Box 111, Hanna-McCormick Papers.

17. Ruth McCormick speech, February 13, 1920, op. cit.

18. Ruth McCormick ms. of speech, Box 111, [undated] Hanna-McCormick Papers.

19. Cott, *Grounding of Feminism*, pp. 101–2; Suzanne La Follette, *Concerning Women* (New York: Boni, 1926) p. 268; Jane Addams, *Woman Citizen*, April 19, 1924, pp. 14–16.

20. Dorothy M. Brown, *Setting a Course: American Women in the 1920s* (Boston: Twayne, 1987) p. 50; Harriet Taylor Upton, General Letter to Committee, December 14, 1921 and June 29, 1922, Box 13, Hanna-McCormick Papers; Ruth McCormick, mss. of speeches, Box 111, Hanna-McCormick Papers; Ruth McCormick to Mrs. Milan H. Hulbert, July 19, 1922, Box 13, Hanna-McCormick Papers; Brown, *Setting a Course*, p. 52.

21. *Chicago Tribune*, October 31, 1930.

22. Medill McCormick, mss. of various speeches, Box 7, Medill McCormick, ms. of speech February 14, 1922, Box 109, Hanna-McCormick Papers.

23. McCormick Diary, February 7, 12, 1922.

24. Medill McCormick to Lord Eustace Percy, June 23, 1922, Box 7; Ruth McCormick Form Letter, August 7, 1922, Box 14; Ruth McCormick to Mrs. Knight, June 16, 1922, Box 13; Ruth McCormick to Lilias Wilson, July 1922, Box 13; Ruth McCormick to Mrs. Milan H. Hulbert, op. cit., Hanna-McCormick Papers.

25. Ruth McCormick to Mrs. B. J. Arnold, July 21, 1922, Box 13; Ruth McCormick to Mrs. Albert W. Evans, July 19, 1922, Box 13; Ruth McCormick to Flora Witkowsky, July 21, 1922, Box 13; Ruth McCormick to Mrs. Joseph Bowen, July 25, 1922, Box 13, Hanna-McCormick Papers; Wilson, *Memoir*, p. 169.

26. *Chicago Post*, October 30, 1914; Katrina McCormick Barnes, "Miss Forsyth and the Misses Bennett," unpublished ms.; Barnes conversation with author, September 1985.

27. Barnes conversation with author, February 1987; Peter Miller, Jr., conversation with author, July 1984; McCormick Diary, March 14–15, 1923;

Graham White and John Maze, *Harold Ickes of the New Deal: His Private Life and Public Career* (Cambridge: Harvard University Press, 1985) p. 189; Ruth McCormick to Martha Connole, [July 1928] Box 41, Hanna-McCormick Papers.

28. Tankersley conversation with author, September 1984, February 1985, October 1987; Margaret Ailshie in Simmses' guest book, November 28, 1936, McCormick Collection.

29. Barnes to author, December 18, 1984.

30. Ruth McCormick to Ella Steward, July 19, 1922, Box 13, Hanna-McCormick Papers; *Chicago Tribune*, October 14, 1922; Cott, *Grounding of Feminism*, pp. 162, 196.

31. Hicks, *Republican Ascendancy*, pp. 57–59; McCormick Diary, November 1922.

32. McCormick Diary, November 15, 17, 18, 23, 1922.

33. McCormick Diary, November 15, 18, 19, 25, 1922.

34. McCormick Diary, November 26–28, December 1, 1922.

35. McCormick Diary, December 6–7, 1922.

36. McCormick Diary, December 11, 14, 24, 26, 1922.

37. McCormick Diary, February 1–5, 1923.

38. Elisabeth Israels Perry, *Belle Moscowitz* (New York: Oxford University Press, 1987) p. xii; McCormick Diary, March 1, 9, 14, 1923.

39. *Chicago Tribune*, March 20, 1923; McCormick Diary, March 14–19, April 18, 20, 1923; Flexner, *Woman's Rights Movement*, p. 340.

40. McCormick Diary, April 14, 22, 1923.

41. McCormick Diary, May 6, 9, 1923.

42. McCormick Diary, May 10, 11, 1923.

43. McCormick Diary, October & June 1923.

44. McCormick Diary, October 23, 1923.

45. Cott, *Grounding of Feminism*, pp. 85–86.

46. Anne Forsyth, "Ruth Hanna McCormick Simms," ms., Box 119; Ruth McCormick to John T. Adams, November 6, 1923, Box 14, Hanna-McCormick Papers.

47. Harriet Taylor Upton to Ruth McCormick, November 12, 1923, Box 14, Hanna-McCormick Papers.

48. McCormick Diary, November 9, 1923.

49. Medill McCormick to Samuel Gompers, December 19, 1923, Box 10; Medill McCormick to Charles M. Wheeler, [1924], Box 12; J. T. Williams to Medill McCormick, May 15, 1924, Box 12, Hanna-McCormick Papers.

50. Medill McCormick to Ruth McCormick, April 6, 1924, Box 1, Hanna-McCormick Papers.

51. Medill McCormick to General Frank McCoy, October 3, 1924, Box 12; Medill McCormick to J. T. Williams, May 28, 1924, Box 12, Hanna-McCormick Papers.

52. McCormick Diary, August 21, 1924.

53. Medill McCormick to Horace Wade, April 29, 1924; Medill Mc-

Cormick to B. M. Makey, October 23, 1924, Box 12; Medill McCormick to Ruth McCormick, May 29, 1924; Medill McCormick to Ruth McCormick, July 7, 1924; Box 1, Hanna-McCormick Papers; McCormick Diary, August 21, 1924.

54. Harriet Taylor Upton, June 20, 1922, Box 14, Hanna-McCormick Papers; McCormick Diary, February 13, 1923.

55. *Chicago Tribune*, May 19, 1923; Helen Bennett, "National Committee Woman," ms. Box 14, Hanna-McCormick Papers; Upton, November 12, 1923, op. cit.

56. Harriet Taylor Upton to Ruth McCormick, June 17, 1923, Box 14; "Legal and Political Status of Women in the United States," National League of Women Voters, November 1927, Box 130; Katherine Phillips Edson to Ruth McCormick [undated] Box 14, Hanna-McCormick Papers.

57. Ruth McCormick to Louise Bowen, April 16, 1924, Louis O. Bowen to Ruth McCormick, April 16, 1924, Box 14, Hanna-McCormick Papers.

58. Ruth McCormick to Lawrence Y. Sherman, May 28–29, 1924, Box 14, Hanna-McCormick Papers.

59. Ruth McCormick telegram to Emily N. Blair, May 27, 1924; Emily N. Blair to Ruth McCormick, Box 14, Hanna-McCormick Papers; Forsyth, "Ruth Hanna McCormick Simms."

60. *Chicago Tribune*, March 13, 1924.

61. Bennett, "National Committeewoman"; Mildred Adams, "Ruth McCormick, Politician and Farmer," *The Woman Citizen*, February 1926, pp. 11 ff.

62. McCormick Diary, 1924.

63. Sallie Hert to Ruth McCormick, August 27, 1924, Box 14, Hanna-McCormick Papers; Barnes, "Rock River"; McCormick Diary, August 26, 1924.

64. McCormick Diary, September 11, 17, 1924.

65. Ickes Papers, Box 35; McCormick Diary, October 12, 1924.

66. McCormick Diary, October 14–16, 19, 1924; W. B. McKinley to Medill McCormick, November 5, 1924, Box 12, Hanna-McCormick Papers.

67. McCormick Diary, November 11, 1924.

68. Medill McCormick to G. Dawson, November 12, 1924, Box 12, Hanna-McCormick Papers.

69. McCormick Diary, November 26, 1924.

CHAPTER 6

1. Arthur Brisbane to Medill McCormick, June 12, 1924, January 12, 1925, Box 12; Medill McCormick to S. R. Guggenheim, December 6, 1924, Box 12, Hanna-McCormick Papers; McCormick Diary, October 14, 1924, January 1925; K. M. McCormick to Medill McCormick, [undated] McCormick Collection.

2. Helen Throckmorton, "Woman's World's Fair Marks Epics," *The Woman's Viewpoint*, Woman's World's Fair Scrapbook, Chicago Historical Society;

Helen Bennett, "Women's World's Fair," ms., Box 14, Hanna-McCormick Papers.

3. Bennett,"Women's World's Fair;" *Chicago Tribune*, February 3, 1925.

4. Robinson, "Cutting Sex Out," pp. 23–29.

5. *New York Times*, February 26, 1925; Barnes conversation with author, September 1985.

6. George Porter also killed himself exactly two years later. Barnes conversation with author, September, 1984; *New York Times*, February 25, 1925; K. M. McCormick telegram to Ruth McCormick, *Chicago Tribune* Archives.

7. Barnes conversation with author, September 1984; Seymour conversation with author, September 1985; Peter Miller, Jr. conversation with author, September 1984; *New York Times*, February 25, 1925.

8. *New York Times*, February 26, 1925.

9. Barnes conversation with author, September 1984.

10. C. G. Jung to Ruth McCormick, March 12, 1925, Box 124, Hanna-McCormick Papers.

11. Bennett, "Women's World's Fair;" Tankersley conversation with author, 1985.

12. Kessler-Harris, *Out to Work*, pp. 218–19, 224, 227.

13. *Illinois State Historical Society Journal* 18, no. 2: 452; Woman's World's Fair Souvenir Program, Chicago Historical Society.

14. Bennett, "Women's World's Fair;" *Illinois State Historical Society Journal*, op. cit.; Throckmorton, "Woman's World Fair."

15. Cott, *Grounding of Feminism*, p. 135; Financial Records, Box 14; Medill McCormick to Ruth McCormick, [undated] Box 1, Hanna-McCormick Papers.

16. McCormick Diary, October 22, 1924; *Chicago Tribune*, June 14, 1925; *The Woman Citizen*, Des Moines, reprinted in Rockford [IL] *Register*, July 4, 1925; *Chicago South Shore News*, July 17, 1925; *Duluth Herald*, June 13, 1925.

17. Barnes conversation with author, September 1984.

18. *Salem* [OR] *News*, August 12, 1925; *Rockford* [IL] *Star*, August 20, 1925; *New York Sun*, August 20, 1925; E. Andris to Ruth McCormick, June 27, 1925; A. Gibbons to Ruth McCormick, June 29, 1925; Jay S. McCarthy to Ruth McCormick, June 29, 1925, Box 14; Stella Whitmore to Ruth McCormick July 8, 1925, Box 15, Hanna-McCormick Papers.

19. *El Paso Times*, September 12, 1925; Adams, "Ruth McCormick," pp. 11 ff.; *Glen Ellyn News*, October. 2, 1925.

20. *New York World*, November 24, 1925; *Chicago American*, October 19, 21, 1925.

21. *Birmingham Age-Herald*, December 12, 1925; *Orlando Reporter Star*, November 25, 1925; *Dallas Times Herald*, November 3, 1925; *New York Evening World*, November 21, 1925; *Baltimore Sun*, October 31, 1925.

22. *Missoula Missoulian*, February 24, 1925; *Washington Star*, February 9, 1926.

23. McCormick Diary, January-March, 1926; *Tower Hill Times*, January

28, 1926; *Canton News,* February 7, 1926; *Chicago Tribune,* March 5, July 7 and October 18, 1925; *Springfield Journal,* September 13, 1925; *Peoria Star,* March 7, 1926; *Belleville News Democrat,* March 18, 1926.

24. McCormick Diary, April, 1926; Tankersley to author, October 16, 1985.

25. *Rayne [LA] Tribune,* April 24, 1926; *Mason [GA] Telegraph,* April 15, 1926; *New York Times,* April 10, 1928.

26. Theo. Marsters, "Peoria As We Go Along," p. 24 of unidentified Peoria [IL] newspaper, in McCormick Scrapbook, 1925–1927, McCormick Collection; Adams, "Ruth McCormick."

27. Stuart A. Rice and Malcom M. Willey, "American Women's Ineffective Use of the Vote," *Current History* 20 (July 1924): 641, quoted in Brown, *Setting the Course,* p. 70; *Elgin Courier,* November 11, 1925; *Chicago Post,* November 11, 1925; *Chicago Herald Examiner,* November 12, 1925.

28. *Chicago Herald Examiner,* January 31, 1926; *Danville News,* February 18, 1926; *Chicago Tribune,* July 12, 1926; *Chicago News,* November 30, 1925.

29. C. W. Gilbert, "Daily Mirror of Washington," *Philadelphia Public Ledger,* November 19–20, 1925; Adams, "Ruth McCormick"; McCormick Diary, May 28, 1926.

30. McCormick Diary, November 18, December 3–4, 1926; *Chicago Tribune,* December 4, 1926.

31. McCormick Diary, August–October, 1926; December 7, 1926.

32. McCormick Diary, October 10, November 28, December 13, 1926; Ruth McCormick to Perry B. McCullough, May 21, 1928.

33. *Chicago Journal,* May 2, 1927; *Chicago Tribune,* June 3, 1927; *Macon Telegraph,* April 15, 1927; *New York Times,* January 15, 1928; Joseph L. Bache to Ruth McCormick, June 3, 1927, Box 15; Ruth McCormick to J. A. Ayres, July, 1927, Box 15, Hanna-McCormick Papers; Ruth McCormick to Alice Longworth, June 11] 1927, McCormick Collection.

34. *Time,* April, 18, 1927, p. 13; Ruth McCormick to A. H. Owens, December 1927, Hanna-McCormick Papers.

35. Ruth McCormick to Mary Mooreson, September 26, 1927, Box 15, Hanna-McCormick Papers.

36. Ruth McCormick, ms. of speech, October 15, 1927, Box 111, Hanna-McCormick Papers.

37. *New York Times,* September 29–30, 1927.

38. Ruth McCormick to Cyril E. Reed, November 17, 1927, Box 22; Ruth McCormick to Mary E. Busey, December 13, 1927, Box 64; Fred H. Gibbs to Ruth McCormick; Ruth McCormick to Edward A. Jones, December 24, 1927, Box 15, Hanna-McCormick Papers.

39. *New York Times,* January 15, 1928; Ruth McCormick to R. N. Huff, Box 25, December 22, 1927.

40. Letters and notes on talk with Jim Snyder, Boxes 15–22, Hanna-McCormick Papers.

41. Tankersley conversations with author, September 1984, April 1985.
42. Ibid.
43. *New York Times Magazine*, June 9, 1929; Mary King Patterson to Ruth McC. Miller [Bazy], November 2, 1950, Box 109, Hanna-McCormick Papers; Medill McCormick to Ruth McCormick, various letters, McCormick Collection; Ruth McCormick, "Politics: A Prescription," Box 111, Hanna-McCormick Papers.
44. Robinson, "Cutting Sex Out," pp. 23–29; Tankersley conversation with author, September 1984; Barnes conversation with author, September 1984.
45. Janet White Barnes Lawrence conversation with author, March 1985.

CHAPTER 7

1. *New York Times*, January 15, 1928.
2. Ruth McCormick, "How I Live on Twenty-Four Hours a Day," unidentified magazine article, Box 131, Hanna-McCormick Papers; *Chicago Tribune*, October 31, 1930.
3. Ruth McCormick staff to Mrs. R. D. Omer, February 21, 1928, Box 29; Katherine Hamill to Mrs. Casewell S. Jones, February 15, 1928, Box 31, Hanna-McCormick Papers; Raymond Moley, *27 Masters of Politics* (New York: Funk & Wagnalls, 1949) p. 181; Katherine Hamill to Mrs. Caswell Jones, February 15, 1928, Box 31, Hanna-McCormick Papers.
4. Ruth McCormick to Carrie Partridge, May 17, 1928, Box 40; Olive M. Williams to Ruth McCormick, October 12, 1928, Box 43; Ruth Miller [Bazy] to Ray Moley, Jr., June 6, 1949; Jim Snyder to George M. Miley, March 31, 1928, Hanna-McCormick Papers; Tankersley to author, September 1984.
5. Unidentified magazine clipping, Box 74, Hanna-McCormick Papers.
6. Robinson, "Cutting Sex Out," pp. 23–29; *Christian Science Monitor*, February 2, 1928; Ruth McCormick to Mrs. Otter Heper, March 3, 1928, Hanna-McCormick Papers; Shirer, *Twentieth Century Journey*, vol. 1, p. 421.
7. Helen Bennett, "Methods of Ruth Hanna McCormick," ms., Hanna-McCormick Papers; Ruth Miller to Ray Moley, Jr., June 6, 1949, Hanna-McCormick Papers.
8. *Chicago Tribune*, April 8, 1928; Anne Forsyth to Mrs. Graham Thompson, February 2, 1928, Hanna-McCormick Papers; Selden, "Father Complex," pp. 6 ff.
9. Bennett, "Methods," Box 108, Hanna McCormick Papers; Mary King Patterson to Ruth Miller, November 2, 1950, Box 109, Hanna-McCormick Papers; *Chicago Tribune*, April 1, 1928.
10. Elaine Showalter, ed. *These Modern Women: Autobiographical Essays from the Twenties* (Old Westbury: Feminist Press, 1978) pp. 12–13, quoted in Brown, *Setting a Course*, p. 32; Elizabeth Fraser, "Here We Are—Use Us," *Good Housekeeping* 71 (Sept. 1920): 161, quoted in Brown, *Setting a Course*, p. 67.

11. McCormick, "Politics"; Anne Forsyth to Mrs. E. O. Richards, January 28, 1928, Box 26, Hanna-McCormick Papers.

12. *Chicago Tribune*, March 19, June 18, 1928; Anne Forsyth to Mrs. L. B. Gregory, March 10, 1928, Box 35, Hanna-McCormick Papers.

13. Mr. Weinrank to Ruth McCormick, [Jan. 1928]; John Palandech, April 20, 1928, Box 40, Hanna-McCormick Papers; *Chicago Today*, November 12, 1927; *New York Times*, April 13, 1930; *Chicago Tribune*, November 3, 1927, January 19, February 19, 1928.

14. Harold L. Ickes to Ruth H. McCormick, March 27, 1928, Ickes Papers, Box 36.

15. *New York Times*, April 8, 1928; William T. Hutchinson, *Lowden of Illinois: the Life of Frank O. Lowden* (Chicago: University of Chicago Press, 1957) p. 581.

16. *New York Times*, April 9–11, 1928; Anne Forsyth to Mrs. E. A. McKenzie, March 28, 1928, Box 35, Hanna-McCormick Papers.

17. *New York Times*, April 8–11, 1928; *Chicago Journal*, March 27, 1928; Howard Gosnell, *Machine Politics: Chicago Model* (Chicago: University of Chicago Press, 1937; New York: Greenwood Press, 1968), pp. 37–38, 88, 138.

18. Fred A. Smith, article for *Independent Woman*, March 26, 1929, typescript; William Hard, article for *Standard Examiner*, typescript, Hanna-McCormick Papers; *Milk Market Reporter*, April 7, 1928; *Chicago Tribune*, March 30, April 9, 1928; *Chicago News*, April 6, 1928.

19. *New York Times*, April 11, 1928; Selden, "Father Complex," pp. 6 ff.

20. *Chicago Tribune*, April 11, 1928, October 23, 1928.

21. *New York Times*, April 8, 11–12, 1928.

22. *Time*, April 23, 1928, pp. 11–12.

23. Hutchinson, *Lowden*, pp. 564–65, 572–79, 585, 589; Brown, *Setting a Course*, p. 15; *New York Times*, May 31, 1928.

24. William Hard, "A Woman Senator?" *Review of Reviews*, March 1930, pp. 62–67.

25. Hutchinson, *Lowden*, pp. 593, 600; *Chicago Tribune*, June 6, 1928.

26. *New York Times*, June 12, 1928.

27. *New York Times*, August 21, 1928; *Rockford Register-Republic*, Simms biography, Box 131, Hanna-McCormick Papers; Barnes to author, September 1984.

28. *Chicago Tribune*, September 8, 1928; *Chicago Evening American*, April 3, 1928.

29. Ruth McCormick campaign literature, 1930, Hanna-McCormick Papers; *Chicago Tribune*, November 8, 1928.

30. *Chicago Tribune*, November 8, 1928; Ruth McCormick to Jim Snyder, November 27, 1928; Ruth McCormick to O. P. Farr, December 3, 1928, Box 46, Hanna-McCormick Papers.

31. Hard, "A Woman Senator?"

32. *Chicago Tribune*, January 22, 31, February 1, 6, 1929; Tankersley conversation with author, June 1985.

33. *Chicago Tribune*, April 11, 1929; *New York Times*, April 10, 1929.

34. *Congressional Record*, 71st Congress, 1st Session: Senate, March 4, 1929, pp. 5–7.

35. *New York Times*, April 15, 1929; unidentified clipping, June 9, 1929, McCormick Scrapbook.

36. *New York Times*, May 30, 1929; Sophinisba Breckenridge, pp. 275–78, in Brown, *Setting a Course*, p. 69.

37. *New York Times*, December 18, April 13, 1930; *Chicago Tribune*, December 5, 1929.

38. *Congressional Record*, 71st Congress, 1st Session: House, April 15, 1929, p. 25; Jim Snyder to Barney Thompson, April 17, 1929; Ruth McCormick, ms. of speech April 27, 1929, Hanna-McCormick Papers.

39. Albert G. Simms II, M.D., conversation with author, September 1985.

40. *Congressional Record*, 71st Congress, 1st Session: House, April 26, 1929, p. 610; Hicks, *Republican Ascendancy*, pp. 217–23.

41. Brown, *Setting a Course*, p. 20; *Chicago Daily Tribune*, June 17, 1929, clipping, Box 52, Hanna-McCormick Papers.

42. Ruth McCormick campaign pamphlet, 1930; Ruth McCormick to J. E. Dertinger, July 23, 1929, Box 52, Hanna-McCormick Papers; *Congressional Record*, 71st Congress, 1st Session: House, pp. 261–62, HR 12743.

43. Ruth McCormick to O. P. Tuttle, December 3, 1928, Box 46; Ruth McCormick to C. L. Logan, October 15; Jim Snyder to Judge Miller, April 24, 1929, Box 48, Hanna-McCormick Papers.

44. *New York Times*, May 12, 1929; *Chicago Tribune*, May 12, 1929; Ruth McCormick to J. E. Dertinger, May 16, 1929, Box 50, Hanna-McCormick Papers.

45. Jim Snyder to O. M. Farr, January 23, 1929, Box 47; Jim Snyder (?) to Ruth McCormick, April 24, 1929, Box 48; Jim Snyder to Judge Fred E. Carpenter, May 28, 1929, Box 50; Jim Snyder (?) to Fred Smith, May 24, 1929, Box 50; G. W. Hill to Ruth McCormick, May 11, 1929, Box 49; Ruth McCormick to C. E. Gullett, July 2, 1929, Box 52; Jim Snyder to Judge C. H. Miller, July 29, 1929, Box 52, Hanna-McCormick Papers.

46. Ruth McCormick to Mrs. L. A. Rider, July 6, 1929, Hanna-McCormick Papers; *Chicago Tribune*, September 1, 1929.

47. *Chicago Tribune*, April 27, September 22–23, November 2, December 12, 1929; *New York Times*, August 20, September 23, 1929.

48. Ruth McCormick to Mark E. Penney, September 30, 1929, Box 56; Ruth McCormick to [?] December 10, 1929; Jim Snyder to Ruth McCormick, September 9, 1929; Judge Charles H. Miller to Ruth McCormick, September 19, 1929, Box 57; R. H. McCormick Press Release, December 9, 1929, Box 69, Hanna-McCormick Papers; *New York Times*, June 30, 1929, November 17; *Chicago Tribune*, September 23, 1929.

49. Ruth McCormick to Dr. H. L. Green, October 7, 1929, Box 69; Jim Snyder to O. M. Farr, November 4, 1929; O. M. Farr to Fred Smith, November 13, 1929, Box 64; Ruth McCormick to Mrs. Emma Rosselot, October 31, 1929, Box 63, Hanna-McCormick Papers.

50. Ruth McCormick to Rev. Benjamin E. Chapman, November 23, 1929, Box 65; Jim Snyder to Judge William Radliff, December 5, 1929, Box 69, Hanna-McCormick Papers.

CHAPTER 8

A shorter version of this chapter appeared in the *Illinois Historical Journal* 81, no. 3 (1988):191–210.

1. *Chicago Tribune*, September 3, 1929; Gosnell, *Machine Politics*, pp. 163–64; Irene McCoy Gaines, ms. of speech, November 25, 1929, Chicago Historical Society; Weekly report of Irene Gaines, November 30, 1929, Box 67, Hanna-McCormick Papers.

2. *New York Times*, November 7, 1929, January 14, April 14, 1930; *Chicago Tribune*, January 14, 1930.

3. Perry, *Belle Moscowitz*, p. 160; *Chicago Daily News*, April 10, 1930; *New York Times*, January 13, February 23, 1930.

4. *Chicago Tribune*, January 14, 1930; *New York Times*, January 14, 1930; various items, Boxes 70, 72, Hanna-McCormick Papers; Tankersley conversation with author, September 1984.

5. Fred Smith to O. M. Farr, January 16, 22, 1930; "Shall She Be Senator?" clipping from *Christian Science Monitor*, January 16, 1930; various items, Box 71, Hanna-McCormick Papers; *Chicago Tribune*, January 21, 1930.

6. *Chicago Tribune*, January 26, March 18, 1930; Ruth McCormick to M. A. Myers, March 18, 1930, Box 83, Hanna-McCormick Papers.

7. Jim Snyder to C. E. Gullett, February 8, 1930; Jim Snyder to Judge C. A. McNeill, February 26, 1930; Jim Snyder to E. L. Hiser, March 4, 1930, Box 76; Jim Snyder to T. A. Oakes, March 14, 1930, Box 79; Natalie H. Pegram to Ruth McCormick, Box 84, Hanna-McCormick Papers.

8. Mary Church Terrell to Jim Snyder, February 5, 1930, Box 74; Rosa Gordon Newton to Ruth McCormick, March 11, 1930, Box 80; Irene Gaines to Ruth McCormick, February 22, 1930; Jenny Lawrence, February 10, 1930, Box 74; O. M. Farr to F. A. Smith, February 28, 1930, Box 75; Katherine Hamill to Mrs. Eunice O. Steele, March 6, 1930, Box 82, Hanna-McCormick Papers.

9. *New York Times*, February 11, 1930.

10. Rodney Dutcher, NEA syndicated column, February 15, 1930, McCormick Scrapbook; *Chicago Tribune*, April 1, 6, 1930.

11. Natalie H. Pegram to Katherine Hamill, Box 82, Hanna-McCormick Papers; William Hard, clippings in McCormick Scrapbook; *New York Times*, February 23, 1930; *Chicago Tribune*, April 6, 1930.

12. Katherine Hamill to Helen McMackin, February 11, 1930; Katherine Hamill to Mrs. Caswell S. Jones, February 18, 1930, Box 74; Nellie F. Cooley to Helen Hood, Box 78; ms. of speech written for Fannie Worthing by F. A. Smith, February 12, 1930, Box 78, Hanna-McCormick Papers.

13. *Chicago Tribune*, March 17, 19, April 3, 6, 1930; Gosnell, *Machine Politics*, pp. 163–64.

14. *Chicago Tribune*, March 23, 1930.

15. *Chicago Tribune*, April 2, 6, 1930.

16. *Chicago Tribune*, April 6 and undated clipping, 1930, McCormick Scrapbook; other clippings, Hanna-McCormick Papers.

17. *Chicago Tribune*, March 3, March 19, 1930; *New York Times*, March 23, 1930; Nye Committee Hearings, Box 113, Hanna-McCormick Papers.

18. Republic Press Service, March 11, 1930, clipping, Box 81.

19. *Chicago Tribune*, March 11, 23, 24, 27, 1930.

20. *New York Times*, March 23, 1930; *Chicago Tribune*, April 7, 1930; H. E. Morgan to Ruth McCormick, March 20, 1930, Box 81, Hanna-Mc-Cormick Papers.

21. *Chicago Tribune*, April 1, 1930; U. P. Column, April 3, 1930, clipping, McCormick Scrapbook.

22. *Chicago Tribune*, April 6, 9, 1930.

23. *Chicago Tribune*, April 9, 1930; *Washington Times Herald*, April 10, 1930.

24. Barnes conversation with author, September 1984.

25. *New York Times*, April 9, 11, 1930; *Chicago Tribune*, April 9, 1930.

26. *Chicago Tribune*, April 10, 1930; *Chicago Daily News*, April 10, 1930; *Times Recorder*, April 1930, clipping, McCormick Scrapbook; "Analysis of Votes in the 1930 Election," Illinois League of Women Voters, Box 87, Hanna-McCormick Papers.

27. *New York Times*, April 10, 16, 1930; *Times Recorder*, April 16, 1930.

28. *Chicago Daily News*, April 10, 1930; *Chicago Tribune*, April 9, 1930; "Mirrors of Washington," *Wall Street Journal*, April 25, 1930, typescript, Box 87, Hanna-McCormick Papers.

29. *New York Times*, April 10, 1930.

30. *Chicago Tribune*, April 11, 1930; *Washington Times Herald*, April 10, 1930; *New York Times*, April 11, 12, 15, 1930; Fred Smith to Jim Snyder, April 14, 1930, Box 84, Hanna-McCormick Papers.

31. Will Rogers, quoted in *Kansas City Times*, April 25, 1940.

32. Jim Snyder to Henry Coens, April 11, 1930, Box 86, Hanna-Mc-Cormick Papers; Hiram Johnson to Maj. Archibald M. Johnson, April 9, 1930, in Robert Burke, ed., *The Diary Letters of Hiram Johnson*, vol. 5, *1929–33* (New York: Garland, 1984).

33. Ruth McCormick, ms. of statement at the Lincoln Hotel, Box 103, Hanna-McCormick Papers; *New York Times*, April 15, 20, 1930.

34. Charles H. Miller to R. H. McCormick, April 30, 1930, Box 88, Hanna-McCormick Papers.

35. *New York Times*, April 10, 20, June 5, 1930; various letters, Box 88, Hanna-McCormick Papers.

36. *Chicago Tribune*, April 19, 1930; *Times Recorder*, April 16, 1930; Hicks, *Republican Ascendancy*, p. 88; U.P. Column, May 2, 1930, McCormick Scrapbook; Harold Ickes to Gerald Nye, May 16, 1930, Box 36, Ickes Papers; *New York Times*, April 16, May 2, 1930.

37. *Chicago Tribune*, May 7, 9, 10, 15, 24, 25, 26, August 3, 1930; *New York Times*, May 13, June 30, 1930; Jim Snyder to Mable Reineke, May 21, 1930, Box 88; Jim Snyder to Ruth McCormick, June 21, 1930, Box 90, Hanna-McCormick Papers.

38. *Plain Dealer Wire*, July 14, 1930; Nye Committee Hearings, July 14, 1930, Box 113, Hanna-McCormick Papers.

39. Nye Committee Hearings, op. cit.; *Chicago Tribune*, July 14–17, 1930; *New York Times*, July 15, 1930.

40. *Chicago Tribune*, July 19, 1930; *New York Times*, July 18, 1930; U.P. column, July 18, 1930, Box 97, Hanna-McCormick Papers.

41. Ruth McCormick to Mrs. Maud Dennis, July 29, 1930, Box 91, Hanna-McCormick Papers; *Chicago Tribune*, July 18, 1930; *New York Times*, July 18, 1930.

42. *New York Times*, August 31, September 2, 1930; *Chicago Tribune*, August 31, Sept. 2, 1930.

43. *New York Times*, September 2, 18, 1930; U.P. story, September 4, 1930, McCormick Scrapbook; *Chicago Tribune*, September 3, 18, 1930.

44. *Chicago Tribune*, September, 3, 17, 1930; *New York Times*, September 17, 21, 1930; unidentified cartoon, McCormick Scrapbook; various letters, Box 97, Hanna-McCormick Papers.

45. *New York Times*, August 22, 24, 1930.

46. *New York Times*, August 22, Oct. 19, 1930; *Chicago Tribune*, August 30, September 7, 10, 15, 24, October 21, 1930.

47. Gosnell, *Machine Politics*, pp. 3, 94; *Chicago Tribune*, September 26, 27, October 19, 21, 30, 31, November 1, 1930.

48. Martha Connole to Ruth McCormick Miller [Bazy], [November 4] 1950, Box 109, Hanna-McCormick Papers.

49. Ruth McCormick to Will C. Carson, October 6, 1930, Box 99; Nye Committee Hearing, Box 113; Katherine Hamill to Effie Stephenson, September 12, 1930, Box 97; Justus L. Johnson to Ruth Miller, November 4, 1930, Box 109; L. D. Lowell to Ruth McCormick October 29, 1930, Box 99; Hanna-McCormick Papers; *Chicago Tribune*, October 10, 1930.

50. *New York Times*, October 23, 29, 30, 1930; *Chicago Tribune*, October 1, 12, November 2, 1930.

51. *Chicago Tribune*, October 12, November 5, 1930; *New York Times*, November 5, 1930; Barnes conversation with author, September 1984.

52. W. D. Hardy to Ruth McCormick, December 29, 1930, Hanna-McCormick Papers; *New York Times*, October 25, November 5, 1930.

53. Gosnell, *Machine Politics*, p. 164. *Chicago Tribune*, November 2, 1930; Bennett, "Methods," Box 108, Hanna-McCormick Papers.

54. Barnes conversation with author, September 1984.

CHAPTER 9

1. See Cott, *Grounding of Feminism*, especially pp. 215–24.

2. Jim Snyder to Judge C. H. Miller, November 6, 1930, Box 102; Ruth McCormick to Letitia Myles, November 12, 1930, Box 102; Ruth McCormick to C. E. Gullett, November 25, 1930, Box 102; Ruth McCormick to Lawrence Sherman, November 10, 1930, Box 102; Ruth McCormick, Editorial for Republican Women of Illinois, ms., Box 102, Hanna-McCormick Papers.

3. Kraditor, *Ideas of Woman Suffrage Movement*, p. 23; Clare H. Treadway to Ruth McCormick, December 3, 1930, Box 103, Hanna-McCormick Papers.

4. Barnes conversation with author, September 1984.

5. Katherine Hamill to Jim Snyder, January 13, 1931, Box 104, Hanna-McCormick Papers; *New York Times*, March 2, 1931; Alice Longworth, "What Are the Women Up to?" *Ladies Home Journal*, March 1934, p. 9; Tankersley conversation with author, September 1984.

6. *New York Times*, March 27, 1931, March 9, 1932; Frank D. Reeve, *History of New Mexico* (New York: Lewis Historical Publishing Co., 1961) p. 361; Albert G. Simms II, M.D. conversation with author, September 1985.

7. Barnes conversation with author, September 1984; *New York Times*, March 27–28, 1931; Albert Simms to Ruth McCormick, May 28, 1931, McCormick Collection.

8. *Chicago Tribune*, July 13–14, 1931; Albert Simms II to author, November 22, 1985; Francis Froelicher to Ruth Miller [Bazy], December 21, 1950, Box 109, Hanna-McCormick Papers; Robert Dietz conversation with author, September 1985.

9. Bronson Cutting to Olivia Cutting, October 30, November 13, 1931, Box 9, Bronson M. Cutting Papers, Manuscript Division, Library of Congress, Washington, D.C.

10. Paul Horgan conversation with author, October 1984.

11. Tankersley conversation with author, September 1984, September 1985; Barnes conversation with author, September 1984.

12. Albert Simms II conversation with author, September 1985; Paul Horgan conversation with author, October 1984; Kathryn Kennedy O'Connor, *Theatre in the Cow Country* (South Bend: Creative Service for Publishers, 1966) p. 40; George Byrnes conversation with author, August 1985.

13. Albert Simms II conversation with author, September, 1985; *Yakima* [WA] *Republic*, April 11, 1940; Tankersley conversation with author, September 1984.

14. *New York Times*, January 5, 1932; *Chicago Tribune*, June 14, 1932; Bronson Cutting to Olivia Cutting, October 21, November 11, 1932, Box 10, Cutting Papers; Moley, *Masters of Politics*, p. 182.

15. *New York Times*, October 2, 1934; *Literary Digest*, November 3, 1934, p. 13; Peter Miller, Jr. conversation with author, November 1984; Tankersley to author, December 1990.

16. Ruth McCormick to Eva Pope, April 20, 1936, Box 107; *Chicago Tribune*, October 31, 1939; unidentified clipping, McCormick Scrapbook.

17. *New York Times*, June 7, 9, 1936; Tankersley conversation with author, September 1984; Ickes, *Autobiography*, pp. 236–39.

18. *Chicago Tribune*, October 5, 31, 1936; unidentified clipping, McCormick Scrapbook; Ruth McCormick to Eva Pope, November 14, 1936, Box 107, Hanna-McCormick Papers; Herbert Hoover to Ruth Simms, November 1936, McCormick Collection.

19. *Amarillo News*, May 8, 1940; Bennett, "The Lady from Illinois," Box 13, Hanna-McCormick Papers; Tankersley conversation with author, September 1984 and September 1985.

20. Johnny McCormick to R. R. McCormick, September 10, 1936, McCormick Collection.

21. Ruth McC. Simms to Paul Horgan, [undated], Paul Horgan Private Collection; Ruth McC. Simms to Eva Pope, November 14, 1936, Box 107, Hanna-McCormick Papers; Ruth McC. Simms to Alice Longworth, [undated] McCormick Collection.

22. J. D. Hunley, *History of the Kirtland West Officers Club*, Kirtland Air Force Base, Albuquerque, NM, October 1984, pp. 1–9; Sandia School catalog, McCormick Collection.

23. Albert Simms II conversation with author, September 1985; letters, Box 132, Hanna-McCormick Papers; McCormick Diary, November 18, 1937; Elizabeth Wood Seymour conversation with author, September 1985.

24. O'Connor, *Theatre*, pp. 21–51; Byrnes conversation with author, August 1985.

25. Horgan conversation with author, October 1984; *Chicago Tribune*, April 22, 1929.

26. Horgan conversation with author, October 1984; Ruth McC. Simms to Horgan [undated] Horgan Collection; Barnes conversation with author, September 1984; Reeve, *History of New Mexico*, p. 346; Irene Kuhn conversation with author, April 1984.

27. Seymour conversation with author, September 1985; Ruth McC. Simms to Eva Pope, July 1, 1935, Box 107, Hanna-McCormick Papers; Horgan conversation with author, October 1984; Robert Metzger, ed., *My Land Is the Southwest: Peter Hurd Letters and Journals* (College Station: Texas A & M University Press, 1983) p. 115; Peter Hurd to Paul Horgan, January 27, 1936, Metzger, *Hurd Letters*, p. 160; Peter Hurd to Henriette Wyeth Hurd, Metzger,

Hurd Letters, p. 185; McCormick Diary, August 22, 1937; Henriette Wyeth Hurd conversation with author, September 1985.

28. Hurd conversation with author, September 1985; Albert Simms II conversation with author, September 1985; Horgan conversation with author, October 1984; Barnes conversation with author, September 1984; Byrnes conversation with author, August 1985; Tankersley conversation with author, October 1987; McCormick Diary November 11, 1937.

29. Robert Mann conversation with author, May, 1986.

30. Barbara Jamison Dietz, [November 6, 1950] to Ruth Miller [Bazy], Box 109, Hanna-McCormick Papers.

31. McCormick Diary, summer, 1937; August 26, September 13, 1937.

32. McCormick Diary, July 12–16, 1937.

33. McCormick Diary, July 21, 31, August 19. 25, 28, September 19, 1937.

34. Albert G. Simms to Ruth Tankersley [Bazy], June 14, 1951, McCormick Collection.

35. Byrnes conversation with author, August 1985; Seymour conversation with author, September 1985; George Baldwin conversation with author, September 1985; Lawrence conversation with author, March 1985; Tankersley conversation with author, September 1984, June 1985; Hurd conversation with author September 1985; Dietz conversation with author, September 1985.

36. Ruth McC. Simms to Eva Pope, [June] 1937, Box 107, Hanna-McCormick Papers; Dietz conversation with author, September 1985.

37. Tankersley conversation with author, September 1984; Dietz conversation with author, September 1985.

38. Katrina McCormick Barnes, "Mr. Kelly," unpublished ms.

39. Tankersley conversation with author, September 1984; *New York Times*, June 24, 1938; Dietz conversation with author, September 1985.

40. Tankersley conversation with author, September 1984.

41. Barnes conversation with author, November 26, 1987; Ruth McC. Simms to Ken Adams, Box 109, Hanna-McCormick Papers.

42. *New York Times*, June 26–July 1, 1938; Barnes, "Mr. Kelly;" Dietz conversation with author, September 1985; Tankersley conversation with author, September 1984.

43. Ruth McC. Simms to Fanny [Robbins], [undated], Box 108, Hanna-McCormick Papers; Horgan conversation with author, October 1984.

44. Ruth McC. Simms to Katrina McC. Barnes [Triny], [undated], McCormick Collection.

45. Ruth McC. Simms to Ruth McCormick [Bazy], [undated] McCormick Collection.

46. *Chicago Tribune*, October 27, 1938; *New York Times*, October 28, 1938.

47. Ruth McC. Simms to Ruth McCormick [Bazy], Thanksgiving Day, 1938, and others, McCormick Collection.

48. Tankersley conversation with author, September 1984; various items, Box 107, Hanna-McCormick Papers; McCormick Diary.

49. Barnes to author, October 17, 1984.

CHAPTER 10

1. Tankersley conversation with author, September 1984.

2. Susan Estrich managed the presidential campaign of Michael Dukakis in 1988.

3. Tankersley conversation with author, September 1984; Herbert S. Parmet and Marie B. Hecht, *Never Again: A President Runs for a Third Term* (New York: Macmillan, 1968) p. 17; Richard Norton Smith, *Thomas E. Dewey and His Times* (New York: Simon and Schuster, 1982) p. 278.

4. *Washington Times Herald*; Wendt, *Chicago Tribune*, pp. 609, 612.

5. Smith, *Dewey*, p. 276.

6. Parmet & Hecht, *Never Again*, pp. 66-68.

7. Barry K. Beyer, *Thomas Dewey, 1937–1947: A Study in Political Leadership* (New York: Garland, 1979) p. 35; Earl Browder, *The Way Out,* (New York: International Publishers, 1941) p. 136; Parmet and Hecht, *Never Again,* pp. 66–67.

8. Tankersley conversation with author, September, 1984; John Richmond, "Men Who Would Be President, Part II, Thomas E. Dewey," *Nation*, March 16, 1940, pp. 356–60.

9. Janet Davis, *Chicago Times*, December 15, 1939; *New York Herald Tribune*, April 16, 1940; *Tacoma Times*, April 9, 1940; Seattle newspaper, unidentified clipping, April 9, 1940, McCormick Scrapbook; James P. Selvage to Ruth McC. Miller [Bazy], November 6, 1950, Box 109, Hanna-McCormick Papers.

10. Barnes conversation with author, September 1984, and December 1984; *Chicago Times*, May 8, 1940; Tankersley conversation with author, September 1984.

11. Irene Kuhn conversation with author, October 1984; Ruth Simms to Ruth McCormick [Bazy], [undated] McCormick Collection.

12. Moley, *Masters of Politics*, p. 56; Beyer, *Dewey*, pp. 167, 290; Kuhn conversation with author, October 1984; Wolcott Gibbs and John Bainbridge, "St George and the Dragnet," *New Yorker*, May 25, 1940, pp. 24–38; Edwin Jaeckle conversation with author, December 1984.

13. Hamilton Basso, "Young Mr. Dewey," *The New Republic*, February 12, 1940, pp. 201; Stanley Walker, *Dewey, An American of This Century* (New York: McGraw Hill, 1944) p. 110; unidentified clipping, Seattle newspaper, April 9, 1940, McCormick Scrapbook.

14. Beyer, *Dewey*, pp. 177–78; McCormick Diary, October 25, 31, 1939.

15. Smith, *Dewey*, pp. 302–3.

16. *New York Herald Tribune*, October 7, 1939; *Washington Star*, November

8, 1939; McCormick Diary, October 31, 1939; Ruth Simms to Ruth McCormick [Bazy], [undated] McCormick Collection.

17. *Christian Science Monitor*, January 10, 1940; Ruth McC. Miller [Bazy] to Ray Moley, June 6, 1949, McCormick Collection; Tankersley conversation with author, September 1984.

18. Woolf, "Dewey's Right Hand Woman," p. 10.

19. Ruth Simms to Thomas E. Dewey, February 2, 1940; Ruth Simms to Thomas E. Dewey, February 2, 1940, Thomas E. Dewey Papers, Department of Rare Books and Special Collections, University of Rochester Library, Rochester, NY.

20. *Boston Globe, New York Times, New York Herald Tribune*, November 24, 1939; Irene Kuhn conversation with author, October 1984. Kuhn later became a well-known journalist and was a senior editor of *Gourmet* magazine until she was ninety. McCormick Diary, November 25, 1939.

21. *Christian Science Monitor*, December 1, 1939; *New York Times*, December 3, 1939; Elisabeth Perry to author, October 1990.

22. Tankersley telephone conversation with author, January 1985; *A Dewey Bibliography* (Washington D.C.: Press Research, 1944) p. 79; Burton R. Rubin conversation with author, October 1984; Kuhn conversation with author, March 1984; Jaeckle conversation with author, December 1984; *New York Post*, December 6, 1939.

23. *New York Telegraph*, December 20, 1939; *Kansas City Times*, April 25, 1940; Kuhn conversation with author, September 1984; *New York Times*, January 20, 1940.

24. *Chicago Times*, December 15, 1939; *New York World Telegram*, December 20, 1939; Kuhn conversation with author, March, September 1984; Peter Miller, Jr. conversation with author, December 1984.

25. *New York Journal American*, December 8, 1939; *New York Post*, December 6, 7, 1939; "The Hare and the Tortoise," *Time*, December 19, 1939, pp. 13–14; Parmet and Hecht, *Never Again*, p. 74.

26. *New York Times*, February 23, 1940; Parmet and Hecht, *Never Again*, pp. 51–65.

27. *Great Neck Record*, February 29, 1940; Tankersley conversation with author, September 1984; Smith, *Dewey*, p. 306.

28. *Kansas City Times*, April 25, 1940; *Amarillo, [TX] News*, May 8, 1940; Ruth Simms to Paul Lockwood, April 10, 1940, TED Collection; Smith, *Dewey*, p. 300; Ruth Simms to Thomas E. Dewey, Thomas E. Dewey to Ruth Simms, February 9, 1940, TED Collection; Basso, "Young Mr. Dewey," p. 201.

29. Harold L. Ickes, "Dewey The Clamor Boy," *Look*, March 26, 1940; Gibbs and Bainbridge, "St George and the Dragnet," p. 27.

30. Jaeckle conversation with author, December 1984; Raymond Clapper, *Washington Daily News*, April 11, 1940; Ruth Simms to Ruth McCormick [Bazy], [undated] McCormick Collection.

31. *Seattle Daily Times*, April 10, 1940; *Raton, [NM] Reporter*, April 19,

1940; Horgan conversation with author, October 1984; Ruth Simms to Ruth McCormick [Bazy], [undated] McCormick Collection.

32. Parmet and Hecht, *Never Again*, pp. 79–80; *New York Times*, March 29, 1940, quoted in Beyer, *Dewey*, p. 225; Ruth Simms to Ruth McCormick [Bazy], [undated] McCormick Collection.

33. *Washington Daily News*, April 11, 1940; *Minneapolis Star Journal*, April 14, 1940; *Buffalo Courier Express*, February 5, 1940; *Centralia Chronicle*, April 6, 1940; *Aberdeen World*, April 9, 1940.

34. *Seattle Post Intelligencer*, April 10, 1940; *Seattle Star*, April 10, 1940; *Spokane Chronicle*, April 12, 1940.

35. *Seattle Star*, April 13, 1940; *Portland Journal*, April 12, 1940; *Kansas City Times*, April 25, 1940.

36. *Albuquerque Journal*, April 17, 1940; *Rockford Labor News*, May 8, 1940; *Amarillo News*, May 8, 1940.

37. *Los Angeles Express*, May 13, 1940; *Kansas City Times*, April 10, 1940; *Seattle Daily Times*, April 10, 1940; "The Rising Tide: Chronology of Highlights of the Thomas E. Dewey Preconvention Campaign"; Ruth Simms to Thomas E. Dewey, May 6, 1940, TED Collection; Beyer, *Dewey*, p. 183.

38. Jaeckle conversation with author, December 1984.

39. TRB, "Washington Notes," *The New Republic*, April 22, 1940.

40. Ruth Simms to Elizabeth Wood, May 23, 1940; Ruth Simms to Gordon Ewen, May 31, 1940, Hanna-McCormick Papers.

41. Beyer, *Dewey*, p. 226; *Nassau Rev. Star*, June 13, 1940, McCormick Scrapbook, McCormick Collection; Parmet and Hecht, *Never Again*, pp. 111.

42. Parmet and Hecht, *Never Again*, p. 48; Beyer, *Dewey*, pp. 116–17; Hugh Ross, "Was the Nomination of Wendell Willkie a Political Miracle?" *Indiana Magazine of History*, June 1962, p. 83.

43. *New York Times*, May 3, 1940; Parmet and Hecht, *Never Again*, p. 94–111.

44. Arthur Krock, *Memoirs: Sixty Years on the Firing Line* (New York: Funk and Wagnalls, 1968) p. 195; Smith, *Dewey*, pp. 290–91, 306.

45. Parmet and Hecht, *Never Again*, pp. 100–101, 107–22.

46. *Philadelphia Enquirer*, June 19, 1940; Parmet and Hecht, *Never Again*, p. 116; Smith, *Dewey*, p. 308-9; Beyer, *Dewey*, 185–86.

47. Parmet and Hecht, *Never Again*, p. 120; Smith, *Dewey*, pp. 308–9.

48. Peter A. Odegard, *Prologue to November 1940* (New York: Harper & Bros., 1940) p. 50.

49. Beyer, *Dewey*, p. 186; *Philadelphia Enquirer*, June 19, 1940.

50. Odegard, *Prologue to November*, pp. 58–60; Smith, *Dewey*, p. 311–12; Tankersley conversation with author, September 1984.

51. *New York Herald Tribune*, June 27, 1940, quoted in Beyer, *Dewey*, p. 187; Smith, *Dewey*, p. 312.

52. Ross, "Nomination of Wendell Willkie," p. 83, 90–94; Odegard, *Prologue to November*, pp. 58–60.

53. Drew Pearson and Robert S. Allen, "Washington Merry Go Round," *Worcester Evening Gazette*, July 5, 1940; Smith, *Dewey*, p. 311; Jaeckle conversation with author, December 1984; Beyer, *Dewey*, pp. 187–88.

54. Odegard, *Prologue to November*, pp. 58–61; Smith, *Dewey*, p. 312; Ross, "Nomination of Wendell Willkie," pp. 81, 96–97; Tankersley conversation with author, September 1984; Parmet and Hecht, *Never Again*, pp. 95–6; Alfred E. Eckes and Eugene Rosebloom, *A History of Presidential Elections from George Washington to Jimmy Carter* (New York: Macmillan, 1979) p. 176; Beyer, *Dewey*, pp. 186–87; Moley, *Masters of Politics*, pp. 46–49.

55. Smith, *Dewey*, pp. 313–14; Walker, *Dewey*, pp. 113–15; Kuhn conversation with author, October 1984; Ruth Simms to Elizabeth Wood, December 17, 1943, Box 108, Hanna-McCormick Papers.

56. Ruth Simms to Thomas E. Dewey, [June 29, 1940] TED Collection; Barnes to author, December 18, 1984.

57. Hazel E. Henning to Lillian Rosse, July 11, 1940, TED Collection.

58. Thomas E. Dewey to Ruth Simms, July 9, 1940, TED Collection.

59. Moley, *Masters of Politics*, p. 183; Smith, *Dewey*, 328; Ruth Simms to Thomas E. Dewey, July 16, 1940, TED Collection.

60. Ruth Simms to Thomas E. Dewey, July 16, 1940, TED Collection.

61. Thomas E. Dewey to Ruth Simms, July 26, 1940, TED Collection; Parmet and Hecht, *Never Again*, pp. 200–230 passim., 234.

62. Ruth Simms to Ruth McCormick [Bazy], [undated] McCormick Collection; Ruth Simms to Ruth McCormick [Bazy], November 5, 6, 1940, McCormick Collection.

63. Parmet and Hecht, *Never Again*, p. 275.

64. Smith, *Dewey*, 296, 334–35; Ruth Simms to Thomas E. Dewey, December 2, 1940; Ruth Simms to Thomas E. Dewey, January 9, 1942, TED Collection.

65. Ruth Simms to Thomas E. Dewey, May 26, 1942; Thomas E. Dewey to Ruth Simms, January 19, 1942, TED Collection.

66. Jaeckle conversation with author, December 1984.

67. Ruth Simms to Thomas E. Dewey, May 26, 1942, TED Collection; Ruth Simms to George Byrnes, September 22, 1942, Box 108, Hanna-McCormick Papers.

68. Peter Miller, Jr. conversation with author, December 1984; Ruth Simms to Thomas E. Dewey, [undated]; Ruth Simms to Thomas E. Dewey, May 26, 1942; Ruth Simms to Thomas E. Dewey, August 16, 1942, TED Collection.

69. Ruth Simms to Ruth McC. Miller [Bazy], [undated]; Ruth Simms to Ruth McC. Miller [Bazy], September 29, 1942, Box 108, Hanna-McCormick Papers.

70. Thomas E. Dewey to Ruth Simms, January 17, 1943; Irene Kuhn to Thomas E. Dewey, April 2, 1943; Thomas E. Dewey to Ruth Simms, April 8, 1943; Ruth Simms to Thomas E. Dewey, April 20, 1943, TED Collection;

Smith, *Dewey*, p. 371; Ruth Simms to Elizabeth Wood, April 19, 1943, Hanna-McCormick Papers.

71. Ruth Simms to Betty and Osborne Wood, December 17, 1943, Box 108; Ruth Simms to Bazy and Peter Miller, September 21, 1943; Ruth Simms to Eva Pope, June 26, 1943, Hanna-McCormick Papers; Ruth Simms to Thomas Dewey, July 12, 1943, TED Collection.

72. Smith, *Dewey*, p. 387; Jaeckle conversation with author, December 1984.

73. Jaeckle conversation with author, December 1984.

74. Ruth Simms to Thomas E. Dewey, [undated] TED Collection; Ruth Simms to E. G. Bennett, [undated], Box 108, Hanna-McCormick Papers; *Kansas City Times*, April 25, 1940.

75. Thomas E. Dewey to Ruth Simms, December 17, 1943, TED Collection; Smith, *Dewey*, p. 386.

76. Ruth Simms to Thomas E. Dewey, December 7, 1943; Ruth Simms to Thomas E. Dewey, March 1944, TED Collection; Ruth Simms to Elizabeth Wood, March 15, 1944, Hanna-McCormick Papers; Herbert Brownell conversation with author, March 1985.

77. Beyer, *Dewey*, p. 43; Ruth Simms to Thomas E. Dewey, April 20, 1943; Ruth Simms to Thomas E. Dewey, April 24, 28, May 22; Ruth Simms to Paul Lockwood May 29, 1944; Thomas E. Dewey to Ruth Simms, May 26, 1944; Ruth Simms to Thomas E. Dewey, June 5, 1944; Ruth Simms to Thomas E. Dewey, [undated], TED Collection.

78. *Chicago Tribune*, June 19, 1944; Smith, *Dewey*, pp. 401–3.

79. Jaeckle conversation with author, December 1984.

80. Ruth Simms to "Gordon," July 20, 1944; Ruth Simms to Francis Froelicker, September 8, 1944; Ruth Simms to Elizabeth Wood, [October 30, 1944], Box 108, Hanna-McCormick Papers.

81. *Chicago Tribune*, December 6, 1944; Tankersley conversation with author, September 1984.

82. Ruth McC. Miller [Bazy] to George and Gracie Byrnes, November 17, 1944; Ruth Simms to Elizabeth Wood, [October 30, 1944]; Ruth Simms to "Gus," November 24, 1944, Hanna-McCormick Papers.

83. Barnes conversation with author, September 1984; Peter Miller, Jr. conversation with author, November 1984.

84. Tankersley conversation with author, September 1984.

85. Peter Miller conversation with author, November 1984; Barnes conversation with author, September 1984.

86. Barnes, "Mr. Kelly."

Bibliography

MANUSCRIPT SOURCES

Chicago Tribune archives and morgue. Tribune Tower. Chicago, Illinois.

Bronson M. Cutting Papers. Manuscript Division. Library of Congress. Washington, D.C.

Thomas E. Dewey Papers. Department of Rare Books and Special Collections. University of Rochester Library. Rochester, New York.

Mark A. Hanna Papers. Case Western Reserve Library. Cleveland, Ohio. Most of Hanna's papers were apparently lost in a fire.

Hanna-McCormick Family Papers. Manuscript Division. Library of Congress. Washington, D.C. Includes Ruth Hanna McCormick's papers.

Harold L. Ickes Papers. Manuscript Division. Library of Congress. Washington, D.C.

Harriett Laidlaw Papers. Schlesinger Library. Radcliffe College. Cambridge, Massachusetts.

McCormick Family Papers. Held by Kristie Miller. Includes family correspondence; the correspondence between C. G. Jung (published in *Spring 50* (Dallas: Spring Publications, 1990); letters of condolence to Ruth Simms after the death of her son Medill; seven scrapbooks of newspaper clippings on Ruth and Medill's wedding, Ruth's suffrage activities in 1913–14, her campaigns in 1927–1930, her farm, the 1940 Dewey campaign; a diary that Ruth kept sporadically in the 1920s and 1930s. The bulk of Medill McCormick's papers were given to a journalist friend who was commissioned by Ruth to write Medill's biography. The book was never written and the papers were lost. It has been difficult, therefore, to document the role Ruth McCormick played in Medill's political career.

MICROFILM SOURCES

Carrie Chapman Catt Papers. Manuscript Reading Room. Library of Congress. Washington, D.C.

National American Woman Suffrage Association. Manuscript Reading Room. Library of Congress. Washington, D.C.

New York Times. 1890–1945. Library of Congress. Washington, D.C.

PUBLISHED SOURCES

Addams, Jane. *Twenty Years At Hull House.* New York: Macmillan, 1910; Signet Edition, 1961.

Allen, Frederick Lewis. *Only Yesterday: An Informal History of the 1920s.* New York: Harper & Row, 1931.

Alsop, Jospeh. *F.D.R.: A Centenary Remembrance 1882–1945.* New York: Washington Square Press, 1982.

Banks, Olive. *Faces of Feminism: A Study of Feminism as a Social Movement.* New York: St. Martin's Press, 1981.

Beer, Thomas. *Hanna.* New York: Octagon Books, 1973.

Beyer, Barry K. *Thomas Dewey, 1937–1947: A Study in Political Leadership.* New York: Garland, 1979.

Blair, Karen. *The Clubwoman as Feminist: True Womanhood Redefined, 1868–1914.* New York: Holmes & Meier, 1980.

Browder, Earl. *The Way Out.* New York: International Publishers, 1941.

Brown, Dorothy M. *Setting a Course: American Women in the 1920s.* Boston: Twayne, 1987.

Buechler, Steven M. *The Transformation of the Woman Suffrage Movement: The Case of Illinois 1850–1920.* New Brunswick: Rutgers University Press, 1986.

Burke, Robert, ed. *The Diary Letters of Hiram Johnson.* Vol. 5, *1929–33.* New York: Garland, 1984.

Butt, Archibald Willingham. *Taft and Roosevelt.* Port Washington: Kennicat, 1971.

Cott, Nancy F. *The Grounding of Modern Feminism.* New Haven: Yale University Press, 1987.

Croly, Herbert. *Marcus Alonzo Hanna: His Life and Work.* Hamden: Archon Books, 1965.

Davis, Allen Freeman. *Spearheads for Reform: The Social Settlements and the Progressive Movement, 1890–1914.* New York: Oxford University Press, 1967.

Dawes, Charles G. *A Journal of the McKinley Years.* Chicago: The Lakeside Press, R. R. Donnelly and Sons, 1950.

Dewey Bibliography, A. Washington D.C.: Press Research, 1944.

Eckes, Alfred E., and Eugene Rosebloom. *A History of Presidential Elections from George Washington to Jimmy Carter.* New York: Macmillan, 1979.

Evans, Sara M. *Born for Liberty: A History of Women in America.* New York: The Free Press, 1989.

Flexner, Eleanor. *Century of Struggle: The Woman's Rights Movement in the United States,* rev. ed. Cambridge: Belknap Press, 1975.

Gable, John Allen. *The Bull Moose Years: Theodore Roosevelt and the Progressive Party.* Port Washington: Kennikat Press, 1978.

Gies, Joseph. *The Colonel of Chicago.* New York: E. P. Dutton, 1979.

Ginger, Ray. *Altgeld's America.* New York: M. Wiener, 1986.

Gosnell, Howard. *Machine Politics: Chicago Model.* Chicago: University of Chicago Press, 1937; New York: Greenwood Press, 1968.

Gould, Lewis L. *Reform and Regulation: American Politics from Roosevelt to Wilson.* Second Edition. New York: Alfred A. Knopf, 1986.

Green, Marguerite. *The National Civic Federation and the American Labor Movement, 1900–1925.* Washington, D.C.: Catholic University of America Press, 1956.

Hagedorn, Hermann, ed. *The National Edition of the Works of Theodore Roosevelt,* vol. 17. New York: Charles Scribner's Sons, 1926.

Hagedorn, ·Hermann. *The Roosevelt Family of Sagamore Hill.* New York: Macmillan, 1954.

Hanna, Mark. *His Book.* Boston: Chapple Publishing Co., 1904

Harper, Ida Husted. *Suffrage Snapshots.* Washington, D.C.: Leslie Judge Publishing, 1915.

Harriman, Florence Jaffray (Mrs. J. Borden). *From Pinafores to Politics.* New York: Henry Holt, 1923.

Hicks, John D. *Republican Ascendancy 1921–1933.* New York: Harper and Row, 1960.

Hunley, J. D. *History of the Kirtland West Officers Club.* Kirtland Air Force Base, Albuquerque, NM, October 1984.

Hutchinson, William T. *Lowden of Illinois: the Life of Frank O. Lowden.* Chicago: University of Chicago Press, 1957.

Ickes, Harold L. *The Autobiography of a Curmudgeon.* Chicago: Quadrangle Books, 1943.

Irwin, Inez Haynes. *Angels and Amazons: A Hundred Years of American Women.* New York: Garden City, 1933.

————.*The Story of the Woman's Party.* New York: Harcourt, Brace, 1921.

James, Edward T., and Janet Wilson James, eds. *Notable American Women.* Cambridge: Harvard University Press, 1971.

Johannesen, Eric. *Cleveland Architecture 1876–1976.* Cleveland: Western Reserve Historical Society, 1979.

Kessler-Harris, Alice. *Out To Work: A History of Wage-Earning Women in the United States.* New York: Oxford University Press, 1982.

Kohlsaat, H. H. *From McKinley to Harding; Personal Recollections of Our Presidents.* New York: Charles Scribner's Sons, 1923.

Kraditor, Aileen S. *The Ideas of the Woman Suffrage Movement, 1890–1920.* New York: W. W. Norton, 1981.

Krock, Arthur. *Memoirs: Sixty Years on the Firing Line*. New York: Funk & Wagnalls, 1968.

La Follett, Robert M. *La Follette's Autobiography: A Personal Narrative of Political Experiences*. Madison: Robert M. La Follette, 1913.

La Follette, Belle Case, and Fola La Follette. *Robert M. La Follette*, vol. 1. New York: Macmillan, 1953.

La Follette, Suzanne. *Concerning Women*. New York: Boni, 1926.

Lauer, Solon. *Mark Hanna: A Sketch From Life*. Cleveland: Nike Publishing House, 1901.

Leech, Margaret. *In the Days of McKinley*. New York: Harper and Brothers, 1959.

Livermore, Seward W. *Politics Is Adjourned: Woodrow Wilson and the War Congress, 1916–1918*. Middletown: Wesleyan University Press, 1966.

Longworth, Alice Roosevelt. *Crowded Hours*. New York: Charles Scribner's Sons, 1933.

Mary McDowell and Municipal Housekeeping: A Symposium. Chicago: University of Chicago Settlement League, 1938.

McGerr, Michael E. *The Decline of Popular Politics: The American North, 1865–1928*. New York: Oxford University Press, 1986.

McGivena, Leo E., et al. *The News: The First Fifty Years of New York's Picture Newspaper*. New York: News Syndicate, 1969.

Metzger, Robert, ed. *My Land Is the Southwest: Peter Hurd Letters and Journals*. College Station: Texas A & M University Press, 1983.

Moley, Raymond. *27 Masters of Politics: In a Personal Perspective*. New York: Funk and Wagnalls, 1949.

Morgan, David. *Suffragists and Democrats: The Politics of Woman Suffrage in America*. Ann Arbor: Michigan State University Press, 1972.

Morgan, H. Wayne, ed. *The Gilded Age*. Syracuse: Syracuse University Press, 1970.

———. *From Hayes to McKinley: National Party Politics 1877–1896*. Syracuse: Syracuse University Press, 1969.

O'Connor, Kathryn Kennedy. *Theatre in the Cow Country*. South Bend: Creative Service for Publishers, 1966.

Odegard, Peter A. *Prologue to November 1940*. New York: Harper & Bros., 1940.

Park, Maud Wood. *Front Door Lobby*. Ed. Edna Lamprey Stantial. Boston: Beacon Press, 1960.

Parmet, Herbert S., and Marie B. Hecht. *Never Again: A President Runs for a Third Term*. New York: Macmillan, 1968.

Perry, Elisabeth Israels. *Belle Moscowitz*. New York: Oxford University Press, 1987.

Rhodes, James Ford. *The McKinley and Roosevelt Administrations, 1897–1909*. New York: Macmillan, 1922.

Roosevelt As We Knew Him: The Personal Recollections of 150 of His Friends and Associates. Philadelphia: John C. Winston, 1927.

Roosevelt, Mrs. Theodore Jr. (Eleanor Butler). *Day Before Yesterday.* Garden City: Doubleday, 1959.

Ross, Isabel. *An American Family: The Tafts.* Cleveland: World Publishing, 1964.

Shaw, Anna Howard. *The Story of a Pioneer.* New York: Harper & Bros., 1915.

Shirer, William L. *Twentieth Century Journey: A Memoir of a Life and the Times.* Vol. 1, *The Start, 1904–1930.* New York: Bantam Books, 1985.

Sinclair, Andrew. *The Better Half.* Westport: Greenwood Press, 1965.

Smith, Richard Norton. *Thomas E. Dewey and His Times.* New York: Simon and Schuster, 1982.

Stone, Ralph. *The Irreconcilables: The Fight Against the League of Nations.* New York: W. W. Norton, 1973.

Sullivan, Mark. *Our Times: The United States 1900–1925.* 6 vols. New York: Charles Scribner's Sons, 1927; Syndicate Co., 1969.

Thomasville, Georgia: A Place Apart. Dallas: Taylor Publishing Company, 1985.

Trout, Grace Wilbur. "Sidelights on Illinois Suffrage History." *Illinois State Historical Journal* 13, no. 2 (July 1920):145–79.

Tuchman, Barbara W. *The Proud Tower: A Portrait of the World Before the War, 1890–1914.* New York: Macmillan, 1966.

Victory: How Women Won It, A Centennial Symposium, 1840–1940. NAWSA. New York: HW Wilson Co., 1940.

Walker, Stanley. *Dewey, An American of This Century.* New York: McGraw Hill, 1944.

Ware, Susan. *Partner and I: Molly Dewson, Feminism, and New Deal Politics.* New Haven: Yale University Press, 1987.

Wendt, Lloyd. *Chicago Tribune: The Rise of a Great American Newspaper.* Chicago: Rand McNally, 1979.

Wheeler, Adade Mitchell, and Marlene Stein Wortman. *The Roads They Made: Women in Illinois History.* Chicago: Charles H. Kerr, 1977.

White, Graham, and John Maze. *Harold Ickes of the New Deal: His Private Life and Public Career.* Cambridge: Harvard University Press, 1985.

White, William Allen. *A Puritan in Babylon: The Story of Calvin Coolidge.* Gloucester: Peter Smith, 1973.

———. *The Autobiography of William Allen White.* New York: Macmillan, 1946.

———. *The Old Order Changeth.* Rev. ed. Milwaukee: The Young Churchman, 1917.

Whitlock, Brand. *Her Infinite Variety.* Indianapolis: Bobbs-Merrill, 1904.

Willert, Sir Arthur. *Washington and Other Memories.* Boston: Houghton-Mifflin, 1972.

Wilson, Edith Bolling. *My Memoir.* Indianapolis: Bobbs, Merrill, 1938.

Wilson, Howard E. *Mary McDowell, Neighbor.* Chicago: University of Chicago Press, 1928.

Ziegler, Elsie Reif. *Light a Little Lamp.* New York: John Day, 1961.

Index

Addams, Jane, 37–38, 41, 55, 73, 96, 153; and woman suffrage, 81–82, 92–93, 129

African-American politicians, 16–17, 88, 92, 117, 131–32, 189–90, 207–8, 211–12, 232–33

Ailshie, Margaret Cobb, 132–33, 238

Anthony, Susan B. amendment. *See* Bristow amendment

Baumann, Gus, 247–48

Barnes, Courtlandt, 242, 252

Barnes, Katrina McCormick, 236, 242, 250–51; childhood of, 75, 95, 105, 145, 151–52, 158; and McCormick, Ruth, 165–66, 192, 218, 234, 288, 289–90

Barthelme, Mary, 139, 159

Baur, Bertha, 194–95, 241

Beard, Mary, 83

Benedict, Crystal Eastman, 83, 89

Bennett, Estelline, 132, 136, 242, 247–48

Bennett, Helen, 81, 234, 247–48; and McCormick campaigns, 110–11, 132, 136, 164, 187–88, 213; and Woman's World's Fair, 149–50, 152, 154

Blair, Emily Newell, 143

Blake, Margaret, 43, 133, 151

Blatch, Harriot Stanton, 91

Booth, Elizabeth K., 76–78, 80–81, 85–86

Borah, William, 114–15, 117–19, 126, 145, 149, 155, 157

Bowen, Louise de Koven, 73, 92–93, 131, 143, 150

Brandegee, Frank, 114, 119, 125–26, 147

Breckenridge, Sophinisba, 38

Bristow amendment, 90, 97, 105

Bristow, Joseph L., 90

Brownell, Herbert, 280, 284

Burns, Lucy, 83–85, 87

Catt, Carrie Chapman, 103, 155

Campaign financing, 141, 224–29

Chavez, Dennis, 240, 253

Chicago Equal Suffrage Society, 92

Chicago Political Equality League, 76, 80

Chicago Tribune, 15, 141, 242, 282–83. *See also* McCormick, Medill; McCormick, Robert R.

Child labor laws, 103, 130, 136, 140, 189

Congressional Committee. *See* NAWSA: Congressional Committee

Congressional Union, 83, 89, 102, 107, 121; NAWSA, split with, 85, 87, 91–

92, 98; Democratic party, threatens, 83–87, 96–98, 106
Connole, Martha, 132, 232
Coolidge, Calvin, 134, 147, 149, 155, 194; and McCormick, Ruth, 144, 146, 150–52, 161
Consumers' League, 40–41, 103
Crowe, Robert, 190–93, 216–17
Cutting, Bronson, 238–40, 242

Dawes, Charles Gates, 128, 145, 164, 189
Dean, Emily, 144, 198
De Lee, Joseph, 105, 133, 150
Democratic National Committee: women on, 142–43
Deneen, Charles S., 56–57, 111, 140–41, 161; 1928 campaign of, 190–91, 193, 195, 198; 1930 campaign of, 201, 203–4, 207, 210, 212–13, 216–21, 224, 226
Dennett, Mary Ware, 82, 85
Depression of 1930s, 198, 204, 237, 244–45, 247; and 1930 election, 214, 225–26, 228, 231–33
de Priest, Oscar, 207, 232
Dewey, Thomas E.: as governor, 279, 280–82, 284; 1940 campaign of, 257–77; 1944 campaign of, 279–80, 282–85
Dewson, Molly, 152, 209
Dietz, Robert III, 237–38, 250–51

Easley, Ralph M., 24, 41–42
Eastman, Crystal, 83, 89
Emmerson, Lou ("Lop Ear Lou"), 190–93, 197, 201, 215, 218, 231–32
Equal Rights Amendment, 129, 195

Farm issue, 133, 140, 146; in 1928 campaign, 186, 194; 1929 Farm Bill, 198, 200, 203; in 1930 campaign, 209–10, 214
Felton, Rebecca, 97, 203
Forsyth, Anne, 132, 136, 138–39, 164, 187–88
Fountain Valley School, 237–38, 244, 248

Funk, Antoinette, 77–78, 85, 89, 92, 97, 99, 102–3

Gaines, Irene McCoy, 92, 131, 207–8, 211
General Federation of Women's Clubs, 93, 130, 156
Gilpin, Laura, 243, 248; photo by, 177
Gompers, Samuel, 24, 42–43, 140

Hamill, Katherine ("Sis"), 164, 186, 212
Hanna, Augusta Rhodes ("Gussie"), 9–13, 27, 30, 33, 111, 137
Hanna, Daniel R., 10, 14, 137
Hanna, Mabel, 10, 14, 27, 30, 158
Hanna, Marcus Alonzo ("Mark"): before 1896, 10–16; and 1896 campaign, 17–20; and labor, 12, 19, 23–24; and Roosevelt, Theodore, 9, 22–23, 25, 28, 33–34; in Senate, 20, 21. See also McCormick, Ruth
Hanna, Ruth. See McCormick, Ruth Hanna
Hard, William, 38, 108, 151, 192, 194, 197, 213
Harding, Florence, 119, 127–28, 134
Harding, Warren G., 125–28, 133–34
Harriman, Florence J. ("Daisy"), 41, 52–53, 56, 112–13
Hays, Will, 121, 124, 126
Hoover, Herbert, 198, 233; 240; and McCormick, Ruth, 195, 220, 222, 236, 239, 241
Horgan, Paul, 239, 242, 245–47
Hurd, Henriette, 246, 250
Hurd, Peter, 246

Ickes, Harold L., 92, 126, 146, 263, 267; McCormick, Ruth, views on, 76, 97, 146, 190, 225, 241, 267–68
Illinois Equal Suffrage Association, 76, 80, 93–96, 102
Illinois Republican Women's Clubs, 122, 131–32, 138–39, 149, 153–54, 187, 195–98, 200, 239

Jaeckle, Edwin, 260, 265, 268, 271–72, 276, 280, 282–83, 286–87

Johnson, Hiram, 37, 114, 117–18, 223
Jung, Carl, 44–45, 152

Kahn, Florence, 199–200, 222
Kelley, Florence, 38, 41
Kellogg-Briand pact, 187, 210
King, Mary, 36–37
Knox, Philander, 114, 118, 124, 126
Kuhn, Irene Corbally, 260, 263, 265–66

La Follette, Robert, 37, 48–51, 114, 146–47
Landon, Alfred M., 240–41, 274, 276
League of Nations: McCormicks oppose, 113–19; 1920s campaign issue, 123, 127, 155, 210, 214, 223
League of Women Voters, 126, 143, 156, 220; McCormick, Ruth's views on, 135–37, 139, 159, 236; successor to NAWSA, 113, 130, 139
Lewis, James Hamilton, 76, 110–12, 221, 223–24, 228–34
Little Theater of Albuquerque, 243–45, 248
Lodge, Henry Cabot, 22, 97, 114, 119, 125, 127
Longworth, Alice Roosevelt, 51–53, 110, 128, 150–51, 156; bon mots of, 159, 238, 273; and League of Nations, 115–19; and McCormick, Ruth, 26, 29–30, 34–35, 43, 49, 107, 124, 126, 132, 151, 162, 192–95, 218
Longworth, Nicholas, 43, 53, 156, 200, 222–23
Lowden, Frank O., 124, 126, 145, 161, 193–94

McBride, Lucia, 13, 20, 41, 280
McCormick, Edith Rockefeller, 150
McCormick, Katherine Medill, 15, 26 (fn.), 146; and McCormick, Medill, 26–27, 30, 36, 44–45, 47–49, 134, 137, 145, 151; and McCormick, Ruth, 27, 44–46, 137, 158, 163
McCormick, Katrina ("Triny"). See Barnes, Katrina McCormick
McCormick, Joseph Medill ("Medill"), 9, 15, 29, 44, 93, 117, 130, 232; and

Chicago Tribune, 26, 36, 44–49; in Congress, 109–10, 113–14, 119–20, 128, 130, 140, 189; death of, 151; in Europe, 103, 109, 127, 134–35; in Illinois legislature, 57, 76, 78–79, 97; mental health of, 35, 44–48, 101, 142, 146–47; 1916 campaign of, 104; 1918 campaign of, 110–12; 1924 campaign of, 135–41, 146–47; in Progressive party, 49–57; and Roosevelt, Theodore, 48–52, 57, 76. See also League of Nations; McCormick, Katherine; McCormick, Ruth
McCormick, Medill ("Johnny"), 237, 242, 249; death of, 250–55; early years of, 105, 136, 145, 166, 218, 222
McCormick, Robert R. ("Bert"), 26 (fn.), 30, 45, 101; and Chicago Tribune, 46, 49, 241–42
McCormick, Ruth ("Bazy"). See Tankersley, Ruth McCormick
McCormick, Ruth Hanna: arts, supports the, 244–48; and children, 95, 135–36, 139–40, 145, 160–61, 165–66, 218, 242, 248, 288–89; and Dewey, Thomas E., 278–80, 283–87; finances, 35, 133, 154, 195, 239, 244, 265–66; and Hanna, Mark, 4, 10, 13–15, 17, 19–25, 27, 29–31, 33, 41, 51–52; and labor, 41–43, 50–51, 75, 103, 136, 189, 207; and McCormick, Medill, 14–15, 26–31, 35, 45–48, 93–95, 99, 101, 104, 108–13, 120, 127, 130, 137–39, 143, 145–47, 149, 152, 154; and NAWSA, 83–103; and partisan politics, 2–4, 17–18, 43, 52, 55, 99, 123–31, 137–41, 158–60, 166–67, 188–89, 196, 209; politics: 1931–1938, 239–42; political style of, 81–82, 185–88, 202–3, 212–17, 233–34, 261–63, 283–84; and Progressive party, 52–57, 73, 104; and Republican National Committee, 113, 120–21, 125, 128–30, 142–46, 157; and Roosevelt, Theodore, 9, 26, 29–30, 34, 42, 48, 52, 54, 57, 75–76; and Simms, Albert, 236–38, 249–51, 253–

54, 257; war, views on, 4–5, 22, 103, 257–58, 260–61, 272, 279–80
McCulloch, Catharine Waugh, 76, 78, 81, 94
McDowell, Mary, 38–39, 41, 55, 73, 75
McKinley, William (IL), 79–80, 139, 146, 154, 157–58, 161
McKinley, William (OH), 16–20, 22–23, 25
McNary-Haugen Bill, 186, 194, 196

Mann, Robert, 247
Medill, Joseph, 15, 26 (fn.)
Meem, John Gaw, 238, 243–45, 248
Miller, Ruth ("Bazy"). See Tankersley, Ruth McCormick
Miller, Peter, Jr., 281, 287–88, 290
Mitchell, Albert, 241, 253
Moscowitz, Belle, 2, 136, 152, 209, 264

National American Woman Suffrage Association (NAWSA), 74, 84–86, 94, 102, 107, 130, 139; Congressional Committee of, 82–100
National Civic Federation, 24–25, 140; Women's Committee of, 41–43, 50–51
National Woman's Party, 113, 121, 129, 155, 195, 209
Nye, Gerald, 224–29, 234

O'Neill, Lottie Holman, 159, 195–98, 223, 229, 232
O'Connor, Kathryn Kennedy, 244
Outlawry of war, 186, 187, 210
Owen, Ruth Bryan, 199, 209, 213, 222

Parsons, Mabel Hanna. See Hanna, Mabel
Patterson, Eleanor ("Cissy"), 26 (fn.), 29–30, 47, 151
Patterson, Joseph, 26 (fn.), 44, 49, 141, 151, 188, 219
Patterson, Mary King, 36–37
Paul, Alice, 74, 83, 85, 87, 98, 129. See also Congressional Union; National Woman's Party
Perkins, Francis, 98, 136, 209, 278
Pratt, Ruth Baker, 198–99, 222, 241

Progressive party, 37–38, 48, 54–57, 73, 76. See also McCormick, Medill; McCormick, Ruth
Prohibition, 123, 141, 186, 236; in 1930 campaign, 213–14, 221–24, 229–31, 233

Quaker beliefs, 11, 16, 22, 213, 258

Rankin, Jeannette, 96, 106–7, 220
Rathbone, Henry, 162–64, 189, 193
Reineke, Mabel, 159–60
Republican National Committee, 113, 121–22, 128, 139, 142–45, 156. See also McCormick, Ruth
Republican Women's Clubs. See Illinois Republican Women's Clubs
Rhodes, Augusta ("Gussie"). See Hanna, Augusta Rhodes
Robins, Margaret Dreier, 55, 73, 82
Rock River Farm, 99, 104, 131, 147, 202, 227
Rockford Register-Republic, 99, 195
Rogers, Will, 192, 223
Roosevelt, Alice. See Longworth, Alice Roosevelt
Roosevelt, Eleanor, 136, 143, 152, 209, 268–69
Roosevelt, Franklin D., 126–27, 132, 232, 241, 279, 280–81; in 1940 campaign, 258, 272, 276
Roosevelt, Theodore, 22–23, 25, 33–34, 37, 43, 109–12; in 1912, 49–56, 74. See also McCormick, Medill; McCormick, Ruth
Rush, Olive, 243, 248

Samson, Belle ("Sam"), 104–5, 165, 242, 248
Sandia School, 239, 243, 248
Shafroth, John F., 90
Shafroth-Palmer Amendment, 88, 90–91, 93, 95–99, 103
Shaw, Anna Howard, 83, 86, 92, 101
Sheppard-Towner Maternity Bill, 130
Sherman, Lawrence Y., 76, 114, 143, 235
Shonnard, Eugenie, 243

Simms, Albert G., 200, 234, 236–38, 240, 246, 249–53, 268, 270, 288
Simms, Ruth Hanna McCormick. *See* McCormick, Ruth Hanna
Sisson, Charles, 265, 268
Small, Lennington, 138–40, 143, 158, 161–62, 190–91, 193
Smith, Frank L., 144–45, 157–58, 160, 190, 193, 225
Snyder, Jim, 164–65, 186, 199, 204–5; in 1930 campaign, 202, 211, 223, 226, 231
Sprague, J. Russel, 264, 268, 272, 274, 280
Swanson, John A., 190–91, 193, 216

Taft, Robert, 258–59, 266, 271, 276
Tariff, 133, 198, 203, 209–10
Tankersley, Ruth McCormick ("Bazy"), 127–28, 218, 222, 237, 242, 275, 281, 287; and McCormick, Ruth, 135, 165–66, 248, 253–54, 257; McCormick, Ruth, views on, 132, 239, 287, 289–90; Simms, Albert, views on, 238, 251, 257
Terrell, Mary Church, 208, 211
Thompson, T. B. ("Barnie"), 195, 199, 228, 290
Thompson, William Hale, 11, 131, 139, 162, 164, 190–93; in 1930 campaign, 220–21, 225–26, 232
Treadwell, Harriet Taylor, 79–80
Trinchera Ranch, 243, 249, 253, 257, 281–82
Trout, Grace Wilbur, 76–81, 88, 91–96, 102

University of Chicago Settlement House, 38–40
Upton, Harriet Taylor, 82, 128, 139, 142

Vandenberg, Arthur, 258–59, 266, 270–71, 284
Vittum, Harriet, 73, 92, 94
Volstead Act. *See* Prohibition

Wells-Barnett, Ida, 88
White, William Allen, 50, 109, 120, 126
Willebrandt, Mabel Walker, 195
Willert, Arthur, 106–7, 115, 118, 125
Willkie, Wendell, 266, 271–79, 284
Wilson, Woodrow, 106–7, 111, 113, 118, 123–24, 128; and League of Nations, 109, 113–17; and woman suffrage, 74, 84, 86, 98, 101–2, 112
Woman suffrage, 73–103, 105, 112, 121, 126–27; effect of, 82, 84, 129, 157, 188–89, 220. *See also* NAWSA, National Woman's Party
Woman's Party. *See* National Woman's Party
Woman's World's Fair, 149–50, 152–54
Women's Christian Temperance Union (WCTU), 213
Women's City Club of Chicago, 41, 82, 92
Women's club movement, 37. *See also* Consumers' League; National Civic Federation Women's Committee; Women's Trade Union League; Women's City Club of Chicago
Women's Trade Union League, 40
World Court, 198, 154–58; and 1930 election, 203, 209–10, 213–14, 217, 219–20, 222–23, 229
World War One, 96, 103, 106–11
Wyeth, Henriette, 246, 250

Yates, Richard, 164, 193